PREFACE

It is well recognised that company law is a large and complex subject which has expanded rapidly in volume in recent years. Added to this is the continual reform to the existing law. This is partly due to the need to comply with obligations imposed on the United Kingdom from Brussels but partly because of the increasing complexity of commercial life generally. There is no sign that the growth and reform is at an end. In addition, there are now two established series of specialist company law reports (*Butterworths Company Law Cases* and *British Company Cases*) which have obviously resulted in many more cases reaching the public domain for comment and analysis. This places enormous pressure on any undergraduate course which bears the general title of company law especially if it is accompanied by the increasing time constraints placed on undergraduate law courses with the move towards modular degrees. To a certain extent, some topics, such as securities regulation and insolvency, can be isolated and treated separately, but there is a considerable, interrelated core to company law which simply has to be covered. From the point of view of the student some kind of perspective needs to be maintained of the subject as a whole so that this core can be understood and applied.

I have attempted in this book to present the core principles of company law in a readable and intelligible form focussing particularly on important cases and extracting key passages of judgment. This is to acknowledge that despite being a statute based subject, like any subject in a common law jurisdiction the law 'lives in' the cases. Further, a more immediate pragmatic reason for doing so, for most of the readers of this book, is that examination questions tend to focus around issues which have received judicial attention.

I have been ably assisted by Jennifer James of the University of Reading and Gil Brazier, Solicitor, who have written the chapters on Company Charges and Insider Dealing respectively. Both areas are examples of where the law has experienced considerable changes in the last few years. Overall responsibility for the accuracy of the book, however, remains mine. I would like to express my gratitude to all at Cavendish who have worked on the book, especially Kate Nicol and Jo Reddy for their patience. I am deeply indebted to my secretary Beverley Hodges at the University of East Anglia for typing the almost indecipherable manuscript with a high degree of accuracy and speed. I am also indebted to my wife, Esther, for the lost weekends while I was putting this project together.

I have attempted to state the law as at 1 May 1996.

References to the 1985 Act and the 1989 Act throughout the book are to the Companies Act 1985 and the Companies Act 1989 respectively.

Simon Goulding

Norwich

May 1996

FOR OLIVER

CONTENTS

TABLE OF CASES

TABLE OF STATUTES

CHAPTER ONE

INTRODUCTION

GENERAL

Between 1844 and 1856 the legislature laid down the foundations of a form of business association which was to become the most important and powerful in the economy. This form of association was the registered company, the law relating to which is the concern of this book.

The basic idea of using the registered company as a tool or medium for trade and commerce is straightforward. A company is formed or 'incorporated' by a promoter. Shares are issued by the company to shareholders, (who are initially 'the subscribers' to the company's constitution) who then enjoy control over the company by voting in meetings in proportion to the number of shares they hold.

The day-to-day running of the company's business is then normally delegated to directors who are appointed by the shareholders and are usually, but not necessarily, from among their number. In the simplest model the company acquires its money and assets by issuing shares. The consideration which is used to pay for the shares is then known as the 'capital'. But in many cases the money provided by issuing shares is irrelevant to the amount of money which the company actually uses in its business which will be provided by loans. Even the corporators may, for instance, prefer just to take one share each and then lend money to the company under a formal loan.[1] Crucially any assets accumulated by the company are owned both legally and beneficially by the company alone and the shareholders have no direct interest in them at all. This is as a result of the registered company being an incorporated association and that on its formation a new legal personality with its own legal rights and obligations is created in addition to and separate from those persons who are associating together. It is this new personality or entity which owns the accumulated assets.[2] As an illustration of this, a person who owns all the shares in a company can still be convicted of stealing from the company.[3]

While the company remains a small enterprise, with one or two persons owning all the shares, and those persons also being the only directors, the 'ownership' of the company and the control of it remain in the same hands; but once the company becomes larger with a more diverse shareholding, inevitably the proportion of shares held, (and hence the proportion of ownership) by those in day-to-day control of the company, namely the board of directors, diminishes.[4] This gives rise to the possibility

---

1   See, for example, *Re Ghyll Beck Driving Range Ltd* [1993] BCLC 1126.
2   *Macaura v Northern Assurance Co Ltd* [1925] AC 619.
3   *Attorney General's Reference (No 2 of 1982)* [1984] QB 624; *R v Philippou* (1989) 89 Cr App R 290.
4   Berle and Means, *The Modern Corporation and Private Property* 1968.

of the use of the company's assets in a way which the shareholders do not agree with, or which is contrary to the interests of the company. Given this structure, a significant part of company law, as will become apparent, is concerned with the issues of control of the company and the use or abuse of its powers.

Further, the larger the company becomes, the less important the relationship between the shareholders themselves. In these circumstances the shareholders regard their position as that of investors, rather than as members of a business association with a say in how the company is run. Despite the very different factual situations which exist in small family or 'one-person' companies, on the one hand, and large enterprises, on the other, it is a notable feature of English company law that the same basic laws, whether statutory or judge-made, apply to all types of registered company. The Companies Act 1985, presently the main consolidated company law statute, encompasses both the largest and the smallest business enterprises. The division between these two types of situation corresponds broadly, but not always, to the distinction between public and private companies.

PUBLIC AND PRIVATE COMPANIES

Generally speaking, public companies are ones which can raise money by inviting the public to purchase their shares. This is a considerable advantage for public companies, but not every public company will be able to make the fullest use of it since they will not have access to a market. A company's shares will be much more attractive to investors if they can be traded on a properly regulated market, because not only will they be easily and safely purchased, but also they will be easily disposed of. The major market place for shares in the United Kingdom is the Stock Exchange,[5] but by no means all public companies have access to this market. Companies can only gain admission to it by complying with certain conditions, and notably by demonstrating a satisfactory trading record.

The distinction between public and private companies first appeared in the Companies Act 1907. A 'private company' was defined as one which by the company's constitution restricted the right to transfer its shares, limited the number of its members to 50 and prohibited any invitation to the public to subscribe for any shares or debentures of the company. The 1907 Act was concerned with increasing the protection for investors who were considering subscribing for shares in a company by requiring it to provide relevant information when offering shares for sale to the public. This was to be done either through the established practice of issuing a prospectus, or in lieu of that, by requiring the company to furnish the Registrar of Joint Stock Companies with a statement containing the same information as would have been included in the prospectus. A private company was exempt from filing this statement. Thus the distinction was born as a recognition of the existing state of affairs which had by then emerged and it was, by the beginning of the 20th century, too late to separate

---

5   Its full title being The International Stock Exchange of the United Kingdom and the Republic of Ireland Limited: see Financial Services Act 1986, s 142.

the provisions applying to each type of association into different statutes. The approach to company law reform is almost always inherently conservative lest anything is done which jeopardises the use of registered companies by businesses and thereby hinders the development of the economy. Certainly nothing as radical as the enactment of two entirely different statutes, one applying to small companies and one applying to companies which offered shares for sale to the public, could then be contemplated.

The way in which the distinction was framed, namely by defining private companies and classifying the remainder as public, lasted until the Companies Act 1980, when considerable amendments to the law were made, again for the protection of the public and those dealing with public companies; this time, though, as a response to the Second Directive of the European Community.[6] Now it is the public company which is defined in the Companies Act, and all other companies are private.[7] A public company is one which states in its constitution that it is a public company and which complies with all the requirements laid down in the Companies Act for registration or re-registration of a company as a public company. Further, a public company cannot begin business or exercise any of its borrowing powers unless the Registrar has certified that the company has an allotted share capital of not less than £50,000[8] (of which at least one quarter must have been paid up).[9] There has never been any such minimum capital requirement on private companies. The 1980 Act also introduced the mandatory requirement that the name of a public company should end with the words 'public limited company' (which can be abbreviated to plc) to distinguish it more openly from a private company.[10]

So the approach of the legislature has been to lay down the overall framework of company law in the Companies Acts, yet to make exceptions for private companies and generally subject them to a less strict regime. The rules, for instance, which regulate what a company can do with its capital, make important relaxations for private companies and will be dealt with in Chapter 7, but among the other concessions to private companies in the Act are: that a private company need only have one director whereas a public company must have two;[11] the directors of a private company have no obligation imposed on them to ensure that the company secretary is a qualified person and possesses the requisite knowledge and experience to discharge the functions of a secretary;[12] and the provisions relating to the preparation, keeping and presentation of the accounts are less onerous.[13]

In addition, provisions in the Companies Act which require persons acquiring interests in the shares of a particular company to make disclosure of those interests to

---

6   Article 6 of 77/91/EEC.
7   Companies Act 1985, s 1(3).
8   Companies Act 1985, ss 117,118.
9   Companies Act 1985, s 101.
10 Companies Act 1985, s 25.
11 Companies Act 1985, s 282.
12 Companies Act 1985, s 286.
13 See, for example, Companies Act 1985, s 222(5).

the company to prevent sudden and unexpected takeover bids, only apply to the shares of public companies.[14]

The one major drawback of the private company is the inability to go to the market to raise capital. When a business run by a private company expands and needs further investment capital, one obvious course for it to take is to re-register as a public company so that further shares can be offered and sold to the public.[15] Such re-registration is necessary since the offering or advertising of its shares for sale to the public by a private company is a criminal offence, and any officer who makes such an offer or any person who causes such an advertisement to be issued is liable to be prosecuted unless the Secretary of State makes an exemption order.[16]

There are currently approximately one million registered companies in England, Wales and Scotland. Only about 10,000 of these are public companies, of which only 2,000 are listed on the Stock Exchange.[17] This means, of course, that overwhelmingly it is the private company which is used as the medium through which to conduct business. However, it must be borne in mind that many of the private companies will be subsidiaries of public companies, so the number of independent businesses is much lower than the figures suggest.

COMPANIES AND PARTNERSHIPS

In contrast to the company, the other main type of business association is the partnership. This is an unincorporated association where two or more persons associate for the purposes of business. No other separate legal personality is brought into existence on the formation of the partnership and the business and all its assets remain the property of the partners. The Partnership Act 1890 defines a partnership as '[t]he relation which subsists between persons carrying on a business in common with a view of profit' and it specifically excludes the relationship which exists between the members of a company.[18] But while companies can never be considered as partnerships, companies themselves can be the partners in a partnership, for example as part of a joint venture with other companies.

Each partner is an agent for the others and hence can affect the legal rights and obligations or matters connected with the business.[19] Partnerships can be formed by deed or quite informally, and in contrast to companies, simply in writing, orally or even by conduct. It is normal, however, to have a partnership agreement which sets out the terms on which the partners are associated. In the absence of any agreement to the contrary, when one partner wishes to leave or retire, the partnership has to be dissolved and then perhaps re-formed among remaining partners. Further, when a new

---

14 Companies Act 1985, ss 198–220. See p180.

15 Companies Act 1985, ss 43–48.

16 Companies Act 1985, s 81 and Financial Services Act 1986, ss 170 and 171.

17 Companies in 1994/95, HMSO.

18 Partnership Act 1890, s 1.

19 Partnership Act 1890, s 5.

partner wishes to join, there has to be unanimous consent of the existing partners. Again, as we shall see this is in contrast to the registered company.

FEATURES OF THE REGISTERED COMPANY

The most substantial differences between a company and a partnership can be appreciated by an examination of the main features of the modern registered company.

Incorporation by registration

Incorporation of associations prior to the passing of the Joint Stock Companies Act 1844 was restricted, and it occurred in only two major circumstances. First, when the Crown granted a royal charter as an act of prerogative power, conferring corporate status, for example, on trading associations such as the South Sea Company or the East India Company. Second, a practice which occurred more commonly from the late 18th century onwards, when a statute incorporated a company, usually to construct and run public utilities such as gas and water supplies and the canals and railways. The incorporating statute was a private Act of Parliament and the sections of the Act gave the company its constitution. For Blackstone the King's consent was absolutely necessary for the creation of a corporate body, hence the idea that in England, incorporation and the creation of a non-natural legal person was a concession. Blackstone described the above two methods of incorporation as being with the express consent of the King.

Another less frequently occurring method was by prescription, where the King's consent was presumed. This was because, although the members could not show any charter of incorporation, the corporation had purported to exist as such from a 'time whereof the memory of man runneth not to the contrary', and therefore the law was willing to presume that the charter had been originally granted but subsequently lost. An example of this type of incorporation was the City of London.

Finally, where the King's consent to incorporation had been implicitly given, although not a method of incorporating an association, was where the common law by custom recognised that certain officeholders had a separate legal personality in addition to their own natural personality. Such offices included bishops, vicars and even the King himself. On the death of the officeholder, the office and the corporate personality are transferred to the successor. These are known as 'corporations sole' to distinguish them from incorporated associations which are known as 'corporations aggregate'.

Quite apart from these corporations, though, during the 18th century there grew up an entirely different form of business association which, because of its importance in commercial enterprise, ultimately provided much of the impetus for reform. This became known as the 'deed of settlement' company.

As a result of the difficulties in obtaining corporate status and because an unincorporated body of persons could not hold property, except as partners, and because the Bubble Act of 1720 made it illegal to pretend to act as a corporate body,[20] the device of the trust was used so that money property of a group of persons associating together for the purposes of business could be put into a trust and trustees could be appointed to administer it. There was therefore a 'joint stock' held under trust and although there was in fact no corporation, all the parties for all practical purposes acted as if there were one. Shares in 'the company' could be issued to the persons contributing property to the joint stock, and each person would execute a covenant that he would perform and abide by the terms of the trust. The difference between these unincorporated companies and partnerships was that they enjoyed continuous existence with transmissible and transferable stock, but unlike partnerships no individual associate could bind the other associates or deal with the assets of the association.

The ingenuity of the legal draftsmen in drawing up the trust deeds brought about a situation where groups of associating persons achieved corporate status for all practical purposes, so that as Maitland was able to say:

'in truth and in deed we made corporations without troubling King or Parliament, though perhaps we said we were doing nothing of the kind'

and that the trust:

'in effect enabled men to form joint stock companies with limited liability, until at length the legislature had to give way.'[21]

The legislature did give way in a major and significant way in the Joint Stock Companies Act 1844, which introduced for the first time, albeit in a rather long-winded form, the notion of the formation and incorporation of a company for a commercial purpose by the act of registration by a promoter. No longer did would-be corporators have to obtain a royal charter or await the passing of an incorporating statute. Incorporation could be obtained by the administrative act of registration. The equivalent section in the 1985 Act reads:

'Any two or more persons associated for a lawful purpose may, by subscribing their names to a memorandum of association and otherwise complying with the requirements of this Act in respect of registration, form an incorporated company, with or without limited liability.'

and by s 13(3):

'From the date of incorporation mentioned in the certificate, the subscribers of the memorandum, together with such other persons as may from time to time become members of the company, shall be a body corporate by the name contained in the memorandum.'

The act of registration creates the corporation.[22] The drafting of these sections inherited from previous Companies Acts seems to imply that the body corporate is simply the aggregate of the subscribers and members, and this is why in the 19th

---

20   6 Geo I, c18.

21   Maitland, *Collected Papers*, Vol III p 283.

22   *Arab Monetary Fund v Hashim (No 3)* [1991] 2 AC 114 at 160.

century a company is referred to in judgments as 'they' or 'them'. This view is wholly superseded by the view that a company is separate from, and additional to, the members, and is now always referred to as 'it'. The former view seems especially strange now that there is the possibility of companies being formed with a single member.

Among the disadvantages of the old deed of settlement companies was the difficulty in suing and enforcing judgments against them, since they essentially remained large partnerships. But from this very first statute introducing the notion of incorporation by registration, the option of continuing to carry on trade in the form of a large partnership was severely circumscribed to deal with this problem. The 1844 Act required partnerships of more than 25 persons to register, thus compelling the use of the new form of business association.[23] Thus there is one readily identifiable legal persona which can sue to enforce the rights of the business and which can be sued to be held accountable for the obligations of the business. The present-day successor to this provision is s 716 of the CA 1985, and the number of partners has been reduced to 20. There are, however, express exceptions contained in the section, allowing, for instance, solicitors and accountants to practise in partnerships of unlimited size.[24]

Transferable shares

A crucial element in the success of the registered company as a form of business association is the idea of the transferable share. Shares in a company are transferable in the manner provided for in the company's articles.[25]

Those persons who are originally involved in setting up and running the business may wish to leave it or to leave their 'share' of the business to their beneficiaries on their death, but usually all parties, particularly those remaining involved in the business, will want to affect the company as little as possible. A serious disadvantage with the partnership is that, unless express provisions are made in a formal partnership deed as to what should happen in the event of there being a change in the composition of the partnership, when any partner dies or wishes to leave, or when a new partner is admitted, the partnership has to be dissolved and re-formed. In respect of the registered company, in theory changes of the shareholders can be accomplished conveniently and with a minimum of disruption to the company's business. When a shareholder sells his shares to another person that person becomes the new shareholder, and the only involvement of the company is to change the appropriate entry in the register of members. Thenceforth the new person becomes a new member.

Further, because the company is a corporate body and a recognised legal entity, it survives the death of one or even all of the members.[26] The shares of any deceased member are simply transferred to their personal representatives. The company therefore

---

23   7 & 8 Vict c110, s 2.

24   Companies Act 1985, s 716(2).

25   Companies Act 1985, s 182.

26   *Re Noel Tedman Holdings Pty Ltd* [1967] Qd R 561.

has a potentially perpetual existence.

In practice, in respect of private companies, the position with regard to the transmissibility of shares is likely to be more complicated by the presence in the company's constitution of a clause which states that any member wishing to sell his or her shares must first offer them to existing members who have an option to purchase them, or possibly are obliged to purchase them. This is an important restriction for the small family company to include in its regulations since the members will obviously wish to retain control over who comes into the company. Again this does not directly affect the company but it can lead to disputes, especially as to the mechanism for the valuation of the shares. Formerly there was a requirement in the Companies Acts that in order for a company to qualify as a private company there had to be such a restriction on the transfer of shares[27] but this was removed in the Companies Act 1980.

These clauses are not usually found in the constitution of public companies which do not in the normal case have any restrictions on transfer.[28] This reflects the reality that the shares in the public company are an investment only and that the shareholder has little or no interest in the business of the company or the identity of the other shareholders.

Limited liability

Corporations, as already described, existed long before the Companies Acts of the mid-19th century. As early as 1612, in *Sutton's Hospital*,[29] Coke had stated that corporations were distinct from their members and later in the century, in the case of *Edmunds & Tillard v Brown*,[30] it was recognised, as a result of this distinction, that the members of a chartered company were not directly personally liable for the debts and obligations incurred by the company in its own name and likewise nor was the company liable for the members' debts and obligations. Hence the recognition of the important advantage of trading through the medium of a corporation rather than in a partnership, where each partner remains both jointly and severally liable for the debts of the business, or even as a member of the old deed of settlement company where, since there never was in law a distinct body brought into existence, the members remained liable for debts incurred.

The position, however, was not so straightforward as this because as a case such as *Salmon v The Hamborough Company*[31] shows the courts were willing to make orders to the effect that should a company not be able to pay a judgment debt, then the company could make 'calls' on the members of the company so that sufficient money was collected. In this way members could be made indirectly liable for a proportion of

---

27 Companies Act 1948, s 28.

28 The Listing Rules of the Stock Exchange prevent a listed company from having such restrictions on the transferability of its shares.

29 (1612) 10 Co Rep 1.

30 (1668) 1 Lev 237.

31 (1671) 1 Ch Cas 204, HL.

the company's unpaid debt. Many charters of incorporation, however, contained an express clause exempting members from any such liability.

When the legislature first established the registered company in 1844 it was initially envisaged that members would not escape liability for the debts of the company, but there was a clear and significant difference between the position that existed with chartered corporations. By s 66 of the 1844 Act a creditor had to proceed first against the company for the satisfaction of his debts, and if that did not recover the required amount, the creditor could then proceed directly against the members of the company personally. Further, a member would remain under such personal liability for three years. But this state of affairs did not last long and the hurriedly passed Limited Liability Act 1855 provided that, as long as a number of conditions were satisfied, a member was absolved from liability for the debts of the company.

So the position now is that members are said to enjoy limited liability, although the meaning of this phrase and the way it works in practice depends on what sort of registered company is being considered. Overwhelmingly the most popular and important form of company for trading purposes is the company limited by shares. Here each share is given a nominal value and a member of this form of company is liable only up to that full nominal value of each share he holds or has agreed to purchase. Most shares today are issued to shareholders on a fully paid up basis, so that in the event of the company being wound up insolvent there is no further liability on the part of the member, no matter how much the company owes to its creditors. If, however, the member is holding partly paid shares (which was the case with some recent Government 'privatisations') and the company goes into insolvent liquidation, then the member will be called upon to pay the outstanding amount on each share.

The other form of registered company which can be formed under the Act where the members can enjoy limited liability is the company limited by guarantee. Here the company does not issue shares, but instead the members each agree to pay a fixed amount should the company be wound up insolvent. The amount is usually only nominal but in any event this form of company is only really appropriate for charitable or educational purposes rather than for commercial ventures.

Limited liability and the registered company are not inevitably and inextricably linked in English company law. Section 1(2)(c) states that a company can be formed without a limit on the liability of its members. So, in the event of such a company going into insolvent liquidation, the members could be called upon to make a contribution to the company's assets. The advantage of such a company is that there is an exemption from the disclosure requirements in the Act. However, not surprisingly, this form of company is not particularly popular and at present there are fewer than 4,000 registered at Companies' House.[32]

Disclosure and formality

---

32   Companies in 1994/95, HMSO.

A major feature of the law relating to registered companies, which is immediately apparent to anyone forming and running a company, is the amount of information about the company which has to be compiled and disclosed. Thus the formalities and the publicity associated with the registered company can be considered disadvantageous, and to some extent form a disincentive for a businessman to incorporate his business. The information required of a sole trader, or by the partners in a normal partnership, is much less and may only be the information which is required for the purposes of taxation and this is not available for public inspection. But as regards the registered company, from its inception the idea of incorporation by registration was seen as a privilege or concession to businessmen, and in return for this there had to be a certain amount of documentation which had to be open for public inspection and scrutiny. So the 1844 Act established the Registrar of Companies who is still with us today and whose offices are located in Cardiff. The reasoning behind this requirement was perhaps best encapsulated by the American judge, Justice Brandeis, who once said that '[s]unlight is the best of disinfectants; electric light the best policeman'. Furthermore, and specifically in the context of English company law, the 1973 White Paper on Company Law Reform stated it was the government's view that 'disclosure of information is the best guarantee of fair dealing and the best antidote to mistrust'.[33]

So the reasoning behind the disclosure requirements is that fraud and malpractice are less likely to occur if those in control of corporate assets have to be specifically identifiable and know they have to disclose what they have been doing. This means that public disclosure is intended to protect investors and creditors who either put money into the company or who deal with it.

For public companies which are listed on the Stock Exchange there is the additional, extra-legal requirement to disclose information to the Stock Exchange. In addition to prospectuses and the regular reports which have to be filed, it is also necessary for a company to give the Stock Exchange 'any information necessary to enable holders of the company's listed securities and the public to appraise the position of the company and to avoid the establishment of a false market in its listed securities'.[34]

The issue of disclosure in company law has another aspect to it and that is the disclosure of information by the directors to the members both in and out of general meeting. The aim here goes beyond that in relation to public disclosure to the registrar, which is largely concerned with the protection of investors and creditors, and generally has more to do with ensuring that the members of the company are satisfied with the efficiency of their management and are able to scrutinise the conduct of the directors. So the directors have a duty to lay the annual accounts, the directors' and the auditors' reports before the company in general meeting every year.[35] Furthermore, every member of the company is entitled to receive a copy of these documents not less than

---

33 Company Law Reform, 1973, Cmnd 5391, para 65.
34 Admission of Securities to Listing (known as the 'Yellow Book'), s 5, ch 2, para 1.
35 Companies Act 1985, s 241.

21 days before the date of the meeting at which they are to be laid before the company.[36]

Also a company must keep a register of its members at its registered office which is open to inspection not only to any member (free of charge) but also to any other person (on payment of the prescribed fee).[37]

Officers of a company who fail to comply with the provisions in respect of disclosure are likely to have committed a criminal offence and more particularly directors who are in 'persistent default' in complying with disclosure requirements can be disqualified from holding office as a director for up to five years.[38]

There has been some trenchant criticism of the disclosure system, in particular that the present level of disclosure cannot be justified.[39] There has indeed been a steady growth in the volume of documents required from each company, without perhaps a thorough examination of whether the further disclosure meets the overall aims of the system. In addition further disclosure is constantly being required by EC directives. Originally, under the 1844 Act, a company only had to send a copy of its constitution, a list of members and a copy of any prospectus to the registrar. In addition, there was a requirement to present balance sheets to the registrar, but somewhat surprisingly this requirement was dropped in the 1856 Act and not re-introduced until 1907. But the list of members, on the other hand, very important during the time when members were liable for the company's debts, has remained. Now, in addition to the keeping and filing of annual accounts,[40] it is necessary to prepare a directors' and an auditors' report, lay them before the general meeting and deliver them to the registrar,[41] as well as annual returns,[42] containing particulars of the directors, company secretary and the address of the registered office,[43] copies of any special or extraordinary resolutions,[44] and valuations of company property.[45]

Some reform has begun to be made, especially to remove the bureaucratic burden from private companies. The Companies Act 1989 introduced the 'elective resolution' which allows a company, if it passes such a resolution, to dispense with certain specified formalities required by the 1985 Act. Most important in this context is the ability of a private company to pass an elective resolution to dispense with the laying of accounts and reports before the general meeting.[46] Elective resolutions will be dealt with in greater detail later. This is part of the move towards the deregulation of small

---

36 Companies Act 1985, s 238.
37 Companies Act 1985, s 356.
38 Company Directors (Disqualification) Act 1986, s 3.
39 See, for example, Sealy (1981) 2 Co Law 128.
40 Companies Act 1985, s 242.
41 Companies Act 1985, ss 234, 235, 241 and 242.
42 Companies Act 1985, s 363.
43 Companies Act 1985, s 364.
44 Companies Act 1985, s 380.
45 Companies Act 1985, s 111.
46 Companies Act 1985, ss 252, 379A.

businesses, which, if the present Government's intention is implemented, looks likely to continue.[47]

A further relaxation which was introduced by the 1989 Act is that public companies listed on the Stock Exchange may send shareholders a summary financial statement instead of the full audited accounts.[48]

The advantages of forming a company

Most of the reasons why those running a business would wish to form a company through which they can run their businesses flow from the above features either directly or indirectly. It is able to enjoy a perpetual existence, the death or retirement of the members having no necessary effect on its continued existence, a fact which obviously is not the case with the partnership. Similarly, a change of members by a transfer of shares can be accomplished without affecting the company.

The management of the company can be assigned to specific persons, the directors, so that other members do not have the authority to represent or legally bind the business with third parties. Obviously, in addition, limited liability against the trading debts can be enjoyed by those investing in the business. In a recent empirical study of small businesses it was discovered that overwhelmingly the most important reason given by the respondents for the formation of a company was the advantage of limited liability.[49] It must be appreciated that in practice this will only mean protection for the directors and members against liabilities incurred to trade suppliers. This is because if banks lend money to small, under-capitalised companies they will almost certainly demand personal guarantees to be given by the directors.

A normal partnership cannot offer either of these features although they can in effect be achieved by forming a partnership under the Limited Partnership Act 1907 which is in fact very little used. Under this Act an investor in a partnership business can limit his liability to the amount actually invested or pledged. This limited partner then takes no part in the management or the running of the business. If he does, he loses the protection of the Act and becomes fully liable in the normal way. Such limited partnerships have to be registered and in 1994 there were only about 4,000 on the Register.[50] By the time the legislation was introduced, the 'one-person' limited company had become commonplace, which with the sanction of the House of Lords' decision in *Salomon v Salomon Ltd* was able to achieve limited liability for all persons concerned with the business.[51]

Lastly, an advantage which is enjoyed by companies over sole traders or

---

47 Most likely through the use of the powers under the Deregulation and Contracting Out Act 1994.

48 Companies Act 1985, s 251.

49 *Alternative Company Structures for the Small Business*, Hicks, Drury and Smallcombe ACCA Research Report No 42.

50 Companies in 1994/95, HMSO.

51 [1897] AC 22. See Chapter 3.

partnerships, which emerged during the last century without design on the part of the legislature, is that companies can give what is known as a floating charge as security for a loan.[52] This can be an important reason for deciding to incorporate a business, especially if that business has at any one time a significant part of its capital tied up in chattels or moveable property. A floating charge is a security given over assets which in the normal course of business change from day to day, eg raw materials or stock-in-trade. The company can continue to trade and deal with the assets comprised in the charge because it does not, while the charge is floating, affect them or interfere with the company's ability to give good title to a buyer if they are sold. So a company, by granting such a charge to a lender, increases the assets against which it can borrow. Without the ability to use such a device the company could only borrow money against the security of fixed assets, ie land. This is the position of sole traders and partnerships because of, *inter alia*, the Bills of Sale Acts 1878 and 1882. A floating charge would fall within the definition of a bill of sale within the meaning of the Acts, and therefore it would need to be registered in statutory form in the Bills of Sale Registry; in this form all the movable property subject to the charge would need to be set down in the schedule to the bill. Since the whole point of the charge is that the property charged can continually change this would be totally impractical. The reason why companies can create these charges without registering them as bills of sale is that the Acts do not apply to corporate bodies.

In the empirical survey mentioned above, none of the respondents gave as a reason for incorporating the ability to grant a floating charge, so it may be that this advantage is significantly over-estimated. In any event, as mentioned above, in the case of the 'one-person' company there is probably no impetus for the bank to demand a floating charge since it has taken a personal guarantee from the businessman anyway.

The purpose of company law

The objective of a good system of company law should be, first, to provide a framework within which entrepreneurs can be encouraged to take commercial risks and develop new businesses. This will also provide passive investors with a mechanism by which they can invest capital in a business or industry, again without the possibility that they will incur unlimited liability which may potentially bankrupt them. The justification for this must be that it will be for the good of the economy as a whole, even though there will be individuals who will lose out by dealing with such companies. Therefore, the second objective must be to provide sufficient controls on the persons forming and running companies, so that an outsider who deals with the company does not lose out unfairly as a result of fraud or sharp practice or abuse of the Companies Act.

Achieving the right balance between these opposing interests is not easy. Usually the legislators of any system of company law adopt a mixture of measures which provide on the one hand *ex ante* protection so that, for instance, minimum

---

52 See Chapter 11.

capitalisation requirements are laid down for the formation of a company and then strict rules are enacted for the maintenance of that capital to provide a sum for the satisfaction of creditors. Further, there could be scrutiny of the constitution and the proposed activities of the company and the reputation and character of the persons who will be running the company on its formation by a central agency. And on the other hand *ex post* protection, whereby mechanisms are set in place, for example, to dislodge the security of various pre-liquidation transactions which are entered into to cheat *bona fide* creditors, or procedures are established for fixing those who have been running companies fraudulently or recklessly with a liability to contribute to the company's debts. Further, steps can then be taken to disqualify these persons from running companies in the future. In the UK, as will be seen in the following pages, despite the fact that there are lengthy and complicated rules concerning the maintenance of capital, the emphasis is very definitely on *ex post* remedies, whereas in continental jurisdictions much stronger use is made of *ex ante* protection, with all other European jurisdictions apart from the UK and the Republic of Ireland having significant minimum capitalisation requirements for the equivalent of both private and public companies. In the UK there are no minimum capital requirements for private companies, with such requirements for public companies only being introduced in 1980.

The sources and reform of company law

Legislation

Not surprisingly, the most important source of company law is legislation and it is a source which has been enormously fertile. The increase in the sheer volume of statutory provisions which apply to companies has been phenomenal. The 1844 Act, which first provided for the incorporated registered company, contained only 80 sections with 10 schedules. The latest consolidating Act, the Companies Act 1985, contains nearly 700 sections with 25 schedules, and now this Act is far from being considered as the complete or even latest word on the law relating to companies. The general pattern in this development of legislation has been the passing of several Acts reforming parts of the law as it relates to companies followed by a large consolidating Act attempting to incorporate all the relevant provisions. So the first consolidating Act was as early as the Joint Stock Companies Act 1856, but this was soon replaced by the Companies Act 1862. This survived until 1908 when it was replaced by the Companies (Consolidation) Act of that year. Two more consolidating Acts were passed, in 1929 and 1948, before the current statute, which is the Companies Act 1985. Unfortunately much reform of the law relating to insolvency was underway simultaneously with the passage of the Companies Act 1985, following the recommendations of the Cork Committee, which reported in 1982. This resulted in the short-lived Insolvency Act 1985 which was repealed to make way for the consolidating Insolvency Act 1986. This latter Act took with it large amounts of Parts XVIII, XIX, XX and XXI of the Companies Act 1985. Further, all the provisions of Companies Act which dealt with the disqualification of directors were removed and replaced in the Company Directors Disqualification Act 1986. In addition the provisions relating to insider dealing were placed into a separate Act, the Company Securities (Insider Dealing) Act 1985. This itself has now been repealed and replaced by Part V of the Criminal Justice Act 1993. The Companies Act 1989 effected many important changes and inserted new provisions into the 1985 Act.

It should be borne in mind that subordinate legislation forms an important source of company law and practice and its role is increasing. This is probably inevitable due to the pressures on parliamentary time and the increasing complexity and specialisation of company law matters, but in any case increasing use is being made of s 2(2) of the European Communities Act 1972 to enact the substance of EC company law directives. So that, for example, s 1 of the 1985 Act was recently amended by statutory instrument to include a new s 1(3A), which provides for the first time in English law that a company can be incorporated with a single member.[53] Part III of the 1985 Act was repealed and replaced by the Public Offers of Securities Regulations 1995,[54] so that provisions which were formerly contained within the statute are now to be found in a subordinate legislation.

The process is not confined simply to measures enacting community directives. By s 117 of the 1985 Act, the Secretary of State is given power to make regulations further extending the scope of elective resolutions to relieve the administrative burden on private companies, and he is given a similar power in the Deregulation and Contracting Out Act 1994.[55]

Reform

The genesis of company law reform until recently has been the law reform committees which have reviewed various areas of company law and the introduction of major company legislation has been preceded by the report of such a committee. The 1844 Act itself was preceded by a committee under Gladstone;[56] the 1908 Act followed the report of the Loreburn Committee;[57] the 1929 Act followed the Wrenbury and the Greene Committees[58] and the 1948 Act followed the Cohen Committee.[59] The last of these large-scale company law reviews was by the Jenkins Committee[60] which reported in 1962; some of its recommendations were then enacted in the Companies Act 1967 and some, notably the provision which is now s 459, in the Companies Act 1980. The Companies Bill 1973, which would have implemented the remaining recommendations of the Jenkins Committee, fell with the Conservative Government in 1974. The Bolton Committee[61] was commissioned by the Board of Trade in 1969

---

53 Companies (Single Member Private Limited Companies) Regulations 1992 (SI 1992 No 1699) implementing the Twelfth Directive 89/667/EEC.

54 SI 1995/1537.

55 See pp 108 and 151.

56 1844 BPP, Vol VII.

57 1906, Cmnd 3052.

58 1918, Cd; 1926, Cmnd 2657.

59 1945, Cmnd 6659.

60 1962, Cmnd 1749.

to look generally into the small firm but its report did not lead to any significant changes in company law.

In November 1992 the Department of Trade and Industry announced that it was to carry out a review of a number of areas of company law. Amongst the areas selected for consideration were: the law relating to private companies; the law on directors' duties; the law relating to financial assistance by a company for the acquisition of its own shares; on the registration of company charges; on disclosure of interests in shares; and the law relating to groups of companies. This review has as its broad objective the simplification of the law and the reduction of unnecessary burdens on business. It has already produced a number of consultation documents on the above areas and the review is already beginning to have an effect on the legislation; see, for example, the Order under the Deregulation and Contracting Out Act 1994, in relation to elective resolutions.[62]

Many of the topics selected for review relate to small businesses but in addition the DTI in April 1994 invited the Law Commission to carry out a study into the reform of the law applicable to private companies, with special reference to determining whether the present law was meeting the needs of small businesses and whether a new form of incorporation for them was desirable. The conclusions published in a consultative document in November 1994 were broadly that it was not necessary to institute an entirely new form of business association with limited liability, since the main problems for small businesses were not in company law, although it was thought desirable to reform the law of partnership in a number of respects.[63]

Following the insertion by the Companies Act 1989 of a new s 8A into the 1985 Act, empowering the Secretary of State to promulgate regulations introducing a new standard set of articles for what are described as 'partnership companies', the DTI has recently conducted a consultation process over the form that these new articles might take.[64]

'Partnership company' is simply defined in the section as a company limited by shares whose shares are intended to be held to a substantial extent by or on behalf of its employees. The idea behind the partnership company is that members of the workforce participate in the company as 'owners' as well as employees and have a role in its management, although there are a variety of structures through which this is achieved. Usually, though, they will employ some sort of trust which holds shares for the benefit of employees. This has brought various tax advantages since the early 1970s, but now the hope is that the partnership company will be developed further so that it is not only used as a vehicle for tax avoidance but also to promote employee involvement further. If this is to be achieved successfully it is thought that there needs to be a new standard form constitution which can be adopted by such companies which, for instance, would

---

61   (1971) Cmnd 4811.

62   See p 98.

63   Company Law Review: The Law Applicable to Private Companies URN 94/529.

64   Model Articles of Association for Partnership Companies (Table G) March 1995: A Consultative Document URN 95/609.

have more appropriate regulations concerning management and voting rights and the rights of those employee shareholders wishing to leave the company. It is this new constitution, a proposed Table G, which the DTI is now currently drafting.

The European Union

After 1972 and the UK's accession to the Treaty of Rome, followed by the UK's joining of the European Community in 1973, the greatest impetus towards the introduction of new statutory provisions have been the directives issued by the Council of the European Community (now the European Union). Strictly speaking, almost all European action in company law is not a source since there needs to be implementation by national legislation on the part of Member States to bring the substantive proposals into force, but the effect of the European Union on company law cannot be ignored. Also a limited amount of action taken by the Commission does have direct effect in Member States and recent decisions both by the European Court of Justice and the House of Lords mean that reference to and knowledge of the directives will become increasingly important. Significant parts of Chapters 2, 5 and 10 have been affected by European initiatives and Chapter 12 examines in detail the process of European action.

Case law

Despite the enormous volume of legislation relating to companies, and however wide-ranging the provisions appear to be, they cannot be said to amount to a code of company law in the civil law sense. A significant contribution to company law has come from the judgments of company law cases. Around the framework of the statutes the courts have often found themselves in a position where they not only have to interpret the statutory provisions but also they have found it necessary to extrapolate the intention of Parliament and develop rules around this intention (eg in *Ashbury Rly Carriage and Iron Co v Riche* (1875)[65] and the *ultra vires* rule) or to formulate wholly new principles totally independent of the provisions of the Act (eg the fiduciary obligations of directors). While some of the rules developed by the courts (eg the capital maintenance rule laid down by *Trevor v Whitworth*)[66] have been subsequently adopted by the legislature and are now in statutory form, some provisions of the Act refine and presuppose the continued existence of the independent judge-made principles (eg the Companies Act 1985, s 317).

---

65   (1875) LR 7 HL 653. See p 122.
66   (1877) 12 App Cas 409. See p 142.

CHAPTER TWO

FORMATION AND PROMOTION

FORMATION

The formation of a company is a straightforward administrative process involving the delivery to the companies' registrar of the company's memorandum and articles and an accompanying statement in the prescribed form of the name and residential address of the person or persons who are to become the first directors and the first secretary of the company.[1] In addition those persons named as the first directors will have to state their nationality, date of birth, business occupation and other current directorships held by them.[2] This statement has to be signed by or on behalf of the subscribers of the memorandum who are the persons who have agreed to take a certain number of shares to become the first members of the company and has to contain a consent signed by each of the persons named as director and secretary.[3] There is also a fee of £50.00 for registration.[4]

By s 12(1) the registrar is required not to register a company's memorandum unless he is satisfied that all the requirements of the Act have been complied with. But by s 12(2) if he is so satisfied he is under a duty to register the memorandum and articles. So when the registrar receives an application for registration, although it has been said that he is exercising a quasi-judicial function, his discretion to refuse registration is severely limited.[5] It has been held on an application for a writ of *mandamus* that the registrar was correct in refusing to register a company whose proposed object was unlawful.[6] It has been stated *obiter* that if the objects of a proposed company are lawful then the registrar might still have a discretion to refuse registration if the proposed name were scandalous or obscene, but this issue is now expressly dealt with by s 26(1)(e).[7] This paragraph states that a company shall not be registered with a name which in the opinion of the Secretary of State is offensive.

If the registrar is satisfied then on registration of the company's memorandum he shall issue a certificate of incorporation.[8] But the granting of the certificate of incorporation is no guarantee by the registrar that the objects of the company are lawful.[9] On the date of incorporation (which is stated in the certificate) the company is

---

1   Companies Act 1985, s 10.

2   Companies Act 1985, s 10(2), Schedule 1.

3   Companies Act 1985, s 10(3).

4   Companies (Fees) Regulations 1991 (SI 1991 No 1206).

5   *R v Registrar of Companies, ex parte Bowen* [1914] 3 KB 1161.

6   *R v Registrar of Companies, ex parte More* [1931] 2 KB 197.

7   *R v Registrar of Companies, ex parte Bowen* (*supra*).

8   Companies Act 1985, s 13(1).

9   *Bowman v Secular Society Ltd* [1917] AC 406.

'born' and is capable of exercising all the functions of an incorporated company,[10] except that if it is a public company it cannot commence business or exercise any borrowing powers unless the registrar has issued a certificate that he is satisfied that the nominal value of the company's allotted share capital is not less than the authorised minimum.[11]

Section 13(7) provides that:

'A certificate of incorporation given in respect of an association is conclusive evidence –

(a) that the requirements of this Act in respect of registration and of matters precedent and incidental to it have been complied with, and that the association is a company authorised to be registered, and is duly registered, under this Act ...'

Once the certificate of incorporation has been granted and the corporate entity brought into existence it used to be thought that the only way in which the company could be destroyed or extinguished was by winding up in accordance with the provisions of the Companies Acts, but it was suggested in *Bowman v Secular Society Ltd*[12] that as the Crown was not bound by the Companies Act and hence the formation of a company under it, the Attorney General in judicial review proceedings could apply for a writ of certiorari to quash a certificate. This is what occurred in *R v Registrar of Companies, ex parte Attorney General*[13] in which the incorporation of a company formed for the purpose of providing the services of a prostitute was quashed. In this procedure the Attorney General will be arguing that the registrar has acted *ultra vires* or has misdirected himself on the law in granting a certificate of incorporation to a company whose objects are wholly unlawful. As the above case demonstrates, the objects do not necessarily have to involve the commission of criminal offences but it is sufficient if they are illegal in the sense of being void as contrary to public policy.

This procedure, in effect, gives rise to the possibility of nullity, which because of the conclusiveness of s 13(7), had been thought not to be an issue in the UK. This doctrine is well known in jurisdictions in continental Europe where, for example, on the discovery of a defective incorporation, a court declares the incorporation null and void. This can have serious consequences for any persons who dealt with the company before the declaration of nullity, since if the company was never properly incorporated it could never have been a party to any contracts with outsiders. Money expended by the outsider would then be irrecoverable. As a result Articles 11 and 12 of the First EEC Directive[14] moved to solve this problem and in particular Article 12(3) prevents the declaration of nullity from having any retrospective effect on commitments entered into by the company before the declaration of nullity. However, the UK government has not considered it necessary to implement these articles. This would become a

---

10 Companies Act 1985, s 13(3) and (4).
11 Companies Act 1985, s 117.
12 [1917] AC 406 at 439 *per* Lord Parker.
13 [1991] BCLC 476.
14 68/151/EEC.

problem if the procedure followed in *R v Registrar of Companies ex parte Attorney General* were to be used more frequently.

Company names

The 1985 Act contains detailed provisions regulating the choice and form of the name of a registered company. By s 714 the registrar is required to keep an index of the names of all companies registered under the Act. Not surprisingly, a company cannot be registered with a name which is the same as that already chosen by a registered company.[15] Even if a company has had its chosen name registered, if the Secretary of State is of the opinion that the name gives so misleading an indication of the nature of the company's business and activities as to be likely to cause harm to the public, he may direct it to change its name, which it must do within six weeks of the date of the direction, although it is given three weeks within which to apply to the court to have the direction set aside.[16] The Secretary of State can also direct a company to change its name within 12 months of it being registered if he is of the opinion that the company has been registered with a name which is the same as or too similar to a name of a company already appearing in the index of company names or one that should have appeared in the index at that time.[17]

A company cannot be registered with a name which gives the impression that the company is connected with the Government or a local authority without the consent of the Secretary of State[18] and the Secretary of State is given the power to make regulations which specify words or expressions which cannot be used by a company as part of its name without his consent or the consent of a specified Government Department.[19] As mentioned above, a company cannot use a name which in the opinion of the Secretary of State would constitute a criminal offence or which is offensive.[20]

By s 25(1) the name of every public company must end with the words Public Limited Company and by s 25(2) the name of every private company which is limited by shares or guarantee must have 'Limited' as its last word. But in both cases s 27 provides an approved statutory abbreviation which are 'plc' and 'Ltd' respectively. The use of these expressions and abbreviations is jealously guarded since it is a criminal offence for a person or company which is not a public company to use the expression 'Public Limited Company'[21] or its abbreviation and it is also an offence for any person which is not incorporated with limited liability to trade or carry on business under a

---

15 Companies Act 1985, s 26(1)(c).

16 Companies Act 1985, s 32.

17 Companies Act 1985, s 28.

18 Companies Act 1985, s 26(2).

19 Companies Act 1985, s 29(1).

20 Companies Act 1985, s 25(d) and (3).

21 Companies Act 1985, s 33(1).

name which uses the word 'Limited' or its abbreviation.[22] In both cases a person convicted is liable to a daily default fine. Additionally a public company commits an offence if, in circumstances in which the fact that it is a public company is likely to be material, it uses a name which may reasonably be expected to give the misleading impression that it is a private company.[23]

A company can change its name by the passing of a special resolution in which case the registrar changes the name on the index and issues a new certificate of incorporation.[24]

In order to protect the public the legislature has policed the use of the company name since primarily this is the way in which the public's attention can be drawn to the fact that it is dealing with a legal person whose liability is limited. If the provisions are not complied with then generally speaking the privilege of incorporation is withdrawn.

So, by s 348 every company shall paint or affix, and keep painted or affixed, a sign with the company's name on the outside of every office or place in which its business is carried on. This sign has to be conspicuous and legible. It is a criminal offence to fail to comply with the section for which both the company and every officer in default can be liable.

By s 349 every company has to have its name on all letters, notices and bills and if it is in default not only is the company liable to a fine but so also is every officer or director of the company who is responsible for such a document. Further, under s 349(4) an officer is not only criminally liable if he signs or authorises to be signed on behalf of the company any bill, cheque, promissory note or order for money or goods if the company's name is not mentioned as required by subsection (1) but also he incurs *personal civil liability* to the holder of the bill, cheque etc. This liability can be incurred even where the name of the company is simply not complete. This occurred, for example, where the name of the company was 'Michael Jackson (Fancy Goods) Ltd' and the director, in signing an acceptance form of the bill of exchange on behalf of the company drawn up by the plaintiff, did not correct a reference to his company of 'M Jackson (Fancy Goods) Ltd'. The company was then in liquidation and it was held that potentially the director could have been personally liable on the bill.[25]

Recently a similar case was brought against a director of a company who had signed cheques on behalf of a company called 'Primakeen Ltd'. But the company's name appeared as 'Primkeen Ltd' and the issue was whether the director was personally liable. It was held that the director was not liable since the misspelling here did not lead to any of the vices against which the statutory provisions were directed and the plaintiff was in no doubt as to which company he was dealing with.[26] This finding is difficult to reconcile with the strictness of the previous case.

---

22 Companies Act 1985, s 34.
23 Companies Act 1985, s 33(2).
24 Companies Act 1985, s 28.
25 *Durham Fancy Goods Ltd v Michael Jackson (Fancy Goods) Ltd* [1968] 2 QB 839.
26 *Jenice Ltd v Dan* [1993] BCLC 1349.

The Insolvency Act 1986 added a new liability to try to control the worst abuses of the so-called 'Phoenix Syndrome'. This is where directors run a company and put it into insolvent liquidation and then shortly afterwards form a new company with the same or virtually same name. They are then in a position to exploit the goodwill of the old company. Often the directors would buy the assets of the original company from the liquidator at a 'knock-down' price. In these circumstances by s 216 of the Insolvency Act the directors will now commit a criminal offence if they were a director 12 months before the company went into liquidation and within five years are concerned with the promotion, formation or management of a company with the same name or a similar name which suggests an association with the original company. What is more interesting is that the director in contravention of s 216 will incur joint and several personal liability for the debts of the company if he is involved in the management of the new company. Further, anyone else who knowingly acts on the instructions of someone who is in contravention of s 216 will also incur joint and several personal liability.

These provisions have recently been considered by the Court of Appeal in *Thorne v Silverleaf*[27] where the court's interpretation and application of the provision is rather ominous for directors. Here the plaintiff had entered into a joint venture with the company and under that agreement had supplied the company with large sums of money. Further, the plaintiff had attended nine or 10 meetings with the defendant where the management of the company was discussed. When the company went into insolvent liquidation owing the plaintiff some £135,000, the plaintiff brought proceedings claiming that, as the name of the company was similar to the name of two previous companies of which the defendant was a director and which went into insolvent liquidation, the defendant was liable to him personally. The Court of Appeal agreed and allowed the plaintiff to recover despite the fact that the plaintiff could hardly be said to be in the range of persons most at risk from the 'Phoenix Syndrome' since he was not misled or confused by the use of the similar name or the victim of fraud – a quite different approach to the one taken in *Jenice Ltd v Dan*. It was also argued that as he had aided and abetted the defendant in the commission of the offence he should on public policy grounds be precluded from recovering. But it was decided that even if he did aid and abet the defendant, that would not preclude him from recovery under s 217, and that the public policy rule only prevented enforcement of rights *directly* resulting from the crime. Here the transactions under which moneys passed from the plaintiff to the company were not in themselves illegal transactions and the plaintiff did not have to plead or rely on an illegality.[28]

---

27 [1994] 1 BCLC 637.

28 *Ibid* at 645.

Promoters

Who is a promoter?

A promoter is someone who forms a company and performs other tasks necessary for it to begin business whether the company is to issue shares or not. This, however, is only a description of what a promoter is. There is no definition of the term 'promoter' in the present Companies Acts,[29] presumably because it has been thought that to produce a definition would ensure that unscrupulous promoters would arrange circumstances so that they always remained outside it. This was also the view of the Cohen Committee when it was suggested to it that the term 'promoter' should be statutorily defined.[30] Any definition would limit rather than expand the scope of what is a promoter or promotion. Persons would then escape who ought to be held liable and a statutory definition cannot be constantly amended. But there are a number of general statements in the cases as to the sort of persons who are considered promoters. One of the most well-known is that of Bowen J in *Whaley Bridge Calico Printing Co v Green*[31] where he states that:

'[t]he term promoter is a term not of law, but of business, usefully summing up in a single word a number of business operations particular to the commercial world by which a company is generally brought into existence.'[32]

But rather than look for a general definition of a promoter in terms of what such a person does, it is preferable in any particular case to ask more broadly, as Bowen J did in *Whaley Bridge*, whether the person in question placed himself in such a position in relation to the company from which equity will not allow him to retain any secret advantage for himself. This is because:

'[t]he relief afforded by equity to companies against promoters who have sought improperly to make concealed profits out of the promotion, is only an instance of the more general principle upon which equity prevents the abuse of undue influence and of fiduciary relations.'[32]

and:

'[i]n every case the relief granted must depend on the establishment of such relations between the promoter and the birth, formation and floating of the company, as render it contrary to good faith that the promoter should derive a secret profit from the promotion.'[32]

Persons who are acting in a purely professional capacity who have been instructed by a promoter, for example a lawyer or accountant, do not become promoters themselves.[33]

---

29 Although there was in the Joint Stock Companies Act 1844.

30 Cohen Committee, Minutes of Evidence, q 7359.

31 (1879) 5 QBD 109.

32 *Ibid* at 111.

33 *Re Great Wheal Polgooth Co Ltd* (1883) 53 LJ Ch 42.

Although if they go beyond this and, for example, agree to become a director or secretary of the company, they will be held to have become promoters.[34]

But a person who is able to instruct persons to form a company, sell property to it or procure the first director to run it would be considered to be a promoter because of the power and influence that that person is able to exert over the company. The company will not have a board of directors at this stage so as to be able to form an independent judgment and therefore it can be forced into transactions which perhaps are not in its best interests and instead to the advantage of the promoter. The duties which are imposed upon a promoter are fiduciary and as such he will be subject to broadly the same judge-made duties which apply to directors. As was clearly stated in *New Sombrero Phosphate Co Ltd v Erlanger* by James LJ:[35]

'A promoter is ... in a fiduciary relation to the company which he promotes or causes to come into existence. If that promoter has a property which he desires to sell to the company, it is quite open to him to do so; but upon him, as upon any other person in a fiduciary position, it is incumbent to make full and fair disclosure of his interest and position with respect to that property.'

Again, in *Lagunas Nitrate Co v Lagunas Syndicate*[36] Lindley MR said:

'[t]he first principle is that in equity the promoters of a company stand in a fiduciary relation to it, and to those persons whom they induce to become shareholders in it, and cannot bind the company by any contract with themselves without fully and fairly disclosing to the company all material facts which the company ought to know.'[37]

The fiduciary duty of a promoter is to the company, but as alluded to in the last quotation ultimately the persons whose money and property are at risk are the investors who are the first persons to buy shares in the new company. In a situation which used commonly to occur, the promoter forced the sale of his own property to the company at substantially more than its true value and paid himself out of the cash received from the sale of shares. The shareholders would then find that the company's assets had already been seriously diminished and thus the value of their shares fell.[38]

Another problem was where a promoter received a commission on a transaction he made for the company. Although the company was not suffering any apparent direct loss it was against the principles of equity that the promoter should keep the commission if undisclosed and unapproved.[39]

Disclosure

So disclosure is the key for the promoter and as long as he has brought his interest to the relevant persons' notice then, except in one special class of case, he will be able to

---

34 *Bagnall v Carlton* (1877) 6 Ch D 371.

35 (1877) 5 Ch D 73 at 118.

36 [1899] 2 Ch 392.

37 *Ibid* at 422.

38 See *Erlanger v New Sombrero Phosphate Co Ltd* (1878) 3 App Cas 1218.

39 *Emma Silver Mining Co v Grant* (1879) 11 Ch D 918.

enforce the contract and retain the profit. But a crucial question is, disclosure to whom? In *Erlanger v New Sombrero Phosphate Co*,[40] a syndicate purchased the lease of an island together with phosphate mineral rights. A company was then formed and the lease and mineral rights were sold to it at a price which was double its true market value. The syndicate had named the first board of directors of the company, the active members of which acted simply as nominees of the syndicate and adopted and ratified the contract. In the words of Lord O'Hagan, their conduct was precisely that which might have been expected from the character of their selection. In these circumstances the House of Lords set the contract aside. The thrust of the speeches is that the promoting syndicate failed in its obligation to the company to nominate an independent board and make full disclosure of the fact that they were the vendors of the property.

> 'I do not say that the owner of property may not promote and form a joint stock company, and then sell his property to it, but I do say that if he does, he is bound to take care that he sells it to the company through the medium of a board of directors who can and do exercise an independent and intelligent judgment on the transaction, and who are not left under the belief that the property belongs, not to the promoter, but to some other person.'[41]

This would, however, only apply in the case of the more ambitious projects where the company is formed with the intention of inviting the public to subscribe for shares (and it might even be too strict for those cases). It would be absurd to attempt to apply this rule to the much more commonly occurring form of promotion where a sole trader or the partners of a partnership incorporate a business and then become the first directors themselves. Of course this was the situation which occurred in *Salomon*.

Here the necessary and sufficient disclosure will be to those persons who are invited to become the shareholders. In *Salomon v A Salomon & Co Ltd*[42] the lower courts had taken an adverse view of the sale of the business to the company at a gross overvalue by Salomon who was obviously the promoter but in the House of Lords an argument that the sale of the business to the company should be set aside on *Erlanger* principles was rejected since the full circumstances of the sale were known by all the shareholders. So it appears that there is no duty on a promoter to provide the company with an independent board but disclosure must be to all shareholders. This view did not only find favour in relation to the 'one-person' or 'family' company situation since, in *Lagunas Nitrate Co v Lagunas Syndicate*,[43] a majority in the Court of Appeal held that disclosure of a transaction in the prospectus issued to the public was sufficient disclosure.

As a result anyone who is occupying the position of promoter and is transferring property to the company would be well advised to make this fact known to all the

---

40   (1878) 3 App Cas 1218.
41   *Ibid* at 1236 *per* Lord Cairns LC.
42   [1897] AC 22.
43   [1899] 2 Ch 392.

shareholders. It need not be done at a formal general meeting if all the shareholders approve of the transaction.[44] If there is not unanimity than a formal resolution in a general meeting should be obtained.

Remedies

Where a promoter is in breach of his duty to the company and is making an undisclosed profit from the sale of an asset to the company, the remedies available to the company are a rescission of the contract, in which case the profit will usually evaporate (but the company will still be able to recover any profit made as an ancillary to the main transaction), or a recovery of the profit from the promoter.

For rescission to be available for the company *restitutio in integrum* has to be possible. This means that the right to rescind will be lost if an innocent third party has acquired an interest in the property (eg the company has mortgaged the property as security for a loan to a third party mortgagee), or there has been a delay by the company in making its election to rescind after discovery of the true position or during that time the position of the promoter has changed.[45]

The right of the company to rescind as a result of an undisclosed interest on the part of the promoter exists whether the promoter acquired the property in question before or after he began to act as promoter.

In respect of a recovery of secret profit by the company where rescission is not available the company, it seems, can only do this where the promoter acquired the interest in the property after he began to act as promoter.[46] This is because the courts have reasoned that to make the promoter account for profits made on the sale of *pre-acquired* property to the company while the contract remained intact would be essentially to force a new contract on the promoter and the company at a lower purchase price. To allow the company to elect to keep the property and insist upon a return of the profit would be to alter the contract and substitute a lower purchase price. This proposition was accepted by a majority in the Court of Appeal in *Re Cape Breton Co*.[47] They reasoned that in these circumstances *either* the claim by the company would be for the difference between what the promoter originally paid for the property and the price paid by the company. But this could not be the correct amount because at the time the promoter acquired the property he was under no duty and he was not acquiring on for and on behalf of the company. *Or*, alternatively, to measure the difference between the real or market value of the property at the time of the sale of the company and the price actually paid by the company. In other words, the price at which the property should have been sold to the company. This was also rejected since if the company is affirming the contract by electing not to rescind, it is adopting the

---

44   See *Salomon v A Salomon & Co Ltd* [1897] AC 22 at 57 *per* Lord Davey.

45   *Re Leeds & Hanley Theatres of Varieties* [1902] 2 Ch 809; *Clough v The London & North Western Rly Co* (1871) LR 7 Ex 26.

46   *Re Cape Breton Co* (1885) 29 Ch D 795; affirmed *sub nom Cavendish Bentinck v Fenn* (1887) 12 App Cas 652.

47   *Supra.*

contract at the sale price. No surreptitious or clandestine profits are made by the promoter because in this sense the profits are only made once the adoption of the contract is made by the company.[48]

Bowen LJ dissenting,[49] held that the reasoning of the majority was fallacious and that by making the promoter/vendor return something which he ought not to have, ie, the profit, is not altering the contract, it is only insisting upon a liability which equity attaches to it because the non-disclosing promoter knew or ought to have known at the outset that it was an incident of equity and fair play attaching to such contract that a promoter was liable to hand back any undisclosed profit.

However, the views of the majority in *Re Cape Breton* have been generally accepted.[50] But in order to avoid injustice in these cases where the promoter sells pre-acquired property to the company and makes a profit because of the unavailability of rescission the courts have held promoters liable in damages for loss caused by a breach of duty or in negligence by causing the company to buy an overpriced asset.[51]

The present day

There has been very little reported litigation involving promoters' liability since the First World War. The decision in *Salomon* meant that, where a company was being promoted to acquire the existing business of a sole trader or a partnership, it was unlikely that the shareholders would not have knowledge of and have assented to what was being done (especially since the Companies Act 1907 reduced the minimum number of members of private companies to two), and so there could be no complaint about contracts which a promoter had caused to be made. In respect of larger ventures, where shares were offered for sale to the public, there was increasing control on the prospectuses or other documents issued to the public inviting them to subscribe for shares. This had begun as early as the Companies Act 1867 with a modest requirement to disclose the promoter's contracts in the prospectus, but was supplemented by the Companies Acts 1900 and 1907 and the Director Liability Act 1890. This increased regulation continued in the 20th century with the Prevention of Fraud (Investments) Act 1939 (replaced in 1958) which made some of the former promoters' activities a criminal offence. More than this, however, was probably the replacement of the private investor by the institutional investor as the dominant source of investment capital and the fact that this latter sort of investor would not buy shares in dubious, untested schemes.

The extra-legal regulation of the main market for shares in the UK by the Stock Exchange means that it is extremely unusual for a public company to be formed and issue shares to the public without a trading record. For a public company to obtain an official listing on the Stock Exchange it has to have at least a three-year record of

---

48 See generally the judgments of Cotton and Fry LJJ.
49 *Ibid* at 806.
50 *Burland v Earle* [1902] AC 83.
51 *Leeds & Hanley Theatres of Varieties (supra)*; *Jacobus Marler Estates v Marler* (1913) 85 LJ PC 167.

trading, and even for the Stock Exchange's Unlisted Securities Market (USM) a two-year record has been required. The USM will soon be closed down by the Stock Exchange after 1996 and replaced by the Alternative Investment Market (AIM) which opened in June 1995. There is no minimum trading record required for admission but companies seeking admission will still have to comply with the Stock Exchange's specific rules for this market.

PROTECTION OF SUBSCRIBERS AND ALLOTTEES OF SHARES

Although there is no necessary connection between the formation and promotion of the company and the allotment of shares to shareholders which can occur at any time during the life of the company, because the law relating to promoters has been considered which affords indirect protection for subscribers of shares, it is convenient to continue with a brief examination of the law relating to public issues of shares which provides a more direct form of protection.

Civil liability

A purchaser of shares in a company may find that he has been misled about the performance and prospects of the company and thereby he suffers or will suffer loss. As is the case with all other contracts a person in this position may have rights under common law and the Misrepresentation Act 1967 to rescind the contract or to seek damages[51a] but some consideration must be given to the special case of a purchaser of shares from the company itself under a contract of allotment, in particular where there is a public issue of shares or other securities.

As mentioned in the preceding section, from very early times there has been an obligation on the company to provide information in a prospectus, which was essentially the advertisement for the company's shares, for the information of potential investors. But the difficulties of providing a purchaser of shares with a damages remedy at common law where he had purchased those shares on the basis of false statements in a prospectus were revealed in the House of Lords decision in *Derry v Peek*.[52] The plaintiff had purchased shares in a company, relying on statements in a prospectus concerning the rights enjoyed by the company which turned out to be false. It was too late for the plaintiff to rescind the contract because the company had gone into liquidation,[53] so an action in the tort of deceit was brought against the directors. This was unsuccessful because it was held that in order to succeed in deceit, fraud must be

---

51a In *Possfund Custodian Trustee Ltd v Diamond* (1996) The Times, April 18, Lightman J stated that when a purchaser in the USM claimed damages at common law for misrepresentation after being misled by defects in a prospectus he had to establish that he reasonably (i) relied on the relevant representation, and (ii) believed that the representation intended him to act on it. That being the case it was at least arguable that a duty of care was owed by those responsible for a prospectus not only to initial suscribers for shares but also to subsequent purchasers in the USM who reasonably relied on the prospectus.

52 (1889) 14 App Cas 337.

53 See *Oakes v Turquand* (1867) LR 2 HL 325.

proved which required actual dishonesty. Here the directors had only been careless and honestly believed the statements to be true. It was to solve this problem that the Directors' Liability Act 1890 was passed to impose liability on promoters and directors for false statements in prospectuses.

Now, the most important legislative regulation of public issues is contained in the Public Offers of Securities Regulations 1995[54] and Part IV of the Financial Services Act 1986 as amended by these Regulations. Which of these will apply and provide remedies for the wronged investor will depend on whether the shares acquired are in a company with an official listing or where there is an application for an official listing or, alternatively, where the shares are unlisted.

The Public Offers of Securities Regulations 1995 were made under s 2(2) of the European Communities Act 1972 to comply with the Prospectus Directive[55] and where shares or debentures which fall within the ambit of that Directive are issued which are neither admitted to an official listing on the Stock Exchange nor subject to an application for such listing the 1995 Regulations apply. These have replaced Part III of the Companies Act 1985 and repealed Part V of the Financial Services Act 1986 (which never came into force). Where there is an offer of a company's shares and that company has an official listing on the Stock Exchange or there will be an application for admission to the Official List then Part IV of the Financial Services Act 1986 applies.

Both regulatory regimes have been heavily influenced in the last ten years by EC Directives concerning the regulation of capital markets.[56] The basic aim of these directives has been to lay down a minimum set of disclosure standards and regulatory framework for securities across the Community, to achieve mutual recognition of propectuses and ultimately to achieve a pan-European market for company securities. The following account is of the basic regulation under the 1995 Regulations. As regards officially listed securities, Part IV of the Financial Services Act 1986 ss 142–57 provides a purchaser of shares with a very similar remedy and is referred to briefly below.

The disclosure requirements

When securities to which the 1995 Regulations apply are offered to the public in the UK for the first time, the 'offeror' has to publish a prospectus by making it available to the public, free of charge, at an address in the UK during the offer period, and deliver a copy of it to the Registrar of Companies.[57]

---

54 SI 1995/1537.

55 89/298/EEC.

56 For example, 79/279/EEC (Admissions Directive); 80/390/EEC (Listing Particulars Directive); 87/345/EEC (Recognition of Listing Particulars Directive).

57 Reg 4.

An offer of securities to the public has to be substantial and offers where the total consideration payable for all the securities offered does not exceed 40,000 ECU are exempted from the regulations.[58] Similarly exempted are offers to persons whose business is to acquire, hold or manage investments,[59] offers to no more than 50 persons[60] and offers 'to a restricted circle of persons whom the offeror reasonably believes to be sufficiently knowledgeable to understand the risks involved in accepting the offer'.[61]

The 'offeror' who must publish the prospectus can, of course, be the company where the company is making a direct offer or 'offer for subscription' to the public or making a 'rights issue'. Or it can be an issuing house or merchant bank where there is an 'offer for sale'. In the latter case the company transfers the shares to the issuing house which then has the task of making the offer. In this situation the issuing house does not become a registered member of the company while it is holding the shares, but it is responsible for the success of the offer. But the regulations might apply also where an existing major shareholder of the company decides to dispose of its shares to the public.

Schedule 1 to the Regulations provides for the form and content of the prospectuses. But regulation 9 states that in addition to this information a prospectus shall contain all such information which is within the knowledge of any person responsible for the prospectus or which it would be reasonable for him to obtain by making enquiries as investors would reasonably require and reasonably expect to find there, for the purpose of making an informed assessment of:

'(a) the assets and liabilities, financial position, profits and losses, and prospects of the issuer of the securities; and

(b) the rights attaching to those securities.'

Liability to pay compensation

By regulation 14 if a person acquires securities in a company to which a prospectus relates and suffers loss as a result of any untrue or misleading statement in the prospectus or the omission from it of any matter required to be included by regulation 9 or 10 then the person or persons responsible for the prospectus will be liable to compensate the acquirer. The word 'acquire' for the purposes of the regulation includes a contract to acquire shares or an interest in them.[62]

The persons responsible for the prospectus are the company itself, each director of the company at the time when the prospectus was published (or is stated as having agreed to become a director), every person who accepts and is stated in the prospectus as accepting responsibility for or for any part of the prospectus, the offeror of the

---

58   Reg 7(2)(h).
59   Reg 7(2)(a).
60   Reg 8(2)(b).
61   Reg 7(2)(d).
62   Reg 14(5).

securities where he is not the company, and any other person who has authorised the contents of the prospectus.[63]

The company and the directors are not responsible for these purposes unless the company has authorised the offer in relation to which the prospectus relates.[64] The definition of persons responsible specifically excludes those persons giving advice as to the contents of the particulars in a professional capacity.[65] So, solicitors simply giving advice to a company on compliance with the regulations would not be responsible as long as, of course, they did not expressly accept responsibility for the particulars or authorise its contents.

There are a number of defences or exemptions available to persons who might otherwise be liable to pay compensation. So, a director is not responsible for any prospectus if it is published without his knowledge or consent and on becoming aware of its publication he forthwith gives reasonable notice to the public that it was so published without his knowledge or consent.[66] Further, if a person has accepted responsibility or authorised only a part of the prospectus he is only responsible for that part.[67]

Regulation 15 provides a defence (although it is actually termed an exemption from liability to pay compensation) where a person satisfies the court that at the time when the prospectus was delivered for registration he reasonably believed, having made such enquiries, if any, as were reasonable, that the statement was true and not misleading or that the matter which was omitted which caused the loss was properly omitted. Further, for the defence to succeed it must be shown that the person continued in this belief up until the time when the shares were acquired or if he did discover the mistake or omission he did all that was reasonable to bring it to the attention of persons likely to acquire shares.[68]

Second, a person is not liable to pay compensation if the loss was caused by a statement made by an expert which was included in the prospectus with the expert's consent and the person satisfies the court that at the time the prospectus was delivered for registration he had reasonable grounds for believing that the expert was competent to make or authorise the statement. Again this defence is subject to all reasonable steps being taken to bring any mistakes or omissions which are discovered to the attention of persons likely to acquire shares.[69]

Third, a person is not liable to pay compensation if he satisfies the court that the person suffering the loss acquired the shares with knowledge that the statement in the prospectus was false or misleading or knew of the omitted matter.[70]

---

63 Reg 13(1).
64 Reg 13(2).
65 Reg 13(4).
66 Reg 13(2).
67 Reg 13(3).
68 Reg 15(1).
69 Reg 15(2).
70 Reg 15(5).

Listed securities

As regards securities for which an official listing will be sought, s 142 of the Financial Services Act 1986 prohibits any shares from being admitted to the Official List except in accordance with the provisions of Part IV and s 142(6) makes the Stock Exchange the 'competent authority' to make listing rules for admission to the Official List.

By s 144(2) the listing rules must make the submission to and approval by the Stock Exchange of a prospectus and publication of that prospectus a condition of the admission of any shares to the Official List where the shares are to be offered to the public for the first time before admission.

In respect of any other securities the listing rules require as a condition of admission to the Official List a document known as 'listing particulars' which must be submitted to and approved by the Stock Exchange and then published.[71]

In both cases, however, the listing rules will require a similar amount of disclosure and there is the same general duty of disclosure in respect of prospectuses and listing particulars in Part IV as there is for prospectuses under the Public Offers of Securities Regulations 1995.

Further, the sanctions on the persons responsible for failing to make proper disclosure and the liability to pay compensation are virtually the same as under the 1995 Regulations as described above. So that by s 150 persons responsible for the prospectus or listing particulars will be liable to pay compensation to any person who has acquired shares and suffered loss in respect of them as a result of any untrue or misleading statement or the omission of any matter required to be included. There are also similar provisions as to who is responsible for the documents and similar defences and exemptions contained in s 151 and s 152 as there are in the corresponding regulations of the 1995 Regulations.

Compensation

The amount of compensation payable under regulation 14 of the 1995 Regulations or s 150 is likely to be the same as the tort measure of damages. That is to say the compensation should be of such an amount as to put the person back into the same position as he would have been in if he had not suffered the loss.

Examples from successful common law actions for damages will be of some assistance. An early example of the payment of damages at common law for non-disclosure by promoters was *Twycross v Grant*[72] where the promoters had not disclosed their contracts with the company as they were obliged to do under s 38 of the Companies Act 1867 and the section deemed the non-disclosure to be fraudulent. The shares turned out to be worthless and damages were recovered by the plaintiff for fraudulent misrepresentation equal to the entire amount which was paid for them.

---

71   Financial Services Act 1986, s 144(2).

72   (1877) 46 LJ CP 636.

Alternatively if, for example, a person had acquired shares for £10,000, and it transpired that a company had not signed a franchise agreement with a third party which the prospectus stated had been signed so that the market value of the shares was only £1,000, then *prima facie* the compensation payable would be £9,000.

So, for example, in *Smith New Court Securities Ltd v Scrimgeour Vickers (Asset Management) Ltd*,[73] shares in F plc had been purchased by the plaintiff following a fraudulent representation to it that other bidders were interested in the shares. This representation was made with the intention of inducing the plaintiff to bid for the shares and indeed had that effect. It was held that the measure of damages should be fixed at the difference between what the plaintiff paid for the shares and their actual value at the time of the transaction. Where shares were quoted on the Stock Exchange *prima facie* the actual true value of the shares was their market value at the time the transaction took place. But this *prima facie* rule will be displaced where there was a false market for the shares on that day, eg the share price was artificially inflated by the publication of false information.

Regulation 14(4) and s 150(4) specifically preserves 'any liability which any person may incur apart from this section', so that a purchaser of shares may still pursue common law remedies for damages or rescission instead of seeking compensation.

Criminal liability

Apart from the civil remedies for issuing a false prospectus or listing particulars there may be criminal consequences as well. By s 47 of the Financial Services Act 1986 any person who makes a statement, promise or forecast which he knows to be misleading, false or deceptive or makes such a statement, promise or forecast recklessly or dishonestly conceals any material facts is guilty of an offence if he makes the statement, promise or forecast or conceals the facts for the purpose of inducing, or is reckless as to whether it may induce, another person to enter into a contract in the UK to buy or sell shares. Further it is also a criminal offence for a person to create a false or misleading impression in the UK as to the market in or the price or value of any shares if he does so for the purpose of inducing another person to acquire, dispose of or subscribe for shares. It will be a defence to this latter offence for the person against whom any charge is brought to prove that he reasonably believed that his act or conduct would not create a false or misleading impression.

An offence under s 47 is triable either way and on a conviction on indictment a person is liable to imprisonment for a term not exceeding seven years or to an unlimited fine or both; and on summary conviction to a term of imprisonment not exceeding six months or to a fine not exceeding the statutory maximum or both.

It should also be mentioned that under s 19 of the Theft Act 1968, a director or other company officer is guilty of an offence if, with intent to deceive members or creditors (which includes debenture holders) of the company about its affairs, publishes

---

73   [1994] 1 WLR 1271. Leave to appeal to the House of Lords has been granted: [1995] 1 WLR 384.

or concurs in publishing a written statement or account which, to his knowledge, is or may be misleading, false or deceptive. On conviction on indictment for an offence under this section a person is liable to a term of imprisonment of up to seven years. This section provides a much more limited liability in the present context than s 47 since the intent to deceive is of existing members of the company, so it might be invoked, for example, where the directors make false statements to members on a rights issue.

PRE-INCORPORATION CONTRACTS

Quite commonly a promoter will have to enter into contracts with third parties on behalf of the proposed company at a time when the company has not yet been formed. A problem which could be faced by third parties in this position if, for instance, the company is subsequently never formed or is formed but goes into liquidation before the bill is paid, is that they do not have anyone to enforce the contract against. This is because the promoter would claim only to be standing in the position of an agent for the company and therefore not personally liable on the contract.

Even if the company were subsequently incorporated and were solvent at the relevant time, it has been the law from very early in the history of the registered company that a contract made for or on behalf of a company at a time when the company did not exist is void.[74] A valid contract requires two parties in existence and possessing legal capacity at the time when the contract is entered into.

Further, even if the company were subsequently incorporated it cannot ratify and adopt the benefit of a contract which has purportedly been made on its behalf.[75] This is the position regardless of whether the purported ratification is by a decision of the directors, a vote of the members in a general meeting or a statement to that effect in the articles. This is because it has been held that the rights and obligations which the purported contract creates cannot be transferred by one of the parties to the contract, the promoter, to the company, which was not capable at the time the contract was made of being a party itself. In order for the contract to be enforced by or against the company there has to be evidence of a novation of it after the company was incorporated. Novation differs from ratification in that essentially a new contract is made on the same terms but this time between the company and the third party. But the courts will not lightly infer that there has been a novation and, for instance, expenditure by the company on the basis of a mistaken belief that the contract is valid will not suffice.[76] In *Howard v Patent Ivory Manufacturing*,[77] the court did infer the existence of a new contract when the board of directors of the newly formed company adopted the agreement in the presence of the third party contractor. Strictly speaking this should not have been sufficient to distinguish this case from previous authority but

---

74 *Kelner v Baxter* (1866) LR 2 CP 174.

75 *Natal Land and Colonisation Co v Pauline Colliery and Development Syndicate* [1904] AC 120.

76 *Re Northumberland Avenue Hotel Co Ltd* (1886) 33 Ch D 16.

77 (1888) 38 Ch D 156.

the judge had clearly taken a view on the merits of the case since the company had enjoyed the benefits of the contract and the liquidator was now seeking to assert that there was never a binding contract.

The case can be distinguished on its facts from previous authority since there had been a subsequent renegotiation of the terms of the contract and the method by which the third party would be remunerated and this would support the view that there was a new contract made.

So, *prima facie*, at common law a pre-incorporation contract is void. But the circumstances have not in all cases been so straightforward. For instance in *Kelner v Baxter*[78] the promoters of a company ordered stock from a supplier and signed a written agreement on behalf of the proposed company. The company was subsequently incorporated but later went into liquidation before the supplier's bill was paid. The court applied the principle that it is better to construe a document as having effect than to make it void, and looking at this situation where at the material time all concerned knew the company did not exist construed the agreement as making the promoters *personally* liable. It cannot have been the intention of the parties to enter into a void agreement or that the supplier contemplated that the payment of his bill was contingent on the formation of the company. The court assumed that the parties contemplated that the persons signing the agreement would be personally liable.

This case was considered in *Newborne v Sensolid (Great Britain) Ltd*[79] where in effect the position was reversed and a promoter was attempting to enforce a contract against a third party buyer. The contract had been signed by the company itself with the promoter's name typed underneath. It was then discovered that on the date the contract was signed the company had not been incorporated so the promoter argued that on *Kelner v Baxter* principles he could enforce the contract personally. But this argument was rejected because in this case looking at the way in which the contract was signed it was the company which purported to make the contract and the promoter did not sign as agent or on behalf of the company but only to authenticate the signature of the company.

The position of the common law was that either it made a difference in the way a promoter signed the contract or, more likely, that as Oliver LJ stated:

> '[t]he question in each case is what is the real intent as revealed by the contract? Does the contract purport to be one which is directly between the supposed principal and the other party, or does it purport to be one between the agent himself – albeit acting for a supposed principal – and the other party? In other words, what you have to look at is whether the agent intended himself to be a party to the contract.'[80]

This unhappy state of affairs was not addressed by the legislature until the UK became a member state of the EEC. Then in 1973 s 9(2) of the European Communities Act 1972 enacted the substance of article 7 of the First Directive. As the UK was not a

---

78   (1866) LR 2 CP 174.

79   [1954] 1 QB 45.

80   *Phonogram Ltd v Lane* [1982] QB 938 at 945.

Member State when the Directive was adopted, there is no official English translation of the text, but in accordance with the general aim of the Directive, which was to protect persons dealing with companies, the provision enables the outsider to enforce the contract against the promoter. The provision is now contained in s 36C of the 1985 Act which provides as follows:

'A contract which purports to be made by or on behalf of a company at a time when the company has not been formed has effect, subject to any agreement to the contrary, as one made with the person purporting to act for the company or as agent for it, and he is personally liable on the contract accordingly.'

The first occasion on which the courts had an opportunity to examine the section was in *Phonogram v Lane*.[81] Here L was going to promote a company called FM Ltd and this company was to manage a pop group called 'Cheap, Mean and Nasty'. L induced Phonogram Ltd to advance £6,000 to L in order to finance the group which would enter into a recording contract with Phonogram. An agreement was signed by L with Phonogram 'for and on behalf of' the proposed company. One of the terms of the contract was to the effect that if FM Ltd was not formed within one month L had to repay the money. In fact FM Ltd was never formed. At first instance the judge, Phillips J, construed the agreement as a pre-incorporation contract and, applying s 9(2) held L personally liable. On appeal the Court of Appeal stated that it would have construed the agreement quite differently since L had clearly undertaken to repay the money personally anyway. But on the basis that the judge had found that this was a pre-incorporation contract and there was no appeal against part of the decision the Court of Appeal proceeded to apply s 9(2) and decided it would cover this situation.

A broad and purposive interpretation of the section by the Court of Appeal is evident by the fact it made no difference that both parties knew the company had not been formed at the material time. Further, that Lord Denning took pains to reject an argument that had been raised in Cheshire & Fifoot's *Law of Contract*[82] to the effect that if a promoter expressly signed as agent for a company this would amount to 'an agreement to the contrary' thus avoiding the effect of the section. It was held that for the purposes of the section there has to be a clear exclusion of personal liability and this will not be made by inferences from the way in which the contract was signed.

Subsequent cases have shown that the courts will not allow the section to be used where for some reason an incorrect name has been used for or by the contracting company. So in *Oshkosh B'Gosh v Dan Marbel Inc Ltd*[83] the Court of Appeal would not allow the section to be applied where a company had passed a resolution to change its name to Dan Marbel Inc Ltd and had entered into contracts under this name but had not at the relevant time registered that new name with the registrar. A successful application of the section would have made the director who acted for the company personally liable but the argument that the company called Dan Marbel Inc Ltd did not exist and was not formed for the purposes of the section until the new name was

81   *Supra.*
82   9th edn (1976).
83   [1989] BCLC 507.

registered could not stand in the light of s 28(7). This provision specifically provides that a change of name by a company shall not affect any rights, obligations or liabilities of the company. The position is that the company has a single, perpetual existence and the name is merely the label of the entity.

Similarly the decision in *Badgerhill Properties Ltd v Cottrell*[84] which is to the effect that if it is clear that a particular company has entered into a contract, the fact that the company's name is misspelt will not allow an argument to be raised in favour of fixing the person who acted for the company with personal liability under the section by reasoning that a company with the misspelt name did not at the time exist.

Another attempt to enlarge the scope of the section failed in *Cotronic (UK) Ltd v Dezonie*,[85] where a contract was signed by D on behalf of a company which, unknown to the parties, had been struck off by the Registrar some five years earlier. A new company with an identical name to the previous one was then formed and D claimed that the agreement had been a pre-incorporation contract and, as such, he could enforce it by relying on what is now s 36C. The argument failed because the contract was not purporting to be made by the new company and *ipso facto* D was not purporting to act as agent for it. The contract was purporting to be made with a company which had been formed long before but was not in existence at the relevant time. No one had thought about the new company.

So what the cases show is that the section will apply only where a contract is purported to be made by or on behalf of a corporate entity which is intended to be a contractual party but which has not at that time been incorporated. In those circumstances the person acting for the company or as agent for it will incur personal liability.

The issue which could have been raised in *Cotronic v Dezonie*, if the court had decided that this was a pre-incorporation contract to which the section could apply, is whether the promoter can rely on the section to enforce the contract against the third party. As the section states that the pre-incorporation contract has effect as a contract made with the promoter, this would certainly seem to be the case, since a contract implies mutuality, but the only doubt raised is that the section ends with the words 'and he is personally liable on the contract accordingly'. These words are superfluous and presumably were inserted for the sake of clarity, but give rise to the possibility that the section could be held not to give the promoter the opportunity to enforce agreements. This is a problem to which the First Directive was not directed.

Finally, it has been held that the section only applies to companies incorporated under the Companies Act 1985 and therefore does not apply to companies formed outside Great Britain.[86] So, in a straightforward case where a contract is made on behalf of an intended company which is to be incorporated outside Great Britain the section cannot apply.

---

84   [1991] BCLC 805.

85   [1991] BCLC 721.

86   *Rover International Ltd v Cannon Film Sales Ltd* [1987] BCLC 540.

CHAPTER THREE

CORPORATE PERSONALITY AND THE REGISTERED COMPANY

THE REGISTERED COMPANY AS A SEPARATE PERSON

Whilst limited liability in the form we know it today might have been an afterthought, for the new registered company in the mid-19th century it soon became an integral part of it. Today many traders would see as the main attraction of forming a company the advantage of avoiding liability for business debts. But the intentions of the legislature were originally to ensure that a business was run by a corporate body which could itself enter into contracts and sue and be sued (and have execution levied against it), as opposed to a partnership with many partners or an unincorporated association, and also to provide a means by which extra capital could be attracted into industry by shareholders buying shares in the corporation and contributing to its joint stock. The Limited Liability Act 1855 was passed to promote the latter aim so as to ensure it was safe for the investor to buy shares in a company. If it were otherwise (as originally conceived in s 66 of the 1844 Act), the purchase of a single share in a company would expose the shareholder to unlimited liability if the company were to fail.

The possibility that a single trader might take advantage of the Act to obtain limited liability for himself, by forming a company which only issued enough shares to satisfy the requirements of the Act, was raised in the debate in the House of Commons on the Limited Liability Act but was thought to be unlikely.[1] Nevertheless this is precisely what did occur, and by the end of the century this type of arrangement was commonplace. The legality of this practice was ultimately put to the test in the celebrated case of *Salomon v Salomon & Co Ltd*.[2] Here a sole trader had formed a company, sold his business to it for £39,000, and had been largely paid for it by taking 20,000 shares in the company and taking £10,000 worth of debentures. The requirement at that time for a limited company to have a minimum of seven members was satisfied by the trader's wife and his five children each being issued with one share. The company declined into insolvent liquidation and there were insufficient assets to satisfy all the creditors. In these circumstances the validity of the debentures issued to Salomon was challenged, especially since, on the evidence, it was established that too high a value had been placed on the business. The liquidator also put in a claim for an order that Salomon be made liable to indemnify the company for its debts.

Vaughan Williams J, at first instance,[3] largely as a result of the control which the trader continued to exercise over the business, held that the company was simply the agent of the trader and therefore under the ordinary laws of agency and agent should be

---

1   *Parliamentary Debates*, 3rd Series, Vol 139, 1855.

2   [1897] AC 22.

3   *Broderip v Salomon* [1895] 2 Ch 323.

indemnified by the principal, Salomon. The Court of Appeal unanimously agreed[4] that the trader should be made liable but they concentrated their judgments on the ground that the use to which the Companies Act had been put was improper. The tenor of the Court of Appeal decision is encapsulated in the judgment of Lopes LJ when he states:

'The Act contemplated the incorporation of seven independent bona fide members, who had a mind and will of their own, and were not the mere puppets of an individual who, adopting the machinery of the Act, carried on his old business in the same way as before, when he was a sole trader. To legalise such a transaction would be a scandal.'[5]

The Court of Appeal went on to suggest that rather than an agent the company was a trustee holding business on trust for Salomon the beneficiary. But all this was swept aside by the House of Lords which unanimously reversed this decision.

The decision of the House of Lords can be summarised in the following way. Once registered in a manner required by the Act, a company forms a new legal entity separate from the shareholders, even where there is only a bare compliance with the provisions of the Act and where the overwhelming majority of the issued shares are held by one person. Further and importantly, that merely because all, or nearly all, of the company's issued shares are held by one individual, there does not arise by reason of that fact an agency relationship between the shareholder and the company. It is also worth noting that these conclusions are premised on the basis that there was no fraud perpetrated by the corporator and their Lordships did not rule out the possibility of an agency relationship arising by virtue of other circumstances. Finally, it was stated that the motives behind the formation of a corporation, once it is registered, are irrelevant in determining the rights and liabilities of the company.

None of the judgments at any level of the litigation really denied that the company existed or that it was a separate legal entity and there was in any case no jurisdiction to do so.

Strong judgments have been given since *Salomon* endorsing the view that the formation of a so-called 'one-person' company leads to the creation of a separate, independent entity with its own rights and liabilities. For example, in *Lee v Lee's Air Farming*[6] it was held by the Privy Council that Lee, who held 2,999 out of the respondent company's 3,000 issued shares and was the only director, could nevertheless be an employee of the company for the purpose of a workers' compensation statute. Lee, although he exercised complete control over the company, could nevertheless cause the company to employ him under a contract of service. Since Lee and the company were two separate entities there was no impediment to them being the parties to a contract.

In *Macaura v Northern Assurance Co Ltd*,[7] despite the fact that Macaura or his nominees held all the shares in a company, the House of Lords held that when Macaura

---

4   *Ibid.*

5   *Ibid* at 341.

6   [1961] AC 12.

7   [1925] AC 619.

sold property to the company he ceased to enjoy any legal or equitable interest in it. The property was wholly and completely owned by the company. Since shareholders have no rights in property owned by the company they cannot take out an insurance policy in respect of it. So here, when the property was destroyed by fire, it was held that Macaura could not claim on his insurance policies as they were invalid.

Finally, in *Henry Browne Ltd v Smith*,[8] the owner of a yacht, chartered it to a company of which he was the sole shareholder. During the period of the charter agreement he ordered steering equipment for the yacht from the plaintiff for the company. The order form stated that the company was the customer. When the plaintiff did not receive payment for the equipment supplied it sued the shareholder but as he was not a party to the contract the action failed.

The separation of the shareholders from the company also underlies decisions such as *Kuwait Asia Bank EC v National Mutual Life Nominees Ltd*[9] where it was held that the shareholders, when appointing or nominating directors to the board, owe no duty of care to third parties who may deal with the company and suffer loss as a result of the negligence of those directors, and *Northern Counties Securities Ltd v Jackson & Steeple Ltd*[10] where it was held that shareholders owe no duty to the company when voting in general meeting and could not be compelled to vote in a particular way even though the resolution passed as a result of the vote may put the company in contempt of court.

CORPORATE LIABILITY

Identification theory

In certain circumstances it is important to know what a person thinks, knows or intends. When that person is a company, an artificial, fictional person, how is it to be determined what the company thinks, knows or intends? The interpretation of the judgment of the leading case of *Lennard's Carrying Co Ltd v Asiatic Petroleum Co Ltd*[11] was that you must look for the 'directing mind and will' of the company. What he or they thought, knew or intended was what the company thought, knew or intended.

In this case a claim was brought against the company by the owners of some cargo which had been destroyed by fire while it was on board a ship belonging to the company. The company had a defence to the claim under what was then s 502 of the Merchant Shipping Act 1894 if it could show that the loss occurred without its 'actual fault or privity'. So the question was then raised as to whether the company was at fault and the way in which the question should be answered was provided by Viscount Haldane LC who stated that:

> '... a corporation is an abstraction. It has no mind of its own any more than it has a body
> of its own; its active and directing will must consequently be sought in the person of

---

8   [1964] 2 Lloyd's Rep 476.
9   [1991] 1 AC 187.
10 [1974] 1 WLR 1133.
11 [1915] AC 705.

somebody who for some purposes may be called an agent, but who is really the directing mind and will of the corporation, the very ego and centre of the personality of the corporation. That person may be under the direction of the shareholders in general meeting; that person may be the board of directors itself, or it may be, and in some companies it is so, that that person has an authority co-ordinate with the board of directors given to him under the articles of association ....'[12]

On the evidence L was the active director of the company but had not been called to give evidence. Viscount Haldane continued:

'[L] therefore was the natural person to come on behalf of [the company] and give full evidence ... about his own position and as to whether or not he was the life and soul of the company. For if [L] was the directing mind of the company, then his action must have been an action which was the action of the company itself within the meaning of s 502.'[13]

In those circumstances, and the onus being placed on the ship owners to rebut the presumption of liability, the company was liable.

So the identification theory proceeds on the basis that there is a person or a group of persons within the company who are not just agents or employees of the company but who are to be identified with the company and their thoughts and actions are the very actions of the company itself.

This was taken further by Denning LJ in *HL Bolton (Engineering) Ltd v TJ Graham & Sons Ltd*,[14] a case concerning the Landlord and Tenant Act 1954 s 30(1)(g), where a landlord challenged the right of a tenant to renew a business tenancy on the ground that it 'intended' to occupy the premises for the purposes of a business to be carried on by it. The landlord was a company and the tenant argued that as no board meeting had been held to consider formally this issue the company could not intend this at all. In the course of dismissing this argument Denning LJ invoked the identification theory in the following way:

'A company may in many ways be likened to a human body. It has a brain and nerve centre which controls what it does. It also has hands which hold the tools and act in accordance with directions from the centre. Some of the people in the company are mere servants and agents who are nothing more than hands to do the work and cannot be said to represent the mind or will. Others are directors and managers who represent the directing mind and will of the company, and control what it does. The state of mind of these managers is the state of mind of the company and is treated by the law as such.'[15]

The analogy with the human body which Denning LJ makes here is unfortunate in one sense, especially from the point of view of those who would like to see an expansion of corporate liability. This is because under this analysis it directs the court to

---

12 *Ibid* at 713.

13 *Ibid* at 713.

14 [1957] 1 QB 159.

15 *Ibid* at 172.

place too much emphasis on only the very senior persons within the company. Lord Justice Denning's judgment was explained in *Tesco Supermarkets Ltd v Nattrass*.[16] Here Tesco was prosecuted under the Trade Descriptions Act 1968 when it was discovered that one of its stores was selling packets of 'Radiant' washing powder which had been marked with a different price from that advertised. Tesco had a defence if the company could show that the offence was committed by 'another person' and it had taken all reasonable precautions and exercised all due diligence to avoid the commission of the offence. In fact the incorrect pricing had been the work of the shelf stacker, and a store manager whose job was to see that packets were properly priced had failed to spot the error. It was held that since the store manager was an employee, or 'hands to do the work' under Denning LJ's formulation, and did not represent the 'directing mind and will' of the company, the act was done by 'another person' separate from the company. Further, that the company itself had taken all reasonable precautions by setting up a system to avoid offences being committed under the Act. As Lord Reid stated:

> 'Normally the board of directors, the managing director and perhaps other superior officers of a company carry out the functions of management and speak and act as the company. Their subordinates do not. They carry out orders from above and it can make no difference that they are given some measure of discretion.'[17]

His Lordship then went on to distinguish the case of the subordinate employee from the case where the board had actually delegated some part of its management functions to a delegate. In the latter case it would be possible to consider the delegate's act as the act of the company.[18] The store manager had not been delegated the duty of setting up and implementing the system. This approach is quite different from cases such as *The Lady Gwendolen*[19] and *The Truculent*[20] where the court focuses on whether the relevant act, thought or intention was that of a person who had been given or assigned the responsibility for a particular task or role.

There is now strong evidence to suggest that the courts are prepared to move away from the *Bolton v Graham* approach. But before looking at these developments, however, some consideration must be given specifically to corporate criminal liability.

Corporate criminal liability

Companies, even though they are fictitious legal persons, can be held to be criminally liable. This was decided as early as the 1840s in two cases concerning statutory railway companies.[21] Today, there are a considerable number of important regulatory statutory offences for which companies are commonly prosecuted, for instance, as employers

---

16   [1972] AC 153.
17   *Ibid* at 171.
18   See also *Seaboard Offshore Ltd v Secretary of State for Transport* [1994] 1 WLR 541.
19   [1965] P 294.
20   [1952] P 1.
21   *R v Birmingham & Gloucester Railway Co* (1842) 3 QB 224; *R v Great North of England Railway Co* (1846) 9 QB 315.

under the Health and Safety at Work Act 1974.[22] There are no company law problems raised by these prosecutions, since the statutory offences are offences of strict liability, so that the issue is whether a certain state of affairs existed and if it did the company can be convicted and fined. Quite a different legal question is raised when the relevant alleged offence is one which requires the prosecution to prove that the accused had the necessary *mens rea*. How can it be shown that a company had a criminal intent? One hundred years after the courts held that it was possible to bring criminal prosecutions against companies in the cases cited above, the courts, in a series of cases in 1944, used what is now referred to as the identification theory to establish the company's *mens rea*. In *DPP v Kent and Sussex Contractors Ltd*[23] the company was charged with doing an act with intent to deceive and making a statement which it knew to be false. The Divisional Court held that the company could be liable and therefore have the necessary intent to deceive. In the words of McNaghten J:

> 'It is true that a corporation can only have knowledge and form an intention through its human agents, but circumstances may be such that the knowledge and intention of the agent must be imported to the body corporate. ... If the responsible agent of a company, acting within the scope of his authority, puts forward on its behalf a document which he knows to be false and by which he intends to deceive ... his knowledge and intention must be imported to the company.'[24]

In *Moore v I Bresler Ltd*[25] the company secretary, who was also the general manager of the Nottingham branch of the company, together with the sales manager of the same branch, caused documents and accounts to be produced which were false and which intended to deceive, so that the company was liable to pay less purchase tax. Both were convicted and so was the company. On appeal by the company the Quarter Sessions quashed the conviction, but this was restored by the Divisional Court of the King's Bench, Viscount Caldecote stating that:

> '[t]hese two men were important officials of the company, and when they made statements and rendered returns ... they were clearly making those statements and giving those returns as the officers of the company, the proper officers to make the returns. Their acts ... were the acts of the company.'[26]

Again, in *R v ICR Haulage Ltd*,[27] it was held by the Court of Appeal that a company could be liable for the offence of common law conspiracy to defraud. Here the acts of a managing director were held to be the acts of the company. The court stated that:

> '[w]here in any particular case there is evidence to go to a jury that the criminal act of an agent, including his state of mind, intention, knowledge or belief is the act of the company, and ... whether the jury are satisfied that it has been proved, must depend on

---

22 See, for example ss 2-6 and 33 of the 1974 Act.
23 [1944] KB 146.
24 *Ibid* at 156.
25 [1944] 2 All ER 515.
26 *Ibid* at 516
27 [1944] KB 551.

the nature of the charge, the relative position of the officer or agent, and the other relevant facts and circumstances of the case.'[28]

In all these cases, what is apparent is that the judges were using the identification theory in a wider and quite different way from the way in which it was subsequently developed and used in *HL Bolton (Engineering) Ltd v TJ Graham & Sons Ltd* and Lord Reid in *Tesco Supermarkets Ltd v Nattrass*. In the latter cases the emphasis is on the seniority of the natural person whose act is in question, ie it is only where the natural person is at the head or centre of the company that his acts can be considered as the acts of the company. In fact Lord Reid criticised statements in the judgment of *R v ICR Haulage Ltd* as being too wide.[29] In the earlier cases the emphasis is on whether the agent or officer is carrying out his role in the company which he was appointed to do. This is in line with even earlier cases which, for example, held that a corporation could act maliciously and could be indicted for criminal libel.[30]

One of the problems with the way in which the law developed for those who favour an extension of corporate criminal liability is that it is much more difficult to prove that the company has the requisite *mens rea* in the common situation where a subordinate employee is responsible for the act even though he was doing what he was paid to do and working within the limitations imposed on him by the company. The larger the company is, the more acute the problem becomes. An employee whose act causes the harm or loss who is far removed from contact with the board or the managing director, will rarely be held to be acting as the company. The problem is nowhere more acute than in relation to corporate manslaughter, where the bigger the enterprise which the company is operating, the greater the potential for loss of life and the more difficult it will be to secure a conviction against the company.

Despite earlier rulings to the contrary it is now accepted that a company can properly be prosecuted for manslaughter. Following the *Herald of Free Enterprise* cross-channel ferry disaster in 1987, which resulted in the deaths of almost 200 people, criminal proceedings were brought against senior managers of the company and the company itself. It was held by the trial judge Turner J that a company in principle could be guilty of manslaughter.[31] In the event, because the managers could not be shown to have had the necessary *mens rea*, which was the only way of establishing that the company had the necessary *mens rea*, the judge directed the jury to return not guilty verdicts against the managers and the company. Subsequently the Law Commission has reviewed the law relating to the liability of corporations for manslaughter and has recommended significant changes in the law.[32] The Law Commission has recommended that there should be a new special offence of corporate killing which would broadly correspond to a new offence of killing by gross carelessness applicable to

---

28 *Ibid* at 559.

29 [1972] AC 153 at 173.

30 *Whitfield v South Eastern Rly Co* (1858) EB & E 115; *Pharmaceutical Society v London & Provincial Supply Association Ltd* (1880) 5 App Cas 857 at 869, 870; *Triplex Safety Glass Co v Lancegaye Safety Glass (1934) Ltd* [1939] 2 KB 395.

31 (1990) 93 Cr App R 72. See also *R v HM Coroner for East Kent, ex parte Spooner* (1987) 3 BCC 636.

32 Legislating the Criminal Code, Involuntary Manslaughter, Law Com No 237.

individuals. It would be committed by a corporation where its conduct in causing the death of someone fell far below that which could reasonably be expected. Further, for the purpose of the new corporate offence, a person's death should be regarded as having been caused by the corporation if it is caused by a failure in the way in which the corporation's activities are managed or organised, to ensure the health and safety of persons employed in or affected by those activities.[33]

There are a number of offences which a company cannot be convicted of by reason of its non-natural, artificial character. So, for example, a company, since it cannot marry, cannot commit bigamy. Similarly it could not commit a sexual offence. Again, it has been held that a company cannot drive a lorry, so it cannot be convicted of offences which may be associated with driving.[34]

Lennard's case reappraised: the attribution theory

Recent decisions have signalled a quite different approach on the part of the courts in their interpretation of the decision in *Lennard's Carrying Co*, and if the Privy Council decision in *Meridian Global Funds Management Asia Ltd v Securities Commission*[35] is followed, the possibilities of obtaining convictions against companies appears to be greater than hitherto.[36]

The changing attitude of the courts to *Lennard's* case is shown by the House of Lords decision in *Re Supply of Ready Mixed Concrete (No 2)*.[37] Here an injunction prevented a company from giving effect to certain existing unlawful agreements made in contravention of s 35(1) of the Restrictive Trade Practices Act 1976 or any other agreements which would contravene this Act. An employee of the company, contrary to express instructions and without the knowledge of the company, made such an agreement and the Director General of Fair Trading then alleged the company was in contempt of court for breaching the terms of the injunction.

It was held that a company had to be judged by its actions and not by its language. So that:

> '[a]n employee who acts for the company *within the scope of his employment* is the company. Directors may give instructions, top management may exhort, middle management may question and workers may listen attentively. But if a worker makes a defective product or a lower manager accepts or rejects an order, he is the company.' (Emphasis added.)[38]

The efforts a company had made to prevent an act by an employee would be taken into account in mitigation but the company could not rely on those measures to deny that the employee's act was the act of the company. In the words of Lord Nolan:

---

33   *Ibid*, para 8.35.

34   *Richmond London Borough Council v Pinn & Wheeler Ltd* [1989] Crim LR 510.

35   [1995] 3 All ER 918.

36   See also *El Ajou v Dollar Land Holdings plc* [1994] 2 All ER 685 on the 'directing mind and will'.

37   *Sub nom Director General of Fair Trading v Pioneer Concrete (UK) Ltd* [1995] 1 AC 456.

38   *Ibid per* Lord Templeman at 465.

'[e]ven in the case of a statute imposing criminal liability, and even without any express words to that effect, Parliament may be taken to have imposed a liability on an employer for the acts of his employees, provided that those acts were carried out in the course of the employment. Further, the liability may be imposed even though the acts in question were prohibited by the employer.'[39]

Lord Hoffmann, in delivering the judgment of the court in *Meridian Global*, focuses on the rules for attributing acts to a company. Since a company is a fictitious person with no real existence, any proposition about a company had to involve a reference to a set of rules. What were the rules which informed one about which acts were to count as acts of the company? These were the 'rules of attribution'. There were not only the primary rules of attribution stemming expressly from the constitution of the company and by implication from company law, for example the giving of powers to the board of directors to manage and represent the company, but also general rules of attribution, that is to say the principles of the ordinary law of agency, enabling the company to function in the commercial world. In most cases these primary and general rules would be enough to determine whether a particular natural person's knowledge and intention should be attributed to and count as the knowledge and intention of the company. Further, liability could also be incurred by the company, as indeed in the same way by a natural person, through the application of the doctrines of estoppel and ostensible authority in contract and vicarious liability in tort. But in exceptional circumstances they would not be enough to determine the matter, for example, in cases where a company was being prosecuted for a criminal offence which required both *actus reus* and *mens rea* to be proved.

In these cases the court would have to interpret the particular section or offence with which the company was being charged to decide what the purpose and policy behind the statute or law were. This accounted for the contrasting decisions in *Tesco Supermarkets Ltd v Nattrass*[40] and *Re Supply of Ready Mixed Concrete (No 2)*.[41] In the former, on a construction of the particular offence, the House of Lords had determined that s 24(1) had intended to give effect to 'a policy of consumer protection which does have a rational and moral justification' and the due diligence defence incorporated into the section reflected that. The company was able to show that the board had instituted systems of supervision and training which amounted to exercising all due diligence to avoid the commission of offences and so it was able to rely on the defence.

In *Re Supply of Ready Mixed Concrete (No 2)* contempt of court was being used to back up undertakings by the company against the background of the Restrictive Trade Practices Act 1976. The whole system of undertakings would be rendered futile if the company could avoid liability by pleading that the breach was by an employee who was not the 'directing mind and will' of the company. Companies could in this way enjoy the benefit of restrictions outlawed by Parliament.

---

39 *Ibid* at 472.
40 [1972] AC 153.
41 [1995] 1 AC 456.

So 'the court must fashion a special rule of attribution for the particular substantive rule'.[42] This had already occurred in *Tesco Stores Ltd v Brent London Borough Council*[43] where Tesco was convicted of supplying a video film with an '18' classification to a boy aged 14. The film was sold by a cashier but the language and content of the relevant section providing for the offence differed substantially from that in *Nattrass*.

It was argued that the defence, namely that the accused neither knew nor had reasonable grounds to believe that the person had not attained the age of 18, had to be the knowledge or belief of the 'directing mind and will'. This was dismissed by the Court of Appeal since the statute would be rendered wholly ineffective in the case of a large company if the relevant knowledge and belief was not that of the actual person who sold the film.

If the act had been carried out or not carried out or carried out with a particular state of mind by the person in the company to whom the company had given that function then quite often that was the most appropriate person whose acts or state of mind could be attributed to the company. The phrase 'directing mind and will' had been used by Viscount Haldane in *Lennard's* case only because on the interpretation of s 502 of the Merchant Shipping Act 1894 he was looking for someone whose functions in the company corresponded to those of an individual shipowner, to whom and in respect of whom the language of the section was primarily drafted. It so happened that in the company in question in *Lennard's* case the 'directing mind and will' was the only person who was carrying out the company's general business and carrying out the functions which an individual shipowner would have done. So it was appropriate to attribute his possible fault or privity to the company.

In *Meridian Global Funds* itself two investment managers who were employees of the Meridian caused it to acquire a 49% shareholding in another company for their own purposes. Meridian did not give notice under s 20(3) of the Securities Amendment Act 1988 of New Zealand which requires 'persons' to give notice to, *inter alia*, the Stock Exchange as soon as they know or ought to know that they are substantial security holders in public companies. On an application against Meridian alleging a breach of this section, since it knew or should have known it was a substantial security holder and had not disclosed this fact, the Privy Council held that there was a breach of s 20(3) since the appropriate person in the company to make disclosure was the person in the company who had been given authority to acquire shares, ie the investment managers, and since the policy of the Act was to ensure immediate disclosure of substantial security holders, the investment managers' knowledge was attributable to the company and therefore there had been a breach of the section. It was irrelevant that because of the self-serving scheme the investment managers did not inform the company.

In summary, and by way of an example of the new approach, if a particular statutory provision required a company to prepare and submit a document to a Government department or official body, and an employee of the company prepared

---

42 [1995] 3 All ER 918 at 924.

43 [1993] 1 WLR 1037.

and submitted a fraudulent document, and if the company were subsequently charged with an offence in relation to this, then the prosecution would not have to show that this employee was the 'directing mind and will' of the company in the sense that he was in actual control of the operations of the company, but simply that he was employed by the company to carry out this particular function, therefore his act and state of mind must be that of the company, even though the company might have instructed him not to make fraudulent submissions.[44]

LIFTING THE VEIL OF INCORPORATION

Together the speeches of the House of Lords in *Salomon* have become immensely influential in English company law. But the decision has not been uniformly approved of, with one distinguished commentator describing it as 'calamitous'.[45] The reason for the criticism of *Salomon* is by and large the opportunities which the decision gives to unscrupulous promoters of private companies to abuse the advantages which the Companies Act gives them by achieving a 'wafer-thin' incorporation of an under-capitalised company and further, to give even the apparently honest incorporators the advantage of limited liability in circumstances in which it is not necessary in order to encourage them to initiate or carry on their trade or business.

In the 100 years since *Salomon* though, the legislature and the courts have not been unaware of the possibilities of abuse and on occasion have responded in various ways to remove the advantages from the corporators of forming a company or of hiding behind one. These 'occasions' are generally described or known as 'lifting the veil' or 'piercing the veil'. For example, it may be decided that in the circumstances it should be ignored that a certain activity or transaction is carried out by a company and the court will regard the activity or transaction as that of the shareholders of the company. Or again, the court may look behind the company to the shareholders in order to extract certain features or characteristics from them and ascribe them to the company itself.

Judicial 'lifting the veil'

It is not possible to distil any single principle from the decided cases as to when the courts will 'lift the veil', nor will any two commentaries categorise the case law in precisely the same way. Nor should we expect to find such a principle or coherent categorisation, because for amongst other reasons these cases are extremely diverse, and although they may all be termed 'lifting the veil' cases, the courts are being requested to undertake a variety of different processes.

A pattern that can be discerned is that the judges, particularly of the Court of Appeal during the 1960s and 1970s, were generally favourably disposed towards 'lifting the veil' in an increasing number of circumstances, which is reflected in the literature of

---

44   *Moore v Bresler Ltd* [1944] 2 All ER 515.
45   O Kahn-Freund, *Some reflections on company law* (1944) 7 MLR 54.

the time.[46] But it is submitted that the lower courts will always show a greater enthusiasm for the process. This was halted by a number of House of Lords decisions in the early 1980s which were much stricter and have produced a very different attitude.[47]

Fraud and the use of equitable remedies

One area of general consensus is that the courts will 'lift the veil' to prevent the use of the registered company for fraudulent purposes or to evade a contractual obligation or liability. So for example in *Gilford Motor Co Ltd v Horne*,[48] H had been employed by the plaintiffs as their managing director. His contract of service had included a restrictive covenant to the effect that after his employment had ended he would not solicit the customers of the plaintiff. The case arose because he did precisely that. One point which was raised in the case was that the solicitation was done by H as an employee of a company which had been formed for the purpose and all the shares of which had been issued to his wife and another employee who were the only directors. The Court of Appeal regarded this company as a 'cloak or sham' and formed merely as a 'device or stratagem', in order to 'mask the solicitation'. An injunction was granted against both H and the company from acting in breach of the covenant.

A case which follows *Gilford Motor Co v Horne* and goes even further is *Jones v Lipman*.[49] Here L entered into a contract to convey a parcel of land to J. Subsequently he changed his mind and in an attempt to avoid being compelled to convey the land he formed a company, A Co, of which he and a clerk employed by his solicitors were the only shareholders and directors. L then conveyed the land to A Co. Russell J granted an order for specific performance against both L & A Co to convey the land to J for two reasons, both of which amount to 'lifting the veil' in the accepted sense. First, because L, by his absolute ownership and control of A Co, could cause the contract to be completed, the equitable remedy could be granted against him. Secondly, the order could be made against the company because it was a creature of L and 'a device and a sham, a mask which he holds before his face in an attempt to avoid recognition by the eye of equity'.

These two cases show that the courts will refuse to allow a person to hide behind the 'veil' of the company and remain anonymous or deny that they have any connection with the company.

Drawing on the authority of *Jones v Lipman* the Court of Appeal in *Adams v Cape Industries plc*[50] was prepared to accept for the purposes of that case that the veil could be lifted where a defendant used the corporate form to evade:

---

46 See, for example, C Schmittoff 'Salomon in the shadow' [1976] JBL 305.

47 See, eg, *Woolfson v Strathclyde RDC* 1978 SLT 159; *Lonrho Ltd v Shell Petroleum Co Ltd* [1980] 1 WLR 627; *Dimbleby & Sons Ltd v NUJ* [1984] 1 WLR 427.

48 [1933] Ch 935.

49 [1962] 1 WLR 832.

50 [1990] Ch 433.

(i) limitations imposed on his conduct; and

(ii) such rights of relief against him as third parties already possess

but rejected the proposition that the veil would be lifted where the corporate form was being used to evade such rights of relief as third parties may require in the future. It was legitimate to use the corporate form to reduce exposure to future potential liabilities. This may be harsh but was an inherent feature of English company law. (But see *Creasey v Breachwood Motors*[51] at p 58.)

Another case where the court would not allow individuals to use a company as cover for improper activities is *Re Darby ex parte Brougham.*[52] Here D & G, two fraudulent persons whose names were well known in the City, formed a company of which they were the sole directors and controllers. This company acquired a licence to exploit a quarry and then a new company was formed to which the licence was sold at a grossly inflated sum. The second company's debentures were then offered for sale to the public and when the subscription money was received the debt to the first company was paid. The prospectus issued to the public stated only that the first company was the promoter. But it was held that in reality D & G were the promoters and, as they received the whole of the fraudulently obtained secret profit, the liquidator of the second company could pursue D & G to account for the profit. The judge could have based his decision, and perhaps would today, on a constructive trust because, as the promoting company broke its duties as a promoter of the second company, and D & G as directors of the first company received the profit knowing of the breach, they would be personally liable as constructive trustees because of their knowing receipt. But Phillimore J based his decision on the finding that they were the real promoters and he was content to ignore the existence of the company.

Is there anything in these cases which is against the spirit or the letter of *Salomon*? In the first two cases the court was not denying the separate entity or the separate existence of the company because in both the court was concerned and obliged to make the order both against the individual and the company. Further, in all three cases the letter of *Salomon* is not infringed since their Lordships' speeches in that case as mentioned above are expressly premised on the basis that there was no fraud.[53] The Companies Acts cannot be used as an engine or instrument of fraud. Certainly the courts would not be averse to holding that the deliberate evasion of a pre-acquired contractual obligation by the formation of a company was a fraud in the wider sense.

The most thorough recent examination of the law was in the Court of Appeal in *Adams v Cape Industries plc.*[54] Here the Court follows the principle laid down earlier in *Woolfson v Strathclyde Regional Council,*[55] that it only permissible for a court to lift the veil where 'special circumstances exist indicating that [the company] is a mere façade concealing the true facts'.

---

51   [1993] BCLC 480.

52   [1911] 1 KB 95.

53   See, for example, [1897] AC 22 at 33 *per* Lord Halsbury.

54   [1990] 1 Ch 433.

55   1978 SLT 159.

Unfortunately little guidance is given as to when a company is a mere façade or the factors which are to be employed in determining whether this is so either in *Woolfson* or *Adams*. But one important issue discussed by the Court of Appeal is the relevance of motive to the question of lifting the veil. It is submitted that the question of why a company was formed, involved or utilised in a transaction is always one of the primary questions. As the Court of Appeal stated:

> 'In our judgment ... whenever a device or sham or cloak is alleged ... the motive of the alleged perpetrator must be legally relevant. ... The decision in *Jones v Lipman* ... was one case where the proven motive of the individual defendant clearly had a significant effect on the decision of Russell J.'[56]

And further on:

> 'Following *Jones v Lipman* ... where a façade is alleged, the motive of the perpetrator may be highly material.'[57]

If the answer to this question is that the corporate form is being used as a vehicle for fraud or the evasion of a pre-existing contractual obligation, the veil is lifted and one can then move forward to describe the company as a mere façade or not. In other words, the finding of 'mere façade' is the end result, and it is meaningless to begin by asking whether the company is a façade in order to decide whether or not to lift the veil.

The question is then what motives are permissible or proper and which are improper? It surely cannot be an improper motive for a corporator to employ the registered company if the only reason for doing so is to avail himself of the advantages which the Companies Acts gives him.[58] This is consistent with the decision in *Henry Browne Ltd v Smith*[59] where there was transparent 'wafer-thin' incorporation but nevertheless the court declined to lift the veil and hold the corporator liable on the contract. Nobody had been misled or defrauded. This was not the case, of course, in *Jones v Lipman*. If this is correct then the judgment in *Re Bugle Press Ltd*[60] cannot represent the law. Here the majority shareholders of company A, who held 90% of the issued shares, formed company B and company B then approached all the shareholders of company A with the intention of effecting a takeover. Of course it acquired 90% without difficulty but the holder of the remaining 10% was unwilling to sell. Company B then sought to exercise its statutory right under what is now s 429 of the 1985 Act to acquire compulsorily the minority. This statutory right could only be exercised by companies, which is why company B had been formed. On an application by the minority shareholder for a declaration that company B was not entitled to acquire his shares, it was held that in the circumstances such a declaration would be made, since

---

56   [1990] 1 Ch 433 at 540.

57   *Ibid* at 542.

58   See, for example, *Hilton v Plustitle* [1989] 1 WLR 149.

59   [1964] 2 Lloyd's Rep 476.

60   [1961] Ch 270.

company B and 90% of company A's shareholders were the same and not to make the order would allow the section to enable majority shareholders to expropriate or evict the minority.

It is submitted that the majority should have been entitled in this case to use the provisions of the Act since there was no proviso preventing its use in this situation, which there could quite easily have been. As it stands the case is irreconcilable with *Salomon*.

☞ *The company as agent or nominee*

Lord Halsbury in *Salomon* expressly refers in his speech to the fact that there was no fraud or agency.[61] Of course if there is an express agency agreement between the shareholder and the company so that the latter is the agent and the shareholder is the principal, the court is obliged to 'lift the veil' and treat the business or the activities of the company as that of the shareholder. This can commonly occur where the shareholder is in fact a parent company.[62] But the strength of the *Salomon* decision has always been that, even in circumstances where one shareholder holds virtually all the issued shares and *de facto* controls what the company does, there is to be no implied agency.

Despite this the courts have on occasion been inclined to find an implied agency agreement, mainly in the context of corporate groups, holding that a parent company is a principal, rather than where the shareholder is an individual. As an isolated example of the latter, however, Lord Denning MR in *Wallersteiner v Moir*[63] was prepared to hold that there was an implied agency between an individual and the companies he controlled:

> '... I am quite clear that [the companies] were just the puppets of Dr Wallersteiner. He controlled their every movement. Each danced to his bidding. He pulled the strings. No one else got within reach of them. Transformed into legal language, they were his agents to do as he commanded. He was the principal behind them. I am of the opinion that the court should pull aside the corporate veil and treat these concerns as being his creatures – for whose doings he should be, and is, responsible.'[64]

Neither of the other two members of the Court of Appeal were willing to support this finding and it is submitted that without more, there is nothing in this passage sufficiently to distinguish the case from Salomon on the agency point alone.

A more reasoned decision on implied agency is to be found in the judgment of Atkinson J in *Smith, Stone and Knight Ltd v Birmingham Corporation*[65] where it was held that the parent company which owned property which was compulsorily acquired by Birmingham Corporation could claim compensation for removal and disturbance even

---

61 [1897] AC 22 at 33.
62 See also Lord Cozens-Hardy MR in *Gramophone & Typewriter Ltd v Stanley* [1908] 2 KB 89.
63 [1974] 1 WLR 991.
64 *Ibid* at 1013.
65 [1939] 4 All ER 116.

though it was a subsidiary company which occupied the property and carried on business there. This was because the subsidiary was operating on the property not on its own behalf but on behalf of the parent company. After asking a number of questions concerning the degree of control and receipts of profits from the business by the parent company, Atkinson J concluded:

> 'if ever one company can be said to be the agent or employee, or tool or simulacrum of another I think the [subsidiary company] was in this case a legal entity, because that is all it was. ... I am satisfied that the business belonged to the claimants, they were ... the real occupiers of the premises.'[66]

Along similar lines is the decision in *Re FG (Films) Ltd*[67] where Vaisey J held that an English company with no significant assets or employees of its own was merely an agent or nominee for its American parent company. Therefore any film nominally made in its name could not be a 'British' film and therefore was not entitled to the advantages provided by the Cinematograph Films Acts 1938-1948.

More recently in *Adams v Cape Industries*[68] a stricter approach by the Court of Appeal can be discerned on the question of implied agency. In holding that a subsidiary company was not acting as the agent of the parent, the Court of Appeal noted that the subsidiary was carrying on business for its own purposes, even though its main purpose was to market goods of the parent in the USA, and at no time did the subsidiary have any authority to bind the parent or affect its legal relations with any third party in any transaction which is the usual hallmark of an agency relationship.

This latter point raises an interesting point, since it is highly unlikely that in either *Smith, Stone & Knight Ltd v Birmingham Corporation* or *Re FG (Films) Ltd* the judges would have been willing to find in different circumstances that the subsidiary companies had any sort of authority to bind the parent companies, yet the terminology of agency is used. It is clear that here the judges had in mind that the companies were transparent nominees rather than agents in the usual sense which were capable of acting within an authority given to them to bind the parent company.

Without express agency agreements, an argument under this head of 'lifting the veil' appears extremely difficult and unlikely to succeed.

Corporate groups

Of course the veil of incorporation may be lifted in the exceptional circumstances discussed in this Chapter between a parent company and a subsidiary in the same way as it can between an individual and a company but *prima facie* the *Salomon* doctrine applies as much to companies within a corporate group. There is concern, however, that the application of the *Salomon* principle to the corporate group presents greater

---

66   *Ibid* at 121.
67   [1953] 1 WLR 483.
68   [1990] Ch 433.

potential for harm because of the greater economic impact it may have. Nowhere is this concern better expressed than by Templeman J in *Re Southard & Co Ltd*:[69]

> 'English company law possesses some curious features, which may generate curious results. A parent company may spawn a number of subsidiary companies, all controlled directly or indirectly by the shareholders of the parent company. If one of the subsidiary companies, to change the metaphor, turns out to be the runt of the litter and declines into insolvency to the dismay of its creditors, the parent company and the other subsidiary companies may prosper to the joy of the shareholders without any liability for the debts of the insolvent subsidiary.'

And even more ominously:

> 'the anxiety of the creditors [of the insolvent subsidiary] will be increased where ... all the assets of the subsidiary company are claimed by another member of the group in right of a debenture.'[70]

As a result of this concern, it is perhaps natural to enquire as to whether the courts have attempted to develop any principle of 'lifting the veil' specifically directed to the corporate group. The answer is yes, but not particularly effectively.

In *Littlewoods Mail Order Stores Ltd v IRC*[71] Lord Denning MR lifted the veil between parent and subsidiary in an income tax case but largely for the same reasons as those in the transparent nominee cases mentioned in the previous section. In declining to treat a subsidiary company as a separate and independent entity from the parent he stated:

> '[t]he doctrine laid down in *Salomon* ... has to be watched very carefully. It has often been supposed to cast a veil over the personality of a limited company through which the courts cannot see. But that is not true. The courts can and often do draw aside the veil. They can, and often do, pull off the mask. They look to see what really lies behind. The legislature has shown the way with group accounts and the rest. And the courts should follow suit. I think we should look at the [subsidiary] and see it as it really is – the wholly-owned subsidiary of Littlewoods. It is the creature, the puppet of Littlewoods in point of *fact*: it should be so regarded in point of *law*.'[72]

The authority of this dictum was doubted in *Adams v Cape Industries plc*[73] especially since the other members of the Court of Appeal did not embrace this same reasoning for their judgments. Further the citation of the group account provisions in the Companies Act to support a wider 'lifting the veil' theory is dubious. Equally it could be argued that, if the legislature has gone out of its way to make provisions which disregard the separate entity principle in certain limited circumstances, it is an indication that, in the absence of those circumstances, the usual principle applies.[74]

---

69   [1979] 1 WLR 1198.

70   *Ibid* at 1208.

71   [1969] 1 WLR 1241.

72   *Ibid* at 1254.

73   [1990] Ch 433.

74   See Cohen LJ in *Ebbw Vale Urban District Council v South Wales Traffic Area Licensing Authority* [1951] 2 KB 366 at 374.

Therefore, no general principle can be derived from this case.

The main English case, again one which came before Lord Denning MR, is *DHN Food Distributors v Tower Hamlets London Borough Council*,[75] the facts of which have a similarity to those of *Smith, Stone & Knight*. A company called Bronze owned freehold property which was compulsorily acquired by the defendants. Bronze was a wholly-owned subsidiary of DHN which carried on a business on the property. A third company, also a subsidiary of DHN, ran the transport side of the business. All three companies had the same directors. Bronze was entitled to compensation for the value of the freehold but not for disturbance to business because it ran no business from the property.

Lord Denning MR swept aside this 'technical point' and after again referring to the statutory provisions which require group accounts to be prepared, and citing this as an example of what Professor Gower stated in *Modern Company Law* (3rd edition) is a growing tendency to look at the economic entity of the whole group, he stated:

> 'These subsidiaries are bound hand and foot to the parent company and must do just what the parent company says. ... This group is virtually the same as a partnership in which all the three companies are partners. They should not be treated separately so as to be defeated on a technical point. ... The three companies should, for present purposes, be treated as one, and the parent company DHN should be treated as that one.'[76]

DHN therefore, although not holding the appropriate interest in the property acquired, could claim compensation for disturbance. Lord Denning MR received lukewarm support for this view from other members of the Court of Appeal.

It can be regarded as somewhat ironic, given the concern expressed above about the possibilities of the abuse of the corporate group, that the strongest English case on corporate economic entity is one where the veil is lifted to the advantage of the group. Further, the counter-argument can immediately be raised, if businessmen seek to take the advantages which accrue to them of running their businesses through a group structure, they must also be expected to take the disadvantages.

The authority of Lord Denning's findings were doubted by Lord Keith in the Scottish House of Lords case *Woolfson v Strathclyde Regional Council*[77] and further doubted and restricted in *Adams v Cape Industries plc*.[78] To the extent that *DHN* might have been construed as authority for the proposition that the courts can generally treat closely connected companies in a group as one economic entity, ignoring their separate personalities, it must be conceded that the decision is no longer good law.

More representative of the current position of the courts are the statements quoted in *Adams v Cape Industries* of Roskill LJ in *The Albazero*[79] that:

---

75 [1976] 1 WLR 852.

76 *Ibid* at 860.

77 (1978) SLT 159.

78 [1990] Ch 433.

79 [1977] AC 774.

'each company in a group of companies (a relatively modern concept) is a separate legal entity possessed of separate legal rights and liabilities so that the rights of one company in a group cannot be exercised by another company in that group even though the ultimate benefit of the exercise of those rights would enure beneficially to the same person or corporate body irrespective of the person or body in whom those rights were vested in law. It is perhaps permissible under modern commercial conditions to regret the existence of these principles. But it is impossible to deny, ignore or disobey them.'[80]

And those of Robert Goff LJ in *Bank of Tokyo Ltd v Karoon*[81] in dealing with an argument that a parent and subsidiary company were economically one person:

'... we are concerned not with economics but with law. The distinction between the two is fundamental and cannot here be bridged.'[82]

Adams v Cape Industries plc is undoubtedly the most influential of recent 'lifting the veil' cases. Here the plaintiffs were attempting to enforce a judgment obtained by default against the defendant English parent company. The judgment had been obtained out of the jurisdiction in a Texas court and English courts could enforce it if the defendant was present within the US jurisdiction. The defendant had a subsidiary company which was incorporated in Illinois so the plaintiffs argued that the companies should be treated as a single economic unit or at any rate the corporate veil should be lifted between the companies, and therefore the defendant could be considered as being present within the US jurisdiction. These arguments were rejected. Previous cases cited to the court where the veil appeared to be lifted between the companies in a group were distinguished and explained as being instances which turned on the particular wording of a contract or statute. So, for example, in *Harold Holdsworth & Co (Wakefield) Ltd v Caddies*[83] it was held that a managing director's service contract with the parent company could be construed as entitling the company to require the director to devote all his time to the business of a subsidiary company and the technical argument that each company in the group was a separate entity notionally controlled by its own board of directors did not prevent this because:

'[T]his is an agreement in re mercatoria and it must be construed in light of the facts and realities of the situation'.[84]

Perhaps overall the strongest point to be taken from the judgment of the court of Appeal in *Adams* on 'lifting the veil' is that it is not objectionable for a parent company (or an individual) to form a company in order to limit its potential future exposure to liabilities. This is a legitimate use of the corporate form.

---

80   *Ibid* at 807.

81   [1987] AC 45.

82   *Ibid* at 64. See also *Re Polly Peck International plc* [1996] 2 All ER 433.

83   [1955] 1 WLR 352.

84   *Ibid* at 367 *per* Lord Reid.

Quasi-partnership cases

The implication from the Companies Act is that once incorporated every company is to be treated in the same way and regarded as the same sort of entity. This is not the case, though, when the courts turn to consider the application of the statutory shareholder remedies, namely unfair prejudicial conduct and just and equitable winding up. In this context the courts do look behind the company to see, for instance, if it is one which is formed and run on the basis of mutual trust and confidence between the corporators or is an 'incorporated or quasi-partnership'. If the company is one of this sort, then in many cases there is a better chance of the shareholder successfully applying for relief, because the court can take into account not just the strict legal rights and position of the shareholder as disclosed in the company's constitution and contained in the Companies Act, but also the legitimate expectations of the shareholder.[85] This topic will be dealt with in greater detail later.[86]

This then is a major but often overlooked way in which the corporate veil is lifted to see what were the circumstances under which the company was incorporated.

Postscript

Cases will continue to come before the courts where the judges will be requested to 'lift the veil' in a wide variety of situations. They will continue to engage in basically *ad hoc* investigations to determine whether the company is or is not 'a mere façade concealing the true facts'. There is an inevitable temptation, though, which *Adams v Cape Industries plc* resists, to lift the veil simply in order to do justice. A recent example of this is *Creasey v Breachwood Motors*[87] where a former employee of A Ltd sought to substitute B Ltd as defendant in a claim for wrongful dismissal. A Ltd and B Ltd had the same shareholders and directors and the assets of A Ltd had been informally transferred from A Ltd to B Ltd after the employee had issued the writ. Any judgment against A Ltd would now be worthless and indeed the company had been struck off under s 652 of the 1985 Act. The judge, Mr Richard Southwell QC, allowed the substitution of B Ltd. It might be argued that those who stood behind these two companies were entitled to use the corporate form to avoid future liabilities in the manner discussed in *Adams v Cape Industries plc*. Here though, although the liability was still contingent, since the action for wrongful dismissal had not been determined, it had at least become more than foreseeable. Further, as the judge stated:

'Nothing I have seen in the evidence could justify their conduct in deliberately shifting [A Ltd's] assets and business to [B Ltd] in total disregard of their duties as directors and shareholders, not least the duties created by Parliament as a protection to all creditors of a company.'[88]

---

85 *Ebrahimi v Westbourne Galleries Ltd* [1973] AC 360.
86 See Chapter 12.
87 [1993] BCLC 480.
88 *Ibid* at 492.

It is possible, therefore, to justify 'lifting the veil' here on the grounds that the use of the corporate form was in connection with disregard of other laws relating to companies. This was also the basis for 'lifting the veil' in *Aveling Barford Ltd v Perion Ltd*.[89] Here L, the director and sole shareholder of two companies, caused one company to enter into a transaction with the other for the sale of an asset at a gross undervalue. It was held by Hoffmann J to be an unlawful return of capital by the vendor company to L. Strictly speaking an unlawful return of capital is to the company's shareholders and the purchasing company did not own any of the vendor's shares. In reality, however, the beneficiary of this transaction was obviously L and Hoffmann J treated the receipt by the purchasing company as receipt by L.

Statutory 'lifting the veil'

If lifting the veil is regarded as removing the advantages which incorporation gives to the corporator, then there are a number of important instances where statutory provisions also bring about this effect. The term corporator here is being used widely to include both shareholders and directors. In most of the cases below the statutory provision is imposing liability on directors or other officers whose general duties and liabilities are considered in Chapter 10, but these provisions are usefully considered here, both because in the small companies to which the provisions usually apply there is an identity between the directors and the shareholders, and also because in respect of fraudulent and wrongful trading it is important to bear in mind that in certain circumstances companies cannot be formed or run to the economic detriment of third parties.

Reduction of members

First, and perhaps least important, is s 24 which provides that if a company, other than a private company limited by shares or by guarantee, carries on business without having at least two members and does so for more than six months, a person who, for the whole or any part of the period that it so carries on business after those six months is a member of the company and knows that it is carrying on business with only one member, is jointly and severally liable with the company for the payment of company's debts contracted during the period or, as the case may be, that part of it.

Given that it is perfectly possible to satisfy the two member requirement by simply issuing one share to a person who will then hold that share as nominee for the other member, this provision does not serve a useful purpose. It became even less important when it was amended to exclude private companies limited by shares or by guarantee following the enactment of the substance of the Twelfth Directive. But it still provides an example where the statute removes the advantage of limited liability from the corporator.

---

89 [1989] 1 WLR 360. See also *Re H (restraint order: realisable property)* [1996] 2 All ER 391 where the veil was lifted to treat the assets of a company as realisable property of the shareholders under s 77 of the Criminal Justice Act 1988 where the company was used as a façade to conceal criminal activities.

Provisions in relation to names

It has already been seen that the advantages of the corporate form can be removed where the director or other officer does not maintain the company's name outside its place of business or where the company's name does not appear on the company's letters, notices and bills etc.[90] A director or shadow director will also incur liability in certain circumstances on the re-use of a company name.[91]

Fraudulent trading

A person will not be able to hide behind the corporate veil and avoid liability for the company's debts if he has used the company to perpetrate fraud and the company has gone into liquidation. In addition, a person who uses a company in such a way commits a criminal offence and on conviction can be fined or imprisoned or both and this offence can be prosecuted regardless of whether or not the company has been wound up.

In respect of the civil liability s 213 of the Insolvency Act 1986 provides that, if in the course of the winding up of a company it appears that any business of the company has been carried on with intent to defraud creditors of the company or creditors of any other person, or for any fraudulent purpose, then the liquidator can apply to the court for a declaration that any persons who were knowingly parties to the carrying on of the business in this way be liable to make such contributions to the company's assets as the court thinks proper.

Fraudulent trading was first introduced as an experiment in the Companies Act 1929 following the recommendations of the Greene Committee. The provision was re-enacted in the Companies Act 1948 with minor amendments but it received a major revision and simplification in the Companies Acts 1981 and 1985.

The meaning of fraud

The first question to be addressed, whether a claim is made under s 213 or an alleged offence is prosecuted under s 458, is what is the meaning of 'fraud' in this context. For this purpose a statement from *Re Patrick & Lyon Ltd*,[92] one of the first cases to consider the new provision in the 1929 Act, is usually cited, to the effect that 'the words 'defraud' and 'fraudulent purpose'... are words which connote actual dishonesty involving, according to current notions of fair trading among commercial men, real moral blame'.[93] Here, for example, the company had never made a trading profit and the directors secured money which was owed to them by the company by causing the company to issue debentures to them but this was not dishonest so that it did not amount to fraud. On the other hand, in *Re Gerald Cooper Chemicals Ltd*,[94] it was held

---

90 Companies Act 1985, ss 348, 349. See Chapter 2.
91 Insolvency Act 1986, s 216. See Chapter 2.
92 [1933] Ch 786.
93 *Ibid* at 790.
94 [1978] Ch 262.

that an insolvent company could be carrying on a business fraudulently where it accepted an advance payment for the supply of goods in circumstances where the directors knew that there was no prospect of the goods being supplied or the payment being repaid. Similarly in *Re William C Leitch Brothers Ltd*[95] Maugham J held that, if a company continues to carry on business and to incur debts at a time when there is to the knowledge of the directors no reasonable prospect of the creditors ever receiving payment of those debts, it was in general proper to infer that the company had been carrying on a business with intent to defraud.

While agreeing with this general proposition Buckley J added confusion by stating in *Re White and Osmond (Parkstone) Ltd*[96] that:

'there is nothing wrong in the fact that directors incur credit at a time when, to their knowledge, the company is not able to meet all its liabilities as they fall due',

and:

'there is nothing to say that directors who genuinely believe that the clouds will roll away and the sunshine of prosperity will shine upon them again and disperse the fog of their depression are not entitled to incur credit to help them to get over the bad time.'

This suggested that ill-founded or reckless optimism could never lead to fraud, because the person concerned was not dishonest, which is an essential ingredient to liability. Such a wide view was rejected by the Court of Appeal in *R v Grantham*,[97] but it remains a problem that because of the requirement of an element of dishonesty there is a high burden not only on the prosecution under s 458 but also on the liquidator under s 213. This problem could have been avoided if a recommendation of the Jenkins Committee had been implemented which would have expanded the civil fraudulent trading provision to include circumstances where directors acted 'recklessly' in relation to the affairs of the company.[98]

Persons who can be defrauded

It has been held, not surprisingly, that the provisions apply not only where all the creditors of the company have been similarly defrauded but also where only one has been so affected.[99]

Also it is no defence to argue that a person supplying goods on credit to a company is not a creditor but at that time only a supplier with a possible future claim against the company. The courts will construe the wording so that 'creditors' includes 'potential creditors'.[100]

---

95 [1932] 2 Ch 71.
96 (1960) unreported.
97 [1984] QB 675. But see *Re EB Tractors Ltd* [1986] NI 165.
98 Cmnd 1749, para 503(b).
99 *Re Gerald Cooper Chemicals Ltd* (*supra*).
100 *R v Kemp* [1988] 1 QB 645.

Who is carrying on the business of the company

It has been held that to be a 'part[y] to the carrying on of the business' of the company, a person must be involved in taking positive steps towards that end or exercising a controlling or managerial function and not just 'advising on' or 'concurring in' or even 'participating in' the business. Therefore a company secretary who was aware that the company was insolvent but who failed to advise the directors that the company should not continue to trade was not a 'party to' the carrying on of the company's business.[101]

Nevertheless in *Re Gerald Cooper Chemicals Ltd*[102] it was held that it was possible for an outsider to be a party to the carrying on of the company's business for the purpose of the section. Here a creditor of the company received a part payment of its debt out of money which was paid to the company in advance in circumstances where there was no intention ever to supply the goods ordered. Templeman J was of the view that 'those who warm themselves with the fire of fraud cannot complain if they are singed'.[103]

The limits of this extension of liability, though, were defined in *Re Augustus Barnett & Son Ltd*[104] where a company had traded at a loss for a number of years and the company was only kept going by support from the parent company in the form of 'letters of comfort'. These were noted in the accounts and were statements by the parent company to provide the company with working capital. Eventually the company went into insolvent liquidation and the liquidator sought to make the parent company liable for fraudulent trading, since it was alleged that it had induced the board of the company to continue trading and thereby it had increased the debts of the company. The claim was struck out because the parent company was not carrying on the business of the company, the board was, and against it there was no allegation of fraud. So even under the more liberal view of the phrase 'parties to' that was taken in *Re Gerald Cooper Chemicals*, there were no fraudulent acts to which the parent company could have been a party, and therefore it would be irrelevant what the motives or intentions of the parent company were for the purpose of fraudulent trading.

Wrongful trading

The difficulties and inadequacies of the law relating to fraudulent trading were examined in the Cork Report into insolvency law and practice which reported in 1982.[105] The main problems with the interpretation and application of the fraudulent trading provisions which prevent them from operating as an effective compensatory remedy is the reluctance of the courts to declare civil liability except in cases where there has been dishonesty and further, the courts insist upon a strict standard of proof. Both of these problems stem from the fact that fraudulent trading has both a criminal and a civil aspect and the courts maintain the same requirements. The Cork

---

101 *Re Maidstone Buildings Provisions Ltd* [1971] 1 WLR 1085. See also *R v Grantham* (1984) 79 Cr App Rep 86 at 91 and *R v Miles* [1992] Crim LR 657.
102 [1978] Ch 262.
103 *Ibid* at 268.
104 [1986] BCLC 170.
105 Report of the Review Committee on Insolvency Law and Practice (1982) Cmnd 8558.

Committee was of the view that civil fraudulent trading should be abolished and that a new provision be enacted which did not require dishonesty to be proven and which would apply in cases of not only fraudulent but also unreasonable trading. This new concept was to be known as wrongful trading, and although the legislature retained civil fraudulent trading it did adopt this main proposal and enacted the wrongful trading provision in the Insolvency Act 1985. It is now to be found in s 214 of the Insolvency Act 1986.

The major advance brought about by wrongful trading is that considerable personal liability can be imposed on those persons who have run a company where the company has gone into insolvent liquidation, even where those persons have not acted dishonestly and, for the purposes of the section, their conduct is to be judged by reference to an objective standard.

The section only applies where a company is in the course of an insolvent liquidation. In these circumstances a liquidator can apply to the court under s 214(1) to have a person who is or was a director or shadow director liable to make such contribution to the company's assets as the court thinks proper. The court can make such an order where at some time before the commencement of the winding up the person against whom the order is sought knew or ought to have concluded that there was no reasonable prospect that the company would avoid going into insolvent liquidation and that person was a director or shadow director of the company at that time. Therefore, if a director resigns his office after the time when there was no reasonable prospect of the company avoiding insolvent liquidation, this will not necessarily save him from having an order made against him even if he resigns before the date of winding up. The court may possibly use its discretion to lower the amount of the contribution from that director if most of the increase in liabilities occurred after that director departed. Alternatively the court may take the view that a director should have acted more responsibly and instead remained in post using his influence to reduce the loss to creditors.

A 'shadow director' to whom the liability under s 214 can be extended is defined by the Insolvency Act 1986 as:

'a person in accordance with whose instructions the directors of the company are accustomed to act (but so that a person is not deemed a shadow director by reason only that the directors act on advice given by him in a professional capacity).'

It has also been held that liability can be extended to a *de facto* director which Millett J explained in *Re Hydrodam (Corby) Ltd*[106] was:

'... a person who assumes to act as a director. He is held out as a director by the company, and claims and purports to be a director, although never actually or validly appointed as such. To establish that a person was a *de facto* director of a company it is necessary to plead and prove that he undertook functions in relation to the company which could properly be discharged *only* by a director.'[107]

---

106 [1994] 2 BCLC 180.
107 *Ibid* at 183.

By contrast a shadow director is someone who claims not to be a director and who is not held out by the company as a director.

The definition of 'shadow director' would obviously catch the sort of person who retires from a company which he has built up over many years but who continues to have influence over the directors. But it may also catch the parent company which is directing the activities of a subsidiary. So wrongful trading may well be able to provide a remedy in situations similar to that in *Re Augustus Barnett Ltd*[108] although care must be taken by the liquidator to bring the claim against exactly the person who is alleged to be the shadow director in the group context. Therefore where a parent company is alleged to be the director of the subsidiary, whether *de jure*, *de facto* or a shadow director, it will not necessarily follow that the directors of the parent company will *ipso facto* be the *de facto* or shadow directors of the subsidiary. Evidence will need to be adduced on this point. The parent company itself must be proceeded against.[109]

In *Re a Company (ex parte Copp)*[110] there was a claim to make a bank liable as a shadow director since it was alleged that it had used its power and position as a debentureholder to exert pressure on the company and the actual directors of the company did not, during the material time, exercise any real authority or free will in the direction of the company's affairs. A claim to have the action struck out as disclosing no cause of action failed, since Knox J was of the opinion that this argument was not obviously unsustainable.[111]

To avoid liability under this section directors or shadow directors may be able to avail themselves of the defence contained in s 214(3), namely that after the time when they first knew or ought to have concluded that there was no reasonable prospect that the company would avoid going into liquidation they took every step with a view to minimising the potential loss to the company's creditors. This does not necessarily mean ceasing all business activity, since that may exacerbate the problem, but it probably means that great care is taken before any further goods are ordered on credit. Almost certainly the correct and safest course of action is to seek independent advice from an insolvency practitioner.

Given the courts' traditional reluctance to make *ex post facto* pronouncements on managerial decisions it is very important to the success of the section to determine what the director 'knew or ought to have concluded' at any particular time. For the purposes of the section:

> 'The facts which a director of a company ought to know or ascertain, the conclusions which he ought to reach and the steps which he ought to take are those which would be known or ascertained, or reached or taken, by a reasonably diligent person having both –

---

108 [1986] BCLC 170.

109 *Re Hydrodam (Corby) Ltd* [1994] 2 BCLC 180.

110 [1989] BCLC 13.

111 But the s 214 claim was later abandoned, see *Re MC Bacon Ltd* (1990) BCC 78 at 79.

(a) the general knowledge, skill and experience that may reasonably be expected of a person carrying out the same functions as are carried out by that director in relation to the company, and

(b) the general knowledge, skill and experience that the director has.'

So the director is to be judged by a mixed objective and subjective standard, with the objective standard being a base line standard of what can reasonably be expected from a person carrying out the functions as the director under examination, and this standard can be raised higher so that even more can be expected from the director as a result of any particular skill and experience that the director possesses.

The first major case to analyse s 214 and to apply it successfully was *Re Produce Marketing Consortium Ltd (No 2)*[112] where the two directors of an insolvent company were held to be liable to contribute £75,000 to the company's assets. Knox J fixed the time at which they ought to have concluded that there was no reasonable prospect that the company would avoid going into insolvent liquidation as the latest possible date on which the accounts for a particular year which disclosed the hopeless financial situation should have been delivered. The fact that the directors had not seen them and had in fact acquiesced in the delay of their delivery was of no relevance.

Knox J also held that the jurisdiction of the court to make orders under s 214 is compensatory rather than penal, so that if wrongful trading is found *prima facie* the appropriate amount that a director should be ordered to contribute is the amount by which the company's assets can be shown to have been depleted by the wrongful trading. So that even though the court has discretion as to how much to order a director to contribute, the lack of fraudulent or dishonest intent should not of itself mean that the court orders a lower sum.

A vexed and as yet unresolved issue is who is to benefit from the orders which the court may make. It is clear that the proceeds of an order under s 214 can be applied for the benefit of the creditors as a whole, in the sense that the court has no power to direct payment to particular creditors or direct that property be given to those creditors who incurred losses during the period of wrongful trading itself.[113] But s 214(1) states that the contribution by the director is to be 'to the company's assets'. If the company's assets have been charged by way of a floating charge then there is a strong argument that the contributions which a director makes under a s 214 order are caught by that charge, in a similar way to the money recovered by the liquidator from directors in misfeasance proceedings where the directors are in breach of their duties.[114] Indeed, that is what Knox J in *Produce Marketing Consortium Ltd* assumed to be the case.[115] If correct, this is widely viewed to be an unfortunate result, since it is plainly against the intention of the Cork Committee, which in proposing wrongful trading wanted to

---

112 [1989] BCLC 520.

113 *Re Purpoint* (1991) BCC 121 *per* Vinelott J at 129.

114 Under the Insolvency Act s 212. See, for example, *Re Anglo-Austrian Printing and Publishing Union, Brabourne v Same* [1895] 2 Ch 891.

115 [1989] BCLC 520 at 554a.

protect creditors generally against unreasonable and reckless commercial behaviour and not simply improve the position of the chargeholders.

Further in the report the Committee specifically stated that under this remedy the courts should be given greater flexibility in awarding compensation than under fraudulent trading and they went on to cite a number of creative methods.[116]

It seems, though, that the courts are now more willing to treat proceedings for compensation under s 214 as being analogous to actions by liquidators under s 239 of the Insolvency Act 1986 to set aside transactions which are a fraudulent preference.[117] Both provisions vest statutory powers in the liquidator and only arise in the winding up of a company. In neither case is the liquidator pursuing rights belonging to the company itself and therefore compensation payable under s 214 should not be considered as the company's property and not subject to a floating charge.

Support for this position comes from the decision of Millett J in *Re MC Bacon (No 2)*[118] and more recently from *Re Oasis Merchandising Services Ltd*[119] which also raises the important related issue of who can pay for the costs of a wrongful trading action. If they are not considered to be a process of realising or getting in assets belonging to the company, then liquidators cannot claim the costs of the proceedings under s 214 out of the company's assets prior to the satisfaction of the floating charge. This means that there will be little if anything to fund the proceedings. In *Oasis Merchandising* the liquidator had assigned the 'fruits' of the s 214 claim to a third party in return for the third party meeting the costs of the proceedings and a share of the 'fruits'. It was held that *prima facie* the agreement was champertous and therefore against public policy so the proceedings were stayed. The liquidator could not justify his action as an exercise of his statutory powers of sale and assignment of the company's property[120] since Robert Walker J held, applying *Re MC Bacon (No 2)*, that the rights conferred on a liquidator to bring a s 214 claim were an incident of his office and not an asset of the company.[121]

Miscellaneous legislative provisions

There are numerous statutory provisions which, in one way or another, have the effect of 'lifting the veil'. First, as regards the Companies Act itself, there are the provisions which define the parent/subsidiary company relationship for various purposes. These generally form an exception to the principle of separate personality since they recognise that a separate company should be treated as having a connection with another body or person, which itself is usually a company.

---

116 See para 1797.
117 *Re Yagerphone Ltd* [1935] 1 Ch 392.
118 [1990] BCLC 607.
119 (1995) BCC 911.
120 Under the Insolvency Act 1986, Sch 4, para 6.
121 Citing *Re Ayala Holdings Ltd* (unreported, 20 May 1993).

First, there are the provisions which Lord Denning referred to in *Littlewoods Mail Order Stores Ltd v IRC*[122] which require the preparation of group accounts. This obligation to prepare group accounts is now imposed on a parent company's directors by s 227 of the 1985 Act. This section provides that the group accounts must be consolidated accounts having:

'(a) a consolidated balance sheet dealing with the state of affairs of the parent company and its subsidiary undertakings, and

(b) a consolidated profit and loss account dealing with profit and loss of the parent company and its subsidiary undertakings.'

Overall the accounts must give a true and fair view of the state of affairs and the profit and loss at the end of the financial year of the group as a whole.[123]

The definition of what constitutes a 'parent company' and a 'subsidiary undertaking' for these purposes is now contained in s 258 of the 1985 Act which was inserted by the 1989 Act. The reform was necessary in order to comply with the requirements of the Seventh EC Directive[124] since in certain respects the previous definition from s 154 of the 1948 Act was too narrow and allowed evasion of the obligation. Section 158 of the 1985 Act now provides (subject to exceptions) that an undertaking is a parent company in relation to another undertaking, a subsidiary undertaking, if:

'(a) it holds a majority of the voting rights in the undertaking, or

(b) it is a member of the undertaking and has the right to appoint or remove a majority of its board of directors, or

(c) it has the right to exercise a dominant influence over the undertaking

    (i) by virtue of provisions contained in the undertaking's memorandum or articles, or

    (ii) by virtue of a control contract or

(d) it is a member of the undertaking and controls alone, pursuant to an agreement with other shareholders or members, a majority of the voting rights in the undertaking,

(e) it has a participating interest in the undertaking and:

    (i) it actually exercises a dominant influence over it, or

    (ii) it and the subsidiary undertaking are managed on a unified basis.'[125]

An 'undertaking' means a body corporate or an unincorporated association carrying on a trade or business, with or without a view to profit. So the parent company has to produce consolidated group accounts to include partnerships over which it exercises control.

---

122 [1969] 1 WLR 1241.

123 See also Companies Act 1985, Schedule 4A.

124 83/348/EEC.

125 See also Companies Act 1985, Schedule 10A for an explanation of the expression used in s 258.

Apart from the requirement to prepare group accounts there are a number of other provisions in the 1985 Act which prohibit certain types of transaction between connected companies. For example, s 23 prevents a company from being a member of a company which is its holding company (the purpose behind this prohibition being to prevent a company from evading the provisions of s 143 against a company buying its own shares), ss 330–42 contain provisions preventing a company from making a loan to a director of its holding company and s 320 applies the safeguards in relation to contracts between a director and a company to a director and the holding company. Before the implementation of the new definition of parent and subsidiary required by the Seventh Directive the one definition sufficed to define the parent (or holding as it then was) company and the subsidiary company relationship. With a more stringent definition formulated as a result of the Seventh Directive for group accounts a new holding/subsidiary relationship has been defined and applied to all other provisions which fall outside the scope of the Directive. This definition is found in s 736 and s 736A, and differs mainly because it is only satisfied as between a holding company and a subsidiary company and item (c) mentioned above in relation to s 258 is not present.

Outside the Companies Acts there are a number of provisions which 'lift the veil' between companies. For instance s 297 of the Trade Union and Labour Relations (Consolidation) Act 1992 provides that two employers shall be treated as 'associated' if one is a company of which the other (directly or indirectly) has control or both are companies of which a third person (directly or indirectly) has control.

Not surprisingly there are provisions in the Taxes Acts which have the effect of treating companies as connected or as a group. See, for example, the group relief provisions in Chapter IV of the Income and Corporation Taxes Act 1988.

CHAPTER FOUR

THE CONSTITUTION OF
THE REGISTERED COMPANY

Every club, society or association needs a constitution or set of rules to regulate the way the business of the association is conducted. The registered company is no different and its constitution is contained in two documents, the memorandum of association and the articles of association. Both are filed with the registrar of companies when the company is formed and they remain open for public inspection. Together they form the complete constitution.

THE MEMORANDUM OF ASSOCIATION

The memorandum is the more fundamental of the two documents and is the one to which the original parties forming the company will subscribe their names.[1] These subscribers agree to take a certain number of shares in the company and become its first members. The memorandum is the more fundamental both because of its content and because, if conflict arises between the terms of the memorandum and the articles, the memorandum takes precedence.[2] Further, the articles cannot modify any of the contents of the memorandum.[3] There was historically always a greater reluctance to allow the clauses of the memorandum to be alterable whereas that was not the case with the articles. Originally no provision was made for any alteration to the memorandum although this position has now significantly changed.[4]

The memorandum is required by s 2 to contain certain basic facts about the company and s 3 requires most companies to have a memorandum in the form specified by the Secretary of State or as near to that form as circumstances admit. The Secretary of State has specified the form of memoranda for the various types of company which may be registered under the Companies Act by promulgating The Companies (Tables A to F) Regulations 1985.[5] These regulations lay down specimen or examples of memoranda, the form of which are to be adopted by registered companies, the most important of which are Table B and Table F which are the specified memoranda for a private company limited by shares and a public company limited by shares respectively. In fact there is only one major difference between the two and that is that the latter memorandum has to state (in clause 2) that the company is a public company and this means that a public company will have a six-clause memorandum whereas the private company will have only five.

---

1   Companies Act 1985, s 2.
2   *Welton v Saffery* [1897] AC 299.
3   *Guinness v Land Corporation of Ireland* (1882) 22 Ch D 349.
4   See p 71.
5   SI 1985/805.

Clause 1 will state the name of the company and clause 2 will state the location of the registered office, although this is done in a very general way by stating the country in which it is located ie England, Wales or Scotland. (Northern Ireland has its own Companies Act under which companies located in the province are registered.)[6]

Clause 3 is the objects clause and is usually the one in practice which deviates most markedly from the corresponding example clauses in Table B or F. This is because, whereas that clause occupies only 4 lines and seeks to encapsulate what business the company formed to undertake, the normal clause in a registered company's memorandum runs to several pages in length so as not to define the objects too narrowly and risk offending the *ultra vires* rule. The reason for and significance of this rule will be explained later[7] but suffice to say at this stage that the length and breadth of these clauses has meant that they are virtually meaningless. Considerable reform has been undertaken of the law in this area and attempts have been made to shorten the length of the objects clause so that s 3A introduced by the Companies Act 1989 gives legislative recognition and validity to an objects clause which states quite simply that 'the company is to carry on business as a general commercial company'. This comes close to saying that the company can do anything and nullifies the point of having an objects clause at all; as Harman LJ once remarked, 'you cannot have an object to do every mortal thing you want, because that is to have no object at all'.[8]

Clause 4 states that the liability of the members is to be limited and clause 5 states what the total share capital of the company is, and into how many shares and of what value it is to be divided up.

The remainder of the memorandum concerns the initial shareholding of the company and is framed in the following way: '[w]e the subscribers to this memorandum of association, wish to be formed into a company pursuant to this memorandum and we agree to take the number of shares shown opposite our respective names'. This declaration has a ring of the 19th century about it when companies were considered primarily as the aggregate of the members rather than or in addition to a single, separate entity. One example of that view is the Court of Appeal judgment in *Broderip v Salomon*[9] where Kay LJ stated that:

> '(t)he statutes were intended to allow seven or more persons *bona fide* associated for the purpose of trade to limit their liability ... and to become a corporation.'

This is also the reason why 'the company' in the older judgments is referred to in the plural and not the singular. The view became rather untenable with the growth of the 'one-person' company and the reduction in the statutory minimum number of members to two when in most cases a second member was found to hold one share as nominee for the incorporator. Further, the artificial nature of the wording in the clause

---

6   See Companies (Northern Ireland) Order 1986 (SI 1986/1032).

7   See Chapter 6.

8   *Re Introductions Ltd* [1970] Ch 199 at 209.

9   [1895] 2 Ch 323 at 345.

of the memorandum becomes even more apparent if 'we' is replaced by 'I' in the case of the newly sanctioned single member company.[10]

As mentioned above, originally it was not possible to effect any change to the memorandum once it was registered. Section 2(7) now provides that 'a company may not alter the conditions contained in its memorandum except in the cases, in the mode and to the extent, for which express provision is made by the Act', and over the years the legislature has provided procedures for altering virtually everything in the memorandum.

The 1862 Act allowed a company to change its name and later it was allowed to alter its nominal capital. The Companies (Memorandum of Association) Act 1890 allowed a company to make alterations to its objects clause and this particular ability was expanded in the 1989 Act.[11]

By s 28 a company may change its name by special resolution but it remains the same 'legal person' so that the change of name does not affect any rights or obligations of the company or affect any legal proceedings which are or could be brought by it or against it.[12] Curiously, no reference is made in the section to any actual alteration of the clause in the memorandum which is what in effect is happening and which is specifically provided for in the other sections concerning alteration. By s 28(6) what happens is that the registrar once duly informed makes the appropriate alteration on the register, ie the index of company names, and issues a new certificate of incorporation which bears the new name. The change of name takes effect from the date on which the altered certificate is issued.

By s 4 a company may alter its objects clause on the passing of a special resolution, but by s 5 a dissenting minority of shareholders may apply to the court for the alteration to be cancelled. Such an application can be made within 21 days after the resolution was passed by the holders of not less in aggregate than 15% in nominal value of the company's issued share capital or any class of it as long as none of them consented to or voted in favour of the alteration complained of. On hearing the application, the court is given very wide discretion as to the order it can make, including confirming the alteration wholly or in part and on such terms and conditions as it may think fit or it can order that the shares of any members be purchased and the capital of the company reduced accordingly.

If a member of a company so requests, the company is obliged to send a copy of the memorandum (and the articles) to him at a cost of no more than 5p, and if the company fails to comply with such a request, it and every officer who is in default is liable to a fine.[13] If the company has made an alteration to its memorandum every copy which is subsequently issued has to take into account that alteration and again, failure to

---

10 Companies Act 1985, s 1(3A).

11 The previous position restricted permissible alterations to a number of itemised headings.

12 Companies Act 1985, s 28(7). See *Oshkosh B'Gosh Inc v Dan Marbel Inc Ltd* [1989] BCLC 507.

13 Companies Act 1985, s 19.

comply will result in the company and every officer who is in default being liable to a fine.[14]

THE ARTICLES OF ASSOCIATION

Every registered company has to have, in addition to a memorandum, articles of association. This document will contain the basic regulations for the management of the company covering such matters as the issue and allotment of shares, the calls on shares, the rules relating to the transfer of shares, the procedures to be followed at general meetings and the regulations relating to members voting, the appointment, removal and powers of directors, the payment of dividends and the capitalisation of profits.

The Secretary of State has prescribed in the same statutory instrument as that containing the specific memorandum a standard set of articles known as Table A (which was formerly contained in Schedule 1 of the Companies Act 1948). The importance of Table A is that, in the case of a company which is limited by shares, if a set of articles is not registered with the registrar together with the memorandum when the company is formed or if any articles are registered in so far as they do not exclude or modify Table A, then Table A shall be the company's articles as if it had been expressly adopted or registered.[15]

The contractual effect of the articles

An issue which has caused a considerable amount of litigation and much discussion among commentators, is the extent to which the terms of the company's constitution can be enforced both by the company and its members.[16] The starting point of the debate must be s 14 which states as follows:

'Subject to the provisions of this Act, the memorandum and articles, when registered, bind the company and its members to the same extent as if they respectively had been signed and sealed by each member, and contained covenants on the part of each member to observe all the provisions of the memorandum and of the articles.'[17]

This has the effect of establishing the memorandum and articles as a 'statutory contract' between the company and its members, the terms of which can be enforced both by the company and the members.

Clear and strong authority for the contractual effect of the articles comes from the House of Lords in *Oakbank Oil Co v Crum*[18] where Lord Selborne LC declared:

'Each party must be taken to have made himself acquainted with the terms of the written contract contained in the articles of association ... He must also in law be taken

---

14 Companies Act 1985, s 20.
15 Companies Act 1985, s 8.
16 See, for example, [1957] CLJ 194; (1972) 35 MLR 362; [1986] CLJ 219.
17 Companies Act 1985, s 14(1).
18 (1882) 8 App Cas 65.

... to have understood the terms of the contract according to their proper meaning; and that being so he must take the consequences whatever they may be, of the contract which he has made.'[19]

So that, for example, if the articles provide that the directors may declare a dividend to be paid to the members in proportion to their shares, the directors cannot pay a dividend to each member in proportion to the amount paid up upon the shares held by him,[20] or declare that instead of paying a dividend that members will be issued with debentures which will be redeemed over thirty years.[21] In cases such as this a member could bring a straightforward claim against the company for what he is entitled to under the articles and the matter becomes purely one of construction of the terms of the 'statutory contract'. This will be the case even though a majority of the members of the company have approved the action proposed by the directors, since this would amount to an alteration of the articles by ordinary resolution.[22]

Conversely, the company will be able to enforce the terms of the statutory contract against the members. So, for example, where the articles provide that any disputes between a member and the company shall be referred to arbitration, the company will be able to obtain an order staying proceedings brought by a member who has not gone to arbitration on such a dispute,[23] or where the articles provide that if a member becomes bankrupt he shall be required to transfer his shares, the company will be able to enforce the article.[24]

The contract which s 14 creates, however, is and remains a special statutory contract with its own distinctive features. The contract derives its force from the statute and not from any bargain struck between the parties and therefore it is subject to other provisions of the Act. Section 9, for instance, provides that the articles, the terms of the statutory contract, can be altered by a three-quarters majority of the members voting in general meeting in contrast to the case of a 'normal contract' where unanimity between the parties would be required for a variation of contractual terms.

There are other contractual principles which are inapplicable to the statutory contract as a result of its special nature. For instance, the court would have no jurisdiction to rectify the articles once registered even if it could be shown that they did not, as they presently stood, represent what was the true original intention of the persons who formed the company.[25] Nor can the court imply terms to supplement the articles under the business efficacy rule.[26]

19   *Ibid* at 70.

20   *Ibid*.

21   *Wood v Odessa Waterworks* (1889) 42 Ch D 636.

22   Which requires a special resolution. See p 78.

23   *Hickman v Kent or Romney Marsh Sheep Breeder's Association* [1915] 1 Ch 881.

24   *Borland's Trustee v Steel Brothers & Co Ltd* [1901] 1 Ch 279.

25   *Scott v Frank F Scott (London) Ltd* [1940] Ch 794.

26   *Bratton Seymour Service Co Ltd v Oxborough* [1992] BCLC 693.

An old common law rule which again served to highlight the difference in the relationship between a member and his company from that of an ordinary contractual relationship has recently been abolished.[27] That was the rule that a shareholder could not sue the company for unliquidated damages while he remained a shareholder. This was most likely to occur where a shareholder wished to sue the company after buying shares in it following a misrepresentation. This rather curious rule was laid down by the House of Lords in a case involving an unlimited company where the consequence of an order for damages would be that the shareholder would be required to contribute to his own damages.[28]

So there is unquestionably a binding of contract which can be enforced by the company against its members and *vice versa*. But do the articles constitute a binding contract between the members *inter se* so that one member can enforce a term against another without involving the company? The answer now is generally recognised to be in the affirmative, but the authority is not particularly strong or straightforward, being a mixture of first instance decisions and *obiter dicta* and even as late as 1960 Vaisey J was declaring that this was a difficult point for which there was 'no very clear judicial authority'.[29] In *Wood v Odessa Waterwork*[30] Stirling J stated quite clearly that the 'articles of association constitute a contract not merely between the shareholders and the company, but between each individual shareholder and every other'. But Farwell LJ in *Salmon v Quin & Axtens*,[31] while approving that statement, stated that the court would not enforce the covenant as between individual shareholders in most cases. Further, Lord Herschell in *Welton v Saffery*,[32] who dissented on the main issue in the case, denied that there was any contract between the individual members of the company and stated that any rights which the articles gave them *inter se* could only be enforced by or against a member through the company:

'It is quite true that the articles constitute a contract between each member and the company, and that there is no contract in terms between the individual members of the company; but the articles do not any the less, in my opinion, regulate their rights *inter se*. Such rights can only be enforced by or against a member *through the company* or through the liquidator representing the company' (emphasis added).

But by 1943 in *London Sack & Bag Co Ltd v Dixon & Lugton*[33] Scott LJ was able to say:

'[i]t may well be, even as between ordinary members of a company who are also in the nominal way shareholders, that [s 14] adjusts their legal relations inter se in the same way as a contract in a single document would if signed by all.'[34]

---

27   Companies Act 1985, s 111A (inserted by Companies Act 1989, s 131(1)).
28   *Houldsworth v City of Glasgow Bank* (1880) 5 App Cas 317 HL.
29   *Rayfield v Hands* [1960] Ch 1 at 4.
30   (1889) 42 Ch D 636 at 642.
31   [1909] 1 Ch 311 at 318.
32   [1897] AC 299 at 315.
33   [1943] 2 All ER 763.
34   *Ibid* at 765.

Then, in *Rayfield v Hands*,[35] though Vaisey J said he found the statement of Lord Herschell 'somewhat cryptic' he enforced an article against the individual director/members in an action brought by another member without joining the company as a party. There is obvious sense in allowing members to bring such an action because it may well be cheaper and quicker not to have to involve the company. Also there is the very real possibility that the members against whom the articles are sought to be enforced have control of or influence on the board of directors who would then be reluctant to authorise the use of the company name to enforce the articles.

Another issue which has caused more difficulty is precisely what type of rights can be enforced as articles by the members or the company. In *Hickman v Kent or Romney Marsh Sheep Breeders Association*,[36] in order to deal with an argument put forward by the plaintiff that the articles do not constitute a contract between the members and the company (and therefore he was not bound by the arbitration clause), Astbury J analysed all the cases relied on by the plaintiff tending to support this proposition as cases involving situations where the article relied upon actually purported to confer the right on a person in a capacity other than that of member, and none of them concerned members who sought to enforce or protect rights in the articles given to them *as members*. In other words they were 'outsider rights'. It was this fact which accounted for the failure in those cases to have the rights enforced.

Support for this line of reasoning can be derived from the case of *Eley v Positive Government Security Life Assurance Co.*[37] Here, on the formation of a company, the plaintiff, who was a solicitor, inserted an article which provided that he should be appointed as the permanent solicitor of the company. When the company subsequently ceased to employ him he brought an unsuccessful action for breach of contract claiming that he had a contractual right to act as the company's solicitor arising from the articles. On one narrow interpretation of the case he failed because he was not a party to the contract since he was not a member: he had not taken shares in the company when it was formed. Subsequently though, he had become a member by taking shares, but this fact was not discussed in the judgments of the Court of Appeal. The interpretation placed on this case and the others by Astbury J is that:

> 'an outsider to whom rights purport to be given by the articles in his capacity as such outsider, *whether he is or subsequently becomes a member*, cannot sue on those articles treating them as contracts between himself and the company to enforce those rights.'[38]

Further, Astbury J is able to extract the following three principles:

1   No article can constitute a contract between the company and a third person.

---

35   [1960] Ch 1.

36   [1915] 1 Ch 881.

37   (1876) 1 Ex D 88.

38   [1915] 1 Ch 881 at 897.

2   No right merely purporting to be given by an article to a person, whether member or not, in a capacity other than that of a member, as, for instance, as solicitor, promoter, or director, can be enforced against the company.

3   Articles regulating rights and obligations of the members generally as such do create rights and obligations between them and the company respectively.

The first and third of these principles are uncontroversial, the first because it is simply a matter of privity of contract and the third because it is extracted from a proper reading of the section and had been established in previous cases. It is the second principle together with the remarkable degree of authority which the *Hickman* judgment has subsequently enjoyed which created the problem. It became what might be described as the orthodox view, once leading textbooks adopted it in successive editions.[39] This view is also reflected in the judgment of Buckley LJ in *Bisgood v Henderson's Transvaal Estates*[40] where he stated that:

> '[t]he purpose of the memorandum and articles is to define the position of the shareholder as shareholder, not to bind him in his capacity as an individual.'[41]

The result of this reasoning is that any article which purports to give a person any right, or fix him with any obligation, which does not relate to or is not connected with his position or capacity as member of the company, cannot be enforced. Some articles therefore, such as the article in *Eley's* case remain as mere unenforceable expressions of intention in the registered articles of the company. So the term 'outsider right' can be misleading in two respects: first, because the person to whom the right belongs is not necessarily an outsider, the right simply does not affect him in his capacity as insider; second, it can hardly be described as a right if it cannot be enforced.

This view was applied in *Beattie v E & F Beattie*[42] where a dispute had arisen between a company and one of its directors concerning an alleged breach of a duty by the director. Again there was a clause in the company's articles obliging all disputes between the company and a member to be referred to arbitration. The appellant director, who was also a member, sought unsuccessfully to rely on this clause to avoid the dispute being aired in court. The claim failed because this was a dispute between the company and the appellant in his capacity as director. As a director and a disputant in this action he had no right to enforce the terms of the article.

The issue has also arisen in cases where the litigation is between members and the company has not been a party. In *London Sack & Bag Co Ltd v Dixon & Lugton*[43] two companies were in dispute over a trading transaction. An argument was put forward by one of the parties that as they were both members of a trade association which was operating as a limited company the parties were bound by one of its articles which stated that:

---

39   See Gower, *Modern Company Law*, 5th edn (1992) pp 283–84.

40   [1908] 1 Ch 743.

41   Ibid at 759.

42   [1938] Ch 708

43   [1943] 2 All ER 763.

'all disputes arising out of transactions connected with the trade ... shall be referred to arbitration.'

In dismissing this claim, the Court of Appeal held that even if members could enforce the terms of the articles directly against other members no rights of action could be created entirely outside the 'company relationship' of the trade association such as commercial trading transactions. That is to say this was a matter which had nothing to do with their membership of the company.

A very different approach was taken in the controversial case of *Rayfield v Hands*,[44] where an obligation in the articles expressly imposing the company's *directors* to buy the shares of a member who wished to transfer his shares was enforced against the directors by such a member. Here there was a share qualification requirement imposed on the directors so that all the directors were also members and Vaisey J was able to say that:

'the relationship here is between the plaintiff as a member and the defendants not as directors but as members.'[45]

Rayfield v Hands, though, appears irreconcilable with other authorities on the issue and perhaps the decision is best supported by viewing it as one of the category of cases involving 'quasi-partnerships' where the courts habitually approach the cases in a different light.

The cases do not consistently follow the *Hickman* view though, even where the dispute is between the company and the member, and the case which most clearly demonstrates this is *Salmon v Quin & Axtens*.[46] Here an article which provided that a managing director could veto a particular type of resolution was enforced by the Court of Appeal in an action brought by that managing director. Clearly the court was at least appearing to enforce a right given to an outsider in the articles and there are other examples in the cases which appear to do the same.[47] The search for a reconciliation of the two lines of authority has occupied considerable space in the law journals with more than one commentator suggesting that only certain types of 'outsider right' in the articles will be enforced; for instance, only those concerned with the management of the company rather than those purporting to appoint certain individuals to positions within the company.[48] This is clearly contrary to the actual wording of the section itself which states that 'all the provisions of the memorandum and articles' should be observed. Further, why enforce certain articles which now appear to the court to be important, and not those which appear trivial if the parties at the time of the formation of the company *bona fide* wished to include these sorts of clauses?

A well known and more wide ranging reconciliation is provided by Wedderburn whose view is that:

---

44 [1960] Ch 1.
45 *Ibid* at 6.
46 [1909] 1 Ch 311.
47 *Pulbrook v Richmond Consolidated Mining Co* (1878) 9 Ch D 610.
48 (1972) 35 MLR 362; (1985) 48 MLR 158; (1980) 1 Co Law 179.

'a member can compel the company not to depart from the contract with him under the articles even if it means indirectly the enforcement of 'outsider rights' vested in either third parties or himself, so long as, but only so long as, he sues *qua* member and not *qua* outsider.'[49]

This view has much to recommend it and is consistent with the argument put forward by Sir Wilfred Greene MR in *Beattie v E & F Beattie*[50] that, if the relevant article had entitled a member to instruct the company to refer a dispute with a director to arbitration, then the appellant would have succeeded, because he would have been enforcing a right common to all the members even though accidentally he was the director in dispute with the company.

So under this view a person would have to sue as member and as long as this was the case he could enforce an article which contained an outsider right even if, coincidentally, he was the beneficiary of the right. The way in which the court can be persuaded that a person is suing as a member is by the bringing of a representative action on behalf of all the members who wish to have the company abide by its constitution.[51]

Despite this, after a reading of the cases on what is, after all, the basic issue of what articles can and cannot be enforced by the shareholders, one has to have some sympathy with the view of Sealy who states that '[o]ur legislators should go back to the drawing-board' and replace s 14 with a much more straightforward provision.[52] The circumstances where the issue has most recently been brought before the courts is in the context of class rights in *Cumbrian Newspapers Group Ltd v Cumberland and Westmorland Herald Co Ltd*,[53] a discussion of which appears on p 173.

Alteration of the articles

The articles of a company can be altered from their original registered form. The relevant enabling section is s 9 which reads as follows:

'(1) Subject to the provisions of this Act and to the conditions contained in its memorandum, a company may by special resolution alter its articles.

(2) Alterations so made in the articles are (subject to this Act) as valid as if originally contained in them, and are subject in like manner to alteration by special resolution.'

It is not possible for a company to restrict its ability to alter its articles by a statement or clause to that effect in the articles or by entering into a contract with a shareholder or third party. Any article which purported to restrict the power given by s 9 would simply be void. The actual legal effect of a contract entered into by a company not to

---

49   [1957] CLJ 194 at 212.
50   [1938] Ch 708.
51   See Rules of the Supreme Court 1965, Order 15, rule 12.
52   LS Sealy; *Cases and Materials in Company Law*, Butterworths (1992, 5th edn) p 96.
53   [1987] Ch 1.

alter its articles has not been entirely clear. It is certainly unenforceable in the manner intended, but the courts have not declared such a contract void. In fact in *Punt v Symons*[54] there was a separate contract with a third party not to alter certain articles and the court refused to grant an injunction to restrain the altering of these articles, but the judge stated that 'it may be that the remedy for the [third party] is in damages only'.

This view cannot stand in the light of the recent House of Lords decision in *Russell v Northern Development Bank Corpn Ltd* which also raised the important issue of the effect of shareholder agreements generally.[55] Here there was an agreement between the shareholders, to which the company was a party, which provided that no further share capital should be created or issued in the company without the written consent of each of the parties to the contract. The agreement also provided that the terms of the agreement should have precedence between the shareholders over the articles of association. In fact, the case arose because an extraordinary general meeting was called to propose an increase in the company's share capital. The Companies (Northern Ireland) Order 1986 contained an equivalent provision to s 121 of the 1985 Act and the articles contained a clause which stated that the company could, by ordinary resolution, increase the share capital. So the issue in the case was whether the agreement could effectively oust the ability of the company to alter its memorandum increasing its authorised share capital. If not, then the agreement was void and the shareholders would be free to vote for an increase. It was held by the House of Lords that the agreement was binding on the original shareholders who were party to it. As Lord Jauncey explained:

> 'While a provision in a company's articles which restricts its statutory power to alter those articles is invalid an agreement *dehors* the articles between shareholders as to how they shall exercise their voting rights on a resolution to alter the articles is not necessarily so.'

On confining the construction of the nature of the agreement to one which simply bound the shareholders as to how they would vote or would not vote on a particular resolution, the House of Lords was able to uphold it. Two further points relevant to the validity of the agreement were: that the agreement only bound shareholders personally who were parties to it and not future, subsequent shareholders who would be able to vote freely to increase capital; and that although a party to the agreement, the company was not bound by it either. The undertaking by the company not to exercise one of its statutory powers was as obnoxious as if it were contained in the articles themselves and was therefore unenforceable. So the *obiter* of Byrne J in *Punt v Symons* cannot now represent the law.

By s 16 a member of a company is not bound by an alteration made in either the memorandum or the articles after the date on which he became a member, if the alteration requires him to take or subscribe for more shares than the member held at the date on which the alteration was made, or increases his liability from that date to

---

54 [1903] 2 Ch 506.
55 [1992] 1 WLR 588.

contribute to the company's share capital, or otherwise to pay money to the company. Although the effect of this section cannot be avoided by a statement in the memorandum or article, a member can agree in writing, either before or after the alteration, to be bound by it. So s 16 affords protection for existing members of a company against incurring further financial commitments where they find themselves in a minority and there is a sufficient majority to alter the memorandum or articles.

In the context of alterations to the articles most of the reported cases have arisen when the majority shareholders have resolved to add a clause allowing the compulsory purchase of a minority shareholding in the company's articles or to add a new way of dismissing a director in circumstances where there is a very obvious target for the immediate use of the altered clause.

Until the turn of the century shareholders who did not possess enough voting strength to block the passing of a special resolution were in a very vulnerable position. Then, in *Allen v Gold Reefs of West Africa*,[56] the Court of Appeal articulated a rule, imported from partnership law, which appeared to improve the position for such minorities. Here the executors of Z brought this action for a declaration that the defendant company had no lien upon the fully paid shares held by them. The company's articles had contained a clause which stated that the company should have a lien for all debts and liabilities of any member on any of the partly paid shares held by that member. Z held partly paid shares in the company and he was the only member to hold fully paid shares. At his death he owed substantial sums of money to the company for arrears of calls on the partly paid shares and it looked unlikely that the executors would satisfy these debts, so the company altered the articles giving it a lien upon both partly paid *and* fully paid shares. The plaintiffs argued that the resolution to alter the article was oppressive and in bad faith because it was a resolution which operated on the general body of shareholders unequally and only Z was affected, and further, that an alteration could not be passed which retrospectively affected a shareholder's rights.

These arguments were rejected and the alteration was upheld by the majority of the Court of Appeal. When a shareholder acquires shares in a company he becomes a party to the statutory contract and he becomes a party not only on the terms of the articles as they then stand, but also on the basis that there is a statutory right to alter them. Lindley LJ, in explaining what the jurisdiction of the court was to interfere with alterations, stated:

> 'Wide, however, as the language of [s 9] is, the power conferred by it must, like all other powers, be exercised subject to those principles of law and equity which are applicable to all powers conferred on majorities and enabling them to bind minorities. It must be exercised, not only in the manner required by law, but also *bona fide* for the benefit of the company as a whole.'[57]

In practice, however, this rule has been extremely difficult to apply and to justify in relating to registered companies. The central problem is that the position of a partner in

---

56 [1900] 1 Ch 656.

57 *Ibid* at 671.

a partnership is quite different from that of a shareholder in a company (except perhaps for certain purposes in those companies which are termed 'quasi-partnerships').[58] In a partnership there are no other persons apart from the partners themselves to consider. The partnership contract is one of good faith between the partners. In *Blisset v Daniel*,[59] where an article of a partnership provided that two thirds or more of the partnership could expel any partner by giving him notice, it was held that this power must be exercised with good faith, and that the power to expel existed not for the benefit of any particular two thirds majority so they could appropriate to themselves the expelled partner's share of the business at a fixed value which was less than its true value, but it existed for the benefit of the whole society or partnership.

When this rule is adopted, and 'society or partnership' is replaced by 'company', one obvious question which arises is: are shareholders supposed to be voting *bona fide* for the benefit of the company as an independent entity or for the members as a general body? If it is to be the former, the then principle is not of much value to the minority as illustrated by *Allen v Gold Reefs* itself. Here the alteration to the article was of obvious benefit to the company as an independent entity because it extended its security for unpaid debts owed to it.

The rule did enjoy some success when a court employed the latter 'partnership' interpretation in *Brown v British Abrasive Wheel Co Ltd*.[60] Here, an alteration of the article to include a compulsory expropriation clause, so that a minority could be bought out by a majority which had indicated it would then invest in the company after the buy-out, was rejected as not being for the benefit of the company (of members) as then composed.

Another case where the rule came to the aid of a minority was *Dafen Tinplate Co Ltd v Llanelly Steel Co*,[61] when a judge took it upon himself to decide the merits of introducing a compulsory expropriation clause and expelling a particular member of a company. The majority wished to add a clause which permitted the majority of shareholders to direct that the shares of any other member (except one named member) should be offered for sale by the directors to such persons as they thought fit.

The underlying reason for this was that the majority wished to buy out the plaintiff member since the plaintiff had formerly been a customer of the company but had since taken its custom elsewhere. Peterson J interpreted the *Allen v Gold Reefs* test as being 'whether in fact the alteration is genuinely for the benefit of the company ...' and in holding that this was not the case here stated:

> '[i]t may be for the benefit of the majority of the shareholders to acquire the shares of the minority, but how can it be said to be for the benefit of the company that any shareholder, against whom no charge of acting to the detriment of the company can be urged, and who is in every respect a desirable member of the company, and for whose

---

58   See p 305.
59   (1853) 10 Hare 493.
60   [1919] 1 Ch 290.
61   [1920] 2 Ch 124.

expropriation there is no reason except the will of the majority, should be forced to transfer his shares to the majority or anyone else?'[62]

These are, however, isolated cases of a successful application of the rule. Subsequently the inherent defects of the rule have prevented it from being used to protect minorities, and it is more likely now that a member who is aggrieved by what he regarded as an oppressive alteration of the articles would bring a petition under s 459.[63]

One reason for the decline of the principle as a useful device for a minority shareholder was the rejection of the objective approach taken by Peterson J in *Dafen Tinplate*. In both *Sidebottom v Kershaw, Leese & Co Ltd*[64] and *Shuttleworth v Cox Brothers & Co (Maidenhead) Ltd*[65] the Court of Appeal favoured a more subjective approach, which is to say that the court will only interfere with a resolution if the majority of shareholders are acting so oppressively that they cannot be acting in good faith for the benefit of the company, or the resolution is one that no reasonable shareholder could possibly believe was for the benefit of the company. In these circumstances the court would be willing to allow a resolution to be passed and an article altered even if the court itself of the opinion that it was not for the benefit of the company.

In the last major analysis of the rule, in *Greenhalgh v Arderne Cinemas Ltd*,[66] the extraordinary and contradictory judgment of Lord Evershed MR failed to provide a lucid set of guidelines for its application. Here the parties had engaged upon a long running and bitter dispute and this was the seventh set of legal proceedings. The articles of a company provided that every existing member had a right of pre-emption over issued shares which a member wished to sell. The managing director, because he wished to sell his shares to an outsider, called a general meeting to alter the articles to add a clause which allowed a member to sell to an outsider if he obtained the sanction of an ordinary resolution of the shareholders. In rejecting the argument that the resolutions were not passed *bona fide* for the benefit of the company as a whole Lord Evershed explained in a famous and often quoted passage:

'... I think it is now plain that '*bona fide* for the benefit of the company as a whole' means not two things but one thing. It means that the shareholder must proceed upon what, in his honest opinion, is for the benefit of the company as a whole. The second thing is that the phrase 'the company as a whole' does not (at any rate in such a case as the present) mean the company as a commercial entity, distinct from the corporators: it means the corporators as a general body. That is to say, the case may be taken of an individual hypothetical member and it may be asked whether what is proposed is in the honest opinion of those who voted in its favour for that person's benefit.'[67]

---

62 *Ibid* at 141

63 See, for example, *Re a Company, ex parte Schwarz (No 2)* [1989] BCLC 427; *Re Blue Arrow plc* [1987] BCLC 585. See p 291.

64 [1920] 1 Ch 154.

65 [1927] 2 KB 9.

66 [1951] Ch 286

67 *Ibid* at 291.

So Lord Evershed begins with a straightforward subjective approach but then confuses the issue by introducing a hypothetical member test which seems to be a mixed objective and subjective test. Further, the confident statement that the authorities show that the 'company as a whole' means the 'corporators as a general body', is certainly not supported by one of the Court of Appeal authorities cited, *Sidebottom v Kershaw, Leese*. Worse still, Lord Evershed himself, later in the judgment refers to the 'benefit of the company as a going concern'.[68]

Lastly, Lord Evershed postulates an alternative approach stating 'that a special resolution of this kind would be liable to be impeached if the effect of it were to *discriminate* between the majority shareholders and the minority shareholders, so as to give the former an advantage of which the latter were deprived'.[69] But this cannot be enough on its own, as the *Greenhalgh* case itself shows, because following the alteration the majority were handed the advantage of being able to sell their shares to outsiders.

What these cases show is that shareholders were in desperate need of some statutory protection, which, correctly framed, would protect them from oppression. In fact by the time the *Greenhalgh* case came before the court, the predecessor of s 459, s 210 of the Companies Act 1948, was already in force and anyway after *Greenhalgh*, in cases where resolutions were attacked, the courts were simply asking the question whether there had been any oppression.[70]

A further problem with the *Allen v Gold Reefs* principle, as was pointed out in *Phillips v Manufacturers Securities Ltd*, is that the share is a piece of property with voting rights attached to it. The general rule is that shareholder can vote on his shares in whatever way he thinks fit for his own benefit even if by doing so he does harm to another,[71] so why should he be restricted to voting bona fide for the benefit of the company on resolutions to alter the articles? Unlike the directors, a shareholder owes no fiduciary duty to the other shareholders or the company. In *Peter's American Delicacy Co Ltd v Heath*,[72] an Australian case and another unsuccessful attempt to challenge an alteration of the articles, the related practical difficulties of applying the rule were discussed. Here Dixon J said:

> '[n]o one supposes that in voting each shareholder is to assume an inhuman altruism and consider only the intangible notion of the benefit of the vague abstraction called ... 'the company as an institution'. An investigation of the thoughts and motives of each shareholder voting with the majority would be an impossible proceeding.'[73]

The issue of the right to vote is discussed generally later in this book. In summary it is easy to overstate the importance of *Allen v Gold Reefs*, and since the introduction of s 459 as a remedy for a shareholder who is a victim of unfairly prejudicial conduct, cases

---

68 *Ibid.*

69 *Ibid.*

70 See *Clemens v Clemens Ltd* [1976] 2 All ER 268.

71 (1917) 116 LT 290.

72 (1939) 61 CLR 457.

73 *Ibid* at 512.

of alteration of articles would almost certainly be brought before the court on a petition under that section, although the old authorities may well be used to determine whether the resolution is unfairly prejudicial, and it has been held that there can still be unfair prejudice even if a special resolution is passed in accordance with the tests expounded in *Greenhalgh*.[74]

The articles and separate contracts

It was stated in section 1 of this Chapter that the orthodox position is that no clause in the articles can be enforced which does not affect the members in their capacity as members or in their personal capacity (subject to *Salmon v Quin Axtens Ltd*[75] and the arguments of the commentators), and in section 2 it was stated that the articles can be altered by the passing of a special resolution, despite the existence of a clause to the contrary in the articles or of a separate contract between the company and outsiders not to alter them. To complete the picture, it is now necessary to consider the position in relation to other sorts of contracts made between the company and an outsider or a member contracting in his personal capacity.

The relationship between an express contractual term and the articles

If an outsider has an express contract containing terms and conditions, then these cannot be overridden by the articles unless the contract is made expressly subject to them. The contractual term must take precedence and cannot be varied or abrogated by an article or the company purporting to act under an article. Many of the cases involve the service contracts executive directors have with their companies. So a managing director whose contract appointed him for so long as he remained a director of the company (subject to certain contingencies which did not at the material time exist) could not be lawfully removed from his post by the board purporting to do so under a clause in the company's articles stating that the board could revoke the appointment of a managing director.[76] He was entitled to recover damages for wrongful dismissal. Again, in *Southern Foundries (1926) Ltd v Shirlaw*,[77] a contract which appointed a managing director for a fixed period of 10 years could not be lawfully brought to an end within the period by a purported termination under the authority of an article. (This was the case whether or not the article was contained in the company's articles at the time of the agreement was made or was subsequently added: see section (c)).

In *Southern Foundries* the articles contained a common clause that a managing director could only hold office as long as he continued to be a director, and if he ceased to be a director then he should *ipso facto* cease to be a managing director. Further articles provided that this company could dismiss a director by the passing of an

---

74 See *Re a Company ex parte Schwarz (No 2)* [1989] BCLC 427.
75 [1909] 1 Ch 311.
76 *Nelson v James Nelson & Sons Ltd* [1914] 2 KB 770.
77 [1940] AC 701.

extraordinary resolution in general meeting and that a director could vacate his office by giving one month's notice in writing. It was held *obiter* that if either the company or the director brought the agreement to an end under this article before the expiring of the 10 year term by use of these methods, there would have been a breach of the agreement. This was on the basis of the common law rule in *Stirling v Maitland*[78] that:

'if a party enters into an arrangement which can only take effect by the continuance of a certain existing set of circumstances, there is an implied engagement on his part that he shall do nothing of his own motion to put an end to that state of circumstances under which alone the arrangement can be operative.'

The clause which was relied on to terminate the agreement was an article, added to the company's articles after the contract was made, which gave power to a named party (the parent company) to remove a director. In the managing director's action for wrongful dismissal this gave rise to an argument by the company that it was the parent company's motion and not its own motion that led to the termination. Nevertheless by a majority of 3:2 the House of Lords dismissed this argument and held that the managing director had been wrongfully dismissed and therefore entitled to damages.

In *Shindler v Northern Raincoat Co Ltd*[79] Diplock J applied *Southern Foundries v Shirlaw*, holding that even though the company's articles gave the board power to revoke a managing director's appointment, where a managing director had been appointed under a separate 10-year service contract it was a breach of contract for him to be removed from office before the expiry of the term. This was because there was an implied term in the contract that the company would do nothing of its own motion to bring the contract to an end.

Contracts which incorporate an article

A situation can occur where a person enters into a contract with the company and an article is either expressly or impliedly incorporated into that contract. If that is the case then the article can be enforced not as an article but as a term of the separate contract. Quite commonly this situation has arisen in relation to directors who have been employed by a company either with no written contract setting out the terms of appointment at all or only an incomplete one. Subsequently either the director or the company wishes to enforce one of the clauses in the articles claiming that the other is bound by it. See, for example, *Guinness plc v Saunders*[80] where it was held that the directors were appointed 'subject to and with the benefit of the provisions of the articles relating to directors'. Therefore in this case the procedure for awarding remuneration to directors was to be derived from a strict interpretation of the remuneration clauses in the articles.

From the authority of *Hickman's* case the articles do not form a contract with the director *qua* director nor can the director, if he holds shares in the company, enforce

---

78   (1864) 5 B & S 840 at 852.

79   [1960] 1 WLR 1038.

80   [1990] 2 AC 663.

the articles *qua* member. The courts on a number of occasions have held that there is an implied contractual relationship between the company and the director and both parties have entered into this contract on the understanding that certain articles were to be incorporated as its terms. So, in *Re New British Iron Co ex parte Beckwith*[81] the directors of a company were appointed but had no written terms which provided for remuneration. A clause in the company's articles stated that '[t]he remuneration of the board shall be an annual sum of £1,000 to be paid out of the funds of the company, which sum shall be divided in such manner as the board from time to time determine ...'. It was held that the directors had been employed 'on the footing of that article' and the terms of it had become embodied into the contract between the company and the directors. So the directors were owed this money as directors and stood in exactly the same position in respect of this money as the other ordinary creditors in the winding up and were not caught by what is now s 74(2)(f) of the Insolvency Act 1986 which provides that '... money owed to members in their character as members is not a debt owed by the company so that members have to wait until all the other creditors have been paid'.

Another example of this situation is found in *Re Anglo-Austrian Printing and Publishing Union (Isaacs Case)*[82] where the articles of a company provided that a director as a qualification for office should take up shares to the nominal value of £1,000 within one month from the date of his appointment and that if he failed to do so he should be 'deemed to have agreed to take the said shares from the company and the same should be ... allotted to him accordingly'. One of the directors served for more than a year without taking up the qualifying shares. When the company was wound up, it was held by the Court of Appeal that the director was bound by an implied contract with the company on accepting and taking up office to have the shares allotted to him. The consequence was that the director then was liable to contribute £1,000 to the company's assets in the winding up.

The Court of Appeal was at pains to distinguish the above case from *Re Wheal Buller Consols*,[83] where there were similar facts, but the relevant article stated that it was a qualification of a director holding office that he held at least 250 shares and his office would have to be vacated if he did not acquire the shares within three months. He did not acquire the shares but continued to act as director after the expiry of three months. In these circumstances (in contrast to *Isaacs Case*) the Court of Appeal could not find that there was any contractual obligation *to take the shares*, simply a clause stating that he should vacate his office. He had not done so, therefore he was in breach of the term, but he could not be forced to take the shares and thus he did not become a contributory for that amount in the winding up. Also in the circumstances of this case an estoppel could not operate simply because he continued after three months without taking the shares.

---

81   [1898] 1 Ch 324.
82   [1892] 2 Ch 158.
83   (1888) 38 Ch D 42.

One consequence of incorporating an article as a term into a separate contract is that the company remains at liberty to alter the article. Therefore, if an article provides for the remuneration of an employee and the article is altered so that the remuneration is decreased, this employee will not be able to complain about the alteration in so far as it affects his future remuneration, although he will be able to claim for remuneration at the old rate up to the date of the alteration.[84]

Another example is *Shuttleworth v Cox Brothers & Co (Maidenhead) Ltd*[85] where the directors were appointed for life by the articles unless they should become disqualified by one of six specified events. The articles were subsequently altered to add a seventh event and the plaintiff was removed under this one. It was held that the contract between the company and the plaintiff derived its force and effect form the articles themselves and therefore as the contractual terms were articles they could be altered. The only question remained was whether the alteration satisfied the *Allen v Gold Reefs* test.[86]

In distinguishing *Nelson v James Nelson & Sons*[87] Scrutton LJ stated:

'The Court [in *Nelson*] held that the contract being outside the articles could not be altered without the consent of both parties. But if a contract is contained in the articles it must be, as the articles themselves are, subject to [s 9 of the Companies Act 1985]. Consequently the plaintiff's contract, if any, is not a contract constituting him a permanent director unconditionally, but is a contract constituting him a permanent director subject to the power of terminating his appointment in accordance with the articles or any modification of the articles sanctioned by the Companies Act.'[88]

But see the next section for the position where an alteration to the articles does infringe an express or implied term in the separate contract because the term is not incorporated from the articles *as* an article.

It may be that a managing director is appointed without any written contract containing the terms as to his appointment and in this case, as *Read v Astoria Garage (Streatham) Ltd*[89] shows, he is very vulnerable. Here the company articles contained an article in the form of the old article 68 of Table A, which gave the board of directors power to appoint a managing director for such term and at such remuneration as they might think fit, and such an appointment should be subject to determination *ipso facto* if the company in general meeting voted to determine his appointment. The plaintiff had been appointed by the board as managing director and had worked as such for 17 years. Nevertheless it was held that he could be validly removed without notice under the article since there was 'no vestige of any contract beyond the minute of the resolution

---

84 *Swabey v Port Darwin Gold Mining Co* (1889) 1 Meg 385.
85 [1927] 2 KB 9.
86 See p 80.
87 [1914] 2 KB 770.
88 [1927] 2 KB 9 at 22.
89 [1952] Ch 637.

[of the board] making the appointment and the article by reference to which ... the appointment was made'.[90]

Contracts which are infringed or affected by an alteration to the articles

It is clear that although a company cannot be restrained from exercising its power to alter its articles it cannot alter them with impunity if to do so breaches the terms of a separate, independent contract with an outsider. A company cannot plead an alteration to the articles if there exists a contract to justify a breach of contract. For example, if a person enters into a contract to subscribe for a company's shares and the company subsequently alters its articles to include a new pre-emption right giving existing members the first right of refusal, making performance of the contract impossible, the subscriber will be able to sue for breach of contract. This principle was stated in *Allen v Gold Reefs*[91] and even more clearly in the Court of Appeal decision in *Baily v British Equitable Assurance Co*,[92] and was approved by the House of Lords in *Southern Foundries (1926) Ltd v Shirlaw*.[93] As Lord Porter stated in the latter case:

> '[It] is ... long-established law that a company cannot forgo its rights to alter its articles, but it does not follow that the alteration may not be or result in a breach of contract.'[94]

and further:

> '[a] company cannot be precluded from altering its articles thereby giving itself power to act upon the provisions of the altered articles – but so to act may nevertheless be a breach of the contract if it is contrary to a stipulation in a contract validly made before the alteration.'[95]

The policy behind this rule is obvious, since as was stated in the judgment of the Court of Appeal in *Baily*:

> '[i]t would be dangerous to hold that in a contract of loan or a contract of service or a contract of insurance validly entered into by a company there is any greater power of variation of the rights and liabilities of the parties than would exist if, instead of the company, the contracting party had been an individual.'[96]

But the company can of course, as mentioned above, avoid this if it is able to show that the clause in the contract was adopted as an article and therefore liable to alteration.

Some care must be exercised over this principle. It is unlikely that an order would be made to restrain an alteration of the articles, either the holding of a meeting for this purpose or the passing of the necessary special resolution, even if the alteration did bring about a breach of contract despite authority to the contrary. In *British Murac*

---

90 *Ibid* at 642.
91 [1900] 1 Ch 656.
92 [1904] 1 Ch 374.
93 [1940] AC 701.
94 *Ibid* at 739.
95 *Ibid* at 740.
96 [1904] 1 Ch 374 at 385.

Syndicate Ltd v Alperton Rubber Co[97] the plaintiff had an agreement with the company that it could nominate two directors to the board as long as it held 5,000 shares. This was repeated in one of the company's articles. The company proposed to delete this article, wishing to appoint directors other than the nominees of the plaintiff. Sargent J granted an injunction to prevent the holding of a meeting to pass the special resolution on the grounds that a company cannot commit a breach of contract by an alteration of its articles.

However, the reliance by Sargent J on the decision of the Court of Appeal in *Baily v British Equitable Assurance Co*[98] was misplaced, since in this latter case the plaintiff only obtained a declaration that the terms of his separate contract were not affected by the company's alteration to its articles and remained intact. It is far from authority for the proposition that a plaintiff can restrain a proposed alteration because of the terms he may have in a separate contract. But the actual decision in *British Murac Syndicate* could now be justified on completely different grounds: see the discussion of class rights.

Therefore, the position seems to be that the company can alter its articles no matter what, but it may well be restrained from acting under the altered article if that would constitute a breach of contract and it may be liable to pay damages.

USING THE CONSTITUTION TO CONTRACT OUT OF COMPANY LAW

An issue which has been raised relatively recently in the cases which have come before the courts is the general question of whether, and to what extent, those persons forming companies can 'contract out' of one or more of the rules of company law. This issue is well known and discussed in the USA[99] but has received little explicit attention in the judgments in the UK. The traditional view would be that the Companies Acts present a 'take it or leave it' set of rules regulating the formation and management of companies. But there has been a number of cases where this issue has arisen. For example, the majority of the House of Lords in *Bushell v Faith*[100] allowed a clause in a company's articles to frustrate the obvious intention of Parliament in enacting what is now s 303.

In *Harman v BML Group Ltd*,[101] the insertion of a clause in the articles giving a member what amounted to a class right, meant that the court was unwilling to exercise its discretion under s 371 to order the holding of a general meeting.

Again, in *Re Abbey Leisure Ltd*,[102] the presence of a clause in the company's articles which provided for what was to happen in the event of a breakdown in the

---

97 [1915] 2 Ch 186

98 [1904] 1 Ch 374

99 See, for example, the collection of papers in 89 *Columbia Law Review* (1989).

100 [1970] AC 1099.

101 [1994] 1 WLR 893.

102 [1989] BCLC 619.

relationship between the shareholders in a company, or the method of valuing a departing member's shares, was held to override the court's ability to make an order under s 459 or to impose its own method of valuation. But the Court of Appeal in *Virdi v Abbey Leisure Ltd*[103] disapproved of these clauses. Lastly, and although not as a result of the constitution itself, in *Russell v Northern Development Bank Ltd*[104] the House of Lords approved a shareholders' agreement which had the effect of restricting the ability of the company to raise further capital, at least so long as the contracting shareholders remained in the majority in general meetings.[105]

This is a feature of company law which can be expected to become more prominent, especially in relation to small companies. Its advantage is that it gives businessmen more flexibility in the structuring of their affairs and providing for future problems.

---

103 [1990] BCLC 342.
104 [1992] 1 WLR 588.
105 See p 79.

CHAPTER FIVE

CORPORATE DECISION-MAKING

At the heart of company law lies the issue of who controls the company. The answer to this question will ultimately determine how the company's property is used, what transactions are entered into or approved and whether persons who have caused harm or loss to the company will be pursued. There are two primary decision-making bodies within a company, the general meeting of shareholders and the board of directors.

In theory there is a great deal of emphasis placed on collective decision-making in company law. The Companies Act places importance on the shareholders' meetings and has a considerable number of provisions regulating when and how they should be held. In reality, though, most important commercial decisions are taken by the board, by a committee of the board or perhaps even the managing director or chief executive who is a delegate of the board, and the Companies Acts in contrast have very little to say prescriptively about the board meeting. In order to obtain an overview as to how power is exercised in the company it is proposed to deal first with the statutory provisions and articles dealing with the general meeting, then those relating to the board and then to the crucial issue of the relationship between the general meeting and the board.

THE GENERAL MEETING

Generally speaking, for there to be a meeting at all, there have to be at least two members present: 'the word 'meeting' *prima facie* means a coming together of more than one person'.[1] So, if a meeting is properly called, but only one member attends, then there cannot be a valid meeting. The position is the same even if the one person present is holding proxies of other members.[2]

In addition there will almost certainly be a quorum requirement for the valid transaction of any business at a general meeting contained in the articles. In article 40 of Table A, two persons entitled to vote at the meeting, each being a member or a proxy for a member, are a quorum, and by s 370(4), which applies if the articles do not provide otherwise, two members personally present are a quorum.

Following the implementation of the Twelfth Directive[3] in relation to single member companies, obviously some amendment had to be made in respect of those companies so s 370A provides that:

'Notwithstanding any provisions to the contrary in the articles of a private company limited by shares or by guarantee having only one member, one member present in person or by proxy shall be a quorum.'

---

1   *Sharp v Dawes* (1876) 2 QBD 26 at 29.
2   *Re Sanitary Carbon Co* [1977] WN 223.
3   89/667/EC.

A problem which sometimes arises is where the meeting is quorate at the outset, but subsequently a member or members leave, reducing the number present to below the minimum required for a quorum. In *Re Hartley Baird Ltd*[4] the quorum set by the company's articles was 10 and the meeting began with that number of members present. Then one member left, but despite this Wynn Parry J held that the departure of the member did not invalidate the proceedings carried on after his departure. Contrast that case, however, with *Re London Flats Ltd*,[5] where two persons were originally present at a meeting and one subsequently left. A decision then taken by the remaining member was held to be ineffective. Here the question was whether or not there was actually still a meeting as defined above, not simply whether, if there were a meeting, it was quorate.

Where the company has articles in the form of Table A, the position is made clear by article 41 which provides that if the quorum is not present within half an hour from the time appointed for the meeting, or if during the meeting such a quorum ceases to be present, the meeting shall stand adjourned to the same day in the next week at the same time and place or to such time and place as the directors may determine.

It has recently been held in *Byng v London Life Association Ltd*[6] that it is possible to have a valid meeting even if all the members attending the meeting are not physically in the same room, if they are connected by audio–visual equipment, as long as this equipment is sufficient to allow members to debate and vote on matters affecting the company. The members would be 'electronically' in each other's presence so as to hear and be heard and to see and be seen. The question which did not arise in Byng, and was left open by Mustill LJ, was whether you could have a valid meeting if none of the members were physically face to face but all were linked by audio–visual transmissions. In this situation the 'meeting' would not be taking place in any single location.

Annual general meeting

Section 366 provides that every company must have an annual general meeting (AGM) every calendar year and that the first annual general meeting must be within 18 months of the formation of the company. Not more than 15 months should elapse between the date of one AGM and the next. At least 21 days' notice in writing is required of the AGM.[7] If the provisions of s 366 are not followed then the company and every officer in default are liable to a fine. Where there is a failure to comply with s 366 then any member can apply to the Secretary of State and ask him to call or direct the calling of a general meeting, and in making any order the Secretary of State can modify or supplement the company's articles in relation to the calling, holding and conduct of the meeting.[8]

---

4   [1955] Ch 143.
5   [1969] 1 WLR 711.
6   [1990] 1 Ch 170.
7   Companies Act 1985, s 369(10)(a).
8   Companies Act 1985, s 367.

Curiously the Act does not go any further to prescribe even the minimum of what has to be done at the AGM. Presumably the original intention was to provide shareholders with at least an opportunity every year to attend and vote on matters affecting the company and to raise matters of policy and concern and seek answers from the board. However, since s 241 requires the directors to lay before the company in general meeting copies of the annual accounts, directors' report and the auditors' report,[9] the AGM will almost always be the occasion on which this is done. It will usually also be the most appropriate time to appoint or re-appoint the directors and auditors of the company.

By s 366A a private company may dispense altogether with the holding of an AGM by elective resolution. But even though this is done, any member may, by notice to the company not later than three months before the end of the year in which the AGM would be required to be held, require the holding of an AGM in that year.

Extraordinary general meeting

Any other meeting of the shareholders will be referred to as an extraordinary general meeting (EGM) and these can be called by the directors by giving 14 days' notice in writing or 21 days' notice if it is the intention to pass a special resolution at the meeting.[10] In addition, shareholders are given certain rights to requisition an EGM in s 368. Despite any clause in the company's articles which may provide to the contrary, the members can requisition a meeting where there is support from members holding not less than one tenth of such of the paid-up capital of the company as at the date of the deposit of the requisition carry voting rights; or, where the company does not have a share capital, members representing not less than one-tenth of the total voting rights. The requisition must state the objects of the meeting and must be signed by the requisitioning members and deposited at the registered office. The directors are then under an obligation to convene a meeting by notice within 21 days of the deposit of the requisition. The actual date of the meeting convened should be not more than 28 days after the notice convening the meeting, otherwise they will be deemed not to have convened a meeting.[11] Article 37 of Table A, which requires directors to proceed to convene an EGM for a date not later than eight weeks after receipt of the requisition, pre-dates the amendment to s 368 by the 1989 Act and has not been amended, so it must be overridden by s 368(8). Further, even though there is now a statutory obligation on the directors to fix a date within a certain time limit, in circumstances where the directors proceed to set a date at the end of the permissible period for no apparent reason, this may well constitute unfairly prejudicial conduct and the court could order an earlier date.[12]

---

9   Companies Act 1985, s 241.

10   Companies Act 1985, s 369(1)(b).

11   Companies Act 1985, s 368(8).

12   *McGuinness v Bremner plc* [1988] BCLC 673. See Chapter 9.

If the directors fail to convene a meeting following a valid requisition, then the requisitioning members, or any of them representing more than one half of the total voting rights of all of them, may themselves convene a meeting within three months of the date of the requisition.[13] Further, any reasonable expenses incurred by the requisitioning members by reason of the failure of the directors to convene a meeting can be recovered from the company which, in turn, can be recovered from remuneration or fees which are paid to the directors.[14] In addition by s 370(3), which applies unless the company's articles provide otherwise, two or more members holding not less than one tenth of the issued share capital, or if the company does not have a share capital, not less than 5% in number of the members of the company, may call a meeting, essentially giving the requisite members the same rights to call a general meeting as enjoyed by the directors.

Notices

The power vested in the directors to call general meetings and send out notices is a power which is potentially open to great abuse. First, the notice given for a meeting may be extremely short, giving shareholders little opportunity to make arrangements to attend or mount an effective opposition to the directors' proposal. Second, the circular accompanying the notice, being drafted by the directors, not only of course will put the directors' views forward but may also not present a true picture. As a result both the courts and the legislature have had to intervene to assist shareholders. It cannot be said, however, that the intervention has been totally successful.

Formerly general meetings, as long as they were not ones at which a special resolution was to be passed, could be called on as little as seven days' notice. Now the legislature has intervened to control the length of notices calling meetings. By s 369(1), any article in the company's articles which purports to provide for the calling of a meeting (other than an adjourned meeting) by a shorter notice in writing than 21 days' in the case of the AGM and 14 days' notice in the case of other meetings (other than meetings for the passing of a special resolution which will have to be held on 21 days' notice), are void. By s 369(2) these periods are made the usual periods of notice for company meetings if the articles do not provide for longer periods. But by s 369(3), even though a meeting be called by shorter notice than either that specified in the section or that specified in the articles as the case may be, the meeting can be deemed to have been duly called if it is agreed, in the case of the AGM by all those members entitled to attend and vote, and in the case of other meetings by members entitled to attend and vote holding not less than 95% in nominal value of the such shares, or in the case of a company without a share capital members holding not less than 90% of the total voting rights of all the members.

In the case of a private company it may elect by elective resolution that a lesser percentage of shareholders is required to consent to short notice for general meetings

---

13   Companies Act 1985, s 368(4).
14   Companies Act 1985, s 368(6).

other than AGMs but this lower percentage cannot be less than 90%.[15] Given that the elective resolution procedure was designed to relax the formalities imposed on private companies, it is scarcely credible that the draftsmen of this provision thought that it was a significant step towards that aim.

The relevant Table A provision, article 38, mirrors the statutory provisions regarding length of notices and approval of short notices and further provides that the longer 21-day notice period is required for meetings to pass a resolution appointing a person as a director. Unless the articles of a company provide otherwise, s 370(2) applies the Table A procedure for serving notice on shareholders.

Circulars

The circulars which are sent to the members of the company with the notice of the general meeting present the directors with an opportunity to strengthen their position. They can put their case to the members first, and at the company's expense; it is also an opportunity to solicit for proxies.[16] However, the courts have often been moved to prevent injustice as a result of a misleading or untruthful circular being distributed, and they can issue an injunction to prevent a resolution taking place until a proper circular is presented to the members, or set aside a resolution already passed.[17]

In addition the members who are not in favour of a proposed resolution have statutory rights to insist on the circulation of their own views. By s 376 it is the duty of the company on a requisition of a certain number of the members to give all members of the company entitled to receive notice of the next AGM, notice of any resolution which is intended to be moved at that meeting. Further again, on the requisition of the members, the company must circulate to all members entitled to be given notice of any general meeting a statement of not more than 1,000 words with respect to the matter referred to in any proposed resolution or the business to be dealt with at the meeting. In both cases the required number of members for a requisition under s 376 is either at least 1/20 of the total voting rights of all the members having at that date the right to vote, or at least 100 members holding shares in the company on which there has been paid up an average sum, per member, of at least £100. In addition to this requirement s 377 proceeds to impose a time limit for serving a valid requisition on the company, normally six weeks in the case of a requisition notice of a resolution and one week before the meeting in the case of statements. Further, the company or any other person who claims to be aggrieved can apply to the court on the basis that the rights conferred under the section are being abused to secure needless publicity for defamatory matter, and if satisfied the court can order that the company need not comply with the requisition and that the company's costs be paid by the requisitionists.

---

15   Companies Act 1985, s 369(4).

16   *Re Dorman Long & Co Ltd* [1934] Ch 635.

17   *Kaye v Croydon Tramways Co* [1898] 1 Ch 358; *Baillie v Oriental Telephone Co* [1915] 1 Ch 503.

On top of all these safeguards the costs of the notice and circulating the statements under s 376 are to be borne by the requisitionists unless the company, presumably in general meeting, resolves otherwise. It is not surprising, therefore, that s 376 is not looked upon as being of great assistance to the objecting member.

Power of the court to order a meeting

The court has power under s 371 to order a meeting to be called, held or conducted in any manner the court thinks fit, if it is for any reason impracticable to call one in the manner in which meetings are supposed to be called or conducted under the articles. The court can make this order of its own motion, or on the application of a director or a member who would be entitled to vote at the meeting. Any such meeting ordered by the court under this section is to be deemed for all purposes as a meeting of the company duly called, held and conducted. The court may under this section give such ancillary or consequential directions as it thinks expedient and an example given in s 371(2) is that the court may direct, contrary to previous authority, that one member present in person or by proxy shall be deemed to constitute a meeting.

This was the order made in *Re Opera Photographic Ltd*[18] where the issued capital of the company was divided between the two directors, 51% to the applicant and 49% to the respondent. The applicant requisitioned a meeting under s 368 for the purpose of considering a resolution to dismiss the respondent as a director under what is now s 303 of the 1985 Act. The respondent did not attend the meeting, so as it was then inquorate no resolution could be passed. The applicant successfully applied under s 371 for the court to order an EGM and that a direction be given that one member present in person or by proxy should be deemed to constitute such a meeting. It appears that the courts will exercise their discretion to make orders under s 371 where shareholders attempt to use the quorum provisions as a means to prevent valid meetings being held. Here, when the respondent did not attend the meeting, the quorum provision operated to give him an unwarranted veto on resolutions to remove directors. It would be the same where, for example, two members of the company hold 75% and 25% respectively; the minority shareholder would not be allowed to frustrate the holding of meetings thereby vetoing the majority's right under s 9 to alter the articles. So, orders will be made under this section not only where it is technically impossible to hold a meeting but also where it is impracticable because of the behaviour of others within the company.[19]

The court can also make an order for a meeting to be held attaching provisos on what can be carried out at or after the meeting. For instance, if new directors are to be appointed at the meeting ordered under s 371, the order may include a proviso that the directors so appointed could not act as such until the hearing of a s 459 petition by

---

18   [1989] 1 WLR 634.

19   *Re EL Sombrero* [1958] Ch 900; *Re HR Paul & Son Ltd* (1973) 118 SJ 166.

another member.[20] The fact that a s 459 petition has been presented does not oust the court's jurisdiction under s 459.[21]

The court can make an order under s 371, ordering a meeting to be held, even if that contravenes a clause in the company's constitution. In *Re British Union for the Abolition of Vivisection*[22] a company, registered under the 1985 Act but without a share capital, had articles which provided that no votes by proxy were allowed at general meetings, but since at a previous EGM a near riot had broken out, it was not practical to hold another meeting because of the threat of a recurrence of disruption. The judge, on the basis that this was a very unusual case, allowed the application and ordered a meeting under s 371 allowing voting by proxy.

A limitation on the courts' willingness to make orders under s 371 appeared in *Harman v BML Group Ltd*[23] where the Court of Appeal would not make an order under s 371 for the holding of a meeting which would override a shareholder's class rights. Here, where a company's shares were divided into 'A' and 'B' shares, a shareholders' agreement provided that a shareholders' meeting should not be quorate unless the holder of 'B' shares was present in person or by proxy. There was only one holder of 'B' shares, so he could effectively frustrate the holding of any valid meeting. It was held that the provisions of the shareholders' agreement conferred class rights on the 'B' shareholder. On an application under s 371 by the majority shareholders who held the 'A' shares Dillon LJ distinguished *Re Opera Photographic Ltd*[24] and *Re HR Paul & Son Ltd*[25] on the grounds that the orders under s 371 only overrode ordinary articles which, for example, made provision for the quorum at general meetings. But an order under s 371 would not be made which overrode class rights because they are deliberately imposed or conferred for the protection of the holders of a minority of shares.

Resolutions

There are four types of resolution which can be passed at a general meeting: ordinary; extraordinary; special and elective.

Ordinary

The ordinary resolution is not defined by the Act and does not have any notice or majority requirements. It can be passed by a bare majority of votes at a meeting.

Special and Extraordinary

On the other hand s 378 defines extraordinary and special resolutions. Both require a majority of not less than 3/4 majority of the votes cast in the meeting on the resolution

---

20 *Re Sticky Fingers Restaurant Ltd* [1992] BCLC 84.

21 *Re Whitchurch Insurance Consultants Ltd* [1993] BCLC 1359.

22 (1995) *The Times,* 3 March.

23 [1994] 2 BCLC 674

24 [1989] 1 WLR 634

25 (1973) 118 SJ 166

(either in person or by proxy where allowed). In calculating whether or not there is a 3/4 majority when a poll is demanded, regard is to be paid only to the numbers of votes cast for and against the resolution, therefore abstentions are ignored.[26]

The main difference between these two types of resolution is that for a special resolution there has to be 21 days' notice of the general meeting at which the resolution is to be proposed as a special resolution, whereas for an extraordinary resolution the notice period required is only that required for the meeting itself. In both cases the notice of the meeting must specify the exact substance of the special or extraordinary resolution to be passed as such. The only changes which will be allowed at the meeting, if it is still to be validly passed, are grammatical changes. No substantive changes will be allowed.[27]

The members of the company can agree to a short notice of less than 21 days for a meeting at which a resolution is to be passed as a special resolution if a majority of not less than 95% in nominal value of the shares giving the right to attend and vote so agree, or in the case of a company not having a share capital members representing not less than 95% of the total voting rights so agree.[28] This majority, as in the equivalent provision in s 369, can be reduced by elective resolution, but to not lower than 90%. Copies of both special and extraordinary resolutions have to be sent to the registrar within 15 days of being passed.[29] They are then recorded by him.

The special resolution is nowadays much more commonly required, although an important instance of when an extraordinary resolution is required is to alter or vary class rights in s 125(2) of the 1985 Act in a class meeting of shareholders.[30]

Elective resolutions

The Companies Act 1989 introduced this new form of resolution, now provided for by s 379A, which can only be passed by private companies. The idea behind these types of resolution is that they allow a private company to elect to dispense with or relax one or more of a specified number of formal requirements imposed by the Companies Act as part of a wider desire to relax the burdens of administration on small businesses. At present private companies can make such elections in respect of the following:

(a) the duration of directors' authority to allot shares (s 80A);

(b) the dispensing of the laying of accounts and reports before the general meeting (s 252);

(c) the dispensing with the holding of an annual general meeting (s 366A);

---

26 Companies Act 1985, s 378(5).
27 *Re Moorgate Mercantile Holdings Ltd* [1980] 1 WLR 227.
28 Companies Act 1985, s 378(3).
29 Companies Act 1985, s 380.
30 See p 172.

(d) the reduction of the majority required to authorise short notice of meetings (s 369(4) or s 378(3));

(e) the dispensing with the annual appointment of auditors (s 386).[31]

An elective resolution can be passed only by the giving of at least 21 days' notice of the meeting, stating that an elective resolution is to be proposed at the meeting and stating the terms of the resolution; the resolution has to be agreed to at the meeting in person, or by proxy by *all* the members entitled to attend and vote at the meeting.[32] A copy of the elective resolution then has to be sent to the registrar in the same way as in the case of special and extraordinary resolutions.[33] The resolution will still be effective if this latter provision is not complied with, but the company and every officer in default are liable to a fine. An elective resolution can be revoked at any general meeting by the passing of an ordinary resolution.[34] It is not possible for a private company to 'contract out' or deprive itself of the ability to pass an elective resolution by inserting clauses to that effect in its memorandum or articles of association.[35]

As part of its ongoing reform of company law, the DTI is currently reviewing the requirement in s 379A(2) which applies even if all the members of the company are in agreement on passing the resolution that at least 21 days' notice in writing be given of the meeting at which it is proposed to pass the elective resolution.[36] This is a somewhat anomalous requirement, given that an elective resolution can be passed in any case by written resolution without any previous notice.[37] So it is proposed to remove this notice requirement where there is unanimous agreement amongst the members that less than 21 days' notice may be given.

Voting

The articles will normally make provision as to the voting rights of members and the procedure to be followed on a resolution put to the general meeting. In the absence of any provision to the contrary in the articles, every member of a company with a share capital has one vote in respect of each share held by him, and in the case of other companies every member has one vote.[38]

Article 54 of Table A provides the usual position adopted by companies that on a show of hands every member present in person shall have one vote, but on a poll shall have one vote for every share of which he is the holder. Article 46 states that when a resolution is put to the vote it shall be decided on a show of hands unless before, or on

---

31 Companies Act 1985, s 379A(1).

32 Companies Act 1985, s 379A(2).

33 Companies Act 1985, s 380.

34 Companies Act 1985, s 379A(3).

35 Companies Act 1985, s 379A(5).

36 Resolutions of Private Companies: A Consultative Document, DTI, February 1995 URN 95/554.

37 Companies Act 1985, s 381A. See p 107.

38 Companies Act 1985, s 370(6)

the declaration of the result of the show of hands, a poll is duly demanded. In these circumstances it is obviously of considerable importance for a member holding a large number of shares to know what constitutes a duly demanded poll, and the legislature has intervened to prevent a company's articles from making the conditions for demanding a poll too onerous. Section 373 makes void any provision in the company's articles which would have the effect either:

a) of excluding the right of members to demand a poll altogether (on any question except the election of the chairman or the adjournment of the meeting);

or

b) making ineffective a demand for a poll on any question (except as above) which is made by either:

   (i) not less than five members having the right to vote; or

   (ii) by a member or members representing not less than one-tenth of the total voting rights; or

   (iii) by a member or members holding shares in the company conferring a right to vote, being shares on which an aggregate sum has been paid up equal to not less than one-tenth of the total sum paid up on all the shares conferring the right to vote.

So, in other words, and by way of example, an article which stated that only six members could duly demand a poll at a general meeting would be void, so too would be an article requiring members holding one quarter of the total number of votes to duly demand a poll, or an article stating that only a demand by members holding an aggregate of one quarter of the total paid up on all shares would be valid. This complex provision attempts to cover the all various ways in which the draftsmen of the company's constitution might seek to make the right to demand a poll difficult to exercise or illusory.

It might be thought preferable, and would certainly be more straightforward, if the legislature repealed this provision and replaced it with a provision which gave a certain number or percentage of members a positive right to demand a poll.

Article 46 of Table A provides that a poll can be duly demanded by:

a) the chairman of the general meeting; or

b) at least two members having the right to vote; or

c) a member or members representing not less than one-tenth of the total voting rights; or

d) a member or members holding shares conferring a right to vote being shares on which an aggregate sum has been paid up equal to not less than one-tenth of the total sum paid up on all the shares conferring voting rights.

By s 373(2), a proxy is deemed to have authority to demand a poll and such a demand by a proxy shall be the same as a demand by the member himself. This is also re-stated in article 46 of Table A. So, for example, a single person attending a general meeting as a proxy for five members can duly demand a poll to be taken.

If a poll is duly demanded, then the chairman will be responsible for conducting it, and Table A provides that with the exception of a poll demanded on the election of the chairman or on the question of an adjournment, which then has to be held immediately, a demand for a poll on any other question can be held either immediately or up to 30 days after the poll is demanded, at such a time and place as the chairman directs.[39]

Where a due demand for a poll by shareholders is ignored by the chairman, it has been held at common law that there is no right to bring an action, because this would be a procedural irregularity in the running of the company which could be 'cured' by the approval of the majority of shareholders voting in a general meeting.[40] The position may well be different after the development of s 459 as an effective shareholder remedy, since an aggrieved shareholder, who has had a proper demand for a poll refused, might be able to allege that this amounted to unfairly prejudicial conduct.

Proxy voting

There may, of course, be shareholders' meetings which not all members are able to attend. The larger the company and more disparate the shareholding, the more likely it is that only a relatively small proportion of the shareholders can attend the meetings in person or even fit into the room where the meeting is being held. If attendance were necessary in order to vote, substantial prejudice may be caused to investors, especially since the directors in normal circumstances have control over the exact date of the meetings. The legislature has provided therefore, in s 372, that any member of a company entitled to attend and vote at a meeting of shareholders is entitled to appoint another person (whether a member or not) as his proxy to attend and vote instead of him. This provision does not apply to companies not having a share capital. Further, the section goes on to provide that in the case of private companies a proxy also has the same right as the member to speak at the meeting. But unless the company's articles provide to the contrary, a proxy is only entitled to vote on a poll and a member of a private company is not entitled to appoint more than one proxy to attend on the same occasion. Table A following the statute only allows a proxy to vote on a poll, but by article 59 a member may appoint more than one proxy to attend on the same occasion. By s 372(3) every notice calling a meeting of the company with a share capital has to contain a statement that a member is entitled instead of attending and voting to appoint a proxy (or proxies where that is permitted) and that 'a proxy need not be a member'.

It is not possible for the company to require that any forms or instruments appointing proxies be received by the company more than 48 hours before the meeting. Any articles which purport to provide for a longer period are void.[41] This

---

39   Article 51.

40   *MacDougall v Gardiner* (1875) 1 Ch D 13.

41   Companies Act 1985, s 372(5).

provision is necessary otherwise the directors could seriously diminish the usefulness of the proxy voting machinery by specifying too short a period for the receipt of the proxy forms. Nor can the directors only send forms to a selected number of members from whom they expect to obtain support.[42]

Usually the articles will provide, as do articles 60 and 61 of Table A, for the form of the instrument appointing the proxy. Once the proxy has been appointed, the member can revoke or determine the appointment, but if the articles follow the form of article 63 of Table A, even if the member does determine, the determination will not be effective and the proxy's vote will be counted unless the notice of the determination is received by the company before the commencement of the meeting. It has been held, though, that at common law, if the member attends and votes at the meeting as well, this will operate to revoke the proxy's appointment and the member's vote will be counted.[43]

The importance of proxy voting should not be underestimated. Section 372 has gone some way towards ensuring that fairness is achieved and although the procedure allows the small shareholder to have his or her say on perhaps the one matter which concerns them without having to attend the whole meeting, it also means that many issues and resolutions have been decided in advance by reason of the proxies which have already been sent to the directors by the large shareholders, thus rendering discussion at the meeting largely redundant. The directors will always be in an advantageous position when it comes to seeking support through the proxy voting procedure since, as explained above, the board will be able to distribute, with the notice of the meeting and the proxy voting forms, a circular prepared at the company's expense, putting forward their views and arguments.

Exercise of the right to vote in general meeting

Freedom to exercise right

It has already been mentioned[44] that there is strong authority, particularly in the older cases, to the effect that the right to vote is a property right being attached or incident to a share which itself is a piece of intangible property or a chose in action. Therefore in voting shareholders can vote in whatever way they think fit and from whatever motive. So in *Pender v Lushington*,[45] concerning a shareholder's right to have his votes recorded, Jessel MR was able to state:

> 'where men exercise their rights of property ... I have always considered the law to be that those who have the rights of property are entitled to exercise them, whatever their motives may be for such exercise.'[46]

---

42   Companies Act 1985, s 372(6).
43   *Cousins v International Brick Co Ltd* [1931] 2 Ch 90.
44   At p 83.
45   (1877) 6 Ch D 70.
46   *Ibid* at 75.

and further on:

> '[t]here is, if I may say so, no obligation on a shareholder of a company to give his vote merely with a view to what other persons may consider the interests of the company at large. He has a right, if he thinks fit, to give his vote from motives or promptings of what he considers his own individual interest.'[47]

Again, in *Northern Counties Securities Ltd v Jackson & Steeple Ltd*,[48] Walton J reiterated the property view:

> '[w]hen a shareholder is voting for or against a particular resolution he is voting as a person owing no fiduciary duty to the company and who is exercising his own right of property, to vote as he thinks fit.'[49]

And in *Phillips v Manufacturers Securities Ltd*,[50] because the right to vote was viewed as a property right, Lord Cozens-Hardy MR was able to cite *Bradford Corporation v Pickles*[51] to support the contention that, as there is no doctrine of abuse of property rights in English law, voting by shareholders could not be impugned on the grounds that it was causing harm or loss to others.[52] It is even the case that a person who is a director can nevertheless vote as a shareholder in general meeting in whatever way he pleases even though he may be ratifying a sale to himself which is otherwise voidable by reason of the fact he holds office as director.[53]

This unrestricted freedom to vote as discussed in Chapter 4 was circumscribed by the principle that, on a resolution to alter the articles, shareholders had to vote 'bona fide for the benefit of the company as a whole', but as was pointed out the practical effect of this principle has been minimal.

In *Clemens v Clemens Bros Ltd*[54] Foster J seemed willing to introduce a much broader principle that would have placed a restriction on voting rights. Here the shares in a company were divided between the plaintiff and her aunt, the latter being one of the directors, in the proportion of 45% to 55%. A proposal was put forward by the board which had to be approved by the general meeting to issue further shares to the non-shareholding directors. This issue would have reduced the plaintiff's shareholding from 45% to below 25%, giving her substantially less 'negative control' over the company and in Foster's J view the calculation of the issue of shares was made specifically to produce this result. The plaintiff alleged that for the aunt to use her voting rights in general meeting to approve the new issue would be oppressive.

---

47 *Ibid* at 75.
48 [1974] 1 WLR 1133.
49 *Ibid* at 1144F.
50 (1917) 116 LT 290.
51 [1895] AC 587.
52 116 LT 290.
53 *North-West Transportation Co Ltd v Beatty* (1877) 12 App Cas 589.
54 [1976] 2 All ER 268.

After a rather confused survey of a number of authorities, Foster J concluded that the aunt could not use her majority voting power to pass the necessary resolutions in general meeting although he refused to state the principle on which he came to this conclusion other than that equity would not allow the legal right to vote in this way.

It is submitted that this case, rather than the dawn of the case law development of a new and important principle of oppression in the use of voting rights, it represents virtually the last attempt by the courts to attempt to do justice between the members of small private companies before the introduction of what is now s 459, first introduced by the Companies Act 1980, and was evidence of the considerable need for an effective statutory remedy.

In a rather exceptional recent case a shareholder has been restrained by injunction from voting on his shares in a way which would have caused the company to collapse and destroy the value of assets available to creditors of the company. In *Standard Chartered Bank Ltd v Walker*[55] a shareholder was proposing to vote as shareholder against a resolution removing him from the board of directors and approving restructuring plans. On the evidence that, if the resolutions were not passed the company would collapse and the shares would become worthless, the plaintiff creditors were granted injunctions on the same principles which underlie the *Mareva* jurisdiction. In acknowledging that it is only in an extreme case that the court will interfere with the right of a shareholder to exercise his voting rights, Vinelott J held here that to oppose or obstruct the reconstruction proposals would be so pointlessly harmful that it would amount to the wilful dissipation of assets.

Loss of right to vote

Where a shareholder sells his shares, he retains the right to vote until he is paid in full for the shares as long as he is still on the register of members.[56] Once he receives payment in full he then becomes a trustee of the shares for the purchaser and has to vote in accordance with the purchaser's wishes.[57] Also a shareholder will normally lose the right to vote if he mortgages his shares so that the mortgagee will be able to exercise the voting rights attaching to the shares.[58]

Voting agreements

shareholders can enter into a contract which restricts the way in which they will vote or bind them to vote in a particular way.[59] These agreements will be enforced by means of both prohibitory and mandatory injunctions by the courts.[60]

---

55 [1992] 1 WLR 561.

56 *Musselwhite v C H Musselwhite & Son Ltd* [1962] Ch 964.

57 *Re Piccadilly Radio plc* [1989] BCLC 683.

58 *Siemens Bros & Co Ltd v Burns* [1918] 2 Ch 324.

59 See *Northern Development Bank Ltd v Russell* [1992] 1 WLR 588; *Puddephatt v Leith* [1916] 1 Ch 200.

60 *Greenwell v Porter* [1902] 1 Ch 530.

Unanimous informal agreement

Notwithstanding the formalities connected with shareholders' meetings outlined above, there is a strong principle running through corporate decision-making to the effect that where a unanimous but informal resolve or assent can be demonstrated on the part of all the members on a matter which is within the power of the company, then the courts will treat this as the equivalent of a formal resolution in a duly convened shareholders' meeting. Examples can be found throughout company law. One of the first references to this principle was made by Cotton LJ in *Baroness Wenlock v River Dee Co*[61] where he stated *obiter* that:

'... the court would never allow it to be said that there was an absence of resolution when all the shareholders, and not only a majority, have expressly assented to that which is being done.'[62]

Then the principle was developed further in *Re Express Engineering Works Ltd.*[63] Here the company's articles disqualified a director from voting in board meetings on any transaction in which he was interested. At a board meeting the five directors of the company, who were also the only shareholders, resolved that the company should buy property from and issue debentures to a syndicate in which they were all interested. When the company went into liquidation, the liquidator sought to have the issue of the debentures set aside. But it was agreed that although the directors could not validly issue the debentures, the shareholders could, and as all the shareholders were in fact present at the board meeting, the Court of Appeal, invoking the principle stated by Lord Davey in *Salomon v Salomon & Co Ltd* that '... the company is bound in a matter intra vires by the unanimous agreement of its members',[64] proceeded to treat the meeting as if it were a general meeting, despite the absence of a formal declaration to that effect.

Again, in *Re Oxted Motor Co Ltd*,[65] it was held that at a shareholders' meeting an extraordinary resolution could be duly passed despite the absence of the required notice of such a resolution where the only shareholders of the company were present and had obviously waived the formalities. This was taken further in *Parker & Cooper Ltd v Reading*[66] where R had lent money to the company and taken a debenture as security. When the company went into liquidation, the liquidator challenged the validity of the debenture on the grounds that the procedure laid down in the articles for sealing debentures had not been followed, and the two directors who had purported to issue it had not been validly appointed at the relevant time. On the assumption that this was an intra vires but irregular transaction, and ratifiable by the general meeting, Astbury J held that it was irrelevant that there had been no actual meeting held to pass a formal

---

61   (1885) 36 Ch D 675n.

62   *Ibid* at 681–2n.

63   [1920] 1 Ch 466.

64   [1897] AC 22 at 57.

65   [1921] 3 KB 32.

66   [1926] Ch 975.

resolution since all the shareholders had assented to the transaction. Further, this assent did not have to be given simultaneously but could be given by all the shareholders at different times.

In *Multinational Gas and Petrochemical Co v Multinational Gas and Petrochemical Services Ltd*[67] it was held that the shareholders of a company could be held to have informally approved the acts of directors, which when carried out might otherwise have given the company or its liquidator a cause of action in negligence against them.

Perhaps the clearest statement of the principle is to be found in the judgment of Buckley J in *Re Duomatic Ltd*[68] where he states:

'... I proceed upon the basis that where it can be shown that all shareholders who have a right to attend and vote at a general meeting of the company assent to some matter which a general meeting of the company could carry into effect, that assent is as binding as a resolution in general meeting would be.'[69]

It must be stressed that this principle can only apply when all the shareholders of a company agree or consent to a course of action or transaction. It cannot apply even if only one minority shareholder dissents or is not shown to assent although it may be possible in that situation to show that he stood by knowing of the irregularity and failing to express dissent and in those circumstances cannot now prevent the principle operating.[70]

If a shareholder does dissent and the principle cannot operate, then a formal meeting must be convened and the formalities complied with.

The question then arises as to whether there are any limitations on the formalities which can be waived or the types of resolution that can be deemed to have been passed by the use of this principle? In *Cane v Jones*[71] it was held that a shareholders' agreement stating that the chairman should not exercise a casting vote in the event of an equality of votes occurring overrode the article in the company's articles of association which provided this right. This effectively brought about an alteration of the articles which under s 9 can only be done by special resolution. If correct, this might be a development which could give rise to concern. The shareholders' agreement was not registered with the registrar. If this had been a proper special resolution and had not been registered, the company and every officer in default would have been subject to a fine.[72]

In *Re Barry Artist Ltd*[73] Nourse J was willing to treat a written resolution signed by all four shareholders of the company as a resolution to reduce the company's capital and cancel its share premium account, which should only be done by special resolution

---

67 [1983] Ch 248.

68 [1969] 2 Ch 365.

69 Ibid at 373.

70 *Re Pearce, Duff & Co Ltd* [1960] 1 WLR 1014.

71 [1980] 1 WLR 1451.

72 Companies Act 1985, s 380.

73 [1985] 1 WLR 1305.

under what is now s 135 of the 1985 Act. Nourse J reached this decision very reluctantly, and only because of the special circumstances of the case, and stated that he would not do so in the future. He made a distinction between a special resolution to reduce capital and an alteration of the articles, because whilst the latter is a matter for the company alone, the former is not effective unless confirmed by the court because of the potential effect on third parties. But even in the latter case, a subsequent purchaser of shares in a company where a shareholders' agreement had *de facto* altered the articles would have no certain way of discovering the complete up-to-date constitution if it could be altered without reference to the registrar. This would seem to negate the whole purpose of a disclosure system.

Further, can the principle of unanimous informal approval apply if the Companies Act specifically requires a meeting to be held? For example, s 319(3) requires certain terms in a director's service contract to be disclosed to and approved by the company in general meeting, and s 121(4) provides that the powers conferred by the section must be exercised by the company in general meeting. In these cases probably not, but contrast that requirement with the provision in s 312 which requires payments to directors for loss of office to be 'disclosed to members of the company and the proposal being approved by the company', to which the principle could apply.

Whatever the view that might be taken by a court at common law there is now the possibility of passing such resolutions as written resolutions without a meeting.

Written resolutions

In addition to the principle of unanimous informal agreement Table A has provided for informal written resolutions. Article 53 provides that a resolution in writing executed by or on behalf of each member who would have been entitled to vote on it if it had been proposed at a general meeting shall be as effective as if it had been passed at a general meeting duly convened and held, and further it does not have to be a single document but can consist of several instruments in like form each executed by or on behalf of one or more members.[74]

The Companies Act 1989 introduced a similar statutory written resolution for all private companies, regardless of the provisions of their articles, as part of the general scheme to relax the formalities to which small businesses were subject. The provisions are now contained in ss 381A, 381B, 381C and 382A. Section 381A begins in promisingly wide terms:

'Anything which in the case of a private company may be done:

(a) by resolution of the company in general meeting; or

(b) by resolution of a meeting of any class of members of the company, may be done, without a meeting and without any previous notice being required, by resolution in writing signed by or on behalf of all the members of the company who at the date of the resolution would be entitled to attend and vote at such meeting.'

---

74 Companies Act 1985, s 381A(2).

As in the case of article 53, the signatures of the members need not be on a single document, but a number of different documents provided each states the terms of the resolution. Also s 381A(6) states that this procedure can be used to pass resolutions which would otherwise be required to be passed as special, extraordinary or elective resolutions.

Section 381B then appears to undermine the value of the new procedure by requiring a copy of any written resolution to be sent to the company's auditors. If the resolution concerns the creditors as auditors, they may within seven days from the day on which they receive the copy of the resolution, give notice to the company stating their opinion that the resolution should be considered in general meeting or, as the case may be, by a meeting of the relevant class of members of the company.[75] Further, the written resolution will not be effective until either the auditors notify the company that in their opinion the resolution does not concern them as auditors or if it does they do not consider it necessary for the resolution to be considered in a meeting, or the seven day period for reply expires.[76] By s 390(2) auditors are then entitled to attend and speak at the subsequent meeting on any part of the business of the meeting which affects them as auditors.

Further limitations on the scope and conditions on use of the written resolution procedure are imposed by Schedule 15A. The written resolution procedure does not apply to a resolution for removing a director from office under s 303 since they are given rights to protest about their removal and make oral representations at the meeting.[77] Nor does the procedure apply to the removal of auditors before the expiration of their period of office under s 391 although in any case a written resolution proposing this would be unlikely to be allowed to become effective without the auditors exercising their rights under s 381B and s 390(2). Schedule 15A also contains a list of resolutions which can be passed under specific statutory provisions which cannot be effectively passed by the written resolution procedure unless certain additional conditions are met. So, for example, where there is a written resolution approving a term in a director's service contract, the requirement in s 319(5), providing that a memorandum setting out the proposed agreement be available for inspection by the members, does not apply but the memorandum has to be supplied to each member before he signs the written resolution,[78]

The DTI is reviewing the current state of the law on written resolutions which it has found from a consultation process is not being used by many companies.[79] The proposal currently under consideration is to remove the auditors' rights to receive copies of the written resolution and to object to it by repealing s 381B and s 390(2) which are probably not necessary for the protection of shareholders as originally intended.[80]

---

75 Companies Act 1985, s 381B(2).

76 Companies Act 1985, s 381B(3).

77 Companies Act 1985, s 304.

78 Companies Act 1985, Sch 15A para 7.

79 See footnote 35.

80 A draft Order under the Deregulation and Contracting Out Act was laid before Parliament in October 1995 and is expected to come into force later this year.

BOARD MEETINGS

Whereas the 1985 Act contains some 26 sections prescribing the form and procedure for holding general meetings and passing resolutions, the Act is relatively silent on the question of board meetings, except to prescribe that certain items should be disclosed to meetings of directors,[81] and that every company has to ensure that in the same way that minutes of general meetings have to be recorded, the minutes of all proceedings of board meetings be entered into a minute book.[82] So for the regulation of board meetings regard must be had primarily to the relevant provisions of the articles and to the common law.

Article 88 of Table A is similarly liberal, stating that subject to the other provisions of the articles 'the directors may regulate their proceedings as they think fit'. Any director can call a meeting of the directors and the quorum for conducting any business is two. Questions are decided by a majority vote and in the case of equality of votes, the chairman of the board has a casting vote.

At common law every director is entitled to notice of directors' meetings and to be able to attend and speak.[83] Meetings called at very short notice, and held at a time when it is known that certain directors will not be able to attend, will not be held to be valid board meetings and therefore decisions taken even when a quorum is present will not bind the company.[84] This point has been stressed on a number of occasions, not only because the shareholders themselves have a right to expect that the company will receive the benefit of every director's advice and expertise,[85] but also because the excluded director may subsequently be held liable with the other directors for a course of action decided upon at the meeting he was unable to attend. So as Jessel MR stated:

> '[a director] has a right by the constitution of the company to take part in its management, to be present, and to vote at the meetings of the board of directors. He has a perfect right to know what is going on at these meetings. It may affect his individual interest as a shareholder as well as his liability as director, because it has been sometimes held that even a director who does not attend board meetings is bound to know what is done in his absence.'[86]

This is even more the case now, following the introduction of the wrongful trading provision.[87] A rather curious qualification in article 88, that it is not necessary to give notice of a meeting to a director who is absent from the UK, is strangely out of place in the age of air travel and in view of the acceptance by the courts of the possibility of using the telephone to assist in the holding of meetings.[88]

---

81 For example, Companies Act 1985, s 317.

82 Companies Act 1985, s 382.

83 *Harben v Phillips* (1883) 23 Ch D 14; *Halifax Sugar Refining Co Ltd v Francklyn* (1890) 62 LT 563.

84 *Re Homer District Consolidated Gold Mines* (1888) 39 Ch D 546.

85 *Re HR Harmer* [1959] 1 WLR 62; see also *Re Portuguese Consolidated Copper Mines Ltd* (1889) 42 Ch D 160.

86 *Pulbrook v Richmond Consolidated Mining Co* (1878) 9 Ch D 610 at 612.

87 See p 62.

88 *Re Equiticorp International plc* [1989] 1 WLR 1010 and see *Byng v London Life Association* [1990] Ch 170.

By article 91 of Table A the directors may appoint one of their number to be chairman and they may at any time remove him from that office.

A valid board meeting can be held informally, as long as all directors who should be informed are informed, and agree to the informality.[89] An informal board meeting cannot be held against the wishes of one or more of the directors, as was shown in *Barron v Potter*,[90] where one of the two directors of the company attempted to convene an informal board meeting on the platform of Paddington Station as the other alighted from a train and against his wishes. It was held that the additional directors who had been purportedly elected at this 'meeting' by the use of a casting vote had not been properly appointed.

Article 93 of Table A provides that a resolution in writing, signed by all the directors entitled to receive notice of a board meeting, shall be as valid and effectual as if it had been passed at a duly convened board meeting. It is also likely that the courts would be willing to apply the principle of unanimous informal agreement to board meetings as well as general meetings. It was certainly the view of Sir James Bacon VC in *Re Bonelli's Telegraph Co*[91] that the directors need not assemble together in the same place but could come to a consensus on an issue by correspondence or other messages, and in *Runciman v Walter Runciman plc*[92] Simon Brown J thought that it was clear that directors, provided they act unanimously, can act informally. Further, in *H L Bolton (Engineering) Co Ltd v T J Graham & Sons Ltd*,[93] Denning LJ was prepared to find what the 'intention' of the company was from the intentions and acts of all the individual directors in spite of the fact that there had been no formal board meeting.

More recently the issue has arisen in respect of s 317, a provision which requires disclosure to the board meeting of a director's interest in a transaction to which the company is a party and the courts have specifically required a 'meeting'. This is apparent from both the decision of the Court of Appeal in *Guinness plc v Saunders*[94] and *Neptune (Vehicle Washing Equipment) Ltd v Fitzgerald*,[95] where Lightman J was even prepared to say that a sole director of a company should still have a director's meeting to:

> 'make the declaration to himself and have the statutory pause for thought, though it may be that the declaration does not have to be read out loud, and he must record that he made the declaration in the minutes.'[96]

The problem is then that the courts have also taken the view, arguably incorrectly,[97] that a failure to disclose under s 317 to the board *ipso facto* makes the transaction in

---

89 *Smith v Paringa Mines Ltd* [1906] 2 Ch 193.
90 [1914] 1 Ch 895.
91 (1871) LR12 Eq 246.
92 [1992] BCLC 1084.
93 [1959] 1 QB 159.
94 [1990] 2 AC 663.
95 [1995] 1 BCLC 352.
96 *Ibid* at 360.
97 See p 237.

question voidable. So, in *Lee Panavision Ltd v Lee Lighting Ltd*,[98] Dillon LJ was unhappy about finding that a technical non-disclosure to the board of an interest which was known to all directors individually would have this inevitable consequence, and so too was Simon Brown J in *Runciman v Walter Runciman plc*[99] where the relevant interest was in a director's service contract, the terms of which were not disclosed to a formal board meeting but known to all the directors.

THE RELATIONSHIP BETWEEN THE BOARD OF DIRECTORS AND THE GENERAL MEETING

To turn now to the power relationship between the directors and the general meeting. The directors derive their powers and functions from the articles of association, and therefore where a dispute arises between the directors and the shareholders as to a particular course of action the company should take, whether the former or the latter should be able to assert supremacy is determined primarily by a construction of the articles. Often the dispute concerns the institution of corporate legal proceedings where the board of directors and the general meeting disagree as to whether litigation should be commenced in the company's name.

Unfortunately the position has not been as clear as it might have been because of the form of the previous relevant Table A article and a first instance decision near the beginning of the century which was out of line with the way in which business practice was developing. Older authority is to the effect that the general meeting of shareholders by ordinary resolution could give instructions to and override the decisions of the directors. Cotton LJ, in *Isle of Wight Rly Co v Tahourdin*,[100] is quite specific in discharging an injunction to prevent a general meeting being held. He states:

'[i]t is a very strong thing indeed to prevent shareholders from holding a meeting of the company, when such a meeting is the only way in which they can interfere, if the majority of them think that the course taken by the directors ... is not for the benefit of the company.'[101]

And the court says to the shareholder:

'[i]f you want to alter the management of the affairs of the company go to a general meeting, and if they agree with you they will pass a resolution obliging the directors to alter their course of proceeding.'[102]

This view treats the directors ultimately as mere agents of the company in general meeting who, while they carry out the day-to-day management of the company's affairs, can still be given instructions by the shareholders and have their authority

---

98   [1992] BCLC 22.
99   [1992] BCLC 1084.
100 (1883) 25 Ch D 320.
101 *Ibid* at 329.
102 *Ibid* at 330.

limited. Again, as another example, in *Pender v Lushington*,[103] where an action had been begun in the name of the company without any authorisation, the Court of Appeal held that the action should not be struck out but that a general meeting should be held to see if the shareholders approved of the action. However, in 1906, a landmark decision was made by the Court of Appeal, one of whose members expressed surprise that this fundamental question of company law had not been resolved earlier. On a narrow interpretation, the case of *Automatic Self Cleansing Filter Syndicate Ltd v Cunninghame*[104] is unremarkable. What is remarkable is that for the first time a court was willing to grasp the nettle and construe the articles in such a way as to deny the right of a majority of shareholders to frustrate a lawful *intra vires* policy of the board. Here the articles vested the management of the business and the control of the company in the directors who could exercise, in addition to the powers given to them in the articles, all powers which may have been exercised by the company, but subject to statutory provisions, the articles 'and to such regulations, not being inconsistent with these presents, as may from time to time be made by *extraordinary* resolution'. The directors were further specifically empowered 'to sell, lease, abandon or otherwise deal with any property rights or privileges to which the company may be entitled on such terms and conditions as they may think fit'.

At a general meeting of the company an ordinary resolution was passed by the shareholders that certain property belonging to the company be sold and directing the directors to carry the sale into effect. The directors declined to comply with the resolution, being of the opinion that this sale would not be in the best interests of the company. The Court of Appeal, distinguishing *Isle of Wight Rly Co Ltd v Tahourdin*, held that on a proper construction of the articles which formed a contract between the members of the company, the directors could not be instructed to sell by ordinary resolution against their better judgment. Lord Collins MR, after construing the relevant articles, continued:

> 'if it is desired to alter the powers of the directors that must be done, not by a resolution carried by a majority at an ordinary meeting of the company, but by an extraordinary resolution. In these circumstances it seems to me that it is not competent for the majority of shareholders at an ordinary meeting to affect or alter the mandate originally given to the directors by the articles of association.'[105]

If the directors are agents, which no doubt for certain purposes they are, it has to be asked for whom are they agents? The answer to this is that it is the company and not the majority of shareholders in general meeting. Once the directors have been appointed, they are entitled to exercise their powers under the company's articles until such time as the articles are properly altered by a special resolution, or in this particular case a regulation is given by extraordinary resolution.

The explanation of *Tahourdin's* case is interesting because there, the company being

---

103 (1877) 6 Ch D 70.
104 [1906] 2 Ch 34.
105 *Ibid* at 42.

a statutory company was subject to the Companies Clauses Act 1845, and s 90 of that Act gave the directors powers of management but also stated that:

> 'the exercise of all such powers shall be subject also to the control and regulation of any general meeting specially convened for the purpose.'

Therefore, for Cozens-Hardy LJ, the decision in that case was entirely understandable (even though s 90 was only referred to in argument in the case and was not mentioned in any part of the judgment).[106]

This decision was cited with approval shortly afterwards by the Court of Appeal in *Gramophone and Typewriter Ltd v Stanley*[107] where Buckley LJ states:

> '[t]his Court decided not long since ... that even a resolution of a numerical majority at a general meeting of the company cannot impose its will upon the directors when the articles have confided to them the control of the company's affairs. The directors are not servants to obey directions given by the shareholders as individuals; they are not agents appointed by and bound to serve the shareholders as their principals. They are persons who may by the regulations be entrusted with the control of the business, and if so entrusted they can be dispossessed from that control only by the statutory majority which can alter the articles.'[108]

The cases subsequent to *Automatic Self-Cleansing* concerning this issue all involved companies which had articles in substantially the same form as each other, but drafted in a materially different way from the equivalent article in Automatic Self-Cleansing Co Ltd's articles. The form in which the management articles tended to be drafted, and the form of the old Table A article, was as follows:

> 80. The business of the company shall be managed by the directors, who may exercise all such powers of the company as are not, by the [Companies Acts 1948 to 1981] or by these regulations, required to be exercised by the company in general meeting, subject, nevertheless, to any of these regulations, to the provisions of [the Companies Acts 1948 to 1981] and to such regulations, being not inconsistent with the aforesaid regulations or provisions, as may be prescribed by the company in general meeting.

The law was thrown into uncertainty by *Marshall's Valve Gear Co v Manning, Wardle & Co Ltd*,[109] the first of these cases shortly after *Automatic Self Cleansing*, where in a first instance decision, Neville J was of the opinion that the absence of any reference to the requirement of an extraordinary resolution in the above article meant that the shareholders could prescribe 'regulations' by ordinary resolution to cause proceedings to be instituted in the name of the company despite objections from the directors (who, in this case, were interested in the third party which was to be sued).

See also *Thomas Logan Ltd v Davis*[110] where the board's right to appoint a particular managing director despite opposition from the general meeting was upheld only by a

---

106 *Ibid* at 46.
107 [1908] 2 KB 89.
108 *Ibid* at 105.
109 [1909] 1 Ch 267.
110 (1911) 104 LT 914.

specific article specifically providing them with this power. It was held that the general management article in the above form in the company's articles would have allowed the general meeting to interfere in other matters not specifically assigned to the board.

Marshall's Valve Gear was followed very shortly afterwards by the Court of Appeal decision in *Quin & Axtens Ltd v Salmon*[111] which declined to take that approach, on the grounds that, despite the exception in the article to management autonomy that allowed shareholders to make regulations, that applied only if the regulation was not inconsistent with the articles, and for the shareholders to give directions to the directors by ordinary resolution would be absolutely inconsistent with the provisions of the articles, namely the management article itself.

There is no doubt that this view was the preferred view adopted by the courts and was applied in *John Shaw & Sons (Salford) Ltd v Shaw*[112] and *Scott v Scott*.[113] Most recently in *Breckland Group Holdings Ltd v London and Suffolk Properties Ltd*[114] Harman J, after a review of the authorities, had little doubt that the decision of Neville J in *Marshall's Valve Gear Co Ltd v Manning Wardle & Co Ltd*, whilst not being directly overruled, could not be considered as good law.

For companies incorporated after 1 July 1985 and adopting the new form of Table A (or companies formed before which have taken the appropriate steps to alter their articles) the position is much clearer. The equivalent management article is article 70 and simply states:

'Subject to the provisions of the Act, the memorandum and the articles and to any directions given by special resolution, the business of the company shall be managed by the directors who may exercise all the powers of the company.'

The learning on the old form Table A article will still be of relevance for those companies which have retained the old article 80, and after *Breckland Group Holdings Ltd* there is unlikely to be a serious challenge to the board's power to manage unhindered by the general meeting. Of course the issue is still ultimately always a construction of the articles and it is possible that a company may wish to reserve day-to-day management powers to the general meeting and this situation is specifically provided for by s 19(3) of the Theft Act 1968.[115] This, however, would be an exceptional case.

The above position relates to circumstances where there is an effective board of directors which can make decisions concerning the management of the company's business. If, however, there is no effective board because there are no directors, or no quorum is possible or the directors refuse to meet, then there is deadlock and it has been held that the powers enjoyed by the board under the articles is retained or reverts

---

111 [1909] AC 442 (affirming *Salmon v Quin & Axtens Ltd* [1909] 1 Ch 311).

112 [1935] 2 KB 113.

113 [1943] 1 All ER 582. See also the discussion of directors' powers of management in *Teck Corp Ltd v Millar* (1973) 33 DLR (3d) 288 at 306 where Laskin J states that the 'directors' power to manage the company is complete'.

114 [1989] BCLC 100.

115 See p 34.

back to the shareholders in general meeting. In *Barron v Potter*[116] the relationship between the only two directors had broken down, one director steadfastly refused to attend any board meeting and there could not therefore be any valid board meetings. The company's articles gave the directors the power at any time to appoint additional directors between general meetings. In those circumstances an EGM of the shareholders was held and resolved to appoint two persons as additional directors. On a complaint by one of the original directors that the general meeting had effectively usurped a power belonging to the directors it was stated by Warrington J that:

> 'I am not concerned to say that in ordinary cases where there is a board ready and willing to act it would be competent for the company to override the power conferred on the directors by the articles except by way of special resolution for the purpose of altering the articles,'[117]

but he went on:

> '[i]f directors having certain powers are unable or unwilling to exercise them – are in fact a non-existent body for the purpose – there must be some power in the company to do itself that which under other circumstances would be otherwise done. The directors in the present case being unwilling to appoint additional directors ... the company in general meeting has power to make the appointment.'[117]

In *Alexander Ward & Co Ltd v Samyang Navigation Co Ltd*[119] Lord Hailsham in the House of Lords was clearly of the opinion that the company could have authorised proceedings to be brought in its name 'in general meeting which, in the absence of an effective board, has a residual authority to use the company's powers'. He cited with apparent approval a passage from the then current edition of *Gower's Modern Company Law*[120] which stated that:

> '[i]t seems that if for some reason the board cannot or will not exercise the powers vested in them, the general meeting may do so,'

and further:

> 'it still seems to be the law ... that the general meeting can commence proceedings on behalf of the company if the directors fail to do so.'[121]

Lord Hailsham's expressed view was that this was the position either where for some reason the directors were unable or unwilling to act or where there were no directors. It is respectfully submitted that this passage from *Gower* is apt to misrepresent the present position. It was in any event based on the assumption that *Marshall's Valve Gear* was correct. Any decision by the House of Lords on the position where there is a

---

116 [1914] 1 Ch 895.

117 *Ibid* at 902.

118 *Ibid* at 903.

119 [1975] 1 WLR 673.

120 Third edn, 1969, pp 136–37. See now 5th edn, 1992, p 152.

121 *Ibid* at 679.

functioning board which refuses to institute proceedings must be *obiter*. *Alexander Ward* was not cited in *Breckland Group Holdings* and now the current view is surely that the residual powers of the general meeting arise only when there is no effective board[122] and do not arise when the board will not commence proceedings following a decision to that effect.

THE RESIDUAL POWERS AND ROLE OF THE GENERAL MEETING

Despite the fact that, from what has been discussed in the previous section, it becomes apparent that companies usually adopt articles giving the board of directors relatively unfettered control of the company in normal circumstances, the decision-making powers and role of the general meeting is not without significance in a number of ways.

Shareholders' powers to remove directors

If the shareholders fundamentally disagree with the policies pursued by the directors or are unhappy with their performance then ultimately a majority of the shareholders can remove the directors from office. This right may appear in the company's articles but in any event s 303 of the 1985 Act provides:

'(1)   A company may by ordinary resolution remove a director before the expiration of his period of office, notwithstanding anything in its articles or in any agreement between it and him.'

But certain safeguards are provided for directors. If such a resolution is proposed under s 303 then it requires special notice to be given, which by s 379 is at least 28 days before the meeting at which the resolution is to be moved. As soon as the company receives notice of an intended resolution under s 303, by s 304 the company must forthwith send a copy to the director concerned and he is entitled, whether or not he is a member of the company, to attend and be heard at the meeting. Further, a director under such a threat is entitled to have representations he makes with respect to his proposed removal circulated to every member of the company or if the company receives these representations too late, the director has the right to have them read out at the meeting. The court can refuse a director these rights in relation to representation if it is satisfied that he is using them 'to secure needless publicity for defamatory material' and can order the director to pay the company's costs on any application under s 304.

Section 303(5) preserves a removed director's right to sue for damages or compensation which may accrue to him by reason of the termination. So if, for example, a director has a fixed term service contract with the company which provides that, as is usual, the contract is enforceable only while he holds office as a director, and a resolution under s 303 removes the director from office which prematurely

---

122 For example, because there cannot be a quorum: *Foster v Foster* [1916] 1 Ch 532.

terminates the service contract, the director may still sue for damages for wrongful dismissal if he is of the opinion that his dismissal was not justified at common law.[123]

The courts have given approval to devices designed purely to avoid the effect of s 303. In *Bushell v Faith*[124] the company had three equal shareholders who were also the only directors. Article 9 of the company's articles provided that:

'In the event of a resolution being proposed at any general meeting of the company for the removal from office of any director, any shares held by that director shall on a poll in respect of such resolution carry the right to three votes per share.'

Section 303(1) appears to render *de facto* void anything contained in a company's articles or in a contract between the company and a director which would prevent that director being removed if a majority of members so wished. But the House of Lords (Lord Morris dissenting) held that the section only provides that a director should always be removable in ordinary resolution, but it does not go further to provide for how that ordinary resolution is obtained or prevent companies giving shareholders special voting rights. Therefore, as the article here did not seek to prevent a director from being removed by ordinary resolution, it was not objectionable. Lord Morris thought that to sanction the article would be to make a mockery of the law:

'[i]ts unconcealed effect is to make a director irremovable ... If article 9 were writ large it would set out that a director is not to be removed against his will and that in order to achieve this and thwart the express provision of section [303] the voting power of any director threatened with removal is to be deemed to be greater than it actually is.'[125]

But Lord Upjohn with the majority disagreed:

'[Article 9] makes no mockery of section [303]; all that Parliament was seeking to do thereby was to make an ordinary resolution sufficient to remove a director. Had Parliament desired to go further and enact that every share entitled to vote should be deprived of its special rights under the articles it should have said so in plain terms by making the vote on a poll one vote one share.'[126]

Parliament has not sought to alter the effect of the decision in *Bushell v Faith* although it has had plenty of opportunity to do so. The decision itself strikes a blow for freedom to contract out of the provisions of the Companies Act and is particularly useful in smaller companies. It becomes more difficult to justify the larger the company becomes, when it is more likely that the shareholders will change from the original corporators who framed the articles.

Another device to entrench a director's position would appear to be to grant a class of shares to a director/shareholder and provide either in the articles or in a shareholders' agreement that the presence either in person or by proxy of the holder of these shares was required in order for a general meeting to be quorate. The director

---

123 See *Southern Foundries (1926) Ltd v Shirlaw* [1940] AC 701.

124 [1970] AC 1099.

125 *Ibid* at 1106.

126 *Ibid* at 1109.

could then prevent a general meeting to dismiss him from being held and the Court of Appeal has indicated that in this situation the courts would not make an order under s 371.[127]

Ratification and approval of irregularities

It has always been recognised that the general meeting has wide powers to ratify or approve acts which are within the powers of the company but which have been carried out in an irregular way and further, to ratify certain breaches of directors' duties. So, for example, if the directors act purportedly on behalf of the company in a matter which is outside their authority under the articles, this can be subsequently ratified by the general meeting. In *Grant v United Kingdom Switchback Railways Co*[128] the directors caused the company to enter into a transaction with a third party in which all of them except one were interested. The company's articles prohibited any director from voting on a transaction in which he was interested, therefore as it stood the transaction was voidable. However, a general meeting was called which duly passed an ordinary resolution approving and adopting the transaction and it was held by the Court of Appeal that no injunction could then be granted to prevent the transaction being carried out. An argument here that upholding the resolution effectively amounted to an alteration of the articles by ordinary resolution failed, Cotton LJ explaining that:

> 'ratifying a particular contract which had been entered into by the directors without authority, and so making it an act of the company, is quite a different thing from altering the articles. To give the directors power to do things in future which the articles did not authorise them to do, would be an alteration of the articles, but it is no alteration of the articles to ratify a contract which has been made without authority.'[129]

This is not to say, however, that the articles do not bind the general meeting. Here the ratification was not in breach of the articles, the general meeting was simply adopting a contract which was within the power of the company to make. By contrast, if the general meeting sought to appoint a director at a higher salary than that provided for by the articles, the court would not uphold the appointments. A special resolution to alter the articles would have to be passed first.[130]

Where the problem concerns a breach of duty by a director in many cases the directors will be able to convene a general meeting to propose a resolution that the company should ratify and approve of what has been done or at least decide that the company should take no proceedings against them.

---

127 *Harman v BML Group Ltd* [1944] 2 BCLC 674. See p 97.

128 (1888) 40 Ch D 135

129 *Ibid* at 138.

130 *Imperial Hydropathic Hotel Co, Blackpool v Hampson* (1822) 23 Ch D 1; *Boschoek Pty Co Ltd v Fuke* [1906] 1 Ch 148.

In *Pavlides v Jensen*[131] it was alleged that directors had negligently sold a mine belonging to the company to a third party at an undervalue, but Danckwerts J was of the opinion that:

> '[i]t was open to the company by a vote of the majority to decide that, if the directors by their negligence or error of judgment had sold the company's mine at an undervalue, proceedings should not be taken by the company against the directors.'[132]

Depending on the circumstances, the effect of the ordinary resolution in general meeting may go beyond simply deciding not to pursue directors for breaches of duty, and be to adopt voidable transactions entered into by directors in breach of fiduciary duty. In *Bamford v Bamford*,[133] where the directors had used their share issuing powers for an improper purpose and an issue of shares was therefore voidable, Harman LJ was able to say quite bluntly:

> '... [i]t is trite law, I had thought, that if directors do acts, as they do every day, especially in private companies, which, perhaps because there is no quorum, or because their appointment was defective, or because sometimes there are no directors properly appointed at all, or because they are actuated by improper motives, they go on doing for years, carrying on the business of the company in the way in which, if properly constituted, they should carry it on, and then they find that everything has been so to speak wrongly done because it was not done by a proper board, such directors can, by making a full and frank disclosure and calling together the general body of the shareholders, obtain absolution and forgiveness of their sins; and provided the acts are not *ultra vires* the company as a whole everything will go on as if it had been done all right from the beginning. I cannot believe that is not a commonplace of company law. It is done every day. Of course, if the majority of the general meeting will not forgive and approve, the directors must pay for it.'[134]

There is some uncertainty concerning the extent to which a shareholders' resolution can effectively ratify and adapt a breach of directors' duties to the company where the directors are able to exercise all or a majority of the voting rights in general meeting. Where the breach of duty is fraudulent and the directors are in a position to control the general meeting then, as discussed, in Chapter 12,[135] this will amount to a 'fraud on the minority' and the courts will not accept that a purported ratification is effective and even a minority shareholder as an exception to the rule in *Foss v Harbottle*[136] will be allowed to bring an action on behalf of the company. But where the conduct of the directors is not fraudulent, even within the wide definition of that term, the position is not so clear. In *Re Horsley & Weight Ltd*[137] Templeman LJ, with whom Cumming-Bruce LJ appeared in substance to agree, expressed the opinion that where directors

---

131 [1956] Ch 565.
132 *Ibid* at 576.
133 [1970] Ch 212.
134 *Ibid* at 237.
135 See p 284 *et seq*.
136 [1843] 2 Hare 461.
137 [1982] Ch 442.

were guilty of 'gross negligence amounting to misfeasance' they would not be able to use their voting rights to ratify where a company was doubtfully solvent and the creditors would be prejudiced. This view received approval from the dissenting judgment of May LJ in *Multinational Gas and Petrochemical Co Ltd v Multinational Gas and Petrochemical Services Ltd*[138] who would have gone further and held that directors could not ratify their own negligence, gross or otherwise, if this was to release gratuitously an asset of the company (ie the cause of action vested in the company) in the winding up. The majority of the Court of Appeal however, whilst accepting the *obiter* of Templeman LJ in *Re Horsley & Weight*, held that a distinction between negligence and misfeasance should be maintained and that the former was ratifiable even by the directors themselves voting on their shares.

Miscellaneous residual statutory powers of the general meeting

Apart from the power to dismiss a director under s 303, the Companies Act gives the general meeting a number of statutory powers to control and scrutinise the activities of directors. So, for example, any director's contract which is to last for more than five years has to be disclosed to and approved by the general meeting[139] So too does any payment to a director by way of compensation for loss of office.[140] A substantial property transaction between a director and the company is voidable at the instance of the company unless it is first approved by a resolution of the company in general meeting or unless it is affirmed by the general meeting within a reasonable period afterwards.[141]

A number of provisions also provide a requirement that the general meeting passes a resolution, usually a special resolution, in order to effect major structural changes to the company. Apart from the special resolutions required to alter the memorandum or articles,[142] special resolutions form part of the requirements to be satisfied if the company is to change its status from a public company and be re-registered as a private company[143] or *vice versa*.[144] A special resolution is also required for a reduction of capital[145] or a change of name.[146]

---

138 [1983] Ch 258.
139 Companies Act 1985, s 319.
140 Companies Act 1985, s 312.
141 Companies Act 1985, s 320.
142 Companies Act 1985, ss 4 & 9.
143 Companies Act 1985, s 53.
144 Companies Act 1985, s 43.
145 Companies Act 1985, s 135.
146 Companies Act 1985, s 28.

CHAPTER SIX

CORPORATE TRANSACTIONS

GENERAL

Since a company is an artificial legal person, created under the Companies Act 1985, special considerations have to be made in relation to how it is to enter into contracts. First, this is because of the way in which the courts have interpreted the role of the registered company's constitutional documents. This interpretation had the effect of limiting the company's overall contractual capacity in contrast to the unlimited capacity of a natural person of full age. Second, the company's articles of association may have limited the powers of those acting for the company or may have imposed certain procedures to be followed in relation to certain types of contract. Third, as the company can only act through the medium of natural persons, the law of agency has to be developed and applied in all company transactions.

Section 36 states that a contract may be made:

(a) by a company, by writing under its common seal, or

(b) on behalf of a company, by any person acting under its authority, express or implied.

Further, any formalities which are required by law in the case of a contract made by an individual are also required where the contract is made by or on behalf of a company (unless a contrary intention appears). A company need not have a common seal but usually will have.[1] In any case though a document which requires to be executed (for example, a transfer of an interest in land) can be executed by a company by the affixing of the seal or by being signed by a director and the secretary of the company or by two directors and expressed (in whatever form of words) to be executed by the company.[2] These provisions only deals with the form in which companies can make their contracts; it does not explain what contracts a company can legitimately enter into, nor who has authority to act for the company. The remainder of this chapter deals with the legal problems arising from these issues and how the courts and the legislature have responded to deal with the problems.

TRANSACTIONS OUTSIDE THE OBJECTS CLAUSE OF THE MEMORANDUM

The history of *ultra vires*

When a company is registered, the incorporators are required to send a memorandum of association to the registrar and as was described in Chapter 2 one of the clauses of

---

1 Companies Act 1985, s 36A(3).

2 Companies Act 1985, s 36A(2) and (4).

the memorandum is the 'objects clause'.[3] The original intention of the legislature was that the incorporators would identify the purposes for which the company was formed and that these would be publicly known. The House of Lords decision in *Ashbury Railway Carriage and Iron Co v Riche*[4] dew the conclusion that this laid down the extent of the company's contractual capacity and that any contract entered into outside the terms of the objects clause was *ultra vires* and therefore void. Further, the contract could not be ratified by the shareholders, even voting unanimously on a resolution to adopt the contract. Here a company, which had clauses in its memorandum stating that the objects of the company were to make and sell etc railway carriages and wagons and all kinds of railway plant and rolling-stock and to carry on the business of mechanical engineers and general contractors, purchased a concession for making a railway in Belgium. Riche was to construct the railway under a contract with the company but subsequently the company repudiated it as being *ultra vires*. This contention was upheld after finding that the contract was outside the terms of the objects clause. Lord Cairns went on to state that:

'It is not a question whether the contract sued upon involves that which is *malum probitum* or *malum in se*, or is a contract contrary to public policy, and illegal in itself. I assume the contract in itself to be perfectly legal. The question is not as to the legality of the contract; the question is as to the competency and power of the company to make the contract. Now, I am clearly of opinion that this contract was entirely, as I have said, beyond the objects in the memorandum of association. If so, it was thereby placed beyond the powers of the company to make the contract. If so, ... it is not a question whether the contract ever was ratified or was not ratified. If it was a contract void at its beginning, it was void because the company could not make the contract. If every shareholder of the company had been in the room, and every shareholder of the company had said, 'that is a contract which we desire to make, which we authorise the directors to make, to which we sanction the placing of the seal of the company', the case would not have stood in any different position from that in which it stands now. The shareholders would thereby, by unanimous consent, have been attempting to do the very thing which, by the Act of Parliament, they were prohibited from doing.'[5]

The clear view of their Lordships was that the rule existed both for the protection of the shareholders both present and future and the persons who might become creditors of the company. Although it is difficult to see that the rule benefited the latter as individuals, since they were at risk of having their transactions impugned, the benefit was presumably to those creditors who were comforted by the knowledge that the assets of the company could not be dissipated on speculative ventures. Even the shareholders might regret the existence of the rule in certain circumstances, since if an unforeseen profitable opportunity presented itself to the directors the company would not be able to pursue it.

The reason why more sympathy was not forthcoming for the persons who were contracting with the company, although unarticulated in the speeches of their

---

3   Companies Act 1985, s 2.

4   (1875) LR 7 HL 653.

5   *Ibid* at 672.

Lordships, must have been that it had by then been established that persons dealing with a company should discover for themselves the contents of the memorandum and articles of association.[6] The high water mark of this approach in relation to *ultra vires* can be seen in *Re Jon Beauforte*.[7] Here a company had been incorporated with an objects clause which authorised the company to carry on business as makers of ladies' clothes, hats and shoes. The company later decided to manufacture veneered panels. To further this latter business, the company contracted with a builder to construct a factory, entered into a contract with a supplier of veneer and ordered coke from a coke supplier to heat the factory. All three remained unpaid when the company went into liquidation and the liquidator rejected their proofs in the winding up on the ground that the contracts were to further an *ultra vires* activity and therefore void. These rejections were upheld by Roxburgh J. The rejection of the coke supplier's proof was particularly harsh, since whereas the builder conceded that the contract was *ultra vires*, the coke supplier was unaware of the purpose for which the coke would be used and it could easily have been used to further legitimate objects. But, as Roxburgh J. pointed out, they had received orders for the coke on letter-headed notepaper which made it clear that the company was now a veneer panel manufacturer and the objects clause, of which the coke supplier would have constructive notice, did not authorise the company to carry on this business. Although this point may have been the 'justification' for the decision, strictly speaking if a contract was void for being *ultra vires* then notice on the part of the third party, whether actual or constructive was irrelevant to the result.[8]

The problem of *ultra vires* was exacerbated by the fact that the objects clause could be altered only within certain specified limits[9] and in any event not so as to affect retrospectively any transaction which was in question. It could prove to have disastrous consequences for a person dealing with a company who was in good faith and was totally innocent apart from failing to obtain and interpret the company's objects clause.

Companies responded to the *ultra vires* doctrine by drafting very wide and lengthy objects clauses which attempted to include every conceivable form of commercial activity.[10] Eventually the Court of Appeal was even prepared to give effect to a clause which provided that the company could 'carry on any other trade or business whatsoever which can, in the opinion of the board of directors, be advantageously carried on by the company in connection with or as ancillary to any of the above businesses or the general business of the company' and held that a particular transaction was *intra vires* even though it had no objective connection with a relationship to the company's main business.[11]

---

6   See *Ernest v Nicholls* (1857) 6 HL Cas 401.

7   [1953] Ch 131.

8   See, for example, *Rolled Steel Products (Holdings) Ltd v British Steel Corporation* [1986] Ch 246 at *per* Browne-Wilkinson LJ.

9   For example, Companies Act 1948, ss 4 and 5.

10 *Cotman v Brougham* [1918] AC 514.

11 *Bell Houses Ltd v City Wall Properties Ltd* [1966] 1 WLR 1323.

Powers

It has long been recognised that not all the contents of the objects clause provided for separate, free-standing objects which constituted the purposes for which the company was formed. There were also powers which were ancillary in the sense that they were present to support the substantive objects of the company.[12] For example, the power to borrow or give guarantees. The courts were also prepared to imply such powers if they were not express if they were fairly incidental to achieving the company's objects.[13] It was at first held that even if express powers were used to further an *ultra vires* purpose, the exercise of the power itself was *ultra vires*. For example, borrowing money to fund an activity not stated in the objects clause.[14] But the most recent cases, most notably *Rolled Steel Products (Holdings) Ltd v British Steel Corp*, narrowed the scope of *ultra vires* and held that the use of an express power could not be beyond the capacity of the company but rather it was an act done in excess or abuse of the powers of the company.[15] The practical difference of this finding was that an act which was *ultra vires*, the company was void and a nullity irrespective of the notice of the third party, whereas an act done in excess or abuse of the company's powers was unenforceable only if the third party had notice of this fact. Further, an *ultra vires* act could not be ratified by the shareholders whereas an act done in excess or abuse of powers could be.[16] See below for the significance of this distinction after the 1989 Act reforms.

Reform of *ultra vires*

Recommendations for the reform of the rule were made as long ago as 1945 by the Cohen Committee where it was described as serving 'no positive purpose' and 'a cause of unnecessary prolixity and vexation'.[17]

The Jenkins Committee also recommended reform, but only to provide protection for third parties contracting with companies in good faith.[18] No action was taken on these recommendations until the UK became a member state of the EEC and was required to implement the First Directive on Company Law. This reform of the law was originally contained in s 9(2) of the European Communities Act 1972 and subsequently became s 35 of the 1985 Act. But a number of difficulties came to light, and after a report was produced by Dr Prentice for the DTI,[19] a much more thorough

---

12   *Cotman v Brougham* [1918] AC 514.

13   *Attorney General and Ephraim Hutchings v Great Eastern Railway Co* (1880) 5 App Cas 473.

14   *Re Introductions Ltd* [1970] Ch 199.

15   See also *Charterbridge Corp Ltd v Lloyds Bank Plc* [1970] Ch 62.

16   *Rolled Steel Products (Holdings) Ltd v British Steel Corp* [1986] Ch 246. The Court of Appeal stated the ratification should be by *all* shareholders but it is unclear what is the basis for this stringent requirement.

17   1945, Cmnd 6659, para 12.

18   1962, Cmnd 1749, para 42.

19   Reform of the *Ultra Vires* Rule: A Consultative Document (DTI 1986).

reform was implemented. This is now contained in ss 35, 35A, 35B, 322A and 711A of the 1985 Act as substituted and provided by the 1989 Act.

Section 35 deals with a company's capacity and the *ultra vires* rule. However, instead of providing that a company has the same powers as an individual, as Prentice had recommended, s 35(1) provides:

> '(1) The validity of an act done by a company shall not be called into question on the ground of lack of capacity by reason of anything in the company's memorandum.'

Thus, *ultra vires* as either a defence by the company or by a contracting party to an action to enforce a contract is no longer possible. This brings about as much protection as is possible for a contractor against the *ultra vires* rule. One should note, however, that subsection (2) provides that:

> '(2) A member of a company may bring proceedings to restrain the doing of an act which but for subsection (1) would be beyond the company's capacity; but no such proceedings shall lie in respect of an act done in fulfilment of a legal obligation arising from a previous act of the company.'

This preserves the right of members to restrain by injunction the company from acting outside the objects clause and therefore in breach of the s 14 contract.[20] But this right is lost once, for example, an *ultra vires* contract proposed by the company has been signed with the contracting party.

This 'internal aspect' to *ultra vires* is further preserved by subsection (3) which provides that:

> '(3) It remains the duty of the directors to observe any limitations on their powers flowing from the company's memorandum; and action by the directors which but for subsection (1) would be beyond the company's capacity may only be ratified by the company by special resolution.'

But as the subsection continues:

> 'A resolution ratifying such action shall not affect any liability incurred by the directors or any other person; relief from any such liability must be agreed to separately by special resolution.'

So directors will be liable to reimburse the company for losses it sustains while engaging upon an activity outside the objects clause, and although it is now provided that the members can ratify and adopt by special resolution an otherwise *ultra vires* act which is quite different from the position which existed before, any such resolution will not of itself relieve the directors from liability and this will have to be done by a separate special resolution. It is difficult to justify a different level of ratification for breaches of directors' duties in relation to observing the terms of the memorandum and all other ratifiable breaches of duty where only an ordinary resolution is required. The section must reflect the view that in relation to the former, constraints on the directors are still regarded as more fundamental.

---

20 See *Parke v Daily News Ltd* [1962] Ch 927 as an example of this sort of action.

A special resolution by the members to ratify an *ultra vires* action which does not relieve the directors of liability might be useful where the company cannot, for a number of reasons, enter into a legal obligation with a contracting party for some time or at all, and the company wishes to preclude a challenge by an individual member under subsection (2).

The requirement on the directors 'to observe any limitations on their powers flowing from the company's memorandum' also presumably still requires the directors to use powers such as borrowing and guaranteeing for the furtherance of the company's objects and not for purposes outside the objects clause which would still be an excessive or abusive use of the powers. Further, as s 35 only validates acts which can be called into question on the ground of lack of capacity a third party dealing with the directors where they have simply acted in excess of the company's powers, as in *Rolled Steel*, will have to bring himself within s 35A to be able to enforce the transaction. As will be seen, the third party in *Rolled Steel* was held not to be in 'good faith' for the purposes of the rule in *Turquand* and therefore may not be in 'good faith' for the purposes of s 35A.

As far as a party to a *transaction* with the company is concerned, they are not bound to enquire as to whether the transaction is permitted by the company's memorandum. This is provided by s 35B, although given the wide-ranging effect of s 35(1), it would be surprising to find this raised as an argument to defeat a transaction purely on grounds of *ultra vires*. It is to be hoped that this would not be successfully raised where there was not a transaction by the company, for instance, where there was a gift. Section 35B also applies to *intra vires* transactions and probably has a larger role to play in clarifying the position in relation to s 35A.

There is also a more comprehensive abolition of the doctrine of constructive notice contained in s 711A which will be considered in relation to s 35A.[21]

The Companies Act 1989 also inserted a new s 3A which provides that companies can be incorporated with the sole object of carrying on business as a general commercial company, a situation which had been previously doubted,[22] and in which case:

(a) the object of the company is to carry on any trade or business whatsoever, and

(b) the company has power to do all such things as are incidental or conducive to the carrying on of any trade or business by it.

Although this provision is primarily a word-saving device, given the inherent conservatism and caution of legal drafting and the use of the word processor, companies are still likely to be formed with extremely lengthy objects clauses, perhaps simply including the statement from s 3A.

There is also a general power to alter the objects clause by special resolution contained in a new s 4 which was substituted by the Companies Act 1989. An

---

21 See p 135.

22 *Re Crown Bank* (1890) 44 Ch D 634.

application can still be made by the holders of not less than 15% in aggregate in nominal value of the company's issued share capital or any class of it (or by the holders of not less than 15% of the company's debentures) for the alteration to be cancelled. No such application can be made by any person who consented or voted in favour of the alteration and the application must be made within 21 days after the date on which the resolution was passed. The court is given a wide discretion as to what orders it can make on such an application, including an order that the company buy the shares of any members.[23]

Gratuitous dispositions and non-commercial transactions

The issue of *ultra vires* was also involved where a company made or was proposing to make a gratuitous disposition or gift either to its employees or ex-employees or by way of a charitable or political donation. There were two different situations. First, where the objects clause itself provided for such dispositions and second, where the objects clause was silent on such matters.

In the latter case, where there were proposed gifts, the courts would only uphold them if they could be regarded as reasonably incidental to the carrying on of the company's business and from which the company would obtain a gain.[24] Therefore, gifts and expenditure on employees to keep and maintain a contented workforce were acceptable,[25] but not after the company had ceased to be a going concern or had gone into liquidation.[26] The company could no longer have an interest in a motivated workforce and therefore gratuitous redundancy payments would be *ultra vires*. Similarly with charitable or political donations: a donation by a chemical company to universities and research institutions could tenuously benefit the company, since there would be a better educated workforce from which to draw employees and a general advancement of scientific knowledge.[27]

Where there was an express provision in the objects clause for the type of disposition in question, there was a much greater chance that it would be upheld, but the courts have scrutinised these dispositions carefully and have not always allowed the disposition to be made.[28] Also, where a company having an express power to pay pensions, determined to pay a pension to the widow of a former company employee which it was not contractually bound to do, the judge held it to be *ultra vires* because it was not reasonably incidental to the carrying on of the company's business and did not benefit the company.[29] The actual finding of *ultra vires* here cannot stand in the light of

---

23   Companies Act 1985, s 5.
24   *Hampson v Price's Patent Candle Co* (1876) 45 LJ Ch 437.
25   *Hutton v West Cork Rly Co* (1883) 23 Ch D 654.
26   *Parke v Daily News Ltd* [1962] Ch 927: subsequently reversed by statute; see Companies Act 1985, s 719.
27   *Evans v Brunner, Mond & Co Ltd* [1921] 1 Ch 359.
28   *Simmonds v Heffer* [1983] BCLC 298.
29   *Re Lee Behrens & Co* [1932] 2 Ch 46; *Re W & M Roith Ltd* [1967] 1 WLR 432.

the decision of the Court of Appeal in *Rolled Steel (Holdings) Ltd v British Steel Corp*,[30] where it was established that an express power to do an act contained in the objects clause precluded a finding of *ultra vires* where that act was done regardless of whether or not the act was of benefit to the company. But the decision might be supportable on the grounds that the directors had abused their powers to pay the pension.

Shortly before the decision in *Rolled Steel* the Court of Appeal,[31] in order to circumvent the problems caused by the above cases, held that a provision in the objects clause of a company which provided the company with the power to pay a pension could actually be construed as a substantive object and not merely an ancillary or incidental power. This meant that it was irrelevant whether the payment of the pension promoted the commercial prosperity of the company since paying pensions was then part of the business of the company.

This rather heavy-handed approach is unnecessary after *Rolled Steel*. The payment of a pension in these circumstances would always be *intra vires* but not necessarily enforceable, because the directors may have abused or acted in excess of their powers to pay pensions (eg where a large payment, described as a pension, is paid to a recently employed person in order to get rid of him: if the recipient knows of this then the transaction becomes voidable at the instance of the company and the recipient might not be able to rely on s 35A because he will not be in 'good faith'). This achieves a balance between protecting the interests of persons transacting or receiving money from the company and protecting the assets of the company from the excesses of management.

Since companies did invariably include clauses in their objects clauses which allowed the company to make gratuitous payments, and now because of the virtual abolition of the ultra vires rule by s 35, the problem of the company's capacity to make gifts is unlikely to arise.[32]

This does not necessarily mean, though, that a third party in all circumstances can enforce an agreement or retain money paid to it by a company, since the court can choose to employ other devices to protect the company. In what became the leading case on the old s 35 (first introduced by the European Communities Act 1972), the court had to examine the effect of the section in a case involving what was in substance a gratuitous disposition. In *International Sales Agencies Ltd v Marcus*[33] the director of a company made payments out of the company's bank account to satisfy the personal debts of a deceased former director and close friend. Lawson J held that the payments were *ultra vires* the company but also that they were made in breach of the director's duty to the company. The defendant recipient was held to be a constructive trustee of the money since he knew of the breach of trust and fiduciary duty by the director. In

---

30 [1986] Ch 246. See p 124.

31 In *Re Horsley & Weight* [1982] 3 All ER 1045.

32 Political and charitable donations made by a company and its subsidiaries which exceed £200 in any financial year must be stated in the directors' report and in the case of political donations the name of the recipient must be given: Companies Act 1985, Sch 7, para 3.

33 [1982] 3 All ER 551.

considering whether what was then s 9(1) of the 1972 Act assisted the defendant, Lawson J held that it could not, because that section only assisted a party *dealing* with a company in good faith, and here the defendant had not been dealing with the company, but simply receiving its money, as a result of an act of generosity. This would not now be a problem under the present s 35 because 'the validity of an act' cannot be impugned on *ultra vires* grounds, thus not requiring the contracting party to show there was any dealing at all. Further, even where the transaction is being challenged on the grounds that the powers of the directors were limited, whilst the protection is afforded only to a person 'dealing' in good faith with a company, 'dealing' is defined very widely.

In any event, though, Lawson J found that the section was of no assistance where there was held to be a constructive trust, and this is likely to be the case with the present section at least where the directors are engaging in fraud or misfeasance.[34] Although the same facts can give rise to both *ultra vires* issues and constructive trusts, this is not necessarily the case and the basic principles governing the two doctrines are wholly different. The section was designed to remove *ultra vires* as a problem for third parties and that continues with the present s 35, but these sections were not intended to prevent the courts from applying constructive trusts principles and imposing constructive trusteeship on certain recipients of company property where there was knowledge of some additional wrongdoing apart from the lack of authority. Further, the courts would be unlikely to hold that an obligation on directors to act in the best interests of the company was a limitation on their powers for the purposes of s 35A, thus entitling a contracting party to claim the protection of that section.[35]

TRANSACTIONS WHERE THERE IS A NON-COMPLIANCE WITH INTERNAL MANAGEMENT PROCEDURES

The doctrine of constructive notice by fixing contracting parties with notice of the contents of its registered documents could have had even worse commercial consequences than it did if it were not for the rule in *Royal British Bank v Turquand*.[36] This case established that, whilst a person dealing with a company might be deemed to know of certain limitations and procedures contained in the constitution which had to be followed before a company could enter into a transaction, he was not obliged to investigate into the internal affairs of the company to see whether the requirements of the constitution and regulations of the company had been complied with. In the *Turquand* case itself a deed of settlement company registered under the Joint Stock Companies Act 1844 was empowered by the deed to borrow money on a bond in such sums as might be authorised by a resolution in general meeting. The company did borrow £2,000 on a bond given to the plaintiff bank, and subsequently in an action on the bond sought to defend itself by pleading that the transaction had been entered into without the consent of the members. It was held that the bond was binding on the company. Jervis CJ stated:

---

34 *Parliamentary Dabates* (Lords), 5th series, Vol 505, 1244–45.

35 See p 135.

36 (1856) 6 E & B 327.

'We may now take for granted that the dealings with these companies are not like dealings with other partnerships, and that the parties dealing with them are bound to read the statute and the deed of settlement [which was registered in a similar way to a company's memorandum and articles]. But they are not bound to do more. The party here, on reading the deed of settlement, would find, not a prohibition from borrowing, but a permission to do so on certain conditions. Finding that the authority might be made complete by a resolution, he would have a right to infer the fact of a resolution authorising that which on the face of the document appeared to be legitimately done'.[37]

There is also a well-known statement of the rule in *Morris v Kanssen*[38] where Lord Simonds approved a passage from Halsbury's *Laws of England* which stated that:

' ... persons contracting with a company and dealing in good faith may assume that acts within its constitution and powers have been properly and duly performed and are not bound to inquire whether acts of internal management have been regular.'[39]

The rule in *Turquand* was particularly useful for a contracting party, where a company's articles fixed the number of directors needed to constitute a quorum for a board to make valid decisions, but unknown to the contracting party a transaction was decided on by an inquorate board;[40] also where the company's articles provided for a certain number of directors' signatures on a document and, although these might have been obtained, unknown to the contracting party none of the directors had been validly appointed.[41]

The scope of the rule in *Turquand* was, however, restricted in the following ways:

1   The rule could only operate in favour of a person acting in good faith without notice of the irregularity and this was interpreted to include absence of grounds for suspicion that there was any failure to comply with internal irregularities.[42]

2   The rule could not operate in favour of an 'insider' (eg a director) who would be deemed to know of any irregularity in the internal management of the company no matter how unrealistic in fact that might be.[43]

3   The rule does not operate to protect outsiders from the consequences of forgery.[44] If a document is discovered to be a forgery, it is a nullity, and no legal consequences can flow from it. The definition of what constitutes a forgery, though, is the subject of some difficulty. Certainly if an unauthorised outsider obtains the company's seal and uses it on a document, forging the signatures of the directors, this will be held to be a forgery. But where there are genuine signatures

---

37   *Ibid* at 332.

38   [1946] AC 459.

39   *Ibid* at 474.

40   *County of Gloucester Bank v Rudry Merthyr Steam & House Coal Colliery Co* [1895] 1 Ch 629.

41   *Mahony v East Holyford Mining Co* (1875) LR 7 HL 869.

42   *B Liggett (Liverpool) Ltd v Barclays Bank Ltd* [1928] 1 KB 48; *Rolled Steel Products (Holdings) Ltd v British Steel Corp* [1986] Ch 246.

43   *Howard v Patent Ivory Manufacturing Co* (1888) 38 Ch D 156; *Morris v Kanssen* [1946] AC 459.

44   *Ruben v Great Fingall Consolidated* [1906] AC 439.

of the directors and simply an unauthorised use of the seal, it is difficult to justify a finding of forgery, since the company is holding out those persons as having authority to represent the document as genuine.[45]

4   Importantly, the rule could not allow a contracting party who dealt with a person who in fact had not been authorised to assume that there had been a delegation of authority to that person under a delegation article. So, for example, in *Houghton & Co v Nothard, Lowe & Wills*,[46] where an agreement with the plaintiffs was made by an ordinary, individual director to whom there had been no actual delegation of authority, the plaintiffs could not rely on the existence of a delegation article in the company's articles and claim that the rule in *Turquand* entitled them to assume that delegation to the director had been made. As Sargant LJ explained:

> 'but even if ... the plaintiffs had been aware of the power of delegation in the articles of the defendant company, this would not in my judgment have entitled ... them to assume that this power had been exercised in favour of a director, secretary or other officer of the company so as to validate the contract now in question ... [T]his [would be] to carry the doctrine of presumed power far beyond anything that has hitherto been decided, and to place limited companies, without any sufficient reason for so doing, at the mercy of any servant or agent who should purport to contract on their behalf. On this view, not only a director of a limited company with articles founded on Table A, but a secretary or any subordinate officer might be treated by a third party acting in good faith as capable of binding the company by any sort of contract, however exceptional, on the ground that a power of making such a contract might conceivably have been entrusted to him'.[47]

The section following deals with the question of when a contracting person *is* entitled to assume that the person he is dealing with has been delegated authority to act for the company.

TRANSACTIONS WHERE THE PERSON ACTING FOR THE COMPANY IS NOT AUTHORISED

The *Houghton* decision above preserves the fundamental rule that the primary agent of the company is the board of directors, which is authorised to manage the company by the articles (in Table A, by article 70); the board will make collective decisions about the management of the company. The board may be and usually will be given powers to delegate its powers to a committee of the board or to a managing director,[48] and if it does make such a delegation then that committee or managing director will have actual authority to act for the company within the terms of the delegation. If no such delegation is made then there is no actual authority given to anyone else to act for the

---

45   See *South London Greyhound Racecourses Ltd v Wake* [1931] 1 Ch 496 which sits uneasily with *Lloyd v Grace Smith & Co* [1921] AC 716, which holds that a principal is vicariously liable for an agent's fraud. See also *First Energy (UK) Ltd v Hungarian International Bank Ltd* (1993) BCC 533.

46   [1927] 1 KB 246.

47   *Ibid* at 266.

48   In Table A, it is given power by article 72.

company but it may be possible for a third party contracting to with the company with a person who purports to represent the company, but who has no actual authority, to claim that that person had apparent or ostensible authority and therefore the company is bound by the agreement. To determine this question, reference must be made to the general law of agency.

The leading case is *Freeman & Lockyer v Buckhurst Properties*,[49] where there were four directors of the company, which had a clause in its articles allowing for the delegation of the board's powers to a managing director. No managing director was ever formally appointed but in reality one of the directors, K, ran the business of the company. K entered into a contract with the plaintiffs, who were a firm of architects, to carry out some work for the company. This work was carried out, but the company subsequently refused to pay the fees on the ground that K did not have authority to enter into the contract on behalf of the company. It was held by the Court of Appeal that although K was not actually authorised he was ostensibly authorised and therefore the contract was binding on the company. In order for a contracting party to be able to raise a valid claim of ostensible authority against the company, Diplock LJ stated that it must be shown:

1   that a representation that the agent had authority to enter on behalf of the company into a contract of the kind sought to be enforced was made to the contractor;

2   that such representation was made by a person or persons who had 'actual' authority to manage the business of the company either generally or in respect of those matters to which the contract relates;

3   that the contractor was induced by such representation to enter into the contract, that is, he in fact relied upon it; and

4   that under its memorandum or articles of association the company was not deprived of the capacity either to enter into a contract of the kind sought to be enforced or to delegate authority to enter into a contract of that kind to the agent.[50]

So the central issue in these cases is whether or not there has been a representation by the board or persons who had actual authority to enter into the contract in question. As Diplock LJ stated:

'The commonest form of representation by a principal creating an 'apparent' authority of an agent is by conduct, namely, by permitting the agent to act in the management or conduct of the principal's business. Thus, if in the case of a company the board of directors who have 'actual' authority under the memorandum and articles of association to manage the company's business permit the agent to act in the management or conduct of the company's business, they thereby represent to all persons dealing with such agent that he had authority to enter on behalf of the corporation into contracts of a

---

49   [1964] 2 QB 480.
50   *Ibid* at 506.

kind which an agent authorised to do acts of the kind which he is in fact permitted to do usually enters into the ordinary course of such business'.[51]

So the principle operates as a form of estoppel, in that a company which holds out a person as someone who is authorised cannot subsequently plead lack of actual authorisation if a contracting party had relied on the holding out. So a company which holds someone out as a finance director, sales director, managing director or company secretary[52] will be representing to the outside world that that person has the authority vested in them which is usual or normal in the ordinary course of business for that type of person.

So, for example, in *British Bank of the Middle East v Sun Life Assurance Co of Canada (UK) Ltd*[53] the court had to examine whether a manager of a branch office of a large insurance company would usually have authority to give an undertaking on behalf of the company. An answer in the negative meant that the branch manager concerned could not have had ostensible authority to represent the company on the undertaking in question. Neither could he represent to a third party that a more junior employee had such actual authority. The second of the Diplock conditions in *Freeman & Lockyer* meant that here this type of undertaking had to be given by the head office of the company for a claim of ostensible authority to succeed. A claim based on ostensible authority also failed in *Armagas v Mundogas SA*[54] where M, who was an employee of the company and who was appointed as 'vice-president (transportation)' and chartering manager, had actual authority to agree a straightforward sale of a ship but no authority to agree a three-year charter-back of the ship. The transaction was known by the persons dealing with the company through M to be one not within the usual authority of an employee in M's position, but they were told, falsely and not by a person with actual authority to manage the business of the company, that he had obtained specific authority for it. It was held that there had been no representation by the company to the contracting party that M had authority, and therefore he was not ostensibly authorised. As Lord Keith stated:

> 'In the commonly encountered case, the ostensible authority is general in character, arising when the principal has placed the agent in a position which in the outside world is generally regarded as carrying authority to enter into transactions of the kind in question.'[55]

In *First Energy (UK) Ltd v Hungarian International Bank Ltd*[56] the Court of Appeal distinguished Armagas in a case where it was known by the contracting party that a senior manager of a branch office of a bank did not have actual authority to sanction a credit facility. Here it was held that though this employee did not have ostensible

---

51 *Ibid* at 505; and see Lord Pearson in *Hely-Hutchinson v Brayhead* [1968] 1 QB 549 at 593.
52 See *Panorama Developments (Guildford) Ltd v Fidelis Furnishing Fabrics Ltd* [1971] 2 QB 711.
53 [1993] BCLC 78.
54 [1986] AC 717.
55 *Ibid* at 777.
56 [1993] BCLC 1409.

authority to make this offer, he was nevertheless, because of his considerable status within the local branch, 'clothed with ostensible authority' to communicate that head office approval had been given for the facility. When he communicated incorrectly that approval had been given to the contracting party, that party was entitled to rely on that statement. It would not have been reasonable to expect that the party should then have checked with head office in London to confirm whether approval had been given.

There is also the possibility that an agent may have implied authority by reason of his being appointed to a particular position. This is a form of actual authority, because the relationship is still between the company and the agent, but it arises where a person is appointed to a particular post and he thereby is vested with all the usual authority of a person occupying that post. An adapted form of the example used by Lord Denning MR in *Hely-Hutchinson v Brayhead Ltd*[57] illustrates the point. If the board appoints one of its number to be the managing director, it invests in him a certain amount of authority. If no authority is expressly delegated to him, then he will have the implied authority to do all such things as fall within the usual scope of that office. He will also have ostensible authority to the same degree. Outsiders seeing him acting as a managing director are entitled to assume that he has the usual authority of a managing director. But, in certain cases, ostensible authority can exceed implied actual authority; for instance, where the board appoints a managing director and expressly limits his authority by stating that he is not to order goods worth more than £500 without the sanction of the board. In that case his actual authority is limited to £500 but his ostensible authority still includes all the usual authority of a managing director, so if he orders goods worth £1,000 this contract will be binding on the company unless the supplier was aware of the limitation. Of course he would have had constructive notice of the limitation if it was contained in the articles, but not if it was contained in the director's service contract. This would also be in accordance with the fourth of the conditions laid down by Diplock LJ in *Freeman & Lockyer*. The reforms enacted by the Companies Act 1989 have addressed not only the problem of *ultra vires*, discussed above, but also *intra vires* authority problems, and it is to this issue that attention must now be turned.

REFORMS IN RESPECT OF LIMITATIONS ON THE BOARD'S POWERS

Section 35A implements the original First EEC Directive requirements, contained in article 9(2), that a limitation on the powers of the organs of the company, arising under the company's constitution or from a decision of the other competent organs, should never be relied on as against third parties, even if they are disclosed. As first enacted in s 9(2) of the European Communities Act 1972, this issue was dealt with in the same section as the reform required by article 9(1) in relation to acts outside the objects of the company, but after the 1989 reforms the two issues have been separated.

---

57 [1968] 1 QB 549.

Section 35A(1) states as follows:

'In favour of a person dealing with a company in good faith, the power of the board of directors to bind the company, or authorise others to do so, shall be deemed to be free of any limitation under the company's constitution.'

Thus, provisions in the memorandum or, more likely, in the articles of association, which purport to limit the powers of the board of directors to bind the company, are ineffective against a person dealing with the company in good faith. This makes the board more akin to an organ of the company in the sense used in many continental jurisdictions rather than an agent which has to be authorised to act for the company by the terms of the company's constitution. The definition of 'dealing' for these purposes is wide, since by s 35A(2)(a) a person 'deals with' a company if he is a party to *any* transaction or other act to which the company is a party. Further, s 35A(2)(b) and (c) provide that a person shall not be regarded as acting in bad faith by reason only of his knowing that an act is beyond the powers of the directors under the company's constitution and that a person shall be presumed to have acted in good faith unless the contrary is proved. Section 35B also provides that, in respect of a party *to a transaction* with a company, that party is not bound to enquire as to whether there are any limitations on the power of the board of directors to bind the company, thus removing any argument that a contracting party is in bad faith because it did not enquire into the possibility of limitations contained in the company's constitution. The 1989 Act also inserted s 711A which is not yet in force. This section is entitled the 'Abolition of doctrine of deemed notice' and provides in subsection (1) that:

'A person shall not be taken to have notice of any matter merely because of its being disclosed in any document kept by the Registrar of Companies (and thus available for inspection) or made available by the company for inspection.'

This effectively reverses the decision in *Ernest v Nicholls*[58] fixing the outside world with constructive notice of a company's public documents. Unfortunately s 711A(2) introduces an element of uncertainty since it states that:

'This does not affect the question whether a person is affected by notice of any matter by reason of a failure to make such enquiries as ought reasonably to be made.'

It is unclear precisely what the effect of this latter subsection is, but what is reasonably clear is that as a result of s 35B 'such enquiries as ought reasonably to be made' do not include an enquiry by a transacting party of whether a particular transaction is permitted by the company's memorandum, or whether there are any limitations on the powers of the board of directors either to enter into the transaction or to authorise others to do so.

The limitations which are made ineffective by this section against a good faith contractor include limitations deriving:

(a) from a resolution of the company in general meeting or a meeting of any class of shareholders, or

---

58 (1857) 6 HLC 401.

(b) from any agreement between the members of the company or of any class of shareholders.[59]

Therefore, for example, if the company in general meeting has given directions by special resolution as envisaged and specifically provided for by article 70 of Table A, limiting the power of the board to act in a particular way, that limitation will be ineffective against the good faith contractor even though the special resolution will have been registered with the registrar.

In the same way as provided by s 35(2) a member of the company can bring proceedings to restrain an act which but for s 35(1) would be *ultra vires*, so a member can bring proceedings to restrain the doing of an act which is beyond the powers of the directors.[60] In both cases, though, the right of the member to bring proceedings is lost where the company has to fulfil a legal obligation arising from a previous act of the company. So, in other words, if a contract has already been signed by the company, it will be too late in either case for a member to be able to bring an action to restrain the company. But, as with s 35, by s 35A(5) the section does not affect any liability on the part of the directors for exceeding their powers. Here s 35A is silent as to the procedure required to relieve a director from liability whereas s 35(3) provides that a separate special resolution is required. It must be presumed, therefore, that an ordinary resolution will be required as under the general law for relieving directors from liabilities for breach of duty.[61]

Section 35A also makes it irrelevant for a person dealing in good faith with the company that there is any limitation on the power of the board to authorise other persons to bind the company. So, for example, a clause in the company's articles which states that the board can delegate its powers to bind the company only to a committee of the board or to an individual director, but only up to a certain maximum sum, would not affect the validity of a contract entered into by a good faith contractor which involved a sum which exceeded that maximum, even if the latter knew of the clause and the limitation.

Section 35A, though, only deals with limitations on the powers to delegate and authorise other persons to bind the company. Its effect on the law of ostensible authority as stated by Diplock LJ in *Freeman & Lockyer v Buckhurst Properties Ltd*[62] is only limited. There can be little doubt that the fourth condition expostulated by Diplock LJ in his judgment, namely that the company was not deprived of the power to delegate authority to enter into a contract of the kind in question to the agent, has been removed. But in a case where a contracting party has entered into a contract with an individual who has not been actually authorised by the company, it will still be necessary to show that there was a representation which was relied on by the contractor. As the representation has to be made by a person or persons who have

---

59   Companies Act 1985, s 35A(3).
60   Companies Act 1985, s 35A(4)
61   See p 118.
62   [1964] 2 QB 480.

actual authority to manage the business of the company, where that person or persons is the board though no limitation under the constitution on their powers would prevent a contractor from establishing that they did have actual authority.

There remains the interesting question of what is 'good faith' for the purposes of the section. For the purposes of the previous s 35, a party dealing in good faith where the transaction was decided on by the directors was not bound to enquire as to the capacity of the company to enter into the transaction or any limitations on the powers of the directors, and was presumed to have acted in good faith unless the contrary was proved. In *TCB Ltd v Gray*[63] Browne-Wilkinson VC, after stating that where the section applied, the doctrine of constructive notice was abolished, rejected an attempt to reintroduce it through the argument that a party could not be in good faith if he did not make the enquiries which ought to have been made. Under the present s 35A this position is made stronger and clearer since s 35A(2)(b) states that a person shall not be regarded as acting in bad faith by reason only of his knowing that an act is beyond the powers of the directors under the company's constitution (as widely defined by s 35A(3)), and as under the previous section, a person shall be presumed to have acted in good faith unless the contrary is proved. Then s 35B removes any obligation on a contracting party to enquire as to whether a transaction is permitted by the company's memorandum or whether there are any limitation on the powers of the directors.

So, if even actual notice of a limitation is not enough to put a contracting party in bad faith, just what is required? According to Nourse J in *Barclays Bank Ltd v TOSG Trust Fund Ltd*,[64] another case where the provisions of the previous section were discussed, good faith was a purely subjective concept and therefore reasonableness, or whether the contracting party had acted reasonably, had no part to play in determining good faith. Rather, it was whether a person had acted genuinely and honestly in the circumstances of the case.

In many cases it would seem that where a person is acting in bad faith for the purposes of the section, he would be likely to be held to be a constructive trustee anyway for acting dishonestly or fraudulently in relation to the company, regardless of whether there were any limitation on the powers of the directors. So, for example, a contracting party who had conspired with the directors to asset strip the company by purchasing company property at an undervalue would not be able to enforce the transaction. This is because it is highly likely in those circumstances that he would be held to be a constructive trustee of the company property.[65] If it transpired, in addition, that there was a limitation on the powers of the directors in the articles to sell this kind of property to the effect, for example, that they required an approval from a general meeting first, then the section would be of little assistance anyway to the contracting party to overcome any problem arising from the limitation because they would be acting in bad faith.

---

63 [1986] Ch 621.

64 [1984] BCLC 1.

65 *Selangor United Rubber Estates Ltd v Cradock (No 3)* [1968] 1 WLR 1555.

Lastly, special provision is made in relation to charitable companies by s 65 of the Charities Act 1993. Sections 35 and 35A of the 1985 Act do *not* apply to the acts of a company which is a charity except in favour of a person who:

(a) gives full consideration in money or money's worth in relation to the act in question; and

(b) does not know that the act is not permitted by the company's memorandum or, as the case may be, is beyond the powers of the directors;

(c) or who does not know at the time the act is done that the company is a charity.

But where a charitable company purports to transfer or grant an interest in property, the fact that the act was not permitted by the company's memorandum or, as the case may be, that the directors exceeded any limitation on their powers, does not affect the title of a person who subsequently acquires the property for full consideration without actual notice of any circumstances affecting the validity of the company's act.[66]

A FUTURE ROLE FOR THE RULE IN *TURQUAND?*

The rule in *Turquand* assisted contracting parties, as we have seen, where there were internal irregularities in the making of a transaction. To the extent that those internal irregularities can be construed as placing *limitations* on the powers of the board of directors or others with purported actual or ostensible authority to enter into transactions, then s 35A makes *Turquand* redundant, since the protection afforded by the section covers this problem and goes further. *Turquand* did not operate where the contracting party was put on enquiry. As Lord Simonds stated in his speech in *Morris v Kanssen*:[67]

'[h]e cannot presume in his own favour that things are rightly done if enquiry that he ought to make would tell him that they were wrongly done.'

But under s 35A it is irrelevant what an enquiry would have revealed to the contracting party.

Section 35A only deals with limitations on the powers of the directors. It is quite reasonable to argue that some of the situations covered by *Turquand* went beyond that and involved more basic questions of what constitutes the board rather than just what its powers are. So, for example, clauses in the articles providing for what is a quorum for a valid board meeting do not provide limitations on the powers of the board but define what the board is. Under this view the rule in *Turquand* would still have a role to play protecting contracting parties who had dealt with a company on the basis of a decision taken by an inquorate board, but those parties would still be prevented from enforcing the transaction if they were put on enquiry that they were dealing with an inquorate board.

---

66 See also *Rosemary Simmons Memorial Housing Association Ltd v United Dominions Trust Ltd* [1986] 1 WLR 1440.

67 [1946] AC 459 at 475.

WHERE THE CONTRACTING PARTY IS A DIRECTOR OF THE COMPANY

Under s 35A it may have been possible for a director of the company concerned to enforce a transaction against the company where the board had exceeded its powers. The possible injustice that this may have caused the company or in certain circumstances ultimately the company's creditors led the legislature to enact s 322A.[68] This section provides that the transaction with the director or persons connected with the director is still voidable at the instance of the company, thus removing the protection of s 35A.

Whether or not the transaction is avoided by the company, the director or the persons connected with him are liable to account to the company for any gain which they have made directly or indirectly by the transaction and to indemnify the company for any loss or damage resulting from the transaction. The company will lose the right to avoid the transaction if restitution is no longer possible, the company is indemnified for any loss or damage resulting from the transaction, there are rights acquired bona fide for value and without notice of the directors' exceeding their powers by a person who is not party to the transaction and who would be affected by the avoidance, or the transaction is ratified by the shareholders in general meeting by ordinary or special resolution as the case may require.[69]

---

68   See *Guinness plc v Saunders* [1990] 2 AC 663.
69   Companies Act 1985, s 322A(5).

CHAPTER SEVEN

CAPITAL

INTRODUCTION

The term 'capital' has special significance in company law. A company which is registered under the Companies Act 1985 with shares is required to have an 'authorised share capital'.[1] This is an amount which is stated in the company's memorandum and is the maximum sum which a company can raise by way of issuing shares. The memorandum will also state how this authorised share capital is to be made up, ie how many shares and of what value. A company does not have to issue all the shares which it is entitled to do but the aggregate nominal value of the shares which it does issue is known as the 'issued share capital'.

The shareholders to whom the shares are issued are not necessarily required to pay for them either in whole or in part although frequently nowadays the shares will be fully paid. So another term, 'paid-up capital', refers to the amount of money paid to the company in respect of the shares. It might be equal to the issued capital but it might be nil in the case of a private company. If the company has issued partly paid shares and wishes to obtain more money it can make a 'call' on the shares, in which case the shareholders are contractually bound to pay the amount specified in the call. By s 737(1) 'called-up share capital' means the aggregate amount of the calls made on the shares (whether or not those calls have been paid), together with any share capital paid up without being called and any share capital to be paid on a specified future date under the articles, the terms of allotment, or any other arrangements for payment of those shares. The terms of allotment and articles provide for the procedure for making calls and article 12 of Table A states that subject to the terms of allotment the directors may make calls upon the members.

A remarkable feature of English company law is that in respect of private companies there is no minimum capital requirement before a company can begin business. In fact the UK and the Republic of Ireland stand alone in the European Union in not having such a minimum capital requirement for private companies. All other Member States do require a minimum contributed capital before their equivalent of a private company can be properly incorporated. The fact that the Companies Act 1985 has a minimum capital requirement for public companies is only as a result of the obligation of the UK to comply with the provisions of the Second EC Directive.[2] This requirement is that a public company must have an allotted or issued share capital of at least the 'authorised minimum'[3] to begin business or exercise any borrowing powers.

---

1   Companies Act 1985, s 2(5).

2   77/91/EEC.

3   Companies Act 1985, s 117.

The authorised minimum is currently £50,000[4] (and necessarily, of course, an authorised share capital of at least this amount) and at least one quarter of this must be paid up.[5]

A curious and somewhat ironic fact then emerges. Despite the absence of a minimum capital requirement for private companies so that companies can be registered for example with two £1 shares being allotted, neither of which are paid up, (and now s 1(3A) allows for a company to be formed with only one share being allotted to a single member), there are a considerable number of intricate and complex provisions which regulate what can be done with the capital once the company acquires it. Many of the provisions are of long standing and pre-date the Companies Act 1980 when the minimum capital requirement for public companies was first introduced. The underlying philosophy for this regulation is that originally, when a company is incorporated, its issued capital is recorded in the publicly available documents with the registrar and the legitimate objects for which the company is formed are also publicly known and as Lord Herschell explained in *Trevor v Whitworth*:[6]

'The capital may, no doubt, be diminished by expenditure upon and reasonably incidental to all the objects specified. A part of it may be lost in carrying on the business operations authorised. Of this all persons trusting the company are aware, and take the risk. But I think [those dealing with the company] have a right to rely, and were intended by the legislature to have a right to rely, on the capital remaining undiminished by any expenditure outside these limits, or by the return of any part of it to the shareholders.'[7]

Again, in the speech of Lord Watson:

'One of the main objects contemplated by the legislature, in restricting the power of limited companies to reduce the amount of their capital as set forth in the memorandum, is to protect the interests of the outside public who may become their creditors. In my opinion the effect of these statutory restrictions is to prohibit every transaction between a company and a shareholder, by means of which the money already paid to the company in respect of his shares is returned to him, unless the Court has sanctioned the transaction. Paid-up capital may be diminished or lost in the course of the company's trading; that is a result which no legislation can prevent; but persons who deal with, and give credit to a limited company, naturally rely upon the fact that the company is trading with a certain amount of capital already paid, as well as upon the responsibility of its members for the capital remaining at call; and they are entitled to assume that no part of the capital which has been paid into the coffers of the company has been subsequently paid out, except in the legitimate course of its business.'[8]

---

4   Companies Act 1985, s 118.
5   Companies Act 1985, s 101.
6   (1887) 12 App Cas 409.
7   *Ibid* at 415.
8   *Ibid* at 423.

But as Buckley LJ explained in *Re Horsley & Weight Ltd*:[9]

> '[i]t is a misapprehension to suppose that the directors of a company owe a duty to the company's creditors to keep the contributed capital of the company intact. The company's creditors are entitled to assume that the company will not in any way repay any paid-up share capital to the shareholders except by means of a duly authorised reduction of capital.'[10]

So although there was no significant capital requirement, and there still is not for private companies, nevertheless if capital is contributed and this is publicly known, the creditor should be able to rely on the availability of a substantial capital sum for the ultimate satisfaction of his debts; a corollary to the theory being that the creditor who advances goods or services on credit to a company with minimal capital and who then suffers loss only has himself to blame. So the fundamental rule is that a company must maintain its capital. This rule has various aspects. For example, a company cannot issue shares at a discount.[11] Section 2(5)(a) provides that in the case of a company having a share capital, the memorandum must state the division of the share capital into shares of a fixed amount. A shareholder who is allotted a share will then be liable up to the full nominal amount of the share even if he has only partly paid for it.[12] As the House of Lords held in *Ooregum Gold Mining Co of India Ltd v Roper*,[13] this system would be rendered wholly redundant if a company could, for example, issue a £1 share for 50p and then treat it as fully paid so there were no more liabilities on the part of the shareholder. The creditors of the company may be seriously misled about the financial standing of the company.

If the company is able to obtain a premium on the sale of its shares over and above the nominal value of them whether in the form of cash or otherwise then s 130 requires a sum equal to the aggregate amount in value of the premiums on those shares to be transferred to a special account known as the 'share premium account'. There are then strict controls on what this money can be used for. It can be used most importantly by the company in paying up unissued shares to be allotted to members as fully paid bonus shares, but otherwise the provisions of the Act relating to the reduction of capital apply as if the share premium account were part of its paid up capital. In particular it cannot be distributed as a dividend to shareholders.

A company cannot return its capital to shareholders except as provided by the Companies Act. The most obvious way in which capital is returned is when a solvent company is wound up and, after all the liabilities have been discharged, the surplus is returned to shareholders in accordance with their relative shareholdings. But where a company is still in existence it can only lawfully return capital to its shareholders under two major groups of circumstances, reduction of capital and redemption or repurchase of shares.

---

9   [1982] Ch 442.

10   *Ibid* at 453.

11   Companies Act 1985, s 100(1).

12   Companies Act 1985, s 100(2).

13   [1892] AC 125.

REDUCTION OF CAPITAL

Section 135 provides that a company limited by shares may if so authorised by its articles reduce its share capital on the passing of a special resolution. The section provides that the capital can be reduced 'in any way' but s 135(2) specifies, without prejudice to the generality of that provision, some of the main ways. So a company may:

(a) extinguish or reduce the liability on any of its shares in respect of share capital not paid up.

This is to say the company will not make further calls on wholly unpaid or partly-paid shares;

(b) either with or without extinguishing or reducing liability on any of its shares, cancel any paid-up share capital which is lost or unrepresented by available assets.

A company whose issued share capital is £100,000 made up of 100,000 £1 shares may wish to reduce its capital if the assets owned by the company are now only worth £25,000. One way to achieve this would be to reduce the nominal value of each share to 25p.

(c) either with or without extinguishing or reducing liability on any of its shares, pay off any paid-up share capital which is in excess of the company's wants.

For example, the company may have sold a large asset and have a substantial amount of cash, more than it could ever need. In these circumstances a reduction of capital could be achieved by cancelling some shares and returning their value to the shareholders or by reducing the nominal value of the shares themselves eg from £1 to 75p and returning 25p to each shareholder.

Where there has been a special resolution passed under s 135 the company must then apply to the court for an order confirming the reduction.[14] Where the proposed reduction of capital involves a diminution of liability in respect of unpaid share capital (point 1 above), or the payment to a shareholder of any paid-up share capital (point 2 above), in which cases the interests of creditors may be affected, and in any case where the court so directs, the court will require the interests of those creditors to be satisfied before confirming the reduction.

The court's role is not just to see that the interests of creditors are protected but it should also see that the procedures were properly carried out and that the shareholders well informed about the proposed reduction when they voted on a special resolution. In *Re Jupiter House Investments (Cambridge) Ltd*[15] Harman J stated that the court's discretion to confirm the reduction would only be exercised in favour of confirmation of the reduction where the court is satisfied

(a) that the proposed reduction affects all shareholders of equal standing in a similar manner, or that those treated in a different manner from their equals have consented to that different treatment, and

---

14 Companies Act 1985, s 136(1).
15 [1985] 1 WLR 975 at 978.

(b) that the cause of the reduction was properly put to shareholders so that on a vote they could exercise an informed choice, and the cause is proved by the evidence before the court.

Creditors of the company are given a statutory right to object to a reduction and a list is drawn up by the company of such creditors and the nature and amount of their debts.[16] The court can order that a notice be published, giving creditors not entered on the list the right to be entered within a certain fixed period. Then the court, if satisfied that every creditor who is entitled to object to the reduction has consented, or that his debt or claim has been discharged or determined or secured, it may make the order confirming the reduction on such terms and conditions as it thinks fit. The court can dispense with the consent of a particular creditor if it is shown that, for example, the company has set aside and deposited a sum which would satisfy the claim made against it by that creditor.[17] The court can even order that the company add to its name the words 'and reduced' after the reduction but in practice this is not required today.[18]

Where a reduction of capital requires the repayment of money to shareholders then the repayment will generally be in the order in which repayment would be made to shareholders if the company were wound up.[19] This will mean that if there are preference shareholders and ordinary shareholders, and the former have priority for repayment of capital in a winding up and there is a reduction of capital by way of repayment and cancellation of shares because the company's assets exceed its needs, then the preference shareholders will be repaid first in full. The courts will not interfere in such a scheme or refuse to confirm such a reduction on complaints by preference shareholders that they may be deprived of a share in the surplus assets in a subsequent winding up of the company or that the reduction will deprive them of a contractual expectation of a fixed higher dividend. The courts have taken the view that these claims are beyond the reasonable expectations of a preference shareholder when he acquires shares in a company.[20] They may share in such surplus assets if there is no reduction before winding up but this would be a 'windfall' and the risk of a reduction of capital is as much an element in the bargain as the right to a preferential dividend. In the Court of Appeal in *Re Chatterley-Whitfield Collieries Ltd*[21] Lord Greene MR expressed the sound business policy on which this practice is based, namely to rid the company of the perhaps onerous obligation of paying a fixed higher rate of dividend every year.

Where the reduction is as a result of a loss or wastage of assets and, for example, the nominal value of the shares is reduced, and again the preference shareholders have priority for repayment in a winding up then normally it would be the ordinary shareholders who would be affected first, since in a winding up the preference

---

16   Companies Act 1985, s 136(4).

17   Companies Act 1985, s 136(5).

18   Companies Act 1985, s 137(3).

19   See, for example, *Re Saltdean Estates Co Ltd* [1968] 1 WLR 1844.

20   *Scottish Insurance Corpn Ltd v Wilsons & Clyde Coal Co Ltd* [1949] AC 462.

21   [1948] 2 All ER 593.

shareholders would have the right to a full repayment of their capital in priority over the ordinary shareholders.[22]

Generally it has been held that reductions taking the form of a proposal to pay off preference shareholders have not involved a variation or abrogation of class rights thus requiring any resolution in favour of the proposal from the holders of the preference shares under ss 125–27.[23] If, however, a class of shareholders does have rights which are varied then there must be a meeting of that class to consider the proposed reduction.[24]

If a company wishes to cancel its unissued shares, in respect of which there has been no agreement to take them, then by s 121(e) a company may do so if it is authorised by its articles and the company in general meeting passes an ordinary resolution to that effect. This cancellation does not for the purpose of the 1985 Act constitute a reduction of capital.[25]

REDEMPTION AND PURCHASE BY A COMPANY OF ITS OWN SHARES

In *Trevor v Whitworth*[26] it was held by the House of Lords that a company had no power to acquire its own shares. The reason was clearly based on the maintenance of capital as Lord Watson explained:

> '[W]hen a share is forfeited or surrendered, the amount which has been paid upon it remains with the company ... whilst the share itself reverts to the company, bears no dividend and may be re-issued. When shares are purchased at par, and transferred to the company, the result is very different. The amount paid up on the shares is returned to the shareholder; and in the event of the company continuing to hold the shares (as is the present case) is permanently withdrawn from its trading capital.'[27]

The rule laid down in *Trevor v Whitworth* is now contained in s 143 which makes it a criminal offence for a company to acquire its own shares whether by purchase, subscription or otherwise. The consequences of contravention of the section are that the company and every officer in default are liable to a fine, and the officer is also liable to imprisonment and the purported acquisition is void. A major exception to this basic prohibition is provided by s 143(3)(a), namely where there is a redemption or purchase of shares in accordance with Chapter VII of Part IV, that is to say ss 159–81.

Redemption

Prior to the passing of the Companies Act 1981, a company could only issue redeemable preference shares, that is to say shares which are issued on the terms that they may be bought back by the company. The 1981 Act extended this power

---

22 *Re Floating Dock Co of St Thomas Ltd* [1895] 1 Ch 691.

23 See p 175.

24 *Re Holders Investment Trust Ltd* [1971] 1 WLR 583.

25 Companies Act 1985, s 121(5).

26 (1888) 12 App Cas 409.

27 *Ibid* at 424.

considerably but in doing so introduced a highly complex series of provisions of which only an outline is provided below. The reason for the complexity is to try to protect the company's creditors against any inappropriate reduction in capital although it has been questioned whether the protection is really necessary.[28] One of the principal reasons why a company may wish to redeem or purchase shares is that the issue of redeemable shares creates the possibility of a temporary membership for an investor in a company with the possibility of being able to withdraw the investment. This is particularly useful where the company is a private company and there is no ready market for the shares. This is obviously not the case with public companies, where the reason for redeeming or repurchasing may be simply to rid itself of unwanted capital.

As far as redeemable shares are concerned, a company may, if authorised to do so by its articles, issue redeemable shares which are to be redeemed or are liable to be redeemed at the option of the company or the shareholder.[29] The shares may be redeemed after a fixed period of time or on the happening of a specified event. Redeemable shares cannot be issued at a time when there are no issued shares of the company which are not redeemable and redeemable shares may not be redeemed unless they are fully paid.[30] The terms of redemption must provide for payment on redemption, otherwise the company may simply change the status of a shareholder into a creditor. As far as public companies are concerned redeemable shares may only be redeemed out of distributable profits of the company or out of the proceeds of a fresh issue of shares made for the purposes of the redemption.[31] Shares which are redeemed are then treated as cancelled on redemption and the amount of the company's issued and paid up capital is diminished by the nominal value of the redeemed shares.[32] In a sense, though, the capital of the company is maintained because there will have been either a fresh issue of shares to finance the redemption so that the capital raised on those shares will 'replace' the redeemed capital or, where the shares are redeemed wholly out of the company's profits, the amount by which the company's issued share capital is diminished on the cancellation of the shares must be transferred to a reserve account, called the 'capital redemption reserve'.[33] This sum is then treated as if it were capital and cannot be distributed.[34] So in effect a company must have twice the amount required to finance the redemption and one half of that will be transferred to the capital redemption reserve and this will 'replace' the amount redeemed. If there is a partial financing of the redemption out of a fresh issue then an amount equivalent to the amount of the balance between the nominal value of the shares redeemed and the

28   See Sealy, *Company Law and Commercial Reality* (1984, London).

29   Companies Act 1985, s 159(1).

30   Companies Act 1985, s 159(2) and (3).

31   Companies Act 1985, s 160(1).

32   Companies Act 1985, s 160(4).

33   Companies Act 1985, s 170(1).

34   Companies Act 1985, s 170(4).

nominal value of the shares of the fresh issue must be transferred out of distributable profits to the capital redemption reserve.[35]

Private companies may, within certain limits, redeem shares out of capital. This is considered under the section dealing with a private company's power to repurchase shares out of capital generally.[36]

The company must give notice in the prescribed form to the registrar within one month of any redemption of redeemable shares and failure to do so is a criminal offence in respect of which the company and every officer in default are liable to a fine.[37]

Purchase

By s 162 a company with a share capital may, if authorised to do so by its articles, purchase its own shares. Article 35 of Table A provides such authority. Sections 163–69 then lay down what additional authority has to be obtained before the purchase can proceed and also imposes certain disclosure requirements. The provisions make a distinction between three types of situation: where the shares are to be purchased in an 'off-market purchase'; a 'market purchase'; and a 'contingent purchase contract'.

Market purchase

This is defined as a purchase by a company of its own shares, where the purchase is made on a recognised investment exchange, and the shares are subject to a marketing arrangement on that investment exchange.[38] By s 166 a company shall not make a market purchase of its own shares unless the purchase has first been authorised by the ordinary resolution in general meeting. This authority must specify the maximum number of shares authorised to be acquired, determine both the maximum and minimum prices which may be paid for the shares and specify a date on which the authority is to expire. This authority can be varied, revoked or renewed by the company in general meeting, but in a resolution to confer or renew authority, the date on which the authority is to expire must not be later than 18 months after that on which the resolution is passed. A resolution under s 166 conferring authority must be sent to the registrar within 15 days.

Off-market purchase

This is defined as a purchase by a company of its own shares where the shares either:

(a) are purchased otherwise than on a recognised investment exchange, or

(b) are purchased on a recognised investment exchange but are not subject to a marketing arrangement on that investment exchange.[39]

---

35 Companies Act 1985, 170(2).

36 See p 150.

37 Companies Act 1985, s 169.

38 Companies Act 1985, s 163(3).

39 Companies Act 1985, s 163(1).

In this case it is perceived that the company requires more protection, and the terms of the proposed contract must be approved in advance by a special resolution before the contract is entered into.[40] In the case of a public company, the authority conferred by the resolution must specify a date on which the authority is to expire, and in a resolution conferring or renewing authority that date must not be later than 18 months after that on which the resolution is passed.[41] A special resolution which is passed conferring authority or varying, revoking or renewing it, shall not be effective if any member of the company who holds shares to which the resolution relates, exercises the voting rights carried by those shares on the resolution and the resolution would not have been passed if he had not done so.[42] A special resolution is also not effective under this section unless a copy of the proposed contract is available for inspection by the members of the company, both at the company's registered office for not less than 15 days ending with the date of the meeting at which the resolution is passed, and at the meeting itself.[43] The document available for inspection must contain the names of any members holding shares to which the contract relates.

Contingent purchase contract

This is a contract entered into by a company which does not amount to a contract to purchase any of its shares but under the company may become entitled or obliged to purchase the shares, for example, where a director retires and the company is obliged in that event to purchase his shares. This type of contract can only be made by a company if the contract is approved in advance by a special resolution before the contract is entered into. The provisions of s 164(3–7) apply to this type of contract.

Disclosure

Where there has been a purchase by a company of any of its shares, it must, within 28 days beginning with the date on which the shares were delivered to it, deliver to the registrar for registration a return in the prescribed form stating the class of shares purchased and the number and nominal value of the shares.[44] Where the company is a public company, this return also has to state the aggregate amount paid by the company for the shares and the maximum and minimum prices paid in respect of the shares of each class purchased.[45] The company also has to keep a copy of a contract approved under ss 164–66 at its registered office for 10 years, and this has to be open to inspection without charge by any member of the company, and in respect of a public company, by any other person.[46] If any of these disclosure requirements are not complied with, then the company and every officer in default are liable to a fine.[47]

---

40 Companies Act 1985, s 164(1) and (2).
41 Companies Act 1985, s 164(4).
42 Companies Act 1985, s 164(5).
43 Companies Act 1985, s 169(1).
44 Companies Act 1985, s 169(1).
45 Companies Act 1985, s 169(2).
46 Companies Act 1985, s 169(5).
47 Companies Act 1985, s 169(6) and (7).

Redemption and purchase of a company's own shares out of capital

In respect of private companies only, the Act allows the use of capital to finance a redemption or purchase of their own shares.[48] The company must however, use its available distributable profits and the proceeds of any fresh issue of shares made for the purposes of redemption or purchase first and then any shortfall can be made up from capital. This is known as the 'permissible capital payment'.[49] The conditions which have to exist before the payment out of capital can be made are that:

(i) there has to be authorisation in the company's articles for redemption or purchase out of capital. Article 35 of Table A does contain such authorisation;

(ii) there must be a statutory declaration by the company's directors specifying the amount of the permissible capital payment for the shares and stating that, having made full enquiry into the affairs and prospects of the company, they have formed an opinion that there will be no grounds on which the company could be found to be unable to pay its debts immediately following the payment of the capital, and that the company will be able to continue to carry on business as a going concern to pay its debts as they fall due during the year immediately following that date;[50]

(iii) there must be attached to the statutory declaration a report addressed to the directors from the company's auditors stating that, *inter alia*, they are not aware of anything to indicate that the opinion expressed by the directors in the declaration is unreasonable;[51]

(iv) there must be a special resolution approving the payment out of capital. The resolution will be ineffective if any member of the company who holds shares to which the resolution relates, exercises the voting rights carried by the shares in voting on the resolution and the resolution would not have been passed if he had not done so.[52]

Within a week immediately following the passing of the special resolution the company must take action to publicise the proposed payment out of capital. It must cause to be published in the *London Gazette* a notice giving details of the payment of capital, and also have a similar notice published in an appropriate national newspaper (ie a newspaper that has a circulation throughout England and Wales) or give the notice in writing to each of its creditors.[53]

Even after the passing of a special resolution to approve any payment out of capital for the purposes of s 171 any member of the company (other than one who consented to or voted in favour of the resolution) and any creditor may apply to the court for a

---

48   Companies Act 1985, s 171.
49   Companies Act 1985, s 171(3).
50   Companies Act 1985, s 173(3).
51   Companies Act 1985, s 173(5).
52   Companies Act 1985, s 173(2).
53   Companies Act 1985, s 175.

cancellation of the resolution within five weeks from the date on which the resolution was made.[54] When the court hears such an application, it has complete discretion to make any order it thinks fit, but s 177 specifically provides that the court can adjourn the proceedings in order that an arrangement be made which the court has to approve for the purchase of the interests of dissentient members or for the protection of dissentient creditors.

FINANCIAL ASSISTANCE BY A COMPANY FOR THE ACQUISITION OF ITS OWN SHARES

General prohibition

There is a general prohibition on a company from giving financial assistance to another person for the purchase of its own shares. This prohibition first appeared in the Companies Act 1929 after a recommendation from the Greene Committee.[55] A practice which had been identified and condemned in the Report was where an asset-stripper agreed to purchase shares from existing shareholders and used a loan from a lending institution to finance the purchase. Once sufficient control had been taken of the company by the asset-stripper he could appoint a new board and use the company's resources to repay or service the loan. This would in effect be to use the company's own money to buy its shares. The Greene Committee felt that this offended against the spirit if not the letter of the rule prohibiting a company from purchasing its own shares. The maintenance of capital rule can be infringed if money or other assistance is advanced to an outsider for these purposes and is not recovered. For example, in a simple case, if a company has an issued and paid up capital of £10,000 comprising 10,000 £1 shares, and the outsider borrowed £10,000 from a bank to approach the existing shareholders with a view to purchasing their shares at par, if the company acts as a surety of the bank loan and the outsider defaults, the company loses its capital of £10,000. There is no necessary reduction of capital, though, if in the above example the outsider himself repays the bank. But because of the risks of the above, the prohibition is very broadly drawn. The original prohibition was on the giving of financial assistance 'for the purpose of or in connection with' an acquisition of shares and this was interpreted surprisingly widely, catching transactions which were otherwise commercially reasonable and unobjectionable. So, for example, where a person sold an asset to a company, and that person received funds from the sale which were used to acquire shares in the company, this was held to be an infringement of the section unless it could be shown that the purchase was in the company's ordinary

---

54 Companies Act 1985, s 176.

55 (1926) Cmd 2657, paras 30–31. The law in this area has recently been the subject of criticism for potentially affecting and prohibiting innocent commercial transactions. The DTI has recently completed a consultation process and a draft Order under the Deregulation and Contracting Out Act is in preparation to reform the legislation.

56 *Belmont Finance Corpn Ltd v Williams Furniture Ltd (No 2)* [1980] 1 All ER 393.

course of business.[56]

Substantial amendments were made to the original provision in the Companies Act 1981 when considerable exceptions to the basis prohibition were introduced for private companies. The basic prohibition is now contained in s 151 which provides that:

(1) Subject to the following provisions of this Chapter, where a person is acquiring or is proposing to acquire shares in a company, it is not lawful for the company or any of its subsidiaries to give financial assistance directly or indirectly for the purpose of that acquisition before or at the same time as the acquisition takes place.

(2) Subject to those provisions where a person has acquired shares in a company and any liability has been incurred, (by that or any other person), for the purpose of that acquisition, it is not lawful for the company or any of its subsidiaries to give financial assistance directly or indirectly for the purpose of reducing or discharging the liability so incurred.

So subsection (1) prohibits the situation where the company makes a loan or a gift to a person to buy its shares before or contemporaneously with the acquisition and for that purpose, whereas subsection (2) prohibits the assistance a company might give to pay off a loan which a person has taken out for the purpose of providing him with sufficient funds to acquire shares. 'Financial assistance' is defined very broadly by s 152(1) to include a gift, guarantee, security, indemnity, loan or 'any other financial assistance given by a company the net assets of which are thereby reduced to a material extent or which has no assets'. The last situation would cover the sale of an asset by a person to a company at an overvalue and for the purpose of providing funds for the acquisition of shares in the company. As succinctly stated by Aldous LJ in *British & Commonwealth Holdings plc v Barclays Bank plc*,[57] the section requires that there should be assistance or help for the purpose of acquiring the shares and that that assistance should be financial.

In *Charterhouse Investments Trust Ltd v Tempest Diesels Ltd*[58] Hoffmann J gave some guidance on what the phrase financial assistance means:

'There is no definition of giving financial assistance in the section, although some examples are given. The words have no technical meaning and their frame of reference is in my judgment the language of ordinary commerce. One must examine the commercial realities of the transaction and decide whether it can properly be described as the giving of financial assistance by the company, bearing in mind that the section is a penal one and should not be strained to cover transactions which are not fairly within it.'[59]

Here Charterhouse was selling off a subsidiary company, Tempest, to A, one of the managers, and the shares in the company were sold to A for £1. Tempest had held tax losses which, as part of the transaction as a whole, were surrendered to Charterhouse. It was submitted that these were a valuable asset belonging to Tempest and the surrender

---

57   [1996] 1 WLR 1 at 15

58   [1986] BCLC 1.

59   *Ibid* at 10. See also *Parlett v Guppys (Bridport) Ltd* (1996) *The Times*, 8 February.

of them to Charterhouse was for the purpose of facilitation of the sale of shares in Tempest, since without the surrender Charterhouse either would not have sold the shares or would have only sold them at a substantially higher price than £1. Hoffmann J held that Tempest had not given financial assistance (even under the wider former section with its wider interpretation). After looking at the commercial realities it was seen that the surrender was part of a composite transaction under which Tempest was receiving benefits and assuming burdens. The benefit it received outweighed the burdens and there was no evidence that at the time the tax losses were of any value to Tempest, since it was unclear that it could make a future profit so as to be able to utilise them.

The giving of advice by the company to a purchaser of its shares would not contravene the section. Further:

'the fact that a company undertakes obligations ... in connection with the proposal for the transfer of its shares does not of itself constitute the giving of financial assistance. ... [T]he fact that a company facilitates a proposal for such a transfer will not involve it necessarily in contravention of [s 151]. Thus, a company may answer requests for information relevant to the proposed transfer knowing that it does so in circumstances such that it be liable for damages if, for lack of care, the information is incorrect. ... But, by answering such requests, the company does not thereby give financial assistance.'[60]

If a company acts in contravention of the prohibition it is liable to a fine and every officer of the company who is in default is liable to imprisonment or fine or both.[61]

Exceptions to the s 151 prohibition

Section 153 contains a number of exceptions to the basic prohibition of s 151. By s 153(1) there is no prohibition on the company from giving financial assistance for the purpose of an acquisition of shares in it or its holding company if:

(a) the company's principal purpose in giving that assistance is not to give it for the purpose of any such acquisition, or the giving of the assistance for that purpose is but an incidental part of some larger purpose of the company; and

(b) the assistance is given in good faith in the interests of the company.

Section 153(2) contains an equivalent exception for the s 151(2) prohibition in relation to reducing or discharging any liability incurred by a person for the acquisition of shares.

There has been an interpretation of this exception by the House of Lords in *Brady v Brady*[62] which favoured a narrow view of its scope. Here a group of companies which had been run by two brothers was split into two, so that the brothers could go their separate ways. As part of the process of division, assets were transferred from one company to its holding company to reduce the liability of the holding company in respect of acquiring shares in the company. One brother refused to execute the

---

60   *Burton v Palmer* (1980) 5 ACLR 481 *per* Mahony J at 492.

61   Companies Act 1985, s 151(3).

62   [1989] AC 755.

agreement, and when the other brother brought proceedings for specific performance, resisted the action on the ground that this agreement infringed s 151(2) and therefore it was illegal. To counter that claim, reliance was placed on the exception contained in s 153(2) to the effect that the financial assistance was an incidental part of a larger purpose of the company, which here was the reorganisation of this whole group to avoid deadlock which resulted from the breakdown in the relationship between the brothers, and avoiding the probable alternative consequence of liquidation. This argument was accepted by the trial judge and the Court of Appeal but it was rejected by the House of Lords. An appeal is made in the course of the speech of Lord Oliver to the mischief at which s 151 is aimed. A wide interpretation of the scope of the exception would deprive s 151 of any useful application if a distinction were not drawn between a purpose and the reason why a purpose is formed.

> 'The ultimate reason for forming the purpose of financing an acquisition may, and in most cases probably will, be more important to those making the decision than the immediate transaction itself. But 'larger' is not the same thing as 'more important' nor is 'reason' the same as 'purpose'. If one postulates the case of a bidder for control of a public company financing his bid from the company's own funds – the obvious mischief at which the section is aimed – the immediate purpose which it is sought to achieve is that of completing the purchase and vesting control of the company in the bidder. The company may have fallen on hard times so that a change of management is considered necessary to avert disaster. It may merely be thought, and no doubt would be thought by the purchaser and the directors whom he nominates once he has control, that he business of the company will be more profitable under his management than it was heretofore. These may be excellent reasons but they cannot, in my judgment, constitute a 'larger purpose' of which the provision of assistance is merely an incident.'[63]

In other words the resolution of the dispute may have been the reason for the division of the business and the giving of the assistance, but it could not be an independent 'purpose'. The only 'purpose' of the transfer of the assets was to give financial assistance for the reduction of a liability incurred in acquiring shares. This interpretation is to reduce considerably the scope for the exception.

Private companies and the relaxation of s 151

In addition to the exceptions provided by s 153 for both public and private companies, ss 155–58 provide additional relaxation of the s 151 prohibition for private companies. The financial assistance may only be given if the company has net assets which are not thereby reduced or, to the extent that they are reduced, the assistance is provided out of distributable profits.[64] Usually the giving of the assistance under s 155 must be approved by special resolution.[65] The directors of the company which is proposing to

---

63 *Ibid* at 779.

64 Companies Act 1985, s 155(2).

65 Companies Act 1985, s 155(4).

66 Companies Act 1985, s 155(6).

give the financial assistance shall, before the assistance is given, make a statutory declaration in the prescribed form.[66] This declaration has to contain particulars of the financial assistance to be given, the business of the company and the identity of the person to whom the assistance is to be given. The declaration must also state that the directors have formed the opinion that immediately after the date on which the assistance is proposed to be given, there is no ground on which the company could then be found to be unable to pay its debts and either:

(a) if it is intended to commence the winding up of the company within 12 months of the giving of the assistance the company will be able to pay its debts in full; or

(b) in any other case, that the company will be able to pay its debts as they fall due during the year immediately following the giving of the financial assistance.

The statutory declaration must also have annexed to it a report addressed to the directors from the company's auditors stating that they have enquired into the state of affairs of the company and they are not aware of anything to indicate that the opinion of the directors is unreasonable in all the circumstances. The statutory declaration and the auditors' report must be delivered to the registrar together with a copy of the special resolution approving the giving of the assistance.[67]

By s 157(2), where a special resolution has been passed approving the giving by the company of financial assistance, an application may be made to the court for the cancellation of the resolution by the holders of not less in the aggregate than 10% in nominal value of the company's issued share capital or any class of it, but such an application cannot be made by a person who consented to or voted in favour of the resolution.

The ability of private companies to give financial assistance for the purchase of their shares is particularly useful where there is a management buy-out of the company's issued shares. A particular management team or board of directors may feel that they would be less hampered and have greater incentives to maximise profits if they owned all the company's shares and there were no passive investors. It is quite likely that they will not be in a position to afford to buy all the issued shares from existing shareholders but will require large loans from a bank in order to do so. In this situation the company itself can guarantee the loans of the directors and this will not be unlawful under s 151 if the procedures laid down in ss 155–58 are followed.

Consequences where a transaction infringes s 151

Originally the criminal penalty for infringing the prohibition against giving financial assistance was a fine of up to £100 maximum. This can hardly have been a deterrent for those who wished to abuse the company's assets in a transaction which may have been worth millions of pounds. This has now been rectified and the penalty for

---

67 Companies Act 1985, s 156.

68 Companies Act 1985, s 151(3).

infringing s 151 is that the company is liable to a fine of unlimited amount and so is every officer who is also liable to imprisonment for a term of up to two years.[68]

More problems have been caused by the need to define what are the civil consequences of infringement. In *Victor Battery Co Ltd v Curry's Ltd*[69] it was held that, where the company had given a debenture as security for money advanced to a person to enable him to purchase shares in the company, the debenture was not illegal and therefore was not void. The reasoning behind the decision was that if it were void, then the company which had contravened the provision would gain a benefit, the avoidance of the security, and the lender would lose. There was also a logical problem in that if the transaction itself was void, it was void *ab initio* and therefore technically no financial assistance could have been given. But this approach was not followed in *Heald v O'Connor*[70] where it was held that a guarantee made in breach of the equivalent provision to s 151 was illegal and void. The problem with this approach is that if the company had actually advanced a sum of money by way of a loan to another person then it cannot sue on the loan because it was a party to the illegal transaction itself and it was held in *Wallersteiner v Moir*[71] that the prohibition was designed for the protection of the company. The solution for the company may be to sue the director and the other persons who have participated in the infringement of s 151. In *Selangor United Rubber Estates Ltd v Cradock (No 3)*,[72] a company was caused by the majority of its directors to pay money to a third party, which was then used by Cradock to acquire the company's shares through an intermediary. Ungoed-Thomas J saw the case as essentially one of the misapplication by the directors of the company's money by way of an unlawful loan. Where the directors act for the company in the illegal transaction with a third party the company is itself a party to the transaction and cannot, because of the illegality, claim any rights arising from the transaction. But if instead the company alleges a breach of trust it is not relying on the transaction at all. The action is against the directors and constructive trustees for perpetrating the transaction and for making the company a party to it in breach of the trust owed to the company by the directors and thereby causing the company loss.

ULTRA VIRES AND THE MAINTENANCE OF CAPITAL RULE

The maintenance of capital rule essentially means that there can be no return of the capital to the shareholders or any other payments to them otherwise than as provided by statute. So, for example, it is permissible to make such payments if there is a reduction of capital pursuant to s 135, or a redemption or repurchase of shares pursuant to ss 159–81, or on a distribution of distributable profits by way of a dividend or on a winding up of the company of surplus assets.

In a number of cases the courts have invalidated or struck down certain payments or transactions between a company and a shareholder on the grounds that what is

---

68 [1946] Ch 242.

69 [1946] Ch 242.

70 [1971] 1 WLR 497.

71 [1974] 1 WLR 991.

72 [1968] 1 WLR 1555; See also *Belmont Finance Corpn Ltd v Williams Furniture Ltd* [1979] Ch 250.

involved is an unlawful return of capital, which the company does not have the power to do, and the payments or transactions are therefore *ultra vires* and void. So, for example, in *Ridge Securities Ltd v IRC*[73] a subsidiary company granted a debenture to its parent company and, under the terms of the debenture, large and wholly uncommercial sums described as interest were payable to the parent company. Pennycuick J held the payments to be *ultra vires* as an unlawful return of the capital of the subsidiary to the parent shareholder. In the well-known case of *Re Halt Garage (1964) Ltd*[74] Oliver J held that certain payments to a non-working director/shareholder could not be genuine payments of remuneration and instead they were dressed-up gifts out of capital. To that extent they were *ultra vires* the company.

More recently in *Aveling Barford Ltd v Perion Ltd*[75] a sale of an asset at an undervalue was characterised as an unlawful return of capital. Here L owned the shares of two companies and was a director and in effective control of both of them. An asset owned by one company was sold to the other at a considerable undervalue. The vendor company went into liquidation and the liquidator successfully brought an action for the purchasing company to be made a constructive trustee of the proceeds of the resale of the asset.

Although there was arguably a clear and obvious breach of fiduciary duty by L to the vendor company, a problem would have been encountered in pursuing that claim because as sole shareholder L both formally and informally approved of the sale so that it could not now be challenged. Hoffmann J overrode this difficulty by employing the maintenance of capital principle:

> '[S]o it seems to me in this case that looking at the matter objectively, the sale to [the purchasing company] was not a genuine exercise of the company's power under its memorandum to sell its assets. It was a sale at a gross undervalue for the purpose of enabling a profit to be realised by an entity controlled and put forward by its sole beneficial shareholder. This was as much a dressed-up distribution as the payment of excessive interest in *Ridge Securities* or excessive remuneration in *Halt Garage*.'[76]

Therefore the sale was *ultra vires* the company, the important consequence of that being that it was incapable of validation by the approval or ratification of the shareholder, L. It is important to bear in mind that the use of the term *ultra vires* in this context differs from its use in relation to corporate transactions. In the latter sense it relates to the problems associated with lack of contractual capacity stemming from the contents of the memorandum and s 35 has substantially removed these altogether. In the present context it relates to the powers of the company as defined by and laid down in the statute. But the development of this doctrine is not without problems. In *Re Halt Garage* the company only had an issued share capital of two £1 shares, one of which the non-working director held. In those circumstances can the payments of £20 per

---

73 [1964] 1 WLR 479.

74 [1982] 3 All ER 1016

75 [1989] BCLC 626.

76 *Ibid* at 632.

week be said to be a return of that capital? And in *Aveling Barford* there was an unexpressed 'lifting the veil' to treat L and the purchasing company as one and the same. L was the shareholder and the purchasing company and the recipient of the proceeds of resale.[77]

DIVIDENDS

The basic common law rule was, not surprisingly having regard to the maintenance of capital rule, that there can be no distribution of dividends to shareholders out of capital.[78] As s 263(3)(1) now provides, a company shall not make a distribution except out of profits available for the purpose. Section 263(3) then states that a company's profits available for distribution (or its distributable profits) are:

> 'its accumulated, realised profits, so far as not previously utilised by distribution or capitalisation[79] less its accumulated, realised losses, so far as not previously written off in a reduction or reorganisation of capital duly made.'

This definition was introduced in the Companies Act 1980 and has the consequence that dividends can only be paid out if 'realised profits' exceed 'realised losses'. These terms are not defined by the Act but are recognised in accountancy and the courts are guided by accounting practices laid down in the relevant Statement of Standard Accounting Practice (SSAP).[80] A company would, for example, have made a realised profit once it receives cash from another person, or is legally and unconditionally entitled to money or other property with a certain value from another person under a transaction, when the value of what it is so entitled to exceeds what has been spent by the company under the transaction. This requirement tightened up the previous rules which allowed a company to make a distribution following revaluation of capital assets which produced a surplus, which in other words produced a 'profit on paper'.[81] Under the present rules, the asset would have to actually be sold in order to realise the profit. Even tighter rules apply to public companies.[82]

The other change made in 1980 was the requirement to look at the past history of profits and losses to calculate the distributable profits for the current year. Previously, the company could calculate the profit available for distribution by simply looking at the profit and loss account for the current year. Now the company must look at how the profits and losses have accumulated over the previous years. For example, if a company has a trading record as follows:

1992–93   £2,000   loss

---

77 See also *Precision Dippings Ltd v Precision Dippings Marketing Ltd* [1986] Ch 447 in relation to the receipt of unlawful dividends by a shareholder. See p 159.

78 *Re Exchange Banking Co, Fitcroft's Case* (1882) 21 Ch D 519; *Verner v General and Commercial Investment Trust* [1894] 2 Ch 239.

79 See p 160.

80 *Lloyd Cheyham & Co v Littlejohn & Co* [1987] BCLC 303.

81 *Dimbula Valley (Ceylon) Tea Co Ltd v Laurie* [1961] Ch 353.

82 Companies Act 1985, s 264.

1993–94   £3,000 profit

1994–95   £4,000 loss

it will have to produce a profit of at least £3,000 in 1995–96 to be in a position to show that its accumulated profits exceed its accumulated losses.

Even where there is a distributable profit in any financial year it will not necessarily be distributed in the form of a dividend to shareholders. The dividend will first have to be 'declared' in accordance with the provisions of the company's articles.[83] The relevant article of Table A is article 102 which provides that the general meeting may, by ordinary resolution, declare dividends but no dividend shall exceed the amount recommended by the directors. So the directors as a matter of management policy decide how much of the distributable profit should be paid out by way of dividend and how much should be retained and invested into the company's business, and it is the general meeting which technically declares the dividend. There is, however, increasing scrutiny of the directors' discretion to recommend dividends and the persistent payment of low dividends without an adequate reason or explanation may be the basis for a s 459 application by the shareholders.[84]

Once declared, the dividend becomes a contractual debt owed to the shareholders for which the limitation period is six years.[85] Dividends should only be paid in cash, unless there is a provision to the contrary in the company's articles, and a member can enforce a payment in cash.[86]

Where there has been an unlawful distribution there is the possibility of two main consequences. First, by s 277, where a distribution made by a company to one of its members is made in contravention of the provisions for calculating distributable profit, then if at the time of the distribution the member knows or has reasonable grounds for believing that it is so made, then he is liable to repay it to the company. But in *Precision Dippings Ltd v Precision Dippings Marketing Ltd*[87] a parent company received a large dividend from the subsidiary company at a time when the accounts of the company were not 'unqualified' as they should have been before a distribution was made.[88] The parent company was held liable to account as a constructive trustee for the dividend received. The Court of Appeal imposed the liability without relying on what is now s 277(1), Dillon LJ stating that:

> 'I do not find it necessary to examine the wording of [s 277(1)] since by subsection (2) the provisions of s 277 are declared to be without prejudice to any other obligation imposed on a member to repay a distribution unlawfully made to him. ... The payment

---

83   *Bond v Barrow Haematite Steel Co* [1902] 1 Ch 353.

84   *Re Sam Weller & Sons Ltd* [1989] 3 WLR 923.

85   *Re Compania de Electricidad de la Provincia de Buenos Aires Ltd* [1980] Ch 136; in contrast to a debt owed by the member to the company which, because it is deemed to be a debt under seal (s 14), has a limitation period of 12 years.

86   *Wood v Odessa Waterworks Co Ltd* (1889) 42 Ch D 645.

87   [1986] Ch 447.

88   See now Companies Act 1985, s 271.

of the £60,000 dividend to Marketing was an ultra vires act on the part of the company. Marketing when it received the money had notice of the facts and was a volunteer in the sense that it did not give valuable consideration for the money. Marketing accordingly held the £60,000 as a constructive trustee for the company'.[89]

This results in the imposition of a personal remedy against the recipient parent company. If it were a volunteer, though, and the funds could be traced, then there could have been a proprietary remedy against it, regardless of its knowledge of the facts.[90]

The other major consequence of the payment of an unlawful dividend is that the directors will be liable to compensate the company for losses. As Jessel MR in *Re Exchange Banking Co (Flitcroft's Case)*[91] explained:

> '[i]t follows then that if the directors who are *quasi*-trustees of the company improperly pay away the assets to the shareholders, they are liable to replace them. ... I am of opinion that the company could in its corporate capacity compel them to do so, even if there were no winding up. They are liable to pay, and none the less liable because the liquidator represents, not only shareholders, but creditors. The body of the shareholders no doubt voted for a declaration of dividend on the faith of the misrepresentation of the directors, so that there was really no ratification at all.'[92]

Since the act of unlawfully repaying money to shareholders is outside the statutory corporate powers and therefore ultra vires, the shareholders even acting unanimously would not be able to ratify and approve of what the directors had done.[93] Certainly directors will be liable if they knew that there was no power to pay dividends at the time and similarly if they were mistaken as to the law in relation to the paying of dividends. But if they act honestly and without negligence in paying dividends while, for example, relying on the accounts, then they will not be liable.[94]

BONUS SHARES

Instead of distributing all the distributable profit by way of dividend the company may decide to 'capitalise' the profit and issue bonus shares to members. This issue is known as a 'capitalisation issue'. The profit is transferred to the share capital account, essentially to pay for the bonus shares, which are then issued to the shareholders as either fully or partly paid up. The issued share capital of the company is then increased by that amount. In this way the shareholders are receiving extra shares rather than cash. However, the individual value of each share may be 'watered down', because in a case where a company has large reserves of profit and a relatively small number of issued

---

89 [1986] Ch 447 at 457.

90 *Re Diplock* [1948] Ch 94.

91 (1882) 21 Ch D 519.

92 *Ibid* at 534.

93 See, for example, *Aveling Barford Ltd v Perion Ltd* [1989] BCLC 626 on unlawful return of capital and ratification.

94 *Dovey v Cory* [1901] AC 477.

shares, a valuer may place a high value on each share. If the profits are capitalised and bonus shares issued, there are necessarily more issued shares, so their individual value is reduced but the overall value of the members' total holding will stay more or less the same.

Article 110 of Table A provides that the directors may, with the authority of an ordinary resolution from general meeting, resolve to capitalise any undivided profits (not required for paying any preferential dividend), whether or not they are available for distribution, or any sum standing to the credit of the company's share premium account or capital redemption reserve.

SERIOUS LOSS OF CAPITAL

Section 142, the predecessor of which was first enacted in the Companies Act 1980, requires the directors of a public company to convene an extraordinary general meeting where the net assets of the company fall to half or less of its called-up share capital. The meeting must be convened not later than 28 days from the earliest day on which that fact is known to a director and the meeting should then be held not later than 56 days from that day for the purpose of considering whether any, and if so what, steps should be taken to deal with the situation. If the directors fail to convene such a meeting then they are each liable to a fine.

CHAPTER EIGHT

SHARES

THE NATURE OF SHARES

A literal construction of the word 'share' is apt to be misleading in relation to the present day registered company. The purchase of shares in a company does not mean that the shareholder has a 'share' in the property of the company. The company's property is owned both legally and beneficially by the company, so shareholders are not joint owners of the company's property,[1] nor can a shareholder even be said to have an equitable interest in the company property. The most famous definition of a share is that of Farwell J in *Borland's Trustee v Steel*[2] where he states that:

> 'a share is the interest of a shareholder in the company measured by a sum of money, for the purpose of liability in the first place, and of interest in the second, but also consisting of a series of mutual covenants entered into by all the shareholders *inter se* in accordance with [s 14]. The contract contained in the articles of association is one of the original incidents of the share. A share is not a sum of money ... but is an interest measured by a sum of money and made up of various rights contained in the contract, including the right to a sum of money of a more or less amount.'[3]

This definition characterises the shares as a bundle of rights stemming from the s 14 contract. Typical of the rights which the shareholder enjoys are the right to vote, participate in dividends when a distribution is made and the return of capital when the company is wound up. There is no doubt that from this bundle of contractual rights the share has emerged as a piece of personal, intangible property, that is to say it is a chose in action. It can be owned, bought and sold, mortgaged and it will form part of the estate of a deceased person. Shares can also be held on trust, thus separating the legal from the equitable, beneficial ownership of them.

The share in a registered company remains personal property regardless of the kind of property owned by a company, so even if the company's only asset is real property the shares will still be personal property. Section 182 confirms this by stating that the shares or other interests of any member in a company are personal estate and are not in the nature of real estate.

There is a common law presumption that all the shares in the company enjoy the same or equal rights and therefore that there is equality between the shareholders. So, for example, in *Birch v Cropper*[4] the House of Lords held that in a winding up of a company which had issued both fully and partly paid shares after the return of capital to

---

1 *Bligh v Brent* (1837) 2 Y & C Ex 268.
2 [1901] 1 Ch 279.
3 *Ibid* at 288.
4 (1889) 14 App Cas 525.

the shareholders they were all to be equally entitled as far as a distribution of the surplus assets of the company was concerned. Similarly, in the absence of anything to the contrary in the company's constitution or the terms of issue, the ordinary and preference shareholders enjoyed the same rights to a return of capital in proportion to the amount paid up on their shares in the winding up.

This presumption of equality can be displaced by provisions in the memorandum or articles or in the terms of issue of the shares providing that different shares will enjoy different rights. Further, where there is no such provision in the memorandum or articles giving the company power to issue shares with different rights, this does not prevent a company from subsequently altering the constitution to give itself the power. In *Andrews v Gas Meter Co*[5] where the company's articles were altered to authorise the issue of preference shares, a claim that there was a condition contained in the memorandum that all shareholders were to be treated equally unless the memorandum itself shows the contrary was rejected.

THE POWER TO ALLOT SHARES

Normally the board of directors will have the powers of management given to them by the articles of association. One of the functions of management will be to decide the question of whether the company needs extra resources and how these are to be obtained and one of the obvious ways is by issuing further shares. So, these management articles, such as article 70 of Table A, give the directors the power to allot or issue further shares in the company. As demonstrated in such cases as *Howard Smith Ltd v Ampol Petroleum Ltd*,[6] this power can be used abusively, and can be used to effect purposes which go beyond the original or main purpose of raising extra finance, for example, to manipulate the voting structure of the general meeting. In the Companies Act 1980 a new section was enacted, which is now s 80 of the 1985 Act, which places controls on the directors' powers to issue shares. This section provides that the directors shall not exercise any power of the company to allot shares, unless they are, in accordance with s 80 or s 80A, authorised to do so by:

(a) the company in general meeting; or

(b) the company's articles.

The authority referred to can be given for a particular exercise of the power or for its exercise generally and may be unconditional or subject to conditions. The authority must, though, state the maximum amount of shares that may be allotted and the date when the authority will expire. This date cannot be more than five years from:

(a) in the case of an authority contained in the company's articles when the company was incorporated, the date of incorporation;

(b) in any other case, the date on which the resolution is passed conferring the authority.[7]

---

5   [1897] 1 Ch 361, not following the decision in *Hutton v Scarborough Cliff Hotel Co Ltd* (1865) 2 Dr & Sim 521.

6   [1974] AC 821.

7   Companies Act 1985, s 80(4).

Any authority conferred on the directors may be revoked or varied by the passing of an ordinary resolution in general meeting.[8] So where the authority is conferred by an article, that authority can be revoked, and hence the article can be altered by an ordinary resolution. Authority can be renewed and further renewed by the passing of an ordinary resolution for a further period not exceeding five years.[9] This renewal must also state the maximum amount of shares that may be allotted and time when the authority will expire. In any case where there is a resolution under s 80 to give, vary, revoke or renew authority to allot shares, a copy of the resolution has to be sent to the registrar within 15 days.[10]

As regards the consequences of a breach of s 80 any director who knowingly and wilfully contravenes, or permits or authorises a contravention is liable to a fine, but the fact that an allotment is made without the directors having authority under s 80 will *not* affect the validity of the allotment.[11]

Section 80A was inserted by the Companies Act 1989 and allows a private company to elect by elective resolution to substitute the provisions of this section in place of s 80(4) and (5) in relation to the giving or renewal of authority. Where such an elective resolution is passed, then the authority given to the directors may be given for an indefinite period or for a fixed period, in which case the authority must state the date on which it will expire.[12] This authority must again state the maximum amount of shares under s 80A, and whether it be given by the general meeting or by the company's articles it can be revoked or varied by ordinary resolution.[13] An authority given for a fixed period may be renewed or further renewed by ordinary resolution and this renewal must state the maximum amount of shares which may be allotted under it, and whether the authority is renewed for an indefinite period or for a fixed period.[14]

Where an election under s 80A ceases to have effect, an authority then in force which was given for an indefinite period or for a fixed period of more than five years:

(a) if it was given for five years or more before the election ceases to have effect, shall expire immediately; or

(b) otherwise, it will have effect as if it had been given for a fixed period of five years.[15]

PRE-EMPTION RIGHTS

Without any rights of pre-emption an existing shareholder in a company would run the risk of the directors allotting new shares to others (either to an outsider or another

---

8   Companies Act 1985, s 80(8).

9   Companies Act 1985, s 80(5).

10   Companies Act 1985, s 80(8).

11   Companies Act 1985, s 80(9) and (10).

12   Companies Act 1985, s 80A(2).

13   Companies Act 1985, s 80A(3).

14   Companies Act 1985, s 80A(4).

15   Companies Act 1985, s 80A(7).

existing shareholder) thus reducing the percentage of votes held by the shareholder and therefore the legal control he was able to exercise in general meeting. Before the Companies Act 1980, the position in private companies was determined by the articles, and the position for public companies listed on the Stock Exchange was governed by the 'Yellow Book' listing rules, which provided that new shares in listed companies should first be offered to the existing shareholders in proportion to the amount of shares they already held. The Companies Act 1980 enacted a new statutory right of pre-emption to protect existing shareholders pursuant to the requirements of the Second EEC Directive.[16] This statutory right is now contained in ss 89–95 of the 1985 Act and it applies to both public and private companies. The provisions are extremely complex and only an outline is given here.

The basic right is contained in s 89(1) and applies to equity securities, which are defined by s 94. It is a complex definition but it basically includes ordinary shares and preference shares which carry a right to participate in the surplus assets of a winding up.

Section 89(1) provides that, where a company is proposing to allot the above shares for cash to any person, it shall not allot them unless it has made an offer by subscription, to each of the existing shareholders who holds these shares on the same or more favourable terms, of a proportion of the shares which is equal to the proportion in nominal value held by him of the aggregate of issued shares. In other words the right gives that existing shareholder the opportunity to purchase enough of the new shares so that he will hold the same proportion of the issued share capital as he did before the new issue. This new issue is known as a 'rights issue'.

So the company will have to offer by subscription the new shares in these proportions to its existing shareholders at the same price and on the same terms. This offer has to be made in writing and must be made to the shareholder personally or by sending it by post.[17] The company must then wait 21 days during which the offer may be accepted, rejected or ignored by the shareholders and then it may allot the shares which have not been taken up either to the other shareholders or outsiders but not at a more favourable price nor on more favourable terms.[18]

There are certain exceptions to this statutory right, the principal ones being as follows:

1   Where the directors are generally authorised for the purposes of s 80 to allot shares, they may be given power either by the articles or by a special resolution to allot shares pursuant to that authority as if the statutory right of pre-emption continued in s 89(1) did not apply.[19]

2   A private company may exclude the statutory right of pre-emption by a provision to that effect in the memorandum or articles of the company.[20]

---

16   77/91/EEC.
17   Companies Act 1985, s 90.
18   Companies Act 1985, s 90(6).
19   Companies Act 1985, s 95(1).
20   Companies Act 1985, s 91.

3 There are special provisions in relation to employee share schemes, ie a scheme for encouraging or facilitating the holding of shares in a company by or for the benefits of *bona fide* employees or former employees of the company or the wives, husbands, widows, widowers, children or step-children under the age of 18 of such employees or former employees. The object of the schemes is to encourage the workforce to participate in the profits which they have helped to make for the company. The shares which are allotted under this sort of scheme are not subject to the statutory pre-emption right, otherwise the scheme could not properly operate. But if shares have already been allotted under a scheme, then the shareholders under the scheme do have the benefit of the statutory right to preserve their position in the same way as other existing shareholders.[21]

Where there is a breach of the pre-emption provisions the company and every officer who knowingly authorised or permitted the contravention, are jointly and severally liable to compensate any person to whom an offer should have been made for any loss, damage, costs or expenses which the person has sustained or incurred by reason of the contravention.[22] No criminal offence is committed by the company or its officers.

PAYMENT FOR SHARES

As stated in the previous chapter, when a company allots shares, they cannot be allotted at a discount, and the allottee must pay the full nominal value for them plus any premium.[23] The general rule is, though, that the shares allotted by a company and any premium on them may be paid up in money or money's worth which includes goodwill and know-how.[24] The position where the company is accepting a non-cash consideration for shares is substantially different depending on whether the company is public or private.

Non-cash allotments by a private company

The common law has always been liberal in respect of non-cash consideration for shares in a company, most famously the House of Lords' benign view of the overvaluation of the business which Salomon was transferring to Salomon & Co Ltd in return for shares and debentures.[25] First, as to the nature of the non-cash consideration, there are no requirements as long as what is being transferred to the company is valuable consideration. So that, for example, an agreement to provide services to the company in return for shares would be acceptable, but not if the services have already been rendered, since that would amount to past consideration.[26]

---

21 Companies Act 1985, s 91.
22 Companies Act 1985, s 92.
23 See p 143.
24 Companies Act 1985, s 99.
25 *Salomon v Salomon & Co Ltd* [1897] AC 22.
26 *Re Eddystone Marine Insurance Co* [1893] 3 Ch 9.

Second, as to the value placed upon the non-cash consideration, the courts will not enquire into the value of this consideration if there appears to be a genuine transaction. As Lindley LJ stated in *Re Wragg*:[27]

> 'As regards the value of the property which a company can take from a shareholder in satisfaction of his liability to pay the amount of his shares, there has been some difference of opinion. But it was ultimately decided by the Court of Appeal that, unless the agreement pursuant to which the shares were to be paid for in property or services could be impeached for fraud, the value of the property or services could not be enquired into. In other words, the value at which the company is content to accept the property must be treated as its value as between itself and the shareholder whose liability is discharged by its means.'[28]

And in the view of A L Smith LJ:

> 'If ... the consideration which the company has agreed to accept as representing in money's worth the nominal value of the shares be a consideration not clearly colourable nor illusory, then, in my judgment, the adequacy of the consideration cannot be impeached by a liquidator unless the contract can also be impeached; and I take it to be the law that it is not open to a liquidator, unless he is able to impeach the agreement, to go into the adequacy of the consideration to show that the company have agreed to give an excessive value for what they have purchased.'[29]

So as long as the directors, in agreeing the terms of the contract of allotment, are genuinely and honestly of the view that the company is receiving property or services of the same value as the nominal value of the shares, the allotment will be valid. If it is clear from the face of the agreement itself that the company is to receive less than the nominal value of the shares in return for an allotment of shares, and the directors could not possibly have been of the view that the company was receiving property of equal value, then the allotment will not be valid.[30]

Non-cash allotments by a public company

As is to be expected there are greater controls on a public company issuing shares for consideration other than cash. The current provisions in the Companies Act were introduced by the Companies Act 1980 in order to comply with the requirements of the Second EEC Directive.

First, by s 99(2) a public company cannot accept at any time an undertaking given by any person that he or another should do work or perform services for the company in payment up of its shares or any premium on them. If a public company does accept such an undertaking, the holder of the shares at the time when they or the premium are treated as paid up by the undertaking is liable:

---

27   [1897] 1 Ch 796.

28   *Ibid* at 826.

29   *Ibid* at 836.

30   *Re White Star Line Ltd* [1938] 1 All ER 607; *Hong Kong and China Gas Co Ltd v Glen* [1914] 1 Ch 527.

(a) to pay the company an amount equal to the nominal value of the shares together with the whole of the premium or, such proportion of that amount as is treated as being paid up by the undertaking; and

(b) to pay interest on the amount payable.[31]

Second, by s 101 a public company cannot allot a share unless it is paid up at least as to one quarter of its nominal value and the whole of the premium on it. This provision does not apply to an employees' share scheme.[32] If a public company does allot a share in contravention of s 101, the share is to be treated as if one quarter of its nominal value, together with the whole of any premium on it, had been received, but the allottee is liable to pay to the company an amount which should have been paid in respect of the share credit being given for any consideration which has actually been paid, with interest.[33]

Third, by s 102 a public company cannot allot shares as fully or partly paid up, as to their nominal value or any premium on them, otherwise than for cash if the non-cash consideration for the allotment is or includes an undertaking which is to be, or may be, performed more than five years after the date of the allotment. If the company does allot shares in contravention of s 102, the allottee is liable to pay the company an amount equal to the aggregate nominal value and the whole of any premium with interest at the appropriate rate. The same liability is incurred by the allottee where there is an allotment for a consideration which consists of or includes an undertaking which is to be performed *within* five years of the allotment, but the undertaking is not performed within the period stated in the contract for the allotment. In this case the allottee is liable to pay at the end of the period provided by the contract.[34]

Fourth, a public company cannot allot shares either as fully or partly paid up, as to their nominal value or any premium, otherwise than in cash unless the consideration has been independently valued and the report concerning the value of the consideration has been made by the valuer to the company during the six months immediately preceding the allotment.[35] A copy of the report also has to be sent to the proposed allottee. If there is an allotment in contravention of this section and either the allottee has not received the valuer's report required by s 103(1) or there has been some other contravention of s 103 or s 108 which the allottee knew or ought to have known amounted to a contravention, the allottee is liable to pay the company an amount equal to the aggregate of the nominal value of the shares and the whole of the premium with interest.[36] Sections 108 to 111 provide for the procedure to be undertaken on valuation and the contents of the valuer's report.

---

31 Currently 5% per annum.
32 Companies Act 1985, s 101(2).
33 Companies Act 1985, s 101(3) and (4).
34 Companies Act 1985, s 102(6).
35 Companies Act 1985, s 103.
36 Companies Act 1985, s 103(6).

The company must deliver a copy of the report to the registrar for registration at the same time that it files the return of the allotments themselves, as it is required to do under s 88. Where shares are issued in contravention of the provisions dealing with payment for shares on allotment and as a result the original owner of them becomes liable to pay a certain amount to the company, a subsequent owner of the shares will also be *prima facie* jointly and severally liable in respect of that amount. But a subsequent owner will be exempted from liability if either he is a purchaser for value and, at the time of the purchase, he did not have actual notice of the contravention, or he derived title to the shares from a person who himself became a holder of the shares after the contravention but was not liable because of the exemption.[37]

A person who is otherwise liable to a company as a result of a contravention of the above provisions relating to the payment for shares in a public company on subscription may make an application to the court under s 113 to be exempted in whole or in part from the liability. The court's power to exempt a person from liability under s 113 is limited in that it must appear to the court to be just and equitable to do so and the court is directed to take into account a number of factors of which the overriding ones are:

(a) 'that a company which has allotted shares should receive money or money's worth at least equal in value to the aggregate of the nominal value of those shares and the whole of any premium, or, if the case so requires, so much of that aggregate as is treated as paid up'; and

(b) subject to this, that where such a company would, if the court did not grant the exemption, have more than one remedy against a particular person, it should be for the company to decide which remedy it should remain entitled to pursue.

Paragraph (a) may be satisfied, for example, where the non-cash consideration was an asset which has since the allotment appreciated in value and has been sold by the company for a cash sum greater than the nominal value of the shares allotted.

CLASSES OF SHARES

As stated in an earlier section of this chapter there is a presumption of equality between the shareholders of a company. But a company does not have to issue shares which all confer the same rights on the shareholders. A company can, and often will, issue shares of different classes conferring different rights in respect of voting, dividends and return of capital in a winding up. The most common classes of shares are ordinary and preference.

Ordinary shares

The term is used to refer to the shares which are not given any special rights. If the company issues shares which all enjoy uniform rights they will be ordinary shares. But should the company confer special rights on some of its issued shares then the shares

---

37 Companies Act 1985, s 112.

not enjoying those rights will be classed as the ordinary shares. The usual position is that the ordinary shares would carry the voting rights in general meeting, carry on entitlement to any surplus assets in a winding up and have no fixed rate of dividend. This gives the ordinary shareholder the power to influence the policies of the company but makes his investment more speculative than the preference shareholder. In a financial year where the company makes a considerable profit and makes a large distribution by way of dividend the ordinary shareholder has a right to participate after the preference shareholder rateably in the funds available. But should the company have a poor year when little profit is made the ordinary shareholder will receive very little or perhaps nothing. The position of the preference shareholder then is significantly better.

Preference shares

The most notable feature of preference shares is that they will normally have an entitlement to a fixed rate of dividend, usually expressed as a percentage of the nominal value of the shares themselves. This fixed rate dividend will be paid in priority to the dividends payable to the ordinary shareholders. The preference shareholder will not have an entitlement to a dividend, though, (unless there is a specific agreement to the contrary), and will only receive a dividend in a particular year if the directors decide to declare one.[38] In that respect they are more like the ordinary shareholder than the debentureholder who will be entitled to a fixed rate of interest every year.

The distributable profit in a poor year can be exhausted entirely in satisfying the claims of the preference shareholders without the ordinary shareholders receiving anything. If the company has performed so badly in a financial year so that there is no distributable profit or not sufficient to satisfy the whole amount to which the preference shareholder is entitled, the preference shareholder may still be in a better position than the ordinary shareholder because the preference share may well be cumulative, in which case arrears of preference dividend will be carried forward and paid out of the distributable profits made in subsequent years, and that is of course before the ordinary shareholder will receive anything. There is a presumption that preferential dividends are to be cumulative unless the terms of issue state otherwise.[39]

A cumulative or non-cumulative preference share will prima facie only be entitled to the fixed, preferential dividend. It is possible though that the preference shares are issued expressly on the basis that they are to have a further entitlement to participate in the surplus profits with the shareholders after their preference dividend has been paid, and after the ordinary shareholders' dividend has been paid up to the same amount. Whether the preference share carries this right will be determined solely by the express terms of issue. As Viscount Haldane LC in *Will v United Lankat Plantations Co Ltd*[40] stated:

---

38 *Bond v Barrow Haematite Steel Co* [1902] 1 Ch 353.

39 *Henry v Great Northern Rly Co* (1857) 1 De G & J 606.

40 [1914] AC 11.

'Shares are not issued in the abstract and priorities then attached to them; the issue of shares and the attachment of priorities proceed *uno flatu* [in one breath]; and when you turn to the terms on which the shares are issued you expect to find all the rights as regards dividends specified in the terms of the issue.'[41]

Again, therefore, unless there is a specific statement to the contrary in the company's constitution or terms of issue, preference shares will not enjoy a priority to the return of capital in a winding up but they will rank equally with the ordinary shareholders.[42]

In the absence of anything to the contrary, the preference shareholders will enjoy the same rights to attend and vote at general meetings as the ordinary shareholders, but often their rights in this respect will be expressly excluded or restricted so that they will only vote in limited circumstances.

VARIATION OF CLASS RIGHTS

Procedure

The legislature has intervened to protect the holders of shares enjoying class rights with a procedure which has to be followed before the class right can be varied or abrogated. This procedure is contained in ss 125–27.

Section 125 applies the statutory procedures where there is a proposed variation of the rights attached to any class of shares in a company whose share capital is divided into shares of different classes. Then, by s 125(2), where those rights are *not* attached to a class of shares by the memorandum and the company's articles do not contain provisions with respect to the variation of the rights, those rights may only be varied if:

(a) the holders of three quarters in nominal value of the issued shares of that class consent in writing to the variation; or

(b) by an extraordinary resolution passed at a separate meeting one of the holders of that class sanctions the variation.

Further, any other requirement (howsoever imposed, but normally contained in the articles) in relation to the variation of rights has to be complied with. So s 125(2) sets a minimum procedure which can be made by even more stringent by any additional procedures which may be laid down in the articles.

Where the articles do contain a provision for variation of class rights then the rights may only be varied in accordance with those provisions in the articles except in specified cases. So the articles may lay down a more relaxed procedure except in those specified cases.[43]

If the class rights are attached by the memorandum, and the memorandum and articles do not contain a provision with respect to the variation of those rights, then

---

41   *Ibid* at 17.

42   *Birch v Cropper* (1889) 4 App Cas 525.

43   Companies Act 1985, s 125(4).

those rights may be varied if all the members of the company agree to the variation.[44] Thus the class rights have a greater unalterability in that case.

Any alteration of a provision in the articles for the variation of class rights or the insertion of such a provision into the articles, is itself to be treated as a variation of those class rights.[45]

By s 127 a dissentient minority of the holders of the class whose rights are being varied are given a statutory right to object to the variation. The right applies where there is a provision in the memorandum or articles for authorising the variation of rights attached to any class of shares which can operate only on the consent of any specified proportion or a resolution of the classholders or the rights are varied under s 125(2). When this is the case then the holders of not less than 15% of the issued shares of that class may apply to the court within 21 days of the consent or resolution to vary the rights to have the variation cancelled. On such an application the variation does not have effect unless and until it is confirmed by the court. The court, after hearing the application can, if it is satisfied that the variation would unfairly prejudice the shareholders of the class represented by the plaintiff, disallow the variation or, if not so satisfied, confirm it.

Meaning of class rights

The next question is to determine precisely what are 'class rights' which will invoke ss 125-127 if there is a proposal for alteration or variation. The leading case is now the first instance judgment of Scott J in *Cumbrian Newspapers Group Ltd v Cumberland & Westmorland Herald Newspapers and Printing Co Ltd.*[46]

Here the plaintiff company acquired 10% of the defendant company's shares. The defendant's articles were then altered giving the plaintiff, which was referred to by name, rights of pre-emption over other issued shares of the defendant and rights of pre-emption over unissued shares and further, the right while it held not less than 10% of the defendant's shares to appoint a director to the board of the defendant. The object of the altered articles was to prevent the defendant from being taken over by a third party without the consent of the plaintiff. It was important to those controlling the plaintiff that the defendant continue to be an independent company publishing an independent local newspaper. Subsequently the defendant company proposed to alter the articles deleting those which conferred the rights on the plaintiff. The plaintiff brought this action for a declaration that the articles conferred class rights on it and therefore they could not be abrogated or varied without compliance with s 125 which in this case would mean obtaining the plaintiff's consent. This claim was upheld by Scott J who analysed the type of rights which can be conferred by the articles into three categories:

---

44   Companies Act 1985, s 125(5).
45   Companies Act 1985, s 125(7).
46   [1987] Ch 1.

1   Rights or benefits which are annexed to particular shares such as dividend rights and rights to participate in surplus assets on a winding up. 'If articles provide that particular shares carry particular rights not enjoyed by the holders of other shares, it is easy to conclude that the rights are "attached to a class of shares" for the purpose of ... s 125.'[47]

2   Rights or benefits which may be contained in articles which are conferred on individuals not in the capacity of members or shareholders of the company. An example would be the article which provided that Eley should be the company's solicitor in *Eley v Positive Government Security Life Assurance Co Ltd*.[48] '[I]f ... rights or benefits conferred by the article were not conferred on the beneficiary in the capacity of member or shareholder of the company, then the rights could not ... be regarded as class rights. They would not be "rights attached to any class of shares".'[49]

3   Rights or benefits that, although not attached to any particular shares, were nonetheless conferred on the beneficiary in the capacity of member or shareholder of the company. The rights which the plaintiffs enjoyed here were of this third category. They would only be enjoyed, on a proper construction of the articles, during the time when the plaintiff was a shareholder of the company, or in respect of the right to appoint a director, while it held at least 10% of the shares.

After an analysis of ss 125–27 Scott J concluded that rights in the first and third category were class rights for the purposes of those sections and that it was the legislative intention not only to extend protection to rights following in the first but also this last category. This was a surprisingly wide interpretation of the phrase 'rights attached to any class of shares'. It would, as Scott J himself pointed out, have the consequences that shares may come into or go out of a particular class on the acquisition or disposal of the shares by a particular individual. The particular shares held by the plaintiff have constituted a 'class for the time being' different from all other shares. Here, for example, the right to appoint a director was conferred on the plaintiff as long as it held at least 10% of *any* of the shares in the defendant. The rights therefore seem to be attached to the plaintiff itself rather than the shares as required by s 125.

Voting at class meetings on a proposed variation

It has been established that when the holders of the class of shares vote on a resolution to vary the class rights they must vote having regard principally to the benefit of the class as a whole. As Viscount Haldane stated in *British America Nickel Corpn Ltd v O'Brien*[50] in a modification of the *Allen v Gold Reefs of West Africa* principle:

> 'There is, however, a restriction of ... powers [to vote on a resolution] when conferred on a majority of a special class in order to enable that majority to bind a minority. They

47   *Ibid* at 15.
48   (1876) 1 ExD 88.
49   [1987] Ch 1 at 16.
50   [1927] AC 369.

must be exercised subject to a general principle, which is applicable to all authorities conferred on majorities of classes enabling them to bind minorities; namely, that the power given must be exercised for the purpose of benefiting the class as a whole, and not merely individual members only ... their Lordships do not think that there is any real difficulty in combining the principle that while usually a holder of shares ... may vote as his interest directs, he is subject to the further principle that where his vote is conferred on him as member of a class he must conform to the interest of the class itself when seeking to exercise the power conferred on him in his capacity of being a member. The second principle is a negative one, one which puts a restriction on the completeness of freedom under the first, without excluding such freedom wholly.'[51]

What may be difficult to accept, however, is the result of this reasoning when the proposed variation of class rights is obviously detrimental to the interests of the class but for the benefit of the company as a whole. At a meeting, subsequent to the class meeting, to pass a special resolution altering the article, the shareholder may have been required to vote for the proposal. At the prior class meeting he is required to vote against the proposal.[52]

What is a variation of class rights?

Section 125(8) and s 127(6) provide that references to variation of class rights are to be read as including references to their abrogation. Apart from this and s 125(7), which provides that an alteration of a provision contained in a company's articles for the variation of class rights is also a variation of class rights, reference must be made to the cases on what constitutes variation.

White v Bristol Aeroplane Co[53] involved a most basic complaint amongst existing shareholders, namely that an issue of further shares in the company would reduce the total voting power of the preference shareholders so that their voting rights were being 'varied'. This was rejected with the Court of Appeal making the distinction between rights and the result of an exercise of those rights:

'the rights [of voting] are conferred by resolution or by the articles, and they cannot be affected except with the sanction of the members on whom rights are conferred; but the results of exercising those rights [ie voting as a certain percentage in general meeting] are not the subject of any assurance or guarantee under the constitution of the company, and are not protected in any way.'[54]

The question of whether or not there has been an abrogation or variation of class rights has arisen in the context of reductions of capital where the company in general meeting resolves by special resolution to reduce capital by, for example, repaying and cancelling all of the preference shares. In the cases, where the preference shareholders have claimed that this is an abrogation of their class rights and therefore there should have

---

51 *Ibid* at 371.
52 See also *Re Holders Investment Trust* [1971] 1 WLR 583.
53 [1953] Ch 65.
54 *Ibid* at 82 *per* Romer LJ.

been a class meeting held to vote on the reduction they, have failed. In *Re Saltdean Co Ltd*[55] Buckley J, citing the judgment of Lord Greene MR in *Re Chatterley-Whitfield Collieries Ltd*[56] for the principle that on a reduction of capital, the shareholders who would receive a prior repayment of capital in a winding up would be the first to be repaid and cancelled on a reduction of capital, said that where here the preferred shareholders did have such rights to a priority, they could not complain of an abrogation to any class right since the prior repayment on a reduction was:

> 'part of the bargain between the shareholders and forms an integral part of the definition and delimitation of the bundle of rights which make up a preferred share.'[57]

Any shareholder who was not aware of this only had himself to blame. Again in *House of Fraser plc v ACGE Investments Ltd*[58] the House of Lords held that the cancellation of preference shares on a reduction of capital was simply the fulfilment or satisfaction of the contractual rights of preference shareholders.

TRANSFER OF SHARES

Unless there are any restrictions placed in the company's articles of association the shares of a company are freely transferable. The former requirement for private companies to restrict the transferability of their shares was abolished in 1980 although many private companies, especially smaller, family companies, will have pre-emption provisions in the articles obliging, for example, an existing member who wishes to sell his shares to offer them for sale to existing members first. These clauses, while *prima facie* perfectly valid, will be strictly construed. Where a public company has a quotation for its fully paid shares then the Stock Exchange's Listing Rules require that there should not be any restriction on the transfer of the shares.[59]

Directors' powers to refuse registration of a new member

Another way of restricting the transferability of shares is to insert into the articles a clause giving the directors the power to refuse to register a transfer of shares. Article 24 of Table A gives the directors the power to refuse to register the transfer of a partly paid share to a person of whom they do not approve, most obviously because the proposed transferee would not be able to satisfy any further calls on the shares. There is no right given to directors to refuse to register transfers of fully paid shares in Table A.

It has been held that, although directors must exercise their discretion under these powers *bona fide* in what they consider to be the interests of the company, if, on a proper construction of the article conferring the power, they are given absolute and

---

55   [1968] 3 All ER 829

56   [1948] 2 All ER 593; affirmed *sub nom Prudential Assurance Co Ltd v Chatterley-Whitfield Colleries Ltd* [1949] AC 512.

57   [1968] 3 All ER 829 at 832.

58   [1987] AC 387.

59   This is a requirement of the Admission Directive (79/279/EEC) and is now contained in para 3.15 of the Listing Rules.

uncontrolled discretion, then the court will give effect to that and not impose any other limitations. The leading case is *Re Smith & Fawcett Ltd*,[60] where Lord Greene MR states as one of the reasons why such clauses should be given full effect that:

'this type of article is one which is for the most part confined to private companies. Private companies are in law separate entities just as much as public companies, but from the business and personal point of view they are much more analogous to partnerships than to public corporations. Accordingly, it is to be expected that in the articles of such a company the control of the directors over the membership may be very strict indeed. There are, or may be, very good business reasons why those who bring such companies into existence should give them a constitution which confers on the directors powers of the widest description.'[61]

Although, as Lord Greene MR also points out, the right of a shareholder to deal freely with his property and to transfer it to whomsoever he pleases, should be cut down only by clear and unambiguous language.[62]

The principle of *Re Smith & Fawcett* means that the directors can refuse to register a transfer without giving any reason. The transferee can only compel a registration if he can show lack of *bona fides*. The court will presume that the directors did exercise their powers honestly and rightly, unless it appears on the face of a document or in a confession by the directors that they have not done so.

Section 183(5) provides that if a company refuses to register a transfer of shares the company shall, within two months after the date on which the transfer was lodged with it, send to the transferee notice of the refusal (this is the position adopted in Table A article 25). If no decision is taken within the two-month period then the rights of the directors to refuse to register the right lapses and the transferee can apply to the court for a rectification to the register of members.[63]

Method of transfer

The articles will provide for the procedures to be followed for the transfer of shares and in addition the provisions of the Stock Transfer Act 1963 will have to be complied with if they are applicable. Section 183(1) of the 1985 Act provides that it is unlawful for a company to register a transfer of shares unless a proper instrument of transfer has been delivered to it, and this applies notwithstanding any provisions in the articles. So, for example, where there was a provision in a company's articles that, on the death of a shareholder his shares were to vest automatically in his widow, the transfer was held to be void.[64] Section 183(2) does not prevent the company from registering as members persons to whom shares have been transmitted by operation of law, so that for

---

60   [1942] Ch 304.

61   *Ibid* at 306.

62   *Re Copal Varnish* [1971] 2 Ch 349.

63   Companies Act 1985, s 359. But see *Popely v Planarrive Ltd* (1996) *The Times*, April 24. See also *Re Swaledale Cleaners* [1968] 1 WLR 1710 a decision under the common law requirement that a decision be taken with a reasonable time which was *prima facie* two months.

64   *Re Greene* [1949] Ch 333.

example, personal representatives and trustees in bankruptcy have a right to be registered as members without delivering an instrument of transfer.

The instrument of transfer itself has to be in writing and signed by the transferor. It does not have to be by deed unless the company's articles so require. Article 23 of Table A does not require a deed; the transfer can be effected 'in any usual form'.

As far as fully paid up shares are concerned a transferor may employ an instrument of transfer provided by the Stock Transfer Act 1963 which was passed to simplify the transfer of shares. In practice these will be the forms used in most transfers of shares. The forms provided by the Act do not replace those which may be provided by the articles but they provide a valid alternative and their use in respect of fully paid up shares of companies registered under the 1985 Act (except companies limited by guarantee and unlimited companies) cannot be excluded by the company's constitution, but the use of the form does not remove the directors' discretion under an appropriate article to refuse the registration of the new member. The instrument provided by Schedule 1 of the 1963 Act must be executed by the transferor but it need not be executed by the transferee. It must contain a description of the shares and the number or amount of them. It must also include the amount of consideration paid for the transfer. The form concludes with a request that such entries in the company's register of members be made as are necessary to give effect to the transfer.

Where the transfer is of unlisted shares then the transferor, after executing the transfer form, delivers the form together with the share certificate to the transferee and then the transferee sends the documents to the company for registration. If the share transfer form is not one provided by the 1963 Act then it will need to be executed by the transferee before being sent to the company. By s 22(2) of the 1985 Act a member is a person who agrees to become a member of a company and whose name is entered in its register of members. The execution by the transferee proves that he has agreed to become a member; when a transferee has not executed the transfer form, because a form under the 1963 Act has been used, the company will need to satisfy itself in some other way that the transferee has agreed to become a member. The transferee will then be entered on the register of members and receive a new share certificate.

The share certificate issued under the common seal of the company specifying any shares held by a member is *prima facie* but not conclusive evidence of the title to those shares.[65] Where, however, the holder of the shares obtained them from a transferor who himself did not have a good title to them, the name of the person who is properly entitled to them will be entered on the register and the holder of the certificate will lose any right to them. But where a *bona fide* purchaser has acquired the shares for value and has relied on a certificate issued to the transferor by the company which was shown to him, then the company will be estopped from denying that the transferor had title to the shares.[66]

---

65   Companies Act 1985, s 186.

66   *Re Bahia and San Francisco Rly Co* (1868) LR 3 QB 584.

It is not until the transferee is registered as a new member that the legal title to the shares will pass to him. This does not apply to share warrants or bearer shares which can be issued under the company's common seal in respect of fully paid shares if the company's articles so provide (Table A does not so provide). By s 188(2) these are transferable by delivery. The bearer or 'holder' of the share warrant may then surrender it to the company, when it will be cancelled and the bearer then registered as a member of the company in respect of the shares in the warrant.

Transfer of shares in a listed company

Currently almost all transfers of listed securities are under a centralised system controlled by the Stock Exchange known as TALISMAN. The main feature of this system is a company incorporated by the Stock Exchange called SEPON Ltd. This company's function is to hold shares as a nominee in listed companies which are in the process of being transferred. It therefore becomes a member of listed companies so that it can hold these shares, but it is not issued with a share certificate.[67]

A person who holds listed securities and who contracts to sell them, transfers them to SEPON by using a 'Talisman Sold Transfer' form. A person then buying listed shares buys through a Stock Exchange member firm from SEPON using a 'Talisman Bought Transfer' form.[68]

It is planned to replace the use of forms entirely by a computerised system of transfer. The original proposal, called TAURUS, was abandoned during its development in 1993 but a new system, CREST, is being developed and is planned for introduction in late 1996.

DISCLOSURE OF INTEREST IN SHARES

The register of members on its own is not a reliable source of information about who is actually beneficially entitled to the shares, or who has interests in it, or who can exercise control over it. This is because the person whose name is registered may only be holding the shares as a nominee for someone else and further, by s 360 no notice of any trust, express, implied or constructive shall be entered on the register or be receivable by the registrar, so that that person could be holding the shares as trustee for someone else, which is a fact not discoverable from the register itself. To attempt to deal with abuses which can result from this situation the Companies Acts have progressively from 1967 added disclosure provisions in respect of certain types of shareholdings.

Directors' shareholdings

By s 324 a director of a company is under an obligation to notify the company in writing of his shareholding in the company including the number of shares of each class

---

67   Companies Act 1985, s 185(4).

68   These forms are prescribed in the Stock Transfer (Addition of Forms) Order 1979.

and the amount of debentures he holds. A director must also notify the company in writing of any changes in his interests in the shares and if he enters into a contract to sell them. By s 325 the company must keep a register to record these interests. This register is open to inspection by any member of the company free of charge and any other person on payment of a fee.[69] The section also applies to shadow directors and is extended by s 328 to the spouse and children of the directors so that a shareholding of the spouse or children is to be treated as that of the director.

A person who fails to comply with the disclosure obligations of s 324 is guilty of an offence and liable to a fine or imprisonment or both.

Disclosure of substantial interests

By ss 198–220 disclosure requirements are laid down, which require persons who acquire substantial interests in shares carrying a right to vote, to disclose to the company the extent of those interests. This is to prevent the surreptitious accumulation of control of public companies through nominees.

The obligation to disclose arises in certain circumstances when a person, either to his knowledge acquires an interest or ceases to be interested in shares carrying an unrestricted right to vote at general meetings, or becomes aware that he has acquired an interest or has ceased to be interested in such shares.[70] For the purposes of the obligation of disclosure, the circumstances when a person has to notify the company are when he has a notifiable interest as defined by s 199. That section provides that a person has a notifiable interest when he has a material interest in shares having an aggregate nominal value equal to 3% or more of the nominal value of the share capital or when he has an interest equal to or more than 10% of the nominal value of the share capital.

By s 202, where the obligation to make disclosure arises, the notification of the company must be performed within two days following the day on which that obligation arises and the notification must be in writing. The notification must contain particulars about the shares in which the interests are held and state the number of shares held. It must also state the names and addresses of the persons who have the interests. There is also an obligation to notify the company if there are any changes in the particulars.

By s 211 every public company must keep a register of these interests and by s 219 the register is available for inspection by any person, member or not, without charge.

'Concert parties'

There are also provisions which seek to prevent 'concert parties', ie two or more persons acting together, to acquire secretly a public company's shares. Section 204

---

69   Companies Act 1985, Sch 13, Part IV, para 25.

70   Companies Act 1985, s 198(1).

provides that the obligation to disclose can arise from an agreement between two or more persons for the acquisition by them of voting shares in a particular public company. To ensure that these deemed undesirable agreements are caught by the obligation, an agreement has to include a provision imposing obligations or restrictions on one or more of the parties with respect to the use, retention or disposal of their interests and any interest in the company's shares is in fact acquired by any of the parties in pursuance of the agreement.[71]

If there is such an agreement each party to it is taken to be interested in all shares in the company in which any other party is interested whether or not those interests were acquired in pursuance of the agreement.[72] Therefore parties to the agreement will be under an obligation to disclose to the company any interests which they or the 'concert party' as a whole hold of 3% or more or 10% or more of the nominal value of the share capital.

Investigation by the company

A public company may, by notice in writing under s 212, require a person whom the company knows or has reasonable cause to believe to be or, at any time during the previous three years to have been interested in voting shares in the company, to confirm whether or not that is or was the case and to give particulars of his past or present interest in the voting shares of the company. The company is required to keep a register of any information supplied to it under a s 212 investigation which is open to inspection to any person without charge.[73] The members themselves can compel the company to exercise its powers under s 212 if a requisition is deposited with the company by not less than 10% of the paid-up voting share capital of the company. The requisition must give reasonable grounds for requiring the company to exercise its powers. The duties of the company are then to carry out the s 212 investigation and then to prepare a report which is then available for inspection at the company's registered office.[74]

Investigation by the Secretary of State

The Secretary of State is given powers under s 442 to require any person whom he has reasonable cause to believe to have obtained or to be able to obtain information as to the present and past interests in the shares of a company to give that information to him where it appears to him that there is good reason to investigate ownership of the company. The failure to give this information or the giving of false information or giving information recklessly will be a criminal offence.[75]

---

71 Companies Act 1985, s 204(2).
72 Companies Act 1985, s 205(1).
73 Companies Act 1985, s 213, 219.
74 Companies Act 1985, s 214, 215, 219.
75 Companies Act 1985, s 444(3).

The Secretary of State can go further and where it appears to him that there is good reason to do so appoint inspectors under s 442 to investigate and report on the membership of any company for the purpose of determining the true persons who are or have been financially interested in the success or failure of the company or able to control or materially influence its policy.

'Freezing orders'

The ultimate sanction for not complying with a notice served by a company under s 212 or failing to disclose information under s 444 to the Secretary of State or to inspectors under s 442 is that a freezing order can be made, by the court in the former case and by the Secretary of State in the latter cases, imposing a number of restrictions on the shares in respect of voting, powers of transfer and receiving dividends.[76]

---

76 Companies Act 1985, ss 454–57.

CHAPTER NINE

THE REGULATION OF INSIDER DEALING

INTRODUCTION

Press notoriety

If a straw poll was taken involving those reasonable men and women on the Clapham omnibus, most (if not all) of them would have some idea of what constitutes 'insider dealing'. Putting to one side the fact that insider dealing seems to have been a problem from the earliest days of the share 'market' which became the London Stock Exchange,[1] the notoriety this practice enjoys is probably due to the fact that at periodic intervals over the years cases of alleged insider dealing have been reported in lurid fashion in the press.[2] It is unfortunate that subsequent reports of successful prosecutions have been much thinner on the ground and perhaps that is as telling a comment as any on the question of whether insider dealing is readily enforceable as a criminal offence. Insider dealing is however a known quantity.

THE MISCHIEF OF INSIDER DEALING

A general definition

A very generalised attempt at defining the criminal offence of 'insider dealing' would be along the following lines: a case of insider dealing in securities will usually involve the buying or selling of certain securities relating to a company by a person connected with that company[3] who, in doing so, is in possession of specific information which relates to those securities and is not generally known but which would be likely, if made public, to have a significant effect on the market price of the securities. There have of course been closely worded statutory definitions.[4] The mischief which insider

---

1   See Chapter 1 for reference to insider dealing in the early days of the share and stockmarket which subsequently became the Stock Exchange in London.

2   One case of alleged insider dealing referred to recently in the press concerned dealing in the shares of Tiphook (the container and trailer leasing transport group) two days before a profits warning was issued which sent its shares into what the *Times* reported on 8 May 1993 as being '... a nosedive'. The incident prompted Paul Myners, the Chairman of Gartmore Investment Management, to call (in a letter to the *Financial Times*) for a more robust approach to the investigation and prosecution of insider dealing in the City. The Surveillance Unit of the Stock Exchange was believed to have investigated the price movement and to have concluded that the price fall was in line with the transport sector as a whole. Shares in Tiphook had been the subject of 'bear raids' in the past whereby speculators attempted to drive their price downwards to make a profit by selling shares short.

3   Such as a director, shadow director, shareholder, employee or professional adviser.

4   See, for historical interest, ss 9–13 and then ss 1 and 2 Company Securities (Insider Dealing) Act 1985 (1985 c8) (CS (ID) A 1985). The latest definition will be explored later in this chapter, 'Through the posting of a bid'.

dealing law is aimed at preventing, however, is clear. Those close to a company must not be allowed to abuse their position by making use of information in their possession, which concerns securities of that company, to some personal advantage.

Some basic examples of insider dealing

A realistic hypothetical scenario in which insider dealing could occur might involve a director of a merchant bank which was advising a company in the process of mounting a takeover of another company. The fact of the announcement of a takeover offer[5] could well have an immediate effect in pushing up the value of shares in the target company and perhaps also in the bidding company. If the merchant banker in question had acquired some of those shares in advance of the bid announcement, at the pre-bid price, he would be indulging in insider dealing if he disposed of them following the announcement of the bid.[6]

Another scenario might involve the imminent announcement by a company of a particularly profitable year. Such news is likely to force up the market value of shares in the company making them more expensive to acquire but also more profitable to sell. Conversely, the news may relate to the fact of an imminent profits warning by a company which would normally have the effect of reducing the value of its securities, making them cheaper to acquire but also less valuable to sell. In either scenario, a shareholder in possession of this information (such as a director of the company) may be tempted to take advantage of it (whether, as the case may be, by buying some more or selling existing securities), either to protect or augment the existing value of his holding.[7]

There are of course many other matters capable of having an effect on the share price of a company. A pharmaceutical company might discover a vaccine against the virus (or viruses) causing full-blown AIDs or perhaps a cure for cancer. A mining company might discover precious metals or oil on recently acquired land. The pension funds of a group of companies may have been pilfered by directors to shore-up the failing businesses of the group. All or any of these scenarios may have an effect on the price or value of related securities.

---

5 Through the posting of a bid. See, too, Rule 2 of the City Code on Takeovers and Mergers.

6 A prosecution involving facts similar to this hypothetical scenario may be found in the case of *R v Titheridge & Titheridge*. In that case, a company called Joseph Stocks & Sons (Holdings) Limited was the object of a takeover bid. Mrs Titheridge was secretary to the chairman of the merchant bank which was advising the bidding company. She passed information to her husband who dealt in securities of Joseph Stocks in December 1980. Both Mr and Mrs Titheridge pleaded guilty to insider dealing and were convicted. They were each ordered to pay a £4,000 fine.

7 A prosecution involving facts similar to these scenarios may be found in the case of *R v Reardon-Smith* (1985) who was a director of a company about to go into liquidation. Just before that stage, in May 1985, Reardon-Smith sold shares in the company. He pleaded guilty to insider dealing and was fined £3,000.

Some cases of insider dealing

One of the best known cases of insider dealing in the United Kingdom concerned an adviser to a company involved in a takeover.[8] That adviser was a man called Geoffrey Collier who was then head of securities at City of London finance house Morgan Grenfell which had been retained by a client to advise on a takeover bid. When the bid was about to be launched, in the autumn of 1986, Mr Collier arranged the acquisition in London on his own behalf of shares of the target company. He did so through a company registered in the Cayman Islands prior to the announcement of the bid and was subsequently convicted on pleading guilty to insider dealing, his prison sentence of twelve months being suspended for two years. He was fined £25,000, ordered to pay £7,000 in costs and was subsequently also expelled from membership of the Stock Exchange in London. Apparently, he only stood to profit in the amount of £15,000 as a result of what he did.

A further example achieved greater notoriety. It involved Ivan Boesky who worked as a risk *arbitrageur* in the United States of America. Risk *arbitrageurs* became prevalent in the last decade. They would acquire holdings of shares in companies in the hope that the market value of those shares would rise enabling them to turn a tidy profit on the disposal of the shares. A common scenario might again have involved the acquisition of shares in a company in anticipation of a takeover. If the takeover went ahead, the *arbitrageur* could either dispose of his shares or, alternatively, retain them in the hope of exercising influence over the company following the takeover. Ivan Boesky had claims to be one of the most successful of this breed of speculator insecurities. In corporate terms, he was often in the right place at the right time and many thought this was due to his superior market analysis. However, subsequently, in many cases it turned out to be due to the receipt of inside information from a number of informants, one of whom[9] subsequently informed on Mr Boesky. Boesky was convicted and sentenced to imprisonment for three years. He also paid over $100 million in settlement to the Securities and Exchange Commission in the United States of America. Approximately half that amount represented a fine while the other half represented the return of ill-gotten gains. If that makes the reader sad on behalf of Mr Boesky, he or she should be aware that Boesky is alleged to have made a minimum profit from insider dealing of $50 million over a period of five years or so. Some newspaper reports at the time estimated his profit to be in the region of $200 million. Also, Boesky profited further in that he came to an agreement with the Securities and Exchange Commission[10] which enabled him to dispose of part of his own portfolio of

---

8   See the case of *R v Collier* where the offences in question were committed in October and November 1986. In proceedings brought in the USA in *SEC v Collier*, Mr Collier admitted the charges laid against him and consented to the issue of permanent injunctions under s 10(b) and r 10b–5 Securities Exchange Act 1934.

9   Dennis Levine, a New York banker. And see various press reports at the time on the activities of Boesky; for instance, 'Secret World of the Inside Stealer' (1986) *Sunday Times,* 23 November.

10   After his activities had been detected.

holdings prior to the public announcement of the charges laid against him. The disposal proceeds are said to have amounted to well over $400 million.

MARKET INFORMATION

The value of information

What may be gleaned from the activities of Geoffrey Collier (in the United Kingdom) and Ivan Boesky (in the United States of America) is the potential value of accurate and timely securities-related information and the effect its presence and use can have. It may not always lead to power and influence but, as has been demonstrated, its prompt use can sometimes give rise to a tidy[11] profit.

'INSIDERS'

The actions of 'insiders'

In the context of insider dealing, what an 'insider' will try to do is to buy or sell (or suggest that others buy or sell) securities when he is in possession of information which may alter their price[12] but he will do so before such information has been made public and has therefore had a chance to have any such effect. Such information will usually relate in particular to the company in question. Its value will depend on its precise nature, exactly who is aware of it and what they are then prepared to do.

Potential 'insiders'

In the first instance, the most usual 'insiders' are persons employed by or connected with a company. They may be directors, other employees or shareholders of that company. Other persons may also find themselves in the position of having unpublished price-sensitive information. Professional advisers[13] or the bankers to a company[14] are more than likely to come into possession of information which they could use to their advantage, by dealing for their own account in the shares of the company, if they were permitted to do so by insider dealing law.

But, what about others who may not be so closely connected with the company? What about an investment manager working in another part of the financial conglomerate which owns the merchant bank which is acting for the company? Should he (or his clients) be prohibited from benefiting if he becomes or is made aware of what is going on? If others are to be prohibited, the answer seems to be that he should also be prevented if, in regulatory terms, there is to be a 'level playing-field'. Taking

---

11 Albeit, potentially ill-gotten.
12 So-called 'price-sensitive information'.
13 Such as the merchant bank acting for a company in relation to a potential takeover.
14 Who lend it money to enable it to develop a new invention.

this scenario a little further, what about the lawyers acting for the merchant bank which is advising the company about a potential takeover? Or those persons even further removed from the company, such as the executive officers of the Takeover Panel who answer initial queries about a potential takeover which is subsequently staged or perhaps even the designers involved in producing the takeover documentation or the printers who print that documentation? If a level playing-field is to be preserved, those people should also be prevented from profiting from being well-informed. But, as a matter of market policy, should insider dealing be prohibited?

SHOULD INSIDER DEALING BE PROHIBITED?

Market egalitarianism

If a securities market is to be efficient, it must be properly equipped to ensure that the price of securities accurately reflects their value. It might be thought that part of that equipment should include the means of preventing or, at least, of discouraging persons who are 'in the know' with unpublished price-sensitive information from taking unfair advantage of their informed position. A 'level playing-field' should be preserved, whereby information is promptly 'made public'[15] and 'insiders' are deterred from abusing their position, if a modern securities market is to preserve credibility. If that is achieved, all investors are then able to deal on the market on an equal footing. Everyone has equal access to all material information. This is the 'ideal' position in what has sometimes been described by economists as the theory of market egalitarianism.

Market efficiency

However, the idea that securities markets should operate on the basis of complete equality between investors and potential investors[16] is generally thought to be too idealistic to be workable in practice.[17] A requirement as to the immediate disclosure of all information would be too all-embracing. The market would be swamped with trivial material. Although most feel that 'insiders' should not be allowed to take unfair advantage of inside information, and investors should have prompt and easy access to important corporate information, there will always be people with informational advantages and disadvantages. This will be so however prompt or wide-ranging is any sensible requirement as to disclosure. Some investors will have greater experience or intuitive ability than others whilst some will simply ensure they always take the very best advice available. But what can be done? The answer seems to be that abuses can be minimised by requiring the prompt disclosure of material information to the market.

---

15 Through disclosure to the market.
16 Between buyers and sellers of securities.
17 See also Carlton and Fischel, 'The Regulation of Insider Trading' (1983) 35 Stan L Rev.
18 Whether primary or secondary legislation.

Laws[18] can also be enacted to discourage persons from taking unfair informational advantages and to punish those who fail to comply. With this approach, market efficiency[19] and the promotion of public confidence in the market is the goal as opposed to market perfection which, in practice, must be impossible to attain.

A 'level playing-field'

An informed layman would say that the effective dissemination of material corporate information coupled with the prohibition of insider dealing was essential for an efficient and credible securities market. 'City' commentators and regulators[20] continue to speak of the need to ensure that London is a 'clean' place to do business or that business may be attracted elsewhere. That argument was obviously accepted by our law-makers some time ago because, since 1980, legislation has been in place which has made insider dealing a criminal offence.[21] It also seems to have been accepted without obvious challenge by companies whose shares are traded in the United Kingdom.

That is because volatile, or even just unexpectedly variable, share prices do not create good 'press' for a company. If, instead, price variability is linked with rumours about the activities of insiders close to the decision-makers of a company, market participants will be wary about dealing in its shares. Such a situation is likely to lower the reputation of the company amongst market analysts and this will cause problems if the company wishes to raise money through share issues and the like. This is therefore another strong argument in favour of prohibiting insider dealing. However, the view that insider dealing should be made subject to the criminal law has not always been held and, indeed, may not be wholly valid today.

An economist's view

In the Sixties, some economists and others propounded the view essentially that there was nothing wrong with insider dealing. In 1966, for instance, Professor Manne[22] argued that insider dealing was beneficial in economic terms and ought not to be prohibited. To many people, insider dealing remains a 'victimless' crime in that it will

---

19 Ensuring investor protection.

20 See, for instance, para 16.7 in Chapter 16 (entitled 'Current Challenges') on p 102 of the review document issued by the Securities and Investments Board in May 1993. That document was entitled 'Financial Services Regulation – Making the Two Tier System Work' and contained the Report of the Chairman of the SIB, Andrew Large, following the request by the Chancellor of the Exchequer in July 1992 that, generally speaking, he undertake a review of the regulatory system in place under the Financial Services Act 1986 (FSA 1986). Reference was made to the 'professional markets' as follows: 'They need a different style of regulation to retail markets. But regulators cannot neglect them. Systemic risks to the financial health of the industry need to be avoided. Clean markets need to be maintained.'

21 See later in this chapter for an account of the move towards insider dealing regulation in the United Kingdom.

22 H Manne, *Insider Trading and the Stock Market* (1966).

usually be hard to establish a direct connection between the activities of an insider and the position of an investor who, as a result of those activities, pays more or receives less[23] for dealing in securities. In some cases, it may be possible[24] for securities to be bought or sold between individuals in direct transactions. In those circumstances, if one of the contracting parties dealt on the basis of inside information, the other could perhaps be regarded as a victim of insider dealing. However, direct acquisitions or disposals are not the norm today.

Most transactions are conducted by and through intermediaries[25] pursuant to the facilities and rules but also subject to the supervision of a relevant securities market. This tends to remove any direct personal contact that might previously have been present[26] and makes it harder to identify a 'victim' of insider dealing. It is also difficult to quantify the 'loss' which would be suffered by such an investor. Although he would not be able to take advantage of fully up-to-date information which may affect the price of the securities with which he is concerned, he would probably have dealt in any event being unaware of the existence of the insider unless dealing by that person had an immediate and noticeable effect on the price of the securities. In doing so, he may have to pay more or receive less for those securities, but that will not usually be caused by any identifiable individual 'insider'. It will simply be the result of movements in the market price of the securities and, as most investment advertising is now required to warn with due prominence,[27] the price of securities can go up as well as down. Investors take the risk of the price moving against them when they deal. Without a connecting link between the insider and the 'outsider',[28] it is hard to see the outsider as a victim of any potential crime committed by the insider. Also, any brokers and market makers involved are professionals and should be well able to look after themselves.

Some economists[29] have argued that insider dealing actually benefits a securities market because it ensures that the market price of affected securities moves[30] in the appropriate direction.[31] In essence, those economists are saying that a securities market with active insiders ensures accuracy in the pricing of the securities so traded. Insider dealing is said to move prices towards a level which correctly reflects the actual position of a company[32] at a given point in time. Economists also argue that insiders have little to gain in delaying the disclosure of information to the market[33] Indeed, unless very close to a company, it would seem that they are rarely in a position where they are able

---

23 That is to say, suffers a quantifiable loss.
24 Particularly where small 'private' companies are involved.
25 Usually both brokers and market makers.
26 Between buyer and seller.
27 See, for instance, rr 5-9 to 5-15 (inclusive) Rules of the Securities and Futures Authority.
28 Being the person not in possession of any inside information.
29 Including Professor Manne. See, for instance, *Insider Trading and the Stock Market* (1966) at pp 77–110.
30 Either up or down.
31 In accordance with a fully informed view of their value.
32 And the value of its stock.

to influence the timing of any such disclosure. So long as an insider has time to deal on the basis of his (or her) inside knowledge, he would normally want the information in question to be made public as soon as possible thereafter, enabling the price of the securities to be affected so fixing any profit from the transaction. In the long run, it is therefore suggested that investors may actually benefit from the activities of insiders.

It might be thought reasonable to assume that few investors[34] would deal with any confidence or frequency on an exchange where the activities of insiders reigned unchecked or were only partially checked. However, in the United Kingdom, where insider dealing is a matter for the criminal law, there seems to be little evidence that the activities of insiders[35] have had much effect on public confidence in the City and the way it is regulated. Likewise, there seems no real evidence that those running companies whose securities have been the subject of alleged or established insider dealing have been regarded as possessing significantly less integrity than those whose companies have escaped.[36] Over recent years, more fuss has been caused over instances of alleged malpractice in corporate governance[37] or where investors have suffered notwithstanding the protections of the Financial Services Act 1986[38] than where the securities of a company may have been subject to insider dealing.

The 'moral' position

Although there may be some doubt as to whether insider dealing should be prohibited if one accepts some of the economic arguments outlined above, there are some 'moral' arguments in favour of its regulation. In a regulatory environment where there are great 'political' concerns to ensure the protection of investors, it is unconscionable that insiders should be allowed to operate unchecked even if their activities may not necessarily be to the direct detriment of all potential investors. If they are allowed to make use of their inside knowledge, there would be no 'level playing-field' whereby all investors operate, relatively speaking, on the same basis. Also, the fact that insider dealing is regarded as dishonest behaviour may well be a reflection of the long-standing common law concern to prevent unjust enrichment and to forestall situations where

---

34 Particularly private individuals.

35 And there is, apparently, only a small incidence of insider dealing on the Stock Exchange in London to the extent that there have been a number of successful prosecutions.

36 The most that seems to occur is the odd sly comment in the financial press. An example occurred (from the *Times* 'Business News' on 17 May 1994) in relation to dealing in the shares of the Portals group. The price of those shares jumped 44p on one day after a spate of buying by so-called 'fringe brokers'. By the end of the same week, after the intervention of the Takeover Panel, Portals was forced to admit that it was involved in bid talks with another company, De La Rue. The Pennington column in the *Times* commented that '... Disregarding a mass outbreak of telepathy, those dealers, presumably, knew something, and that something constituted a leak. *Cui bono?* Well, the potential bidder looks the most embarrassed and the least pleased, which could allow tentative conclusions to be drawn by the uncharitable ... if somebody wanted to strengthen their hand in the negotiations or force the price higher by selective leaks into the market ...'.

37 Directors tampering with pension fund surpluses and the like.

38 See G Brazier, *The Regulation of Insider Dealing in the United Kingdom*, Chapter 2 (Cavendish Publishing Limited, 1996) for more relevant detail on the FSA1986.

people with fiduciary or quasi-fiduciary obligations are able to take advantage of their favoured position. Perhaps, more than anything else, that is why insider dealing remains prohibited.

MOVES TOWARDS INSIDER DEALING REGULATION IN THE UNITED KINGDOM

Early moves

The legislation prohibiting insider dealing took quite a long time in arriving on the statute book in the United Kingdom given that the basic mischief it was intended to prevent had been recognised and commented on as being undesirable for many years. Whatever the 'economic' arguments[39] in favour of or against it, insider dealing has been prevalent as a 'City' practice for some time.[40] The extent to which this contributed to the length of time it took a succession of governments to make it subject to the criminal law can only be speculated upon. If it did, it would not be the first time that 'City' opposition has prevented, or at least delayed, the elected government of the day[41] in taking action against dubious 'market' practices.[42]

Directors' duties

Over recent years, insider dealing has usually involved the directors of a company or those people otherwise closely connected with its management and control or their advisers. In becoming 'insiders', they have used information in their possession as a basis for the prudent acquisition or disposal of shares in the company.[43] However, before enactment of the Companies Act 1980, provided the securities market trading activities of such people did not breach the fiduciary and certain other duties of care which they owed in the circumstances, generally speaking, they were not prohibited. The directors of the company owed duties to the company and not to its individual shareholders nor, for instance, to applicants for shares.[44]

---

39 See G Brazier, *The Regulation of Insider Dealing in the United Kingdom,* Chapter 3 (Cavendish Publishing Limited, 1996) for an outline of some of the arguments put forward by economists in favour of insider dealing.

40 *Ibid,* Chapter 1 for some discussion of the historical origins and development of insider dealing in the United Kingdom.

41 Particularly a Conservative government.

42 A comparatively recent example of 'City' opposition occurred in the run-in to what became known as 'Big Bang' when the basic distinction between 'brokers' and 'jobbers' was abolished along with fixed minimum commission.

43 A recent example of alleged insider dealing concerned the writer and former Conservative Member of Parliament, Jeffrey Archer. He was one of the subjects of an investigation in 1994 by the Department of Trade and Industry into suspected insider dealing in the shares of Anglia Television, a company of which his wife was a non-executive director.

44 See the case of *Percival v Wright* [1902] 2 Ch 421, discussed below.

The common law

An early authority for some of the propositions set out above is the case of *Percival v Wright*.[45] In that case, the directors of a company bought shares from Z. However, they did not disclose to him that negotiations were being conducted for the sale of all the shares in the company at a higher price than that being asked by Z. Those negotiations proved to be abortive but Z sued to have his sale of shares set aside on the grounds that the directors ought to have disclosed the negotiations to him. The court however held that the sale was binding as the directors were under no obligation to disclose the negotiations to Z. Although clearly wrong by the standards of today,[46] what was done was not prohibited at the time notwithstanding the fact that the directors were in possession and dealt on the basis of inside information, being information which was not widely known but which would, if made public, have had a material effect on the market price of the securities in question.

Some learned committees and consultative documents

The Companies Act 1948[47] was based, to a large extent, on the Report in 1945 of the Cohen Committee[48] which reviewed the state of company and related law at the time. So far as share dealing by directors and insider dealing was concerned, the Cohen Committee favoured the imposition on company directors of disclosure requirements relating to the shares they owned in the companies which employed them as directors.[49] The Report also highlighted the use of nominee companies and nominee shareholdings as ways of concealing insider dealing. At the time, nothing much in terms of the regulation of insider dealing occurred as a direct and immediate result of the Cohen Report.

Many of the more important proposals for the reform of company law in the last few decades were made by the Jenkins Committee which reported in 1962.[50] One of the recommendations made by that Committee[51] was that a director, who in any transaction relating to the securities of his employing company[52] made improper use of a particular item of confidential information which might be expected to have a significant effect on the value of those securities, should be liable to compensate a person suffering loss as a result of his action unless the information in question was known to that person. Although some of the recommendations made by the Jenkins

---

45 *Ibid.*

46 Set by insider dealing legislation if not morality.

47 Companies Act 1948 (11 & 12 Geo 6, c 38).

48 The Cohen Report (1945), the Report of the Committee on Company Law Amendment, Cmnd 6659.

49 See Cmnd 6659 at paras 86 and 87. See also ss 323–29 Companies Act 1985 ('Share dealings by directors and their families').

50 The Jenkins Report (1962), the Report of the Company Law Committee, Cmnd 1749.

51 1962 Cmnd 1749 at para 99(b).

52 Or of another company in the same group.

Committee were implemented and became law relatively quickly in a number of later statutes,[53] the recommendation relating to insider dealing was not one of them although, to be fair, an attempt was made in the Companies Bill 1973.[54] This followed a Report in 1972 by Justice, the law reform organisation, which suggested that insider dealing should be made a criminal offence.[55] The Stock Exchange and the Takeover Panel had also issued a joint statement in 1973 recommending criminal sanctions. The Conservative government went with the flow.

The Conservative government White Paper on Company Law Reform[56] was presented to Parliament in July 1973. In it, the government announced its intention to introduce a new Companies Bill. Amongst the reasons given for this proposal was the fact that many of the recommendations made by the Jenkins Committee, which were not included in the Companies Act 1967, were still relevant and important. This included the view that existing arrangements for uncovering and dealing with commercial crime and other malpractices had proved to be inadequate. It was therefore proposed that insider dealing should be made a criminal offence.[57] The White Paper accepted that unfair benefits could be obtained by share dealing on the basis of confidential and price-sensitive information that was not available to the general 'investing' public. It stated that the object of any legislation should be to ensure that 'insiders' in possession of price-sensitive information[58] refrained from dealing until the information had properly been made generally available. The definition of 'insider' suggested[59] was one including directors, employees, major shareholders and the professional advisers of a company together with close relations of those persons.

Some abortive legislation

It was intended that clauses 12–16 Companies Bill 1973[60] would give substantive effect to the recommendations as to insider dealing set out in the Conservative government White Paper. The Bill had a first reading in the House of Commons on 18 December 1973. However, it was lost when Parliament was dissolved on 7 February 1974. The Labour government which was elected decided not to reintroduce the Bill. Instead,

---

53 Such as the Companies Act 1967 which amended the Companies Act 1948 in a number of areas. For instance, amendments were made to provisions governing company accounts so that the accounts of a subsidiary had to disclose the name of its ultimate holding company. Also, the Companies Act 1976 which enacted some of the provisions contained in the Companies Bill 1973 and made amendments concerning the filing of company accounts and the keeping of accounting records.

54 Clauses 12–16 Companies Bill 1973 set out provisions which would have made insider dealing a criminal offence.

55 Justice, 'Insider Trading' (1972), noted by Kay (1973) MLR at p 185.

56 (1973) Cmnd 5391.

57 *Ibid* at para 15.

58 Being information which, if generally known, would be likely to have a material effect on the price of the relevant securities.

59 See (1973) Cmnd 5391.

60 See note 51 above.

they instigated their own review of company law which was also to consider the supervision of securities trading.

Further deliberations

The conclusions of that review were set out in the Labour Party Green Paper on the Reform of Company Law 1974[61] which was published in May 1974. Amongst other matters, the Green Paper criticised existing supervision of the City in its reliance upon self-regulation.[62] The basic conclusion was that the case for a new Companies Commission was overwhelming. It would be a new public supervisory body taking over the Companies and Insurance Division of the Department of Trade. As for insider dealing, the authors of the Green Paper agreed with the objectives of cll 12–16 Companies Bill 1973.

Legislative prohibition

Notwithstanding the impetus given to the proposed prohibition of insider dealing by the above, it still took some time before it became a criminal offence. In 1977, the Takeover Panel and the Stock Exchange issued a further joint statement which emphasised the need for companies participating in or subject to takeovers to take care to see that insider dealing did not occur. The Stock Exchange also issued its Model Code for Securities Transactions by Directors of Listed Companies which set out certain basic standards of good practice.[63] Finally, the Labour government introduced a Companies Bill which provided for criminal penalties and a civil remedy in certain relevant circumstances. As before, that Bill was lost on the dissolution of Parliament.

Insider dealing did not become a criminal offence in the United Kingdom for the first time until the enactment of the Companies Act 1980.[64] Part V of that Act contained 11 separately identifiable offences involving insider dealing. The law relating to insider dealing in company securities was consolidated in the Company Securities (Insider Dealing) Act 1985[65] which entered the statute book on 11 March 1985 and came into force on 1 July 1985.[66] The object of this legislation was to prohibit certain individuals from dealing in company securities in relation to which they were in possession of inside information. A breach of that general prohibition remained a

---

61   The Labour Party Green Paper on the Reform of Company law, entitled 'The Community and the Company'. Drafted in December 1973 and published in May 1974.

62   For instance, by the Stock Exchange and the Takeover Panel.

63   See G Brazier, *The Regulation of Insider Dealing in the United Kingdom,* Chapter 9 (Cavendish Publishing Limited, 1996).

64   The Companies Act 1980. Part V of that Act made insider dealing a criminal offence. The relevant provisions came into force on 23 June 1980 by virtue of the Companies Act 1980 (Commencement) Order 1980 (SI 1980/745).

65   The CS (ID) A 1985 (1985 c 8).

66   See s 18 CS (ID) A 1985.

criminal offence.[67] That Act was subsequently amended by the Financial Services Act 1986[68] and prospectively repealed by the Criminal Justice Act 1993.[69] That restatement of the law resulted from the European Communities Directive of 13 November 1989 co-ordinating regulations on insider dealing,[70] the purpose and *rationale* of which was to ensure the provision of minimum standards for insider dealing laws throughout the European Community. Implementation by the United Kingdom led to the amendment and restatement of the law on insider dealing contained in Part V[71] Criminal Justice Act 1993.

THE DEFINITIONAL BACKGROUND TO INSIDER DEALING

Information is the key

The offence of insider dealing is based upon the misuse of information which relates to securities.[72] In general terms, 'information' has been defined as 'knowledge communicated concerning some particular fact, subject or event.[73]

Inside information

The important expression 'inside information' is defined[74] essentially as meaning information which has four basic characteristics:

- The first is that it must relate to particular securities or to a particular issuer or to particular issuers of securities and not to securities generally or to issuers of securities generally.[75] For the purposes of Part V Criminal Justice Act 1993, it is provided that an 'issuer', in relation to any securities, means any company, public sector body or individual by which or by whom the securities have been or are to be issued.[76] It is further provided, for those purposes, that information shall be

---

67 With the criminal penalties set out in s 8(1)(a) and (b) ('Punishment of contraventions') CS (ID) A 1985.

68 The FSA1986 (1986 c 60). Part VII FSA 1986 contains provisions relating to insider dealing. In particular, ss 177 and 178 set out provisions dealing with investigations into insider dealing.

69 By s 79(14) and Sch 16 Criminal Justice Act 1993 (1993 c 36) (C JA 1993).

70 Council Directive (EEC) 89/592 of 13 November 1989.

71 Entitled 'Insider Dealing'.

72 'Securities' for these purposes are securities to which Part V CJA 1993 applies. Section 54(1) CJA 1993 provides that Part V applies (*per se*) to any security which falls within any paragraph of Sch 2 CJA 1993 and also satisfies any conditions made applicable to it by any order made by the Treasury for the purposes of s 54(1). In Part V CJA 1993, and in this Chapter unless otherwise indicated, any reference to a 'security' is a reference to a security to which Part V is applicable.

73 From the *Compact Oxford English Dictionary* (2nd edn), first published in 1991.

74 By s 56 CJA 1993, for the purposes of ss 56 and 57 CJA 1993. This provision was said by Mr Anthony Nelson, the Economic Secretary to the Treasury, to be '... central to this part of the Bill ...'. See the Report of Standing Committee B, 10 June 1993, at col 172.

75 Section 56(1)(a) CJA 1993.

76 Section 60(2) CJA 1993.

treated as relating to an issuer of securities which is a company not only where it is about the company but also where it may affect the business prospects of the company.[77]

- The second is that the information must be specific or precise.[78] As the Criminal Justice Bill passed through the parliamentary process, the expression 'specific or precise' led to much discussion. When it was considered by Standing Committee B, the Economic Secretary to the Treasury made clear that the '... purpose of the provision is to ensure that inside information does not include information which is mere rumour ...'.[79] He said that the government had been concerned '... that "precise" alone might be interpreted narrowly by the courts, so "specific", which is employed in existing legislation, has been added ...'.[80] Some further guidance was also given. In the context of a takeover bid, 'specific information' might be the fact that a bid was going to be made whilst 'precise information' would be the price at which the bid was going to be fixed. 'Precise information' will be narrow, exact and definitive and thus capable of a narrow interpretation[81] whilst the use of 'specific' was said to keep the integrity of what was required by the directive and was already provided for by existing legislation.[82]

- The third is that the information has not been made public.[83]

- The fourth, more generalised, characteristic for the information in question is that it must be such as would be likely to have a significant effect on the price of any securities if it was made public[84] and, for these purposes, 'price' is specifically said to include 'value'.[85] The requirement that the effect be 'significant' was thought necessary to ensure that the prohibition of insider dealing applied only in respect of major events such as impending takeovers, imminent profits forecasts and dividend announcements out of line with expectations and not in respect of information likely to have only a trivial effect on the price of securities.[86]

---

77 Section 60(4) CJA 1993. The terms 'company' and 'public sector body' are themselves defined by s 60(3)(a) and (b) CJA 1993. information. The Economic Secretary to the Treasury attempted to make it clear that companies (and stock analysts) operating in accordance with existing good 'stock exchange' practice had nothing to fear from the new legislation; see the Report of Standing Committee B, 10 June 1993, at cols 197–99.

78 Section 56(1)(b) CJA 1993.

79 *Per* Mr Anthony Nelson, the Economic Secretary to the Treasury. See the Report of Standing Committee B, 10 June 1993, at col 173.

80 *Ibid.*

81 Also, 'precise' need not necessarily refer to figures. It could refer to a date, an event or another fact. *Per* the Economic Secretary to the Treasury. See the Report of Standing Committee B, 10 June 1993, at col 175.

82 *Ibid* at col 174.

83 Section 56(1)(c) CJA 1993. The expression information 'made public' is itself defined by s 58 CJA 1993.

84 Section 56(1)(d) CJA 1993.

85 Section 56(3) CJA 1993.

86 *Ibid* at col 177.

Information as an insider

In very general terms, the offence is based upon the actions of a person who has 'information as an insider'. For the purposes of Part V of the Act a person has 'information as an insider' if and only if it is 'inside information'[87] and he knows that it is inside information[88] and, also, that he has the information from an 'inside source' and he knows that he has the information from an inside source.[89] It has also been made clear that, for these purposes, the 'person' will be an individual as opposed to a company '... because ultimately it will always be individuals who misuse inside information ...'.[90]

Information from an inside source

For the purposes the last paragraph, a person has information from an inside source[91] if, and only if, he has it through being a director, employee or shareholder of an issuer of securities[92] or through having access to the information by virtue of his employment, office or profession.[93] A person is also regarded as having information from an inside source if the direct or indirect source of his information is a person from one of the categories referred to earlier in this paragraph.[94]

The relevant securities

Part V Criminal Justice Act 1993 is concerned with insider dealing in securities. The 'securities' to which it applies are those falling within any paragraph of Sch 2 Criminal Justice Act 1993[95] which also satisfy any conditions made applicable to them under an

---

87   See s 57 CJA 1993, generally, which is entitled 'Insiders'. Essentially, this provision defines the persons to whom the legislation applies. 'Inside information' is defined by s 56(1) CJA 1993.

88   Section 57(1)(a) CJA 1993.

89   Section 57(1)(b) CJA 1993.

90   *Per* Mr Anthony Nelson, the Economic Secretary to the Treasury. See the Report of Standing Committee B, 10 June 1993, at col 189. See, also, s 61(1) CJA 1993 which outlines the penalties on conviction.

91   And, in general terms, is thus an 'insider'.

92   Section 57(2)(a)(i) CJA 1993. It was made clear by the Economic Secretary to the Treasury that the definition of those 'persons having information as an insider' should include those persons, such as shareholders, who 'own' a company and who are therefore likely to be privy to information which is significant, precise and market-sensitive. Not all such persons will be tempted into insider dealing but they might be and are therefore covered by this definition. See the Report of Standing Committee B, 10 June 1993, at col 190.

93   Section 57(2)(a)(ii) CJA 1993. Whether a person has such access will be a question of fact. A person will be an 'insider' if he obtains information *qua* employee during the course of his employment just as if he did so as a director or shareholder. See the comments of the Economic Secretary to the Treasury in the Report of Standing Committee B, 10 June 1993, at col 190.

94   Section 57(2)(b) CJA 1993.

95   Section 54(1)(a) CJA 1993.

96   For the purposes of s 54(1). Section 54(1)(b) CJA 1993.

order made by the Treasury for those purposes.[96] Such an order was made on 1 February 1994 and took effect on 1 March 1994.[97] Generally speaking, only transactions in securities falling within the overall scope of any paragraph in Sch 2, which are traded on a 'regulated market', are subject to this legislation.[98] 'Regulated markets', for these purposes, are any markets established under the rules of any one of a number of 'specified' investment exchanges.[99]

The various categories of 'securities' are shares and stock in the share capital of a company;[100] 'debt securities';[101] 'warrants';[102] 'depository receipts';[103] 'options' to acquire or dispose of any security falling within any other paragraph of Sch 2;[104] 'futures' contracts;[105] and 'contracts for differences'.[106]

Price, information and securities

The expression 'price-affected securities' is a constituent part of those provisions in Part V Criminal Justice Act 1993 which detail the basic offence of insider dealing.[107] The

---

97 See, generally, the Insider Dealing (Securities and Regulated Markets) Order 1994 (SI 1994/187).

98 *Per* the Economic Secretary to the Treasury. See the Report of Standing Committee B, 10 June 1993, at col 165.

99 See art 9 SI 1994/187. The investment exchanges in question are specified in the Schedule to that Order. They include overseas investment exchanges which are recognised for the purposes of the FSA1986 and the exchanges in other member states on which relevant securities are traded. The 'regulated markets' which are regulated in the United Kingdom for the purposes of Part V CJA 1993 are any markets established under the rules of the International Stock Exchange of the United Kingdom and the Republic of Ireland Limited (other than the market which operates in the Republic of Ireland known as the Irish Unit of the International Stock Exchange of the UK and the Republic of Ireland Limited), LIFFE Administration and Management Limited and OMLX, the London Securities and Derivatives Exchange Limited: see art 10 SI 1994/187.

100 Paragraph 1, Sch 2 CJA 1993. Any such stocks or shares must be officially listed in a State within the European Economic Area or have been admitted to dealing on or have their prices quoted on or under the rules of a regulated market. For these purposes, a 'State within the European Economic Area' means a State which is a member of the European Communities and the Republics of Austria, Finland and Iceland, the Kingdoms of Norway and Sweden and the Principality of Liechtenstein: see arts 2 and 4 SI 1994/187. This requirement, as to listing etc, applies in relation to any security purporting to fall within any paragraph of Sch 2 CJA 1993.

101 Paragraph 2, Sch 2 CJA 1993. And see art 4 SI 1994/187 and s 60(2) CJA 1993.

102 See para 3, Sch 2 CJA 1993. See arts 4 and 5 SI 1994/187. See also the Report of Standing Committee B, 10 June 1993, at col 165.

103 See paras 4(2)(a) and (b) and 4(3), Sch 2 CJA 1993. See arts 4 and 6 SI 1994/187 and, also, the Report of Standing Committee B, 10 June 1993, at col 165 (*per* Mr Anthony Nelson).

104 Paragraph 5, Sch 2 CJA 1993. See arts 4, 7(a) and 7(b) SI 1994/187 and, also, the Report of Standing Committee B, 10 June 1993, at col 165 (*per* Mr Anthony Nelson, the Economic Secretary to the Treasury).

105 See paras 6(1), 6(2)(a) and 6(2)(b), Sch 2 CJA 1993. See also arts 4, 7(a) and (b) SI 1994/187.

106 See paras 7(1)(a), 7(1)(b), 7(1)(c) and 7(2), Sch 2 CJA 1993. See, also, arts 4, 8(a) and 8(b) SI 1994/187.

107 Section 52 CJA 1993.

expression 'price-sensitive information' is relevant to certain of the defences which may be applicable to an individual charged with insider dealing.[108] For the purposes of Part V, securities are 'price-affected securities' in relation to inside information and inside information is 'price-sensitive information' in relation to securities if and only if the information would, if made public, be likely to have a significant effect on the price of the securities[109] and, for these purposes, 'price' is said to include 'value'.[110]

It is difficult to say, in any general sense, what will characterise 'price-sensitive' information and will usually be necessary to consider a variety of factors relevant to each specific case. In addition to the information itself, these may include the existing price and volatility of the shares in question and also the prevailing market conditions.[111] Generally speaking, the more specific the information,[112] the greater the risk that it may be price-sensitive.[113]

Information made public

For these purposes, the expression 'made public' in relation to information is to be construed in accordance with the provisions of s 58 Criminal Justice Act 1993 although it is made clear that those provisions are not to be regarded as being exhaustive as to the meaning of that expression.[114] Essentially, s 58 contains two main elements. The first describes certain circumstances in which information is definitely to be regarded as having been made public.[115] These include where it is published in accordance with the rules of a regulated market for the purpose of informing investors and their professional advisers.[116] The second element provides that, where certain circumstances apply, information may be regarded as having been made public.[117] One instance is where the information may be acquired only by persons exercising diligence or expertise.[118] The *rationale* for this second element was to set out circumstances in which information may be treated as having been made public because it was felt that, unless such instances were made clear, information might well be considered not to have been made public.[119]

---

108 Which are set out in s 53 CJA 1993.

109 Section 56(2) CJA 1993.

110 Section 56(3) CJA 1993.

111 See para 8 of the 'Guidance on the dissemination of price sensitive information' document issued by the London Stock Exchange in February 1994.

112 Particularly financial information such as sales and profits figures.

113 See para 10 Stock Exchange February 1994 guidance document.

114 Section 58(1) CJA 1993.

115 See s 58(1) and (2) CJA 1993.

116 See s 58(2)(a) CJA 1993.

117 See s 58(1) and (3) CJA 1993.

118 See s 58(3)(a) CJA 1993.

119 *Per* the Economic Secretary to the Treasury, Mr Anthony Nelson. See the Report of Standing Committee B, 10 June 1993, at cols 182 and 184.

Whether or not information has been made public will be a question of fact and the point at which information becomes public is crucial because, in the context of insider dealing law, that determines whether the action taken before or after is legal or illegal.[120] The point was well put, as follows: 'If someone possesses inside information and intends to make it public, but deals in the meantime, that is insider dealing. If that person is in receipt of inside information and makes it public so that it is in the public domain when he deals, that is not insider dealing. It is a question of whether the dealing falls on one side or the other of information having been made public ...'.[121]

Professional intermediaries

Generally speaking, the prohibition of insider dealing applies to deals on 'regulated markets'. If dealing takes place 'off-market', it will only be covered by this prohibition if it involves a professional intermediary. It was not thought feasible to go further than that and attempt to catch dealing off-market which was not effected through professional intermediaries. For these purposes, a 'professional intermediary' is defined[122] as meaning a person who carries on a business consisting of a particular defined activity and who holds himself out to the public or to any section of the public[123] as being willing to engage in any such business.[124] It also means a person who is employed by such a person to carry out such an activity.[125] The activities in question are those of acquiring or disposing of securities,[126] whether as principal or as agent, or acting as an intermediary between persons taking part in any dealing in securities.

THE OFFENCE OF INSIDER DEALING

The basic provisions

---

120 See the comments of the Economic Secretary to the Treasury in the Report of Standing Committee B, 10 June 1993, at col 187.

121 *Ibid.*

122 By s 59 CJA 1993. The expression was used, for instance, in Article 2(3) of Council Directive (EEC) 89/592 but HMG considered that a detailed definition was required. See the Report of Standing Committee B, 10 June 1993, at col 192.

123 Including a section of the public constituted by persons such as himself.

124 Section 59(1)(a) CJA 1993. The full expression 'professional intermediary' was used both to conform with Council Directive (EEC) 89/592 and also to ensure that, for example, if a deal was done over the telephone, BT or Mercury did not find themselves acting as an 'intermediary' for these purposes. See the comments of the Economic Secretary to the Treasury in the Report of Standing Committee B, 10 June 1993, at col 192.

125 Section 59(1)(b) CJA 1993.

126 That is to say, securities to which Part V CJA 1993 is applicable. See s 54 and Sch 2 CJA 1993.

127 Section 59(2)(a) and (b) CJA 1993. Whether or not a merchant bank involved in the sale or purchase of a business would be regarded as a 'professional intermediary' for these purposes would depend upon whether it was also acting as a intermediary in any related 'dealing' transaction. See the comments of the Economic Secretary to the Treasury in the Report of Standing Committee B, 10 June 1993, at col 192.

The offence of insider dealing is set out in s 52 Criminal Justice Act 1993.[127] There are three forms which the offence may take: that of acquiring and/or disposing of securities; that of encouraging another to do so; and, also, that of disclosing information.[128] Generally speaking, any relevant acquisition or disposal of securities must take place in certain stated 'circumstances'.[129] Although that single provision contains all three forms of the offence, it relies heavily on many of the definitions examined earlier.[130] Section 52 also has effect subject to various 'defences' to the offence which are set out in s 53 and also in Sch 1 to the Act.[131]

The 'dealing' circumstances

Sections 52(1) and (2)(a) Criminal Justice Act 1993 refer to the occurrence of 'dealing' in securities taking place in certain 'circumstances' which are set out in s 52(3) of the Act. Those circumstances[132] are threefold:

- that the acquisition or disposal in question occurs on a 'regulated market'; alternatively;
- that the person dealing relies on a professional intermediary;[133] or finally
- that the person dealing is himself acting as a professional intermediary.[134]

'Dealing in securities'

For the purposes of the provisions governing insider dealing contained in Part V Criminal Justice Act 1993, a person is regarded as 'dealing in securities' in two main circumstances: first, if he acquires or disposes of the securities, whether as principal or as an agent;[135] or secondly, if he procures directly or indirectly an acquisition or disposal by any other person.[136]

The basic purpose of these provisions, which are central to the offence of insider dealing, is to specify where, when and how 'dealing' may take place. The acquisition of securities of course encompasses the acquisition of legal title to the securities but 'acquire', in relation to a security, is said to include agreeing to acquire the security in

---

128 1993 c 36.

129 See ss 52(1),(2)(a) and (2)(b) CJA 1993.

130 Set out in s 52(3) CJA 1993.

131 In paras 10-31 to 10-41.

132 In paras 10-61 to 10-78.

133 Section 52(3) CJA 1993. Essentially, the 'regulated markets' which are regulated in the United Kingdom for these purposes are The International Stock Exchange of the United Kingdom and the Republic of Ireland Limited, LIFFE Administration & Management and OMLX, the London Securities and Derivatives Exchange Limited. See s 60(1) CJA 1993 and also arts 9 and 10 SI 1994/187, which came into force on 1 March 1994.

134 Section 52(3) CJA 1993. See s 59 CJA 1993 further.

135 See note 134 above.

136 Section 55(1)(a) CJA 1993.

137 Section 55(1)(b) CJA 1993.

question.[137] This ensures, for instance, that a person is not able to avoid the legislation if he agrees to buy securities but then disposes of his rights, making a profit, without having taken legal title to the securities.[138] 'Acquire', in relation to a security, is also said to include entering into a contract which creates the security.[139] This was thought necessary to ensure not only that dealing in existing securities falls within the legislation but also, perhaps mainly in relation to dealing in derivatives such as options, entering into a contract which has the effect of creating a new security.[140]

The disposal of securities, of course, encompasses the disposal of legal title to the securities. 'Dispose', in relation to a security, is also defined more widely for these purposes. It is said to include agreeing to dispose of the security[141] and also the bringing to an end of a contract which created the security.[142]

Territorial extent of provisions

It should be noted that the provisions contained in Part V and Schs 1 and 2 Criminal Justice Act 1993 extend, in terms of application, to the United Kingdom and not merely to England and Wales.[143]

The 'dealing' offence

This is the first form of the offence of insider dealing. An individual who has information as an insider will be guilty of insider dealing if, in the 'dealing' circumstances outlined above, he deals in securities that are price-affected securities in relation to the information.[144] Whether or not this offence of insider dealing has been committed in any given case will therefore depend upon the satisfaction of a number of requirements.

The offence (*per se*) can only be committed by an individual.[145] Although, in some circumstances, a company employing such an individual may itself incur criminal liability this will not be a direct result of the application of Part V Criminal Justice Act 1993. There are however circumstances in which a company could be guilty of an offence connected with insider dealing by an individual. For instance, a securities firm which instructed one of its junior dealers to execute transactions which it knew would

---

138 Section 55(2)(a) CJA 1993.

139 See the Report of Standing Committee B, 10 June 1993, at col 168.

140 Section 55(2)(b) CJA 1993.

141 *Ibid.*

142 Section 55(3)(a) CJA 1993.

143 Section 55(3)(b) CJA 1993.

144 See s 79(2) CJA 1993. The United Kingdom consists of England, Scotland, Wales and Northern Ireland.

145 Section 52(1) CJA 1993. See also s 52(3) CJA 1993.

146 See ss 52(1) and also (2) CJA 1993. Compare ss 47(1) and (2) FSA1986 which refer to 'Any person ...'.

involve insider dealing might be guilty of incitement.

That individual must have 'information as an insider'.[146] The meaning of that expression is derived from the application of two further definitions, those of 'inside information' and where a person has 'information from an inside source'. A person is regarded as having 'information as an insider' if and only if it is and he knows that it is 'inside information' and he has it and knows that he has it from an inside source.[147]

The individual must also 'deal in securities' that are 'price-affected securities' in relation to the information and the dealing must take place in the 'dealing' circumstances. The extended meaning of 'dealing in securities' for these purposes was examined in above whilst the 'dealing' circumstances were outlined in an earlier paragraph. The securities must also be 'price-affected securities' in relation to the relevant information.[148]

When the various requirements outlined above have been satisfied by the circumstances of a particular case, the individual who has so dealt in securities may be guilty of insider dealing. There are however a number of further points to explore if he is to be regarded as falling within the territorial scope of the offence of insider dealing. For instance, he will not be guilty of the 'dealing' offence unless he was within the United Kingdom at the time he is alleged to have done any act constituting or forming part of the alleged dealing.[149] The 'regulated market' on which the dealing is alleged to have occurred must be one identified in an order made by the Treasury, whether by name or by reference to criteria prescribed by the order, as being regulated in the United Kingdom for these purposes.[150] Finally, if relevant, the professional intermediary involved must have been within the United Kingdom at the time he is alleged to have done anything by means of which the offence is alleged to have been committed.[151]

The 'encouraging' offence

The second form of the offence of insider dealing has been regarded as being something of an anti-avoidance measure.[152] It was intended to prohibit a person with inside information from encouraging someone else to deal in securities in circumstances

---

147 Section 57(1)(a) CJA 1993.

148 Section 57(1)(b) CJA 1993.

149 See s 62(1) CJA 1993, generally.

150 Section 62(1)(a) CJA 1993.

151 Section 62(1)(b) CJA 1993. And, see also the Insider Dealing (Securities and Regulated Markets) Order 1994 (SI 1994/187).

152 Section 62(1)(c) CJA 1993.

153 *Ibid* at col 134.

where that 'other' person might or might not have the same inside information. The offence will be committed where an individual, who has information as an insider, encourages another person to deal in securities that are price-affected securities in relation to the information whether or not this is known to that other person.[153] The encourager must however know or have reasonable cause to believe that the dealing would take place in the 'dealing' circumstances outlined above.[154]

The effect of this form of the offence is to prohibit encouragement to deal where the individual knows or has reasonable cause to believe that the person receiving such encouragement will deal in the circumstances covered by the 'dealing' offence. Without a prohibition in these terms, it might have been possible for the individual to circumvent the legislation by saying to someone 'Buy shares in ABC Limited off-market and do not make use of a stockbroker' knowing that the recipient of that encouragement would go and deal through his broker.[155] As with the 'dealing' offence, there are a number of requirements which need to be satisfied before such an individual could be found guilty of the offence.

As with the 'dealing' offence,[156] this form of the offence can only be committed by an individual who has 'information as an insider'. That individual must 'encourage' another person to deal in securities. 'Encouragement' for these purposes is not defined by the Criminal Justice Act 1993 but, in general usage, would require the individual to induce the other to deal or otherwise instigate the dealing. 'Securities' for these purposes means securities falling within Sch 2 Criminal Justice Act 1993 which satisfy any conditions made applicable by a relevant Treasury order.[157]

The relevant securities must be 'price-affected securities' in relation to the information in question whether or not the other person knows that they are price-affected securities.[158] The individual must however know or have reasonable cause to believe that the dealing would take place in the 'dealing' circumstances. He will not however be guilty of the 'encouraging' offence unless he was within the United Kingdom at the time when he is alleged to have encouraged the dealing or, alternatively, the alleged recipient of the encouragement was within the United Kingdom at the time when he is alleged to have received the encouragement.[159]

---

154 Section 52(2)(a) CJA 1993.

155 Section 52(2)(a) CJA 1993. See also s 52(3) CJA 1993.

156 Again, *per* the Economic Secretary to the Treasury. See the Report of Standing Committee B, 10 June 1993, at col 134.

157 From the *Compact Oxford English Dictionary* (New Edition, 1991).

158 Section 54(1) CJA 1993. See, also, the Insider Dealing (Securities and Regulated Markets) Order 1994 (SI 1994/187).

159 Section 62(2)(a) CJA 1993.

160 Section 62(2)(b) CJA 1993.

The 'disclosure' offence

The third form of the offence is also regarded as an anti-avoidance measure.[160] It prohibits the disclosure of information which could be used for insider dealing. An individual who has 'information as an insider' may be guilty of insider dealing simply if he discloses the information to another person, otherwise than in the proper performance of the functions of his employment, office or profession.[161] As with the two other basic forms of the offence, there are a number of requirements which need to be satisfied before an individual may have committed the offence.

As before, this form of the offence can only be committed by an individual[162] and he or she must have 'information as an insider'. The offence is committed where such an individual 'discloses' the information to another person 'otherwise than in the proper performance of the functions of his employment, office or profession'. 'Disclosure', for these purposes, could be in writing but is more likely to be verbal. For instance, an investment analyst with the requisite information as an insider could leave work one evening and go for a drink. He could have one pint too many in a bar and then give a complete stranger the benefit of his inside information. This would seem to be all that is required for commission of the 'disclosure' offence. There is no need for the recipient of the information to deal in securities; although, in practice, a resulting transaction is how the fact of disclosure is likely to come to light. Also, if the recipient does 'deal', he may commit the 'dealing' offence.[163]

However, even if the fact of a relevant disclosure is established, the offence will only have been committed if the individual has disclosed the information otherwise than in the 'proper' performance of the functions of his employment, office or profession. The offence does not apply to someone who discloses information in the proper performance of the functions of his employment, office or profession. It is therefore clear that some of the disclosures which may be made by an individual in the course of his work may not be acceptable. For instance, it would not be in the 'proper performance of his functions' for an individual to disclose confidential information which he had been given in the course of his employment even if his intention was not that the recipient would benefit personally from the information but would instead make use of it for the financial benefit of his employer.[164] If, however, information is disclosed by an individual in the proper performance of his employment, office or

---

161 *Per* the Economic Secretary to the Treasury. See the Report of Standing Committee B, 10 June 1993, at col 134.

162 Section 52(2)(b) CJA 1993.

163 This example is cited by Mr Peter Ainsworth (the Member of Parliament representing Surrey, East). See the Report of Standing Committee B, 10 June 1993, at col 147.

164 Section 52 CJA 1993. This would depend, mainly, on whether the recipient would be regarded as having 'information as an insider' and, in particular, 'information from an inside source'. See ss 56 and 57 CJA 1993.

165 *Per* the Economic Secretary to the Treasury. See the Report of Standing Committee B, 10 June 1993, at cols 134 and also 155–56.

profession, the 'disclosure' offence will not be applicable.[165]

The 'disclosure' offence will also be inapplicable if the individual falls outside its territorial scope. To be more precise, he will not be guilty of that offence unless he was within the United Kingdom at the time when he is alleged to have disclosed the information[166] or, alternatively, the alleged recipient of the information was within the United Kingdom at the time when he is alleged to have received the information.[167]

DEFENCES TO THE OFFENCE OF INSIDER DEALING

'General' and 'special' defences

Section 53 Criminal Justice Act 1993[168] provides 'defences' to the offence of insider dealing. *Prima facie*, it contains a number of relatively generalised provisions[169] which may be applicable where the individual in question has dealt in securities,[170] has encouraged another person to deal in securities[171] or has simply disclosed information to a third party otherwise than in the proper performance of the functions of his employment, office or profession.[172] The legislative intention, however, was that these provisions would, so to speak, 'particularise' the defences available and, in doing so, would thereby reflect '... the anxieties that have been put ... by practitioners since the introduction of the Bill, particularly about the need for greater certainty about the effect of the defences ...'.[173] If any one of these defences is shown to be applicable in any given case, the individual in question will not be guilty of the criminal offence of insider dealing although it may be that other sanctions may be imposed upon him or against the firm employing him.[174]

Schedule 1 Criminal Justice Act 1993 contains three supplemental 'special defences' which may be applicable in certain circumstances to individuals who would otherwise be guilty of the offence of insider dealing. The 'special defences' apply to the 'dealing'

---

166 Section 52(2)(b) CJA 1993. See the Report of Standing Committee B, 10 June 1993, at col 156 where the Economic Secretary to the Treasury states, under pressure from Mr Alistair Darling (the Member of Parliament representing Edinburgh, Central) that the '... adjective "proper" is well understood in the courts. It is difficult to define in every circumstance what will be within or without that term ...'.

167 Section 62(2)(a) CJA 1993.

168 Section 62(2)(b) CJA 1993.

169 1993 c 36.

170 Set out in s 52 CJA 1993.

171 See s 52(1) and then s 53(1) CJA 1993.

172 See s 52(2)(a) and then s 53(2) CJA 1993.

173 See s 52(2)(b) and then s 53(3) CJA 1993.

174 *Per* the Economic Secretary to the Treasury, Mr Anthony Nelson, talking about the Criminal Justice Bill [Lords]. See the Report of Standing Committee B, 10 June 1993, at col 157.

175 For instance, under Chapter 2 of the Rules of the Securities and Futures Authority.

and to the 'encouraging' forms of the offence; two of the defences are specific whilst the other is general. Section 53(4) Criminal Justice Act 1993 provides that the special defences shall have effect although the Treasury may by order amend Sch 1.[175] The 'specific' special defences are capable of being applicable to market makers[176] and also in respect of price stabilisation[177] whilst the more 'general' specific defence relates to information, termed market information, which market participants necessarily possess when involved in major transactions.[178]

The 'general' defences

There are a number of statutory 'defences' to the circumstances in which an individual may be guilty of insider dealing by virtue of 'dealing insecurities',[179] 'encouraging another to deal in securities' or through the 'disclosure of information'. There is no offence of insider dealing if any one of these defences is applicable. The defences in respect of the 'dealing' and 'encouraging' offences are similar. The position differs slightly for the 'disclosure' offence. For instance, the 'closed circle' defence is not applicable to 'disclosure' because that defence itself requires the parties to possess the same information.[180]

No expectation of relevant profit

The first defence, in respect of the 'dealing' offence, is where the individual dealing is able to show that he did not, at the time, expect the dealing to result in a profit attributable to the fact that the information which he possessed was price-sensitive information in relation to the securities in question.[181] For these purposes, it is provided that the reference to a profit must be taken as including a reference to the avoidance of a loss.[182] Accordingly, the individual must be able to show that he did not, at the time, expect the dealing to result in a profit or in the avoidance of a loss which, in either case, was attributable to the fact that the information in question was price-sensitive information.[183] In the context of the 'encouraging' offence, this defence may be applicable if the individual is able to show that he did not, at the time of

---

176 Section 53(5) CJA 1993.

177 See para 1, Sch 1 CJA 1993 which carried forward and replaced existing legislation. See, by way of comparison, s 3(1)(c) and (d) CS(ID)A 1985.

178 See para 5, Sch 1 CJA 1993 which carried forward and replaced existing legislation. See, by way of comparison, s 6 CS (ID) A 1985 as substituted by s 175 FSA1986 with effect from 29 April 1988.

179 Paragraphs 2–4, Sch 1 CJA 1993.

180 They are set out in s 53(1)(a)-(c), inclusive, CJA 1993.

181 Per the Economic Secretary to the Treasury, Mr Anthony Nelson. See the Report of Standing Committee B, 10 June 1993, at cols 159–60.

182 Section 53(1)(a) CJA 1993.

183 Section 53(6) CJA 1993.

184 Section 56(2) CJA 1993 provides that inside information is 'price-sensitive information' in relation to securities if and only if the information would, if made public, be likely to have a significant effect on the price of the securities.

encouraging the other person, expect the dealing which took place to result in a profit or in the avoidance of a loss which was attributable to the fact that the information in question was price-sensitive information in relation to the securities.[184]

Whether this defence will be applicable in any given case will depend upon the relevant facts and circumstances and the individual will need to make his case on a balance of probabilities. Where this defence maybe relevant to the 'dealing' offence, the individual in question will already have dealt in securities resulting in a profit, or in the avoidance of a loss, whilst in possession of price-sensitive information.[185] The defence will only then be applicable if that individual is able to demonstrate that he did not, at the time of dealing, 'expect' the transaction to result in a profit or in the avoidance of a loss which would be 'attributable' to the fact that he possessed information that was price-sensitive to the securities in question. He may, for instance, have sold shares whilst in possession of information which he expected to receive a favourable reaction from the market.[186] He will need to explain why he dealt but, in doing so, he will need to go further. The individual will need to demonstrate, presumably on a balance of probabilities,[187] that he did not expect the profit obtained or the loss avoided to be so attributable. Depending on the circumstances, this may or may not be difficult to establish.

The 'closed circle' defence

The second 'defence' may be in point where the individual is able to show that, at the time of dealing in the securities in question, he believed on reasonable grounds that the information had already been disclosed. For it to be applicable, however, that disclosure of information will need to have been effected widely enough to ensure that none of those taking part in the dealing were prejudiced by not having the information.[188] In the context of the 'encouraging' offence, this 'defence' differs slightly from its equivalent for 'dealing' in securities.[189] It will apply where the individual is able to show that, at the time, he believed on reasonable grounds that the information had been or would be disclosed widely enough to ensure that none of those taking part in the dealing would be prejudiced by not having knowledge of the information.[190] The slight difference is that the defence will still apply where, at the time of giving the encouragement, the information is not thought to have been disclosed but the individual is able to demonstrate that he had reasonable grounds for believing that it would be disclosed sufficiently.

Whether this defence may be applicable will depend upon the facts and

---

185 Section 53(2)(a) CJA 1993. Also s 53(6) CJA 1993.

186 See s 56(2) CJA 1993. 'Price-sensitive information' in relation to securities is inside information which, if made public, would be likely to have a significant effect on the price of the securities.

187 See the Report of Standing Committee B, 10 June 1993, at col 157.

188 Rather than beyond any reasonable doubt.

189 Section 53(1)(b) CJA 1993.

190 In s 53(1)(b) CJA 1993.

circumstances of the case in question. For instance, what disclosure of information had taken place? What was the reason for the dealing? The provision does not specify what will be sufficient but it is thought that this defence may be applicable where the parties to a transaction were in contact with each other immediately prior to the dealing and all possessed information that could or could not then be made public.[191] It may therefore be of particular comfort to corporate financiers in ensuring that those involved in properly conducted transactions, such as underwriting an offer of listed securities, are not running the risk of being found guilty of insider dealing.[192] The legislative intention was that this defence would be concerned with such 'closed circles' as arise in corporate finance transactions where the counterparties to the transaction know the information on which they are agreeing the 'deal' and it is not more widely known outside that circle. If that information is inside information[193] and they would otherwise be prohibited from doing the deal, this defence may enable them to proceed.[194] The provision was not intended to extend further.[195]

Individual would have 'dealt' or 'encouraged' anyway

The third 'defence', where the individual in question has 'dealt insecurities' or has 'encouraged' another to deal is where he is able to show that he would have done what he did[196] even if he had not been in possession of the information.[197] For this defence to be applicable, the individual will therefore need to be able to demonstrate that he had a compelling reason or justification for doing what he did and that he, the individual, would have done so on that basis regardless of the inside information in his possession. Whether he is able to do so will depend on the facts and circumstances of the case. The implicit question for the courts would seem to be whether the circumstances were sufficiently compelling so that a reasonable man would have dealt whether or not he was in possession of inside information.

No expectation of 'dealing' or of 'profit'

The first available defence in respect of the 'disclosure' offence is where the individual is able to show that he did not, at the time of the disclosure, expect any person to deal in securities because of the disclosure in the circumstances mentioned in s 52(3) Criminal Justice Act 1993.[198] For this defence to be applicable, at the time of the disclosure the individual must not expect any dealing insecurities to take place in those

---

191 Section 53(2)(b) CJA 1993.

192 See the Report of Standing Committee B, 10 June 1993, at col 157.

193 See the Report of Standing Committee B, 10 June 1993, at col 157.

194 See s 56(1) CJA 1993.

195 See the Report of Standing Committee B, 10 June 1993, at col 158.

196 'The measure does not go beyond that.' Per the Economic Secretary to the Treasury, Mr Anthony Nelson. See the Report of Standing Committee B, 10 June 1993, at col 158. He would have encouraged the other to deal in the securities.

197 See ss 53(1)(c) and 53(2)(c) CJA 1993.

198 Section 53(3)(a) CJA 1993.

circumstances as a result of his disclosure. The disclosure must be for another purpose. Although this will be a matter for the courts to decide, the test is likely to be whether, in the circumstances, it would be reasonable for the individual to expect such dealing to take place as a result of the disclosure which is made. The second defence for the 'disclosure' offence is where the person disclosing information did expect that dealing in securities would result from his disclosure. He must however be able to show that he did not expect any such dealing to result in a profit attributable to the fact that the information was price-sensitive information[199] in relation to the securities[200] and, for these purposes, 'a profit' must also be taken as including a reference to the avoidance of a loss.[201]

The 'special defences' to insider dealing

There are three scenarios which are thought to merit 'special defences' to the crime of insider dealing. Two of the defences are specific and concern the role of 'market makers'[202] and the question of 'price stabilisation'.[203] The third is more general and relates to the possession of a particular sort of information which is termed 'market information'. These defences are set out in paras 1–5 (inclusive), Sch 1 Criminal Justice Act 1993 and apply to the 'dealing' and to the 'encouraging' forms of the offence.

'Market makers'

The purpose of this defence is to protect market makers carrying on their business as such; holding themselves out, at all normal times, as being willing to buy and sell and thus to make a market in those securities in which they deal. The 'policy' *rationale* is that market makers should be able to continue to quote two-way continuous prices so long as they act in good faith.[204] Without this defence, market makers might well run the risk of insider dealing by dealing in certain circumstances. For the purposes of this

---

199 See s 56(2) CJA 1993.

200 Section 53(3)(b) CJA 1993.

201 Section 53(6) CJA 1993.

202 Carrying forward the provisions in s 3(1)(c) and (d) CS (ID) A 1985.

203 Carrying forward the provisions of s 6 CS (ID) A 1985.

204 *Per* the Economic Secretary to the Treasury, Mr Anthony Nelson. See the Report of Standing Committee B, 15 June 1993, at col 216.

205 In para 1(2)(a) and (b), Sch 1 CJA 1993.

206 Paragraph 1(3), Sch 1 CJA 1993. Paragraph 25B, Sch 1 FSA1986 provides a limited exclusion from investment business where the investment activity of arranging deals in investments is engaged in for the purposes of carrying out the functions of a body or association which is approved under that paragraph as an international securities self-regulating organisation. Such an activity engaged in by the organisation or by any person acting on its behalf is not regarded as constituting the carrying on of investment business in the United Kingdom for the purposes of the FSA1986. See para 25B further.

defence, a 'market maker' is defined[205] as meaning a person who holds himself out at all normal times in compliance with the rules of a regulated market or an approved organisation as willing to acquire or dispose of securities and is recognised as doing so under those rules. Also, an 'approved organisation' means an international securities self-regulating organisation approved under para 25B, Sch 1 Financial Services Act 1986.[206]

The defence is that an individual will not be guilty of insider dealing through dealing in securities or encouraging another person to deal[207] if he is able to show that he acted in good faith in the course of his business as a market maker[208] or his employment in the business of a market maker.[209] There is no requirement that the market maker must have acquired any relevant information that he possesses in the course of his business. How any information was acquired is immaterial.[210] Also, the legislative intention was that this defence should only be applicable to the market making and not all the employees of a market maker.[211] Whether an individual will be able to demonstrate that he had acted 'in good faith', to the satisfaction of the court, will depend on his situation and on the facts and circumstances of the particular case.

'Market information'

The second 'special' defence to a charge of insider dealing relates to the possession by an individual of information which amounts to what is termed 'market information'.[212] This was envisaged as being a specific sort of information which market participants involved in major transactions would necessarily and inevitably possess.[213] An obvious example of market information might concern a person who has sold a large *tranche* of shares. Publication of that information would have an effect on the share price as would the knowledge that someone intended to dispose of the *tranche*.[214] The relevant provisions in fact contain two defences where an individual might otherwise be guilty of insider dealing through dealing in securities or through encouraging another person

---

207 See s 52(1) and (2)(a) CJA 1993.

208 Paragraph 1(1)(a), Sch 1 CJA 1993.

209 Paragraph 1(1)(b), Sch 1 CJA 1993.

210 *Per* the Economic Secretary to the Treasury, Mr Anthony Nelson. See the Report of Standing Committee B, 15 June 1993, at col 216.

211 *Ibid.*

212 *Ibid,* paragraphs 2–4, Sch 1 CJA 1993, inclusive.

213 *Ibid.*

214 *Ibid.*

215 Paragraph 4(a)-(e), Sch 1 CJA 1993.

216 See s 54 CJA 1993.

217 See s 55(2) and (3) CJA 1993.

to deal in securities where the information in question amounts to market information.

For the purposes of this 'special defence, 'market information' will be inside information. It is defined[215] as meaning information consisting of one or more of certain stated matters of fact which are set out in what seems to be an exclusive list. Those facts include where securities[216] of a particular kind have been or are to be acquired or disposed of or that their acquisition or disposal[217] is under consideration or is the subject of negotiation[218] and also the identity of the persons involved or likely to be involved in any capacity in an acquisition or disposal.[219]

The first defence[220] based upon the possession of market information provides that an individual will not be guilty of insider dealing by virtue of dealing in securities or through encouraging another person to deal in securities if he is able to show that the information which he had as an insider was market information[221] and that it was reasonable for an individual in his position to have acted as he did despite having that information as an insider at the time[222] In determining whether it was reasonable for an individual to do any act despite having market information at the time, certain factors (such as the circumstances in which the individual first had the information and in what capacity)[223] shall in particular be taken into account.[224] The second special defence[225] sets out circumstances in which it is considered acceptable for an individual to use market information. It provides that an individual will not be guilty of insider dealing by virtue of dealing in securities or encouraging another person to deal if he is able to show that he acted in connection with an acquisition or disposal which was under consideration or the subject of negotiation or in the course of a series of such acquisitions or disposals.[226] In doing so, he must show that he acted with a view to facilitating the accomplishment of the acquisition or disposal or the series of acquisitions or disposals[227] and it must also be the case that the information which the individual had as an insider was market information arising directly out of his involvement in the acquisition or disposal or series of acquisitions or disposals.[228]

Price stabilisation

The third 'special' defence relates to the securities market practice known as 'price

---

218 Paragraph 4(a), Sch 1 CJA 1993.

219 Paragraph 4(e), Sch 1 CJA 1993.

220 Paragraph 2(1), Sch 1 CJA 1993.

221 Paragraph 2(1)(a), Sch 1 CJA 1993.

222 Paragraph 2(1)(b), Sch 1 CJA 1993.

223 Paragraph 2(2)(b), Sch 1 CJA 1993.

224 Paragraph 2(2), Sch 1 CJA 1993.

225 Paragraph 3, Sch 1 CJA 1993.

226 Paragraph 3(a)(i), Sch 1 CJA 1993.

227 Paragraph 3(a)(ii), Sch 1 CJA 1993. This provision echoes, albeit in different language, the defence provided by s 3(2) CS (ID) A 1985.

228 Paragraph 3(b), Sch 1 CJA 1993.

229 See Appendix E and Part 4 of the Conduct of Business Rules of the Securities and Investments

stabilisation'. This usually involves a 'stabilising manager' supporting the price of newly-issued securities for a limited period following their issue, while they are being offered to the public. The purpose is to ensure the success of the issue by keeping the price steady. The 'stabilising manager' is normally the securities house responsible for the new issue and stabilisation will involve it in purchasing some of the newly issued securities from the market to steady the price and prevent its decline.[229] The *rationale* for allowing stabilisation in controlled circumstances is twofold: to protect investors who might otherwise be affected by price fluctuations in respect of dealings following a new issue of securities and also to ensure the orderly distribution of securities.[230]

As stabilisation involves the price of securities being maintained artificially, it is a form of market manipulation which can be a criminal offence under s 47(2) Financial Services Act 1986.[231] However, s 48(7) Financial Services Act 1986 provides, generally speaking, that s 47(2) will not be regarded as contravened by anything done for the purposes of stabilising the price of investments if it is done in conformity with the Stabilisation Rules promulgated by the Securities and Investments Board and contained in Part 10 Financial Services (Conduct of Business) Rules 1990.[232] In the absence of this third 'special' defence, the actions of a stabilising manager would involve insider dealing. He would have information as an insider[233] and would be dealing in securities[234] that were price-affected securities[235] in relation to that information.[236] The defence however provides that an individual will not be guilty of insider dealing by virtue of dealing in securities or encouraging another person to deal if he shows that he acted in conformity with the price stabilisation rules.[237]

Individuals acting on behalf of public sector bodies

---

230 See *Hansard* for 30 October 1986, at cols 538–47. Also, it has been said that stabilisation was originally excluded from the restrictions on insider dealing to ensure the Eurobond 'market' did not move away from the United Kingdom to a financial centre with a more relaxed attitude. See Ashe & Counsell, *Insider Trading* (Fourmat Publishing) referring to Suter, *The Regulation of Insider Dealing In Britain* (Butterworths) at p 116 and also Rider, Abrams and Ferran, *Guide to the Financial Services Act 1986* (CCH Editions, 2nd edn) at para 730.

231 Generally speaking, market manipulation is made a criminal offence by s 47(2) FSA 1986 which provides that 'Any person who does any act or engages in any course of conduct which creates a false or misleading impression as to the market in or the price or value of any investments is guilty of an offence if he does so for the purpose of creating that impression and of thereby inducing another person to acquire, dispose of, subscribe for or underwrite those investments or to refrain from doing so or to exercise, or refrain from exercising, any rights conferred by those investments'. See Chapter 10, *The Regulation of Insider Dealing in the United Kingdom* by G Brazier (Cavendish Publishing Limited, 1996), for a fuller treatment.

232 See s 48(2)(i),(7),(7A),(8) and (9) FSA 1986.

233 Probably on the basis of ss 56(1) and 57(1), (2)(a)(ii) CJA 1993.

234 Section 55 CJA 1993.

235 Section 56(2) CJA 1993.

236 Section 52(1) CJA 1993.

237 Paragraph 5(1), Sch 1 CJA 1993.

238 Section 63(1) CJA 1993.

239 Section 60(3)(b) CJA 1993.

The offence of insider dealing does not apply to anything done by an individual acting on behalf of a 'public sector body' in pursuit of monetary policies or policies with respect to exchange rates or the management of public debt or foreign exchange reserves.[238] This provision is intended to apply only to 'official' activities in pursuit of monetary policy and the like. The expression 'public sector body' is defined[239] as meaning any one of five bodies which include the government of, and any local authority in, the United Kingdom.[240]

MONITORING, ENFORCEMENT AND PROSECUTION

The usual scenario

If there are unusual price movements or dealings in securities, these matters are likely to be noticed by the market surveillance group of the London Stock Exchange. This unit monitors the securities market by computer. If there is strong evidence of insider dealing, the case will be referred by the Stock Exchange to the Department of Trade and Industry which will consider what took place further. If necessary, inspectors may be appointed pursuant to ss 177–78 Financial Services Act 1986 or, more generally, pursuant to Part XIV Companies Act 1985. If appointed, such inspectors[241] have wide powers and may, for instance, examine on oath any person who they consider may be able to give information concerning insider dealing offences.

The criminal sanction

A prosecution may follow such investigation. Basically, proceedings for offences under Part V Criminal Justice Act 1993 may not be instituted in England and Wales except by or with the consent of the relevant Secretary of State[242] or the Director of Public Prosecutions.[243] In relation to proceedings in Northern Ireland, either the Secretary of State or the Director of Public Prosecutions for Northern Ireland must consent to proceedings being brought.[244] With regard to these proceedings, the Economic Secretary to the Treasury commented[245] that 'The government expect that the arrangements for bringing prosecutions will continue as at present, with the majority of

---

240 Sections 60(3)(b)(i) and (ii) CJA 1993.

241 Usually a chartered accountant and a Queen's Counsel.

242 The Secretary of State for Trade and Industry; presently glorying in the title of the President of the Board of Trade.

243 Section 61(2)(a) and (b) CJA 1993.

244 Section 61(3) CJA 1993.

245 As the Criminal Justice Bill went through the parliamentary process.

246 Per the Economic Secretary to the Treasury, Mr Anthony Nelson. See the Report of Standing Committee B, 15 June 1993, at col 206.

247 Ibid at col 208.

prosecutions being brought by the Secretary of State for Trade and Industry, but the stock exchange will be given permission to bring prosecutions where appropriate'.[246] He mentioned that this had already occurred once. He also thought that it might be feasible for the Securities and Investments Board to prosecute in a case of insider dealing.[247] The arrangements for bringing prosecutions replicate similar provisions in the Company Securities (Insider Dealing) Act 1985[248] which were said to '... have effectively prevented vexatious actions'.[249]

In 1990, in response to the Trade and Industry Select Committee, the Conservative government stated its intention to retain criminal sanctions as the primary means of preventing and punishing insider dealing[250] The Conservative government has continued to believe that '... criminal offences prosecuted in the courts should remain the primary means of action against insider dealers'.[251] The Conservative government also believes that the standard of proof required in prosecutions for insider dealing should remain 'beyond all reasonable doubt' and should not be reduced to the standard required in civil litigation which is that of a 'balance of probabilities'.[252]

On summary conviction, an individual guilty of insider dealing may be liable to a fine not exceeding the statutory maximum or imprisonment for a term not exceeding six months or to both.[253] On conviction on indictment, such an individual may be liable to a fine or imprisonment for a term not exceeding seven years or to both.[254] These provisions carry forward and reapply the penalties which were available under the Company Securities (Insider Dealing) Act 1985[255] and the maximum penalty of

---

248 See s 8(2) CS (ID) A 1985.

249 *Per* the Economic Secretary to the Treasury, Mr Anthony Nelson. See the Report of Standing Committee B, 15 June 1993, at col 206.

250 In response to a suggestion that sanctions imposed by a civil regulator might provide an alternative 'civil' penalty for insider dealing, the point was made that 'The regulator's action would be to impose a sanction on the basis that it was in the public interest to penalise individuals who conducted themselves in a particular way. That is the classic reason for creating a criminal offence. The government accordingly believes that the criminal law remains appropriate'. That passage was quoted by the Economic Secretary to the Treasury, Mr Anthony Nelson. See the Report of Standing Committee B, *ibid* at col 207.

251 *Per* the Economic Secretary to the Treasury, Mr Anthony Nelson. See the Report of Standing Committee B, *ibid* at col 207.

252 *Ibid.*

253 Section 61(1)(a) CJA 1993.

254 Section 61(1)(b) CJA 1993.

255 See s 8(1) CS(ID)A 1985.

256 *Per* the Economic Secretary to the Treasury, Mr Anthony Nelson. See the Report of Standing Committee B, *ibid* at col 206.

257 See s 5 ('Agreements made by or through unauthorised persons') FSA 1986, sub-s (1) of which provides, essentially, that certain agreements which are entered into by a person in the course of carrying on unauthorised investment business or are entered into by a person who is an authorised or exempted person but in consequence of anything done or said by a person in the course of carrying on unauthorised investment business shall be unenforceable against the other party. That other party will be entitled to recover any money or other property paid or transferred by him under the agreement together with compensation for any loss sustained by him as a result of having parted with it. See s 5(7) in relation to the agreements to which s 5(1) is applicable. See Chapter 2, *The Regulation of Insider Dealing in the United Kingdom* by G Brazier (Cavendish Publishing Limited, 1996) in relation to investment business and the need for authorisation.

imprisonment for a term not exceeding seven years and an unlimited fine is said to reflect '... the seriousness with which the government regard the crime of insider dealing'.[256]

Unlike cases involving the carrying on of unauthorised investment business[257] no contract is void simply because one of the parties was an insider dealer. Likewise, no contract is made unenforceable by reason only of the commission of offences involving insider dealing.[258] This has the effect that where a deal by an insider is part of a series of transactions relating to a particular *tranche* of securities, his involvement will not prevent settlement of those transactions.[259]

---

258 Section 63(2) CJA 1993.

259 This example was given by the Economic Secretary to the Treasury, Mr Anthony Nelson. See the Report of Standing Committee B, *ibid* at col 213.

CHAPTER TEN

DIRECTORS

INTRODUCTION

Since a company is an artificial legal person it needs individuals who can act for it, represent it and make decisions concerning how it is to be run. These individuals are the directors, who are officers of the company. But unlike the position in certain other jurisdictions,[1] a director of a company in the UK does not have to be a natural person but can be another company.

As far as the legal requirements in the Companies Acts are concerned, every public company is required to have at least two directors[2] and every private company is required to have at least one director.[3] Apart from these requirements, it will be the articles which will lay down how many directors the company should have and how the directors should be appointed, how their office is to be vacated and how they should be replaced. Table A, article 64 provides that:

> 'Unless otherwise determined by ordinary resolution, the number of directors ... shall not be subject to any maximum but shall not be less than two.'

Articles 73-80 provide the procedures for retirement by rotation, appointment and reappointment and article 81 provides for the disqualification and removal of directors. The articles will also state whether a director must satisfy a share qualification requirement. If a director is required by the articles to acquire a certain number of shares on appointment, then by s 291 he is under a duty to acquire those shares within a two-month period (or such shorter time as may be fixed by the articles) and failure to do so will result in the vacation of his office.

So the director, as well as being an officer, may well be a shareholder, either voluntarily or as the result of a share qualification requirement. He may also be an employee of the company working under a contract of service. The term 'executive director' is normally applied to this sort of director and he will be expected to perform a specified role for the company. The articles will usually empower the board of directors to appoint such employees for instance, Table A article 84 provides that:

> 'the directors may appoint one or more of their number to the office of managing director or to any other executive office under the company and may enter into an agreement or arrangement with any director for his employment by the company or for the provision by him of any services outside the scope of the ordinary duties of a director.'

---

1   For example, Germany and France.
2   Companies Act 1985, s 282(1).
3   Companies Act 1985, s 282 (3).

Non-executive directors, on the other hand, are officers of the company who do not have such an employment relationship with the company and are usually only awarded a relatively small fee for rendering their services. In the recent Cadbury Report on Corporate Governance the important role of the non-executive director was recognised and it was said in particular that they:

'should bring an independent judgment to bear on issues of strategy, performance, resources, including key appointments and standards of conduct.'[4]

The Cadbury Committee was set up to examine the responsibilities of executive and non-executive directors and auditors in relation to financial reporting and accountability, and to make recommendations on good practice, primarily in the context of listed companies, but it expressed the hope that their recommendations would be adopted by others. The larger the company, the more appropriate it is to have an independent voice on the board, and the Cadbury Report emphasises the need to maintain this independence; first by restricting a majority of the non-executive directors' business relationships with the company, and second, keeping the fees paid to them by the company at a level which will not undermine their independence.[5]

It is important to note that the distinction between executive and non-executive directors is not one which is known or recognised by the law in the sense that generally speaking non-executive directors are subject to the same duties and liabilities as executive directors.

The way in which the law controls and regulates the conduct of directors has never been by way of a complete statutory code. Despite an unsuccessful attempt to enact in a statutory provision[6] the general content of a director's duty, instead there has been a gradual increase in the number of statutory provisions, principally in Part IX and Part X of the Companies Act 1985, which lay down specific *ad hoc* duties and obligations on directors, which amongst other objectives seek to enforce fairness by a director in his dealings with the company. These will be examined in detail later in this chapter. Apart from this, though, the courts have been ready to intervene throughout the history of the registered company to protect the company from fraud, bad faith and, historically to a much lesser extent, incompetence. Since there was no specific law of directors' duties laid down, the courts have been guided in the formulation of the principles by analogy from the law of agency and the law relating to trustees. The directors were representing and acting for the company, and possessed the ability to enter into legal relationships with third parties, so there was an obvious reason for the imposition of an agent's duties on the director.

'A corporate body can only act by agents, and it is of course the duty of those agents so to act as best to promote the interests of the corporation whose affairs they are conducting. Such agents have duties to discharge of a fiduciary nature towards their principal.'[7]

---

4   Report of the Committee on the Financial Aspects of Corporate Governance (1992) para 4.11.

5   *Ibid*, para 4.13.

6   See, for example, the Companies Bill 1978, cl 44.

7   *Aberdeen Railway Co v Blaikie Bros* (1854) 1 Macq 461 at 471.

In addition many judges stated that directors occupy a position similar to that of a trustee and are similarly to be subject to a trustee's fiduciary duty. So in *Great Eastern Rly Co v Turner*[8] Lord Selborne LC states that:

'[t]he directors are the mere trustees or agents of the company ... trustees of the company's money and property ... [and] agents in the transactions which they enter into on behalf of the company.'[9]

The origin of this approach may well be the position of the directors who managed the so-called deed of settlement companies which developed after the passing of the Bubble Act in 1720. Here, because the company was unincorporated and had no separate legal personality, the assets had to be vested in the hands of trustees who held them on trust for the subscribers and often these persons would also be appointed the directors as well. After the emergence of the registered company since a director was exercising power over and was essentially in control of assets of which he was not the beneficial owner, it was relatively straightforward for the judges of the Court of Chancery to whom company disputes were assigned to view him as occupying a position similar to that of trustee;[10] one essential difference being, of course, that directors of registered companies do not have the legal title of the company's property vested in them: that remains vested in the company. It has been difficult at times to justify the use of the trustee analogy when directors are required to operate in a commercial environment and produce a profit for the company whereas the trustee's overriding obligation is to preserve the trust assets. Subsequently judges have denied the existence of any strict trustee analogy.[11]

Remuneration

A director is not an employee of the company merely by reason of holding office, further he is not entitled merely by holding office to any remuneration for the services he performs. As McCardie J in *Moriarty v Regent's Garage & Co*[12] stated:

'Not only is a director not a servant of the company, but he is not, *prima facie*, entitled to any remuneration for his service. Therefore, for a director to get remuneration, he must show some contract or agreement to be inferred from the articles of association.'[13]

Again, in *Re George Newman & Co Ltd*,[14] Lindley LJ stated:

'Directors have no right to be paid for their services, and cannot pay themselves or each other, or make presents to themselves out of the company's assets, unless authorised so

---

8   (1872) LR 8 Ch App 149.

9   *Ibid* at 152.

10   See Sealy, *Company Law and Commercial Reality* (1984, London) at pp 38–39.

11   For example, Kay J in *Re Faure Electric Accumulator Co* (1888) 40 Ch D 141.

12   [1921] 1 KB 423.

13   *Ibid* at 446.

14   [1895] 1 Ch 674.

to do by the instrument which regulates the company or by the shareholders at a properly convened meeting.'[15]

Therefore the company's constitution will usually provide for the payment of directors and provide for how the amount is to be calculated.

Table A, article 82 provides that:

'the directors shall be entitled to such remuneration as the company may by ordinary resolution determine ...'

This does not of itself form a contract between the director and the company, although if the articles specify a particular amount and the director has performed services for the company, then the court can find that there was an implied contract which incorporated the remuneration clause into it, therefore, as regards the past the director can sue for the sum as a contractual debt.[16]

On the other hand where the articles simply state that 'remuneration of directors for services will be such a sum to be paid at such times as the directors or the general meeting may determine' and no such determination is ever made, then the directors cannot sue.[17]

Guinness plc v Saunders[18] provides a recent illustration of the importance of the articles to the payment of directors' remuneration. Here the company's articles provided that the board should fix the annual remuneration and also any extra, special remuneration in respect of services which, in the opinion of the board, were outside the scope of the ordinary duties of a director. These articles were construed strictly, so a claim by the director that the remuneration could be fixed by a committee of the board instead of the whole board failed.

Executive directors will be employed under a separate contract of service and Table A, article 84, provides that:

'Any such appointment, agreement or arrangement may be made upon such terms as the directors determine and they may remunerate any such director for his services as they think fit.'

It is quite common in larger companies and public companies for the annual remuneration of the executive directors to be fixed by a 'remuneration committee' of the board. This remuneration committee will normally be composed of non-executive directors who, it is believed, will bring a measure of independence to bear on the question of executive salaries. The Cadbury Committee recommended that remuneration committees should be composed wholly or mainly of non-executive directors, with executive directors playing no part in the fixing of salaries.[19] The articles

---

15   *Ibid* at 686.

16   *Re New British Iron Co ex p Beckwith* [1898] 1 Ch 324.

17   *Re Richmond Gate Property Co Ltd* [1965] 1 WLR 335.

18   [1990] 2 AC 663.

19   Report of the Committee on the Financial Aspects of Corporate Governance (1992), para 4.42.

will then usually provide that the recommendations be approved by the board. The Cadbury Committee considered whether it would be appropriate to give shareholders the opportunity to determine the question of directors' pay in general meeting.[20] It decided against making any such recommendation because it was thought that a director's pay was too complex a matter simply to be reduced to a vote for or against a particular remuneration package. Instead it considered that more opportunities should be given to the shareholders to influence board policies in this matter.[21]

Table A, article 83 allows for the payment to directors of their expenses properly incurred by them in connection with attending meetings of the company or otherwise in connection with the discharge of their duties.

Table A, article 87 allows the company to make provision for a director or any member of his family on his retirement, whether by the payment of a gratuity or pension, including the payment of contributions or premiums. But it must be borne in mind that if the company is not contractually bound to pay these benefits then they will have to be approved by the general meeting under s 312 unless they are a *bona fide* payment by way of pension in respect of past services.[22]

By s 311 a company cannot pay a director remuneration free of income tax, and if any article or provision in a contract purports to pay a director a sum net of tax that sum is deemed to be a gross sum which is subject to income tax.

There is an obligation imposed by s 314 on directors, where the company is being taken over following an offer made to the shareholders, to take reasonable steps to ensure that the particulars of any proposed payment to them by way of compensation for loss of office (or retirement) is included in or sent with any notice of the offer which is circulated or given to any of the shareholders. The consequences of failing to comply with this requirement are that the directors are liable to a fine[23] and any such sum received by the directors is deemed to have been received by them in trust for persons who have sold their shares as a result of the offer.[24]

Once it is established that there is authority to pay a director remuneration, then the amount of that remuneration is not a matter for the courts as long as it can be said to be a genuine payment of director's remuneration and not a disguised gift out of capital. Nor is there any requirement that a director's remuneration be paid only out of profits. In *Re Halt Garage (1964) Ltd*[25] a husband and wife held all the issued shares in a company and were the only directors. In the liquidation of the company, the liquidator sought to recover sums from the directors which had been paid to them as remuneration. The articles provided that directors' remuneration be determined by the company in general meeting.

---

20   *Ibid*, para 4.43.
21   *Ibid*, para 4.45.
22   Companies Act 1985, s 316(3).
23   Companies Act 1985, s 314(3).
24   Companies Act 1985, s 315.
25   [1982] 3 All ER 1016.

The company during the relevant period was suffering a trading loss, but the directors continued to draw sums in respect of remuneration, even though in the case of the wife she took no part in the running or management of the business. In the view of Oliver J:

'[i]n the absence of fraud on the creditors or on minority shareholders, the quantum of such remuneration is a matter for the company. There is no implication or requirement that it must come out of profits only, and indeed, any requirement that it must be so restricted would, in many cases, bring business to a halt and prevent a business which had fallen on hard times from being brought round.'[26]

Further, on turning to the question of quantum:

'... I do not think that, in the absence of evidence that the payments made were patently excessive or unreasonable, the court can or should engage on a minute examination of whether it would have been more appropriate or beneficial to the company to fix the remuneration at £x rather than £y so long as it is satisfied that it was indeed drawn as remuneration. That is a matter left by the company's constitution to its members.'[27]

Therefore in respect of the husband who had been running the business, Oliver J declined to interfere with his drawings. In respect of the wife, though, since the greater part of the payments to her could not be treated as genuine director's remuneration, he substituted a much lower figure to which she was entitled.[28]

It should be noted that cases subsequent to *Re Halt Garage Ltd* have involved situations where a member has challenged alleged excessive payments to directors under s 459.[29]

A director cannot claim a *quantum meruit* from the company if he undertakes work for it as a director but is not paid remuneration under the authority of the articles. A claim for *quantum meruit* failed in *Guinness plc v Saunders*, so too did a claim for an equitable allowance. Lord Templeman found it difficult to conceive of circumstances where a court of equity would exercise its jurisdiction to award such remuneration to a director, who is in a fiduciary position in relation to the company, when the articles of association provide a procedure for awarding remuneration which had not been followed.

Craven-Ellis v Canons Ltd[30] is a decision where a court did award a *quantum meruit* to a person who was appointed as a managing director under a contract, but that case can be distinguished because the company's articles provided that a director satisfy a share qualification requirement within two months of his appointment. When the director concerned failed to acquire the necessary shares, but nevertheless carried out

---

26 *Ibid* at 1023.

27 *Ibid* at 1041.

28 See p 157.

29 For example, *Re Cumana* [1986] BCLC 430.

30 [1936] 2 KB 403.

work for the company, he could claim for a *quantum meruit* since technically he was never a director of the company.

In *Re Duomatic Ltd,*[31] where a director had worked for the company and paid himself remuneration which had not been formally authorised by the general meeting in accordance with the articles, Buckley J stressed that a director is not entitled to a *quantum meruit* but on the facts of this case all the shareholders could be shown to be assenting to the payments and therefore the director was excused from liability to repay the money drawn.

Lastly, the 1985 Act requires a certain amount of disclosure in respect of directors' salaries. But instead of requiring each director's salary to be stated, s 232(1) and Sch 6, Part I require the aggregate amount of directors' emoluments to be shown in the accounts. Schedule 6 requires the chairman's salary to be disclosed and also, if any of the directors' emoluments exceed the chairman's, the emoluments of the highest paid director. There shall also be shown the number of directors whose emoluments fell into a range of specified bands. The company is also required by Sch 6 para 8 to disclose in the accounts the aggregate amount of any compensation to directors or past directors in respect of loss of office.

DUTIES AND OBLIGATIONS OF DIRECTORS GENERALLY

Duties are owed to the company

It is important to appreciate that whatever duties the directors are subjected to, they owe those duties to the company and not to shareholders as individuals. This is because in recent times the company has been viewed as the 'corporators as a general body'.[31a] This is readily understood if the directors are viewed simply as agents for the company, since the company as a separate entity with its own rights and liabilities is the principal, but even in 1902 in the case of *Percival v Wright*[32] it was being argued that the directors were trustees both for the company and for the shareholders who were the real beneficiaries, and therefore the directors owed duties to shareholders. This was easily rejected by Swinfen Eady J, who stated that directors were not under any fiduciary duty to individual shareholders. Here shareholders sought to have share transfers to the directors set aside on the ground that at the time they were entered into, the directors had not disclosed to them the existence of negotiations with a third party for the purchase of the company's shares thus increasing their value. This rule has been departed from in certain special circumstances where, for instance, the directors have acted in such a way that they have become implied agents for the shareholders in negotiations with third parties.[33]

---

31   [1969] 2 Ch 365.

31a See Lord Eversham MR in *Greenhalgh v Arderne Cinemas Ltd* [1951] Ch 286 and see the discussion of Laskin J in *Teck Corp Ltd v Millar* (1973) 33 DLR (3d) 288 at 313 *et seq.*

32   [1902] 2 Ch 421.

33   See, for example, *Allen v Hyatt* (1914) 30 TLR 444.

In the special case of a company which has become a 'target company' in a takeover bid, the question arises as to the position of the director in giving advice to the shareholders on whether to accept or reject a particular offer for their shares, or in a contested takeover, which of two or more competing bids to accept. Obviously in certain situations it may be of benefit to the directors themselves for the company not to be taken over or for one bidder to succeed rather than another. In *Gething v Kilner*[34] it was held by Brightman J that the directors in this situation have a duty towards their shareholders which includes a duty to be honest and not to mislead.

This was taken further in *Heron International Ltd v Lord Grade*,[35] where the judgment of the Court of Appeal seemed to suggest that the directors would, having decided that it was in the interests of the company that the company should be taken over, have a duty to the current shareholders only to obtain the best price for the shares. But subsequent judgments have not accepted this proposition and instead it has been interpreted as a decision turning on the articles of the company. In *Re a Company*[36] Hoffmann J rejected the proposition that directors were under a positive duty to recommend and obtain the highest possible bid. Here the directors were not in breach of any duty when they had taken the reasonable view that a lower offer for the shares was preferable, and this was the one which was recommended to shareholders. Hoffmann J stated:

> 'I do not think that fairness can require more of the directors than to give the shareholders sufficient information and advice to enable them to reach a properly informed decision and to refrain from giving misleading advice or exercising their fiduciary powers in a way which would prevent or inhibit shareholders from choosing a better price'.[37]

Further in *Dawson International v Coats Paton* there is strong support from Lord Cullen in the Scottish Court of Session for the *Percival v Wright* approach save that if directors do take it upon themselves to give advice to current shareholders then they have a duty to advise in good faith and not fraudulently, and not to mislead whether deliberately or carelessly. If shareholders suffer as a result of a breach of this duty then they would have a personal action to recover this loss from the directors.

Duty to employees

Directors owe no duty to the company's employees. In cases where directors have exercised their discretion for the benefit of employees and, for instance, made *ex gratia* payments to them the courts have considered those payments not in relation to the directors' duties, but actually whether they were *ultra vires* the company. In holding that on the facts the payments were *ultra vires* the company it would also be a breach of the directors' duties to the company to make them. Whilst it was recognised in *Hutton v*

---

34 [1972] 1 WLR 337.

35 [1983] BCLC 244.

36 [1986] BCLC 383.

37 *Ibid* at 389.

West Cork Rly[38] that money could be spent on retaining a committed and contented workforce, that would only be proper if the company itself was gaining a benefit.

'[t]he law does not say that there are to be no cakes and ale, but there are to be no cakes and ale for the benefit of the company.'[39]

If the company were in or going into liquidation it would not be an advantage to have a contented workforce, and any such payments would be *ultra vires* and improper.[40] The position in relation to employees was modified by the Companies Act 1980 which introduced two new provisions. To avoid the *ultra vires* problem, what is now s 719 of the 1985 Act provides that the company in any case does have power to make provision for employees or former employees of the company or any of its subsidiaries 'in connection with the cessation or the transfer ... of the whole or part of the undertaking of the company or that subsidiary'. Further, the power can be exercised notwithstanding that its exercise is not in the best interests of the company. If the power is conferred on the company only by reason of this section then it can be exercised only if sanctioned by an ordinary resolution, but the constitution can provide that an exercise of the power can be sanctioned by a resolution of the directors or by some resolution of the company other than an ordinary resolution.

At a more general level, what is now s 309 provides that the matters to which the directors can have regard in the performance of their functions include the interests of the company's employees in general, as well as the interests of its members. But the scope of this section should be carefully noted. By s 309(2) the duty imposed on the directors is owed to the company and not the employees themselves. Further, the duty can only be enforced in the same way as any other fiduciary duty owed to the company. Read as a whole, the section is of at least as much benefit to the directors as the employees, since it prevents the directors being held to be in breach of duty where it is known that they have taken into account the effect on the company's employees when making a particular decision. For the employees, since the duty is not owed to them directly, they have no *locus standi* to enforce it and, in any event, their interests are only one of a competing number of interests which directors have to take into account.

The section does not allow directors to exercise their discretion in favour of particular employees with impunity, since they are to have regard to the interests of employees in general, but it does allow directors, for instance, to consider the effect of competing takeover bids on the company's employees when deciding which one to recommend to shareholders.

In *Re Welfab Engineering Ltd*[41] the directors chose to sell the whole business of the company, together with its debts, in the hope that the business could survive, instead of simply selling the land on which the business was situated, which would have certainly brought about the closure of the business and liquidation but would have achieved a

---

38 (1883) 23 Ch D 654.

39 *Ibid* at 673.

40 *Parke v Daily News Ltd* [1962] Ch 927. See p 127.

41 [1990] BCLC 833.

slightly higher price for the company. When the company subsequently went into liquidation, the liquidator brought misfeasance proceedings against the directors. Hoffmann J held that the directors were not in breach of their duty to the company and that:

> '[the] directors are not entitled to sell the business to save their jobs and those of other employees on terms which would clearly leave the creditors in a worse position than on a liquidation. But I do not think that an honest attempt to save the business should be judged by a stricter standard. This is particularly so against the background of the pressures which must have been imposed on directors of companies like this by the widespread unemployment and industrial devastation in the Midlands at the time.'[42]

Section 309 was not cited in the judgment.

Duty to creditors

Up until a few years ago it would have been confidently declared that in law, directors owe no duties to creditors of the company or other outsiders. The position was as stated by Jessel MR in 1878 that:

> '[i]t has always held that the directors are trustees for the shareholders, that is, for the company. ... But directors are not trustees for the creditors of the company. The creditors have certain rights against a company and its members, but they have no greater rights against the directors than against any other members of the company. They have only those statutory rights against the members which are given them in the winding-up.'[43]

Possibly as a result of increasing concern for creditors, particularly unsecured creditors, in the wake of the Cork Report published in 1984 and the introduction of statutory liabilities such as wrongful trading, some recent judgments have contained statements which seem to alter radically the position of the director in relation to creditors.

The first such statement in England in this direction appears in *Lonrho Ltd v Shell Petroleum Co Ltd*[44] where Lord Diplock stated, without discussion or citing any authority, that the directors must consider what is in the best interests of the company and that these are not exclusively those of its shareholders but may include those of its creditors. He was in fact going no further than Mason J in the High Court of Australia in *Walker v Wimborne*[45] who had stated that:

> 'the directors of a company in discharging their duty to the company must take account of the interest of its shareholders and its creditors. Any failure by the directors to take into account the interests of creditors will have adverse consequences for the company as well as for them.'

---

42 *Ibid* at 838.
43 *Re Wincham Shipbuilding, Boiler and Salt Co, Poole, Jackson and Whyte's Case* (1878) 9 Ch D 322 at 328.
44 [1980] 1 WLR 627.
45 (1976) 137 CLR 1.

Then in *Winkworth v Edward Baron Developments Ltd*[46] Lord Templeman made some extremely wide-ranging suggestions to the effect that a company owes a duty to its creditors, present and future, and that a duty is owed by the directors to the company *and to the creditors* of the company to ensure that the affairs of the company are properly administered, that its property is not dissipated for the benefit of the directors and that it is available for the repayment of creditors' debts. These latter statements went beyond the Commonwealth cases which had foreshadowed these developments in England, since these had been concerned with companies which were at the material time insolvent. Furthermore, the idea that directors in normal circumstances owed duties directly to creditors was difficult to rationalise, since not only would it place the directors in an impossible position in certain commercial situations, it would also mean that creditors would be in a better position than shareholders to pursue breaches of directors duties. In fact though, the leading case in Australia, *Kinsela v Russell Kinsela Pty Ltd*,[47] is quite specific. Here Street CJ stated that:

'[i]n a solvent company the proprietary interests of the shareholders entitle them as a general body to be regarded as the company when questions of the duty of directors arise. ... But where a company is insolvent the interests of the creditors intrude. It is in a practical sense their assets and not the shareholders' assets that, through the medium of the company, are under the management of the directors pending either liquidation, return to solvency, or the imposition of some alternative administration.'[48]

In this case the directors had granted themselves a lease over property owned by the company at a time when the company finances were precarious. The trial judge found that the rent was substantially below a market rental. As the directors were in breach of their duty to the company as the lease directly prejudiced the creditors it was voidable.

Some clarification of the position for English law was made in *West Mercia Safetywear v Dodd*.[49] Here, D was a director of both the company and its parent company. At a time when the company was in financial difficulty and after D had been instructed by an accountant not to use the company's bank account, D transferred £4,000 from the company's account to the parent company. This reduced a debt owed by the company to the parent but the intention behind the payment was to reduce the parent company's bank overdraft which D had personally guaranteed.

In these circumstances the Court of Appeal held that the payment amounted to a fraudulent preference because D had acted in disregard of the interests of the general creditors of the company, and in approving the statement of Street CJ in *Kinsela v Russell Kinsela Pty Ltd* quoted above, held D to be in breach of his duty to the company.

---

46 [1986] 1 WLR 1512.
47 (1986) 4 NSWLR 722.
48 *Ibid* at 730.
49 [1988] BCLC 250.

So instead of owing a duty directly to creditors, the position is that directors have, in fulfilling their duties to the company in certain circumstances, most notably where the company is insolvent, a duty to consider the interests of creditors. Confirmation that a director does not owe duties to creditors as such was made in *Kuwait Asia Bank EC v National Mutual Life Nominees Ltd*[50] where, in the judgment of the Privy Council, it was stated that a 'director does not by reason only of his position as director owe any duty to creditors ... of the company'.

Obligation on directors not to fetter their discretion

The fiduciary duty obliges a director not to allow his duty to the company to come into conflict with either his own personal interest or with the interests of a third party. Therefore, unlike a shareholder, who is free to vote at a general meeting in whatever way he pleases and who can enter into agreements with others as to which way he will vote, a director is bound to act in the best interests of the company and *prima facie* he cannot enter into any arrangements or agreements with third parties as to how he should act or vote at board meetings. This would lead to an unlawful fettering of the director's discretion and the company is entitled to the full, free and unfettered advice of the director in board meetings.[51]

Recently, however, the Court of Appeal has adopted a significant distinction which was made by the High Court of Australia in *Thorby v Goldberg*.[52] Here it was held that directors could enter into an agreement which fettered the exercise of their discretion for the future if they had properly exercised their discretion at the time of making the agreement. So, if at that time:

'they are *bona fide* of opinion that it is in the interests of the company that the transaction should be entered into and carried into effect, I see no reason in law why they should not bind themselves to do whatever under the transaction is to be done by the board.'[53]

In *Fulham Football Club Ltd v Cabra Estates plc*[54] the directors of the company entered into a letter of undertaking with a third party whereby they agreed to use their powers to procure that the company did not object to a planning application submitted by the third party and would, if called upon, procure the company to write in support of the application. In return, the company received £11 million. The directors subsequently applied for a declaration that they were not bound by the undertakings since they conflicted with their duties to the company. The Court of Appeal, adopting the analysis of Kitto J In *Thorby v Goldberg*, refused the application and stated that the undertakings were part of contractual arrangements which, importantly, conferred substantial benefits on the company.

---

50 [1991] 1 AC 187.
51 See p 109.
52 (1964) 112 CLR 597.
53 *Ibid* at 606.
54 [1994] 1 BCLC 363.

The difficulty which directors can find themselves in and a commonly occurring one, is where they have agreed on a course of action which to a certain extent binds their future conduct, for example, to recommend to shareholders the sale of a particular asset belonging to the company which requires shareholder approval, or even to use their best endeavours to ensure that the sale goes ahead, and then subsequently discover that there is another, better offer or that the sale is not in the best interests of the company. This problem was considered in *John Crowther Group plc v Carpets International plc*[55] where the solution adopted by Vinelott J was to construe an agreement such as this as being always subject to the directors' fiduciary duty to act in the best interests of the company anyway, so directors were not in breach of the agreement by recommending a different course of action to the shareholders. In *Fulham Football Club Ltd v Cabra Estates plc* the Court of Appeal noted that *Thorby v Goldberg* had not been cited in *John Crowther Group plc v Carpets International plc* and thought that nothing in the decision meant that directors could not bind themselves as to the future exercise of their fiduciary powers.

So the present position is that, as long as the directors can show a proper exercise of their discretion in the interests of the company at the time they entered into an agreement restricting future exercise of their discretion, and certainly if there are substantial benefits to the company flowing from the agreement, then the directors will be held to the agreement and not be in breach of their duties to the company. This appears to be a position more in accord with the realities of commercial life rather than the strict 'trustee' approach of the directors position taken by Vinelott J. But could the Court of Appeal's view stand in the face of a dramatic change in circumstances after the signing of an agreement affecting the interests of the company? Further the Court of Appeal decision is only concerned with an agreement for certain specific matters affecting the directors' future conduct. It would surely be a wholly different situation if the directors bound themselves to act in accordance with the general directions of a third party.

Nominee and multiple directorships

This leads to the two overlapping problems of the nominee director and multiple directorships. A nominee director is one who is appointed to the board by a shareholder, often a parent company, or under a separate agreement, for instance in a loan agreement between the company and a bank. The obvious purpose of the nominee director is to represent the interests of the appointor on the board but the question then arises as to what extent this is lawful, since the company is entitled to expect that it will receive the benefit of the director's honest, independent judgment. However, this is where the law has to come to terms with the practical realities of commercial life. There is nothing to prevent the appointment of a nominee director, and the nominee can have regard to the position of his appointor when exercising his functions as a director, but only so long as those are consistent with the interests of the

---

55   [1990] BCLC 460. See also *Rackham v Peek Foods Ltd* (1977) [1990] BCLC 895.

company. Certainly a nominee director cannot put the interests of his appointor before the interests of the company nor can he put the interests of a corporate group before the interests of the company if the company is in a group of companies. An illustration of the difficulty which nominee directors can find themselves in is the case of *Scottish Co-operative Wholesale Society v Meyer*,[56] where there was a majority of nominee directors appointed by a parent company on the board of a partly-owned subsidiary. As a result of the nominee directors failing to have proper regard to the interests of the company, the independent shareholders were successful in alleging that the affairs of the company were oppressive to the members.[57]

Similarly, there is nothing in the Companies Acts or the cases[58] which *prima facie* prevents a director from having more than one directorship, even of companies whose businesses are similar. But it may well be that in practice the obligation imposed on a director to make disclosure of information to the board of the company as a result of his fiduciary duties would come into conflict with his duties of confidentiality to another company. In any case an executive director employed under a contract of service will almost certainly have his freedom to take up directorships of other companies curtailed by a contractual term.

THE FIDUCIARY DUTY

General

The fiduciary duty imposed on directors requires them to act *bona fide* and in the best interests of the company. Additionally they must exercise their powers for the proper purposes for which they were conferred and not for any collateral or improper purpose.[59] It is important to distinguish these two different aspects of the fiduciary duty, because in any given situation where the question is raised of whether or not a director is in breach of his duties, they require the application of a different test. The issue of collateral and improper purposes will be addressed separately below, but the general obligation to act *bona fide* and in the best interests means that a director is bound to act in what he perceives and not what a court may perceive to be in the best interests of the company at the time. The essentially subjective approach has to be circumscribed to a certain extent, otherwise a lunatic director acting *bona fide* but completely irrationally could give away the company's money. So, for example, in the words of Pennycuick J in *Charterbridge Corporation Ltd v Lloyds Bank Ltd*:[60]

'The proper test ... must be whether an intelligent and honest man in the position of a director of the company concerned, could, in the whole of the existing circumstances have reasonably believed that the transactions were for the benefit of the company.'[61]

---

56 [1959] AC 324.
57 Under the former s 210 of the Companies Act 1948. See now s 459 at p 291.
58 *London & Mashonaland Exploration Co Ltd v New Mashonaland Exploration Co Ltd* [1981] WN 165.
59 *Re Smith & Fawcett* [1942] Ch 304 *per* Lord Greene MR.
60 [1970] Ch 62.
61 *Ibid* at 74.

As long as a reasonable director could have believed what was done was for the benefit of the company, then the director under scrutiny can claim he has acted *bona fide* and escape liability.

Duty to use powers for a proper purpose

A director must not use his powers for a purpose other than the proper purpose for which they were conferred. To do so would be an abuse of the powers given to the directors and a breach of duty. As Hoffmann LJ has recently stated:

> 'if a director chooses to participate in the management of the company and exercises powers on its behalf, he owes a duty to act *bona fide* in the interests of the company. He must exercise the power solely for the purpose for which it was conferred.'[62]

So where a director used his powers to authorise documents transferring the company's assets to a third party in which he had an interest, for no good corporate purpose or reason, Hoffmann LJ characterised this as a use of the director's powers for an improper purpose.[63]

The power exercised by directors which has most often been called into question, however, is the power to issue new shares in the company. This power is a vitally important one since it could be used to alter the voting strengths of various interest groups within the company, prevent the shareholders from obtaining a resolution to remove the directors or could be used to resist a hostile takeover bid. In *Punt v Symons & Co Ltd*[64] Byrne J was faced with an issue of shares which had clearly been made with the object of creating enough voting power to alter the company's articles. He had no hesitation in holding that this was an improper use of the power since the power was primarily given to directors for the proper purpose of enabling them to raise extra capital when needed by the company. This case was applied in *Piercy v Mills & Co Ltd*[65] where it was held to be a breach of the directors' fiduciary duties to make allotments to maintain control of the company or to defeat the wishes of an existing majority of shareholders.

Subsequent interpretation and application of the rule has led the Commonwealth authorities to depart from the English approach, especially that of Buckley J in *Hogg v Cramphorn Ltd*.[66] Here, despite expressly finding that the directors had acted *bona fide* for the benefit of the company in issuing shares to a trust for the company's employees, so that the additional votes could be used to fight off a takeover bid which the directors believed in good faith was not in the company's interests, Buckley J still went on to ask the question: '[w]as such a manipulation of the voting position a legitimate act ...?' He held that it was not. This went further than the previous cases, because in those cases,

---

62   *Bishopsgate Investment Management Ltd v Maxwell* (1993) BCC 120 at 140.

63   *Ibid.*

64   [1903] 2 Ch 506.

65   [1920] 1 Ch 77.

66   [1967] Ch 254.

on the facts the directors had never had in mind the benefit of the company but only their own interests.

This approach has not been adopted in either Australia or Canada. In the Australian case of *Harlowe's Nominees Pty Ltd v Woodside (Lakes Entrance) Oil Co*[67] the argument that shares could only be issued to raise fresh capital for the company was rejected and it was stated that:

'[t]he principle is that although primarily the power is given to enable capital to be raised when required for the purposes of the company, there may be occasions when the directors may fairly and properly issue shares for other reasons, so long as those reasons relate to a purpose of benefiting the company as a whole, as distinguished from a purpose, for example, of maintaining control of the company in the hands of the directors themselves or their friend.'[68]

It was recognised that the directors may be concerned with a wide range of practical considerations and their judgment, if exercised in good faith and not for irrelevant purposes, would not be open to review.

In the Canadian case of *Teck Corporation v Millar*[69] the approach of *Hogg v Cramphorn* was expressly rejected. Here the Teck Corporation had acquired a majority of the company's shares. The directors of the company were of the view that it would be preferable for another company, Canex, to develop and exploit its mining properties, so they entered into an agreement giving Canex exclusive rights over its copper mines and promising to transfer 30% of the company's share capital in Canex. Teck objected to the agreement since it had the effect of preventing it from controlling the company. Berger J, in holding that the directors had not entered into the agreement for an improper purpose, stated that:

'the directors ought to be allowed to consider who is seeking control and why. If they believe that there will be substantial damage to the company's interests if the company is taken over, then the exercise of their powers to defeat those seeking a majority will not necessarily be categorised as improper ...'[70]

but:

'if they say that they believe there will be substantial damage to the company's interests, then there must be reasonable grounds for that belief. If there are not, that will justify a finding that the directors were actuated by an improper purpose. ... I think that directors are entitled to consider the reputation, experience and policies of anyone seeking to take over the company. If they decide, on reasonable grounds, a takeover will cause substantial damage to the company's interests, they are entitled to use their powers to protect the company.'[71]

---

67 (1968) 42 ALJ R 123.

68 *Ibid* at 125G.

69 (1973) 33 DLR (3d) 288.

70 *Ibid* at 315.

71 *Ibid* at 315 and 317.

The stance taken by the Canadian Court was that it was inconsistent with the injunction to directors laid down in *Re Smith & Fawcett Ltd*[72] that they must exercise their discretion *bona fide* in what they consider – not what a court may consider – is in the interests of the company, and not for a collateral purpose, if the court could not allow them to act on their judgment that a particular takeover bid was not in the interests of the company. The English courts' answer to this would be that the formulation of Lord Greene MR in *Re Smith & Fawcett* has two elements, and whilst there is a general obligation on directors to act in what they subjectively believe is in the interests of the company, when it is a matter of the exercise of a specific power, the court will take an objective view of the proper purpose for which the power was given by, for example, construing the article conferring the power, and measure that against the purpose for which the directors have exercised it in the case in question.

In the Privy Council case of *Howard Smith Ltd v Ampol Petroleum Ltd*[73] the directors of a company issued new shares to one takeover bidder rather than another. Although the judge at first instance found that the directors had not been motivated by any purpose of personal advantage and that the company did need fresh capital at the time, the *primary purpose* of the allotment was to reduce the proportionate shareholding of one takeover bidder and to increase the others, thereby assisting the latter to succeed. In these circumstances the Privy Council held that this was an improper allotment and it was therefore invalid. Lord Wilberforce, in the course of his complex and difficult judgment, seeks to reconcile and draw together the Commonwealth and English authorities. He accepts that, for instance, it is too narrow to state categorically that shares can only be properly issued for the purpose of raising capital.

The court should begin by considering the power whose exercise is in question and then, having defined the limits within which it may be exercised, move on to examine the *substantial* purpose for which it was exercised in the particular case to determine whether it was a proper purpose or not.

When a court considers the substantial motivating purpose in a particular case against a proper purpose, there will be a number of possible improper purposes, the self-interest of the directors being the most common. Where the self-interest of the directors is involved they will not be allowed to plead that their action was *bona fide* for the benefit of the company. Lord Wilberforce considered *Hogg v Cramphorn* to be rightly decided and consistent with *Teck* because *Hogg* involved the self-interest of directors, namely the eventual outcome that they remained in control of the company, whereas in *Teck* the directors wanted to get the best deal for the company. This is difficult to accept in the light of the fact that it was common ground between the parties in *Hogg v Cramphorn* that the directors were not actuated from any personal motive and were honestly of the view that what they were doing was in the best interests of the company. The tenor of the judgment of Berger J is certainly not as narrow as Lord Wilberforce suggests and there is as mentioned above an express rejection of the *Hogg v Cramphorn* approach.

---

72   [1942] Ch 304.

73   [1974] AC 821.

What may be difficult for the courts to decide is that the decision of the directors to retain control or vest it in someone else was reached *bona fide* for the benefit of the company in the absence of evidence that the hostile takeover bidder will simply asset strip the company or otherwise harm the business.

Lord Wilberforce then develops a more fundamental objection to the actions of the directors in this case:

> 'The constitution of a limited company normally provides for directors with powers of management, and shareholders, with defined voting powers having power to appoint the directors, and to take, in general meeting, by majority vote, decisions on matters not reserved for management. Just as it is established that directors, within their management powers, may take decisions against the wishes of the majority shareholders ... so it must be unconstitutional for directors to use their fiduciary powers over the shares in the company purely for the purpose of destroying an existing majority, or creating a new majority which did not previously exist. ... If there is added, moreover, to this immediate purpose, an ulterior purpose to enable an offer for shares to proceed which the existing majority was in a position to block, the departure from the legitimate use of the fiduciary power becomes ... all the greater.'[74]

So the substantial and vitiating purpose in *Howard Smith v Ampol* was the unconstitutional use of the share issuing power to manipulate the voting power.

In *Lee Panavision Ltd v Lee Lighting Ltd*[75] there was another illustration of how the use by directors of their powers for improper purposes can be unconstitutional. This would occur where, as in this case, the directors decide to commit the company to a management agreement whereby a third party runs the company's business and nominates its directors at a time when it is known by the directors that the company's shareholders wish to remove the current directors.

> 'The function of the directors is to manage, but the appointment of the directors who are to do the managing is constitutionally a function of the shareholders in general meeting. Therefore it must have been unconstitutional for the directors, knowing ... that the shareholders were proposing as soon as they could to exercise their constitutional right to appoint new directors, to take all managerial powers away from any new directors who might be appointed by committing [the company] to the ... management agreement.'[76]

Not surprisingly the development of this constitutional justification for interfering with the actions of directors circumvents any objections that the courts should not interfere with the *bona fide* subjective decisions of directors.

In respect of the particular power to issue further shares greater controls on

---

74 *Ibid* at 837.

75 [1992] BCLC 22.

76 *Ibid* at 30.

directors have been introduced since *Howard Smith v Ampol* in the Companies Act 1980. These are now in s 80 of the 1985 Act.[77]

Finally, where as a result of exercising their powers for an improper purpose the directors are in breach of their duties, they can convene a general meeting of shareholders to vote on a resolution approving the directors' actions.[78] Such ratification can be obtained by an ordinary majority of the votes, but where the directors' disputed action is the issue of shares, no votes should be cast by the holders of the disputed allotment in respect of those shares.[79]

Conflict of personal interest and duty

A major aspect of a director's fiduciary duty is that he must not let his duty to the company come into conflict with his personal interests. It is not a breach of duty *per se* for a director to allow such a conflict to occur, but he is under a disability from entering into any transaction where such a conflict exists. Therefore a transaction which a director makes on behalf of the company from which he derives a personal benefit is voidable and can be set aside at the option of the company.

Transactions in which a director has an interest

Generally

To look first at situations where the director has a direct or indirect interest in a contract to which the company is a party: the leading case on this aspect of the law is *Aberdeen Railway Co v Blaikie Bros*,[80] where a company entered into a contract to purchase chairs from a partnership when at the time one of its directors was a partner in the partnership. It was held that the contract could be avoided by the company. Lord Cranworth LC stated the rule thus:

> 'A corporate body can only act by agents, and it is of course the duty of those agents so to act as best to promote the interests of the corporation whose affairs they are conducting. Such agents have duties to discharge of a fiduciary nature towards their principal. And it is a rule of universal application, that no one, having such duties to discharge, shall be allowed to enter into engagements in which he has, or can have, a personal interest conflicting, or which possibly may conflict, with the interests of those whom he is bound to protect.'[81]

The rationale for the rule is then stated to be that:

> '[the director's] duty to the company imposed on him the obligation of obtaining these chairs at the lowest possible price. His personal interest would lead him in an entirely opposite direction, would induce him to fix the price as high as possible. This is the very evil against which the rule in question is directed.'[82]

---

77   See p 164.
78   *Bamford v Bamford* [1970] Ch 212.
79   *Hogg v Cramphorn* [1967] Ch 254.
80   (1854) 1 Macq 461.
81   *Ibid* at 471.
82   *Ibid* at 473.

The rule, which has its origin in the law relating to trustees, is no less applicable in the case of company directors where there may be a number of other disinterested directors on the board. This is because the company is entitled to the benefit of every director's knowledge, skill and opinions in negotiating contracts.

If a transaction is entered into in which one or more of the directors has a personal interest, it is open to the company in the general meeting of shareholders to ratify by ordinary resolution and adopt the transaction company's constitution. This can be done as long as there is full disclosure to the shareholders. In a striking example of ratification, the case of *North-West Transportation Co Ltd v Beatty*,[83] a director was allowed to vote as a shareholder in general meeting on a resolution to ratify a contract for the sale of a ship to the company of which he was the sole owner. He was holding one-third of the shares in the company, but this did not affect the validity of the ratification because on the evidence the company needed this particular ship and the price was fair. It might have been different if the price was extortionate.[84]

It has long been the practice for companies to include in their articles a clause which allows a director to have an interest in a contract with the company, usually provided some procedural safeguards are followed. So, normally, there will have to be disclosure to the board of the interest and a board resolution taken to approve the contract, and further that the director concerned takes no part in the board discussion on the matter and does not exercise a vote at the board meeting. In a case which respected the commercial judgment of businessmen, the Court of Appeal refused to interfere with such a clause in the articles which in effect meant that the company 'contracted out' of receiving the benefit of a fully independent board of directors. As Lord Hatherley LC explained:

> 'the question then remains, whether the company cannot stipulate that this is a benefit of which they do not desire to award themselves, and if they are competent so to stipulate, whether they may not think that in large financial matters of this description it is better to have directors who may advance the interests of the company by their connection, and by the part which they themselves take in large money dealings, than to have persons who would have no share no such transactions as those in which the company is concerned.'[85]

Article 85 of Table A relaxes the general equitable principle and allows directors to be interested in contracts with their company and articles 94 and 95 prevent a particular director from being involved in the decision-making process on the contract.

This is also an area where statute has intervened to enforce fair dealing by directors and to ensure greater control over certain types of transactions in which directors may have an interest. The most general provision is s 317, under which it is the duty of a director who is in any way interested in a contract or proposed contract with the

---

83 (1887) 12 App Cas 589.

84 Where this might constitute a 'fraud on the minority'. See p 284 *et seq*.

85 *Imperial Mercantile Credit Association v Coleman* (1871) 6 Ch App 558 at 568. Reversed by the House of Lords in *Liquidators of Imperial Mercantile Credit Association v Coleman* but on a construction of the particular article.

company to declare the nature of his interest at a board meeting. Generally the director must declare the nature of his interest at the first board meeting at which a proposed contract is considered or where he becomes interested after the proposed contract was discussed, at the next meeting of the board. Further, where he acquires an interest after the contract has already been made, at the first board meeting after that date. A director can give a general notice to the board of directors to the effect that he is a member of a specified company or firm, or connected with a specified person and that after the date of the notice he is to be regarded as interested in any contract with that company, firm or person. A director who fails to comply with the section is liable on indictment to an unlimited fine and on a summary conviction to a fine of up to £2,000.

By s 317(9) nothing in the section prejudices the operation of any rule of law restricting directors of a company from having an interest in contracts with their company.

The relationship between s 317, the general equitable principle developed by the judges, and articles relaxing this principle has caused some difficulty, and it remains to some extent unresolved. The effect of s 317(9) is that the disclosure required by s 317 cannot of itself validate any contract made by a company in which a director has an interest, which under the common law only disclosure to and ratification by the general meeting will do, or following the procedures laid down in the articles. Therefore the section is a purely penal provision. Lord Pearson stated in *Hely-Hutchinson v Brayhead Ltd*:[86]

> '[i]t is not contended that [s 317] in itself affects the contract. The section merely creates a statutory duty of disclosure and imposes a fine for non-compliance; but it has to be read in conjunction with [the equivalent article to article 85 of Table A]. If a director makes or is interested in a contract with the company, but fails duly to declare his interest, what happens to the contract? Is it void, or is it voidable at the option of the company, or is it still binding on both parties, or what? The article supplies no answer to these questions. I think that the answer must be supplied by the general law, and the answer is that the contract is voidable at the option of the company.'[87]

In many cases, though, companies will have relaxed the general equitable principle and will either have adopted article 85 of Table A in their articles, or have articles which require a director to make disclosure to the board in the same manner required by the statutory provision in order for the contract to become binding on the company. In these cases disclosure to the board will serve two purposes, complying with the statutory duty and validating the contract.

Most of the cases which have come before the courts on this issue have involved such a situation and in one of them, *Lee Panavision Ltd v Lee Lighting Ltd*,[88] the directors were all interested in a particular transaction with the company but had failed to disclose their interests formally at a board meeting. Dillon LJ, in remarks which were

---

86 [1968] 1 QB 549.
87 *Ibid* at 594.
88 [1992] BCLC 22.

not necessary for the decision, stated that in cases where every director knows of the interest of a director, and especially in cases where every director shares the same interest, then this would only be a technical breach of the section and would not invalidate the contract.

The question then arises: what if the relevant articles in the company's constitution are specifically more liberal than s 317 and article 85 and only require disclosure to a committee of the board, or the chairman, or do not require any disclosure at all but generally permit directors to enter into contractual relationships with their company?[89] Despite suggestions that the s 317 sets a minimum level of disclosure and that in any case where there was a failure to disclose to the whole board this would automatically invalidate a contract,[90] it would seem that there is no such inter-relationship, and that a director in such a case could comply with the articles to validate the contract but still be liable to a fine for failing to comply with s 317.

This issue arose for consideration in *Guinness plc v Saunders*.[91] Here the company's articles provided that a director who had an interest in a contract with the company should make disclosure 'in accordance with [s 317]'. The company argued that as W, a director, had not made such a disclosure in respect of a contract to provide advice to the company as a takeover consultant, the company was entitled to a repayment of the sum of £5.2 million which W had been paid. This was accepted by the Court of Appeal.[92]

Although the decision was upheld by the House of Lords on other grounds, Lord Goff rejected the reasoning of the Court of Appeal in respect of the effect of s 317. Fox LJ had held that s 317 had civil consequences in addition to the penalty of a fine in the event of non-compliance. The purpose of s 317, Fox LJ reasoned, was to impose a binding safeguard on the company's power to relax the general equitable principle and require there to be disclosure to a full board in any event. As W admittedly had not made disclosure to the full board as required by the statute, W acted in breach of duty in receiving £5.2 million. Lord Goff, citing *Hely-Hutchinson v Brayhead Ltd*,[93] stated that he could not see that a breach of s 317 itself had any effect upon the contract between W and the company. It was therefore as a matter of general law, the failure of W to comply with his duty of disclosure under the *article* (which in this case had adopted the requirements of s 317) that the contract became voidable. This question awaits a final resolution.

In *Neptune (Vehicle Washing Equipment) Ltd v Fitzgerald*,[94] despite the liberal view which Dillon LJ was prepared to take in *Lee Panavision*, Lightman J held that even a sole director should declare at a board meeting an interest which he has in a contract

---

89   See the articles of Niltan Carson Ltd in *Joint receivers and managers of Niltan Carson Ltd v Hawthorne* [1988] BCLC 298.

90   See, for example, Gower, *Principles of Modern Company Law,* 4th ed (1979) p 387.

91   [1990] 2 AC 663.

92   [1988] 2 All ER 940.

93   [1968] 1 QB 549.

94   [1995] 1 BCLC 352. See p 110.

with the company, and record that declaration in the board minutes to comply with s 317, although he was prepared to concede that the declaration did not have to be read out loud if no one else was attending the meeting.

Service contracts

Other statutory provisions are more specific in that they apply to certain types of transactions. The most common transaction which a company enters into in which a director is interested is the director's employment or service contract. It was held in *Runciman v Walter Runciman plc*[95] that s 317 applied to a director's service contract, so that technically it should be disclosed despite the obviousness of a director's interest in the contract. But, in addition, there are specific requirements. By s 318 these service contracts have to be kept at the company's registered office, principal place of business or where the register of members is kept, and they must be open for inspection by any member of the company without charge. Even if there is no written contract of service and the contract is merely oral, a written memorandum setting out the terms has to be produced and be open for inspection. These requirements are enforced by criminal sanctions in default.

By s 319 a director cannot incorporate into a contract of service with the company a term where the employment is to last for a period of more than five years and which cannot be terminated by the company by notice or can only be terminated in specified circumstances, unless the relevant term has been first approved by an ordinary resolution of the company in general meeting. By s 319(5) there must be a written memorandum setting out the proposed agreement which is available for inspection by the members of the company both at the company's registered office not less than 15 days before the date of the meeting and available at the meeting itself.

Unlike s 317, a failure to comply with s 319 has express 'civil' consequences since failure to follow the procedure laid down in the section and to obtain the necessary resolution will render the term void and it is deemed to be replaced in the agreement by a term allowing the company to terminate the agreement at any time by the giving of reasonable notice.[96] There are no criminal sanctions for default.

Substantial property transactions

Articles relaxing or excluding the general equitable principle, such as article 85 of Table A, run the risk that contracts in which directors are interested are simply disclosed to and approved by the directors as a matter of course for each other's mutual benefit, without a proper examination of the merits of the transactions and without the shareholders even being informed let alone having the ability to object. This problem was addressed in the Department of Trade White Paper on the Conduct of Company Directors[97] which announced the Government's intention to introduce stricter controls on directors in this area. Therefore the Companies Act 1980 introduced provisions which lay down procedures which have to be followed to approve

---

95   [1992] BCLC 1084.
96   Companies Act 1985, s 319(6).
97   (1977) Cmnd 7037.

significant contracts involving the transfer of an asset between a company and a director (or his family) or vice versa. Sections 320–22 of the 1985 Act provide that in respect of substantial property transactions, regardless of what is provided for in the articles, prior approval of the transaction must be obtained in general meeting to validate a contract. Specifically it is provided that a company cannot enter into an arrangement whereby a director of the company or of its holding company (or a person connected with such a director) acquires a non-cash asset of the requisite value from the company *or* whereby the company acquires a non-cash asset of the requisite value from such a director or connected person *unless* the arrangement is first approved by an ordinary resolution of the shareholders in general meeting.[98] (In addition if the director concerned is a director of the holding company there must also be a resolution of the shareholders of the holding company.)

For the purpose of the section a non-cash asset of the requisite value is one which, at the time of the arrangement, is valued in excess of £100,000 or 10% of the company's asset value, whichever is the lesser, provided that the value is not less than £2,000.[99] The value of the company's net assets is to be determined by reference to the accounts in respect of the last preceding financial year and if there are no accounts then the value is the company's called-up share capital. The burden of proving that the transaction is of the value so as to bring it within the section is on the party bringing the proceedings to make the director accountable and/or to set aside the transaction.[100]

The effect of a contravention of the provisions of s 320 is that any arrangement or contract is voidable at the instance of the company and the director or a person connected with him and any other director of the company who authorised the arrangement is liable to account to the company for any gain which he has made either directly or indirectly from the arrangement and to indemnify the company for any loss or damage resulting form the arrangement.[101]

The right of the company to avoid the arrangement is lost if restitution of any money or other asset which is the subject matter of the arrangement is no longer possible, or the company has been indemnified for the loss or damage suffered by it.[102] Further, the right of the company to avoid is lost if a third party, who is not a party to the arrangement and has acquired rights in good faith without notice of the contravention of s 320, would be affected by an avoidance.[103]

Last, the right of the company to avoid is lost if the arrangement is affirmed by the shareholders in general meting within a reasonable period.[104] This affirmation is not equivalent to obtaining prior approval under s 320 since the director still remains liable

---

98   Companies Act 1985, s 320(1).

99   Companies Act 1985, s 320(2).

100 *Joint receivers & Managers of Niltan Carson Ltd v Hawthorne* [1988] BCLC 298.

101 Companies Act 1985, s 322(1) and (3).

102 Companies Act 1985, s 322(2)(a).

103 Companies Act 1985, s 322(2)(b).

104 Companies Act 1985, s 322(2)(c).

to account for any gain or to compensate the company for any loss. These liabilities arise whether or not the arrangement or transaction has been avoided by the company.

For the purposes of s 320 the main ways in which a person is connected with a director are: if that person is the director's spouse, child or step-child who has not attained the age of 18; a body corporate in which the director holds one-fifth of the share capital or controls one-fifth of the voting power; or a trustee of a trust, the beneficiaries of which include the director, his spouse or any of his children or step-children.[105]

Loans to directors

There are general restrictions on a company's power to make a loan to a director or any person connected with a director. The basic prohibition and exceptions to it are contained in ss 330-44. These sections prevent a company from making a loan to a director of the company or of its holding company, or from entering into any guarantee or indemnity, or from providing any security in connection with a loan made by any other person to the director.[106] There is also a prohibition on the making of quasi-loans to a director where the company pays a debt owed by the director and the director agrees to reimburse the company,[107] and on the entering into credit transactions with a director where, for instance, the company supplies goods to a director under a hire purchase agreement or leases land in return for rent.[108]

For the purposes of ss 330–44 there is a distinction drawn between 'relevant companies' and others, with a 'relevant company' being subject to more stringent rules. A 'relevant company' is a public company or a subsidiary of a public company or a company which has a subsidiary which is a public company.[109]

A general exception to the prohibition is that any company may, by s 334, lend a sum not exceeding an aggregate amount of £5,000 to a director.[110] There are further exceptions for short term quasi-loans not exceeding an aggregate of £5,000 and repayable within two months.[111] and for minor credit transactions not exceeding an aggregate of £10,000.[112] Further, by s 337, any company may lend to a director funds which will meet expenditure incurred or expenditure which will be incurred by him for purposes of the company or for the purpose of enabling him to perform properly his duties as a director. Such a loan must, however, receive prior approval by the company in general meeting following disclosure of the amount of the loan and the purpose of the expenditure, or approval must be obtained at the next annual general meeting after the loan is made, and if such approval is not obtained the loan has to be

---

105 Companies Act 1985, s 346.

106 Companies Act 1985, s 330(2).

107 Companies Act 1985, s 330(3) and 331(3).

108 Companies Act 1985, s 330(4) and 331(7).

109 Companies Act 1985, s 331(6).

110 Companies Act 1985, s 334.

111 Companies Act 1985, s 332.

112 Companies Act 1985, s 335.

repaid within six months of the meeting. In respect of relevant companies a loan under s 337 cannot exceed £20,000.

If a company enters into a transaction or arrangement which contravenes s 330, then it is voidable at the instance of the company unless restitution of any money or asset which is the subject matter of the transaction or arrangement is no longer possible, or the company has been indemnified by the director or connected person against loss, or any rights acquired by a *bona fide* third party without notice of the contravention of s 330 would be effected by the avoidance.[113] Further, any director or connected person with whom the company enters into a transaction or arrangement prohibited by s 330, or any other director who authorised it, is liable to account to the company for any gain which he has made from the transaction or arrangement and is liable to indemnify the company for any loss or damage suffered by the company resulting from the transaction or arrangement.[114] There are exceptions from liability for persons who took all reasonable steps to secure that the company complied with s 330, and for persons who show that at the time the transaction or arrangement was entered into they did not know of the contravention.[115]

Apart from the civil consequences of a breach outlined above, a director of a relevant company will commit a criminal offence if he authorises or permits the company to enter into a transaction or arrangement knowing or having reasonable cause to believe that the company was thereby contravening s 330.[116] The relevant company itself which enters into a transaction or arrangement which contravenes s 330 is guilty of an offence unless it is able to show that at the relevant time it did not know of the circumstances constituting a breach of s 330.[117]

It is also an offence for any person to procure a relevant company to enter into a transaction or arrangement knowing or having reasonable cause to believe that the company was thereby contravening s 330.[118]

Control of directors' profits

There is a broad and general rule imposed on directors that they will not make a profit from their office except by way of receiving duly authorised remuneration (if any) or, as we have already seen in the previous section, entering into an approved transaction with the company. What might be described as the leading case in this area, and possibly the one which goes the furthest, is *Regal (Hastings) Ltd v Gulliver*[119] which demonstrates the extent to which judges have treated the director of a company as being analogous to that of a trustee of a trust fund.

---

113 Companies Act 1985, s 341(1).
114 Companies Act 1985, s 341(2).
115 Companies Act 1985, s 341(4) and (5).
116 Companies Act 1985, s 342.
117 Companies Act 1985, s 342(5).
118 Companies Act 1985, s 342(3).
119 [1967] 2 AC 134 n.

The company, Regal, brought an action against former directors of the company to recover profits which had been made by them on the sale of the shares in a subsidiary company. Regal owned a cinema and the directors had formed a subsidiary with a view to it acquiring the leases of two other cinemas so that all three could be developed or sold together. In the event, the sale of the cinemas themselves fell through, and instead there was a sale of all the shares in the company and the subsidiary. The directors had purchased shares in the subsidiary because it was decided that Regal itself could not afford to buy any more than 40% of the authorised share capital and the landlords required a guarantee for the payment of the rent unless the subsidiary was fully capitalised.

After the sale of the shares the new owners appointed a new board of directors which decided to pursue the former directors for an account of the profits which they had made. The action failed at first instance and in the Court of Appeal, largely due to the fact that there were no allegations made out of any fraud by the directors. The House of Lords took a markedly different approach and held the directors liable. The basis of the decision is the application of the equitable rule originally developed in respect of trustees that:

'insists on those, who by use of a fiduciary position make a profit, being liable to account for that profit,'

and that this liability:

'in no way depends on fraud, or absence of *bona fides*. ... The profiteer, however honest and well intentioned, cannot escape the risk of being called upon to account.'[120]

The case of *Keech v Sandford*[121] is cited heavily by their Lordships as authority for the proposition that the fiduciary cannot use his position to obtain a benefit even where, as here, the person whose interests he is charged to protect is incapable itself of benefitting. Also cited is the case of *Ex parte James*,[122] where Lord Eldon LC explained that the strictness of the rule must be adhered to in the general interests of justice, however apparently honest the fiduciary may be, since:

'no court is equal to the examination and ascertainment of the truth in much the greater number of cases.'[123]

So it is reasoned that it is better to preclude strictly the possibility of benefiting from a fiduciary position rather than allowing the temptation to benefit and then have to engage into the difficult task of deciding whether the director was *bona fide* or not.

Lord Russell acknowledges that there are cases where it is said that the strict analogy of directors to trustees was not absolutely satisfactory, but those were cases which did not involve the question of directors making a profit. The preferred

---

120 *Ibid* at 144, 145 *per* Lord Russell.
121 (1726) Sel Cas Ch 61.
122 (1803) 8 Ves 337.
123 *Ibid* at 345.

approach was that of the Court of Appeal in *Parker v McKenna*,[124] where in relation to another type of fiduciary, an agent, it was stated that:

> 'the rule is an inflexible rule and must be applied inexorably by this court which is not entitled ... to receive evidence, or suggestion, or argument as to whether the principal did or did not suffer any injury in fact by reason of the dealing of the agent; for the safety of mankind requires that no agent shall be able to put his principal to the danger of such an inquiry as that.'[125]

What is necessary for a finding against a director in these circumstances is that the profit was made 'by reason and in the course of' the fiduciary relationship.

Further, the liability to account for the profit does not depend in any way on whether the company was in a position to be able to obtain it for itself or whether the profit was gained at the expense of the company. As Lord Porter in *Regal* stated:

> 'Directors, no doubt, are not trustees, but they occupy a fiduciary position towards the company whose board they form. Their liability in this respect does not depend upon breach of duty but upon the proposition that a director must not make a profit out of property acquired by reason of his relationship to the company ... it matters not that he could not have acquired the property for the company itself – the profit which he makes is the company's, even though the property by means of which he made it was not and could not have been acquired on its behalf.'[126]

Lord Upjohn in the course of his speech in *Boardman v Phipps*,[127] which applied *Regal (Hastings) Ltd v Gulliver*, described it as a clear case which was not laying down any new view but simply applying well settled principles, and that the fundamental rule of equity that a person in a fiduciary capacity must not make a profit out of his trust was part of the wider rule that a trustee must not place himself in a position where his duty and his interest may conflict. Shortly after *Boardman v Phipps* the courts were again required to determine the extent of a director's fiduciary duty.

In *IDC v Cooley*[128] the defendant, a managing director who had been in negotiations with the Eastern Gas Board on behalf of his company concerning contracts for the building of four new depots, was offered an opportunity to carry out this work in a personal capacity. Being under a fixed term contract with the company, the defendant falsely informed the chairman that he wished to resign on grounds of ill health to obtain an early release. In the event the defendant did carry out work for the Gas Board in a personal capacity and made a substantial profit, and the company then brought this action to make him liable to account for it as it was made in breach of the fiduciary duty he owed to the company.

---

124 (1874) LR 10 Ch App 96.

125 *Ibid* at 124 *per* James LJ.

126 [1967] 2 AC 134n at 159. See also *Canadian Aero Service Ltd v O'Malley* (1974) 40 DLR (3d) 371 at 383 *per* Laskin J.

127 [1967] 2 AC 44.

128 [1972] 1 WLR 443.

Roskill J found for the company since the defendant had a duty, once he obtained the information about the Gas Board contract and while he was still a director, to pass it on to the company and not to guard it for his own personal purposes and profit. He had allowed his duty and his interests to come into conflict. Accountability then followed, even though the company would not have obtained the contract anyway since on the evidence the Eastern Gas Board did not like the company's set-up.

An argument to the effect that the *Regal* principle only applied, and the profit must be accounted for, where it is obtained in the course of and owing to the directorship and that here the profit was only obtained when the director resigned, could not relieve the defendant from liability since it was the overriding equitable principle which mattered, not the precise wording of the speeches in *Regal* which obviously referred to the specific facts of that case. As Lord Upjohn stated in *Boardman v Phipps*, the equitable principle must be applied to a great diversity of circumstances.[129]

Therefore a director would be accountable to the company for a secret, personal commission or bribe he may receive from a third party which, for instance, induces the director to cause the company to enter into a contract with the third party.[130] There is also a group of cases which have given rise to the 'corporate opportunity doctrine'. Here the director is liable to account for profit made from an opportunity which it was his duty to obtain for the company. The clearest case is the Privy Council decision in *Cook v Deeks*.[131] Here the plaintiff claimed that the benefit of a contract, which had been entered into by the defendants with the Canadian Pacific Railway (CPR), belonged to the Toronto Construction Co. The plaintiff and the three defendants were the four directors of the company and they each held 25% of the issued share capital. After a series of successfully completed contracts with the CPR, the defendants negotiated another one and took it in their own names forming another company, the Dominion Construction Co, to carry it out. As the trial judge was to state, 'the sole and only object on the part of the defendants was to get rid of a business associate [the plaintiff] whom they deemed, and I think rightly deemed, unsatisfactory from a business standpoint'. Despite the fact that at a general meeting of Toronto Construction the defendants passed a resolution to the effect that the company had no interest in the contract in question, the Privy Council reversed the decision of the Canadian Supreme Court and held that the defendants must hold the benefit of the contract on behalf of Toronto Construction. As Lord Buckmaster, who delivered the opinion of their Lordships, stated:

> 'men who assume the complete control of a company's business must remember that they are not at liberty to sacrifice the interests which they are bound to protect, and, while ostensibly acting for the company, divert in their own favour business which should properly belong to the company they represent.'[132]

---

129 [1967] 2 AC 46 at 123.

130 *Boston Deep Sea Fishing and Ice Co v Ansell* (1888) 39 Ch D 339.

131 [1916] 1 AC 554.

132 *Ibid* at 563.

Another Canadian case which illustrates this principle is *Canadian Aero Service Ltd v O'Malley*.[133] Here two directors of a company were held liable to pay damages to their company for the loss of a surveying and mapping contract with the Guyanan Government. They had been involved in the preparations and the negotiations on behalf of the company and they had taken it up for themselves after resigning from the company. After reviewing the authorities, Laskin J was able to state that the fiduciary principle:

'disqualifies a director or senior officer from usurping for himself, or diverting to another person or company with whom or with which he is associated, a maturing business opportunity which his company is actively pursuing; he is also precluded from so acting even after his resignation where the resignation may fairly be said to have been promoted or influenced by a wish to acquire for himself the opportunity sought by the company, or where it was his position with the company rather than a fresh initiative that led him to the opportunity which he later acquired.'[134]

More recently in England, although the Laskin J formulation of 'maturing business opportunity' has been adopted as the correct approach to be used to determine whether a director who seeks to make a profit after he has left the company is liable, two cases which have come before the courts have both been decided in favour of the director. In *Island Export Finance Ltd v Umunna*[135] it was held that the director's resignation was not motivated by a desire to take up a 'maturing business opportunity' which he was actively negotiating on behalf of the company, and in any case there was no such opportunity at the time. What the cases appear to be recognising is that although a director should be prevented from taking an identifiable opportunity from the company and diverting it to himself, the courts should not prevent a director from using the general knowledge of and skills in a particular business acquired during his working life, even if they are used to compete with his former company. This is in contrast to a director who resigns from a company and subsequently seeks to use what amounts to trade secrets and confidential information belonging to the company which he had access to while he was a director. In that case the courts will restrain the former director by injunction from breaching a duty of confidence.[136]

Again, in *Balston Ltd v Headline Filters Ltd*,[137] it was held that a former director was not liable for breach of fiduciary duty because when he resigned to set up his own business, which admittedly was in competition with that of the company, he did not divert any maturing business opportunity to himself. Further, although the director resigned in order to set up his own competing business without disclosing this intention, this was not an interest which conflicted with his fiduciary duty to the company. A director could even make preliminary steps to forward his intention to set

---

133 (1973) 40 DLR (3d) 371.

134 *Ibid* at 382.

135 [1986] BCLC 460.

136 *Printers and Finishers Ltd v Holloway* [1965] 1 WLR 1; *Cranleigh Precision Engineering Ltd v Bryant* [1965] 1 WLR 1293; *Faccenda Chicken Ltd v Fowler* [1986] IRLR 69.

137 [1990] BCLC 460.

up his own business as long as there was no actual competitive activity while he was a director.

There is some difficulty concerning the extent to which a director can be released from his fiduciary obligation to pursue what is admitted to be an opportunity which he discovered or had knowledge of by reason and in the course of carrying out his duties as director. If the facts of a particular opportunity are fully disclosed to the general meeting of shareholders and a resolution is passed releasing a director then, in the absence of fraud on the minority present in *Cook v Deeks*, it seems that a director may be able to pursue the opportunity for his own benefit.[138] More difficult are the situations where it is only the board of directors which makes the decision to release the director, since it is the company to which the director owes the obligation and the board seems to lack the authority to make such a release. This in fact occurred, though, in the Australian case of *Queensland Mines Ltd v Hudson*.[139]

Another slightly differing situation is where the opportunity is offered to the company and the board consider it, but reject it without giving consideration as to whether any particular director is then free to exploit the opportunity for himself. In *Peso Silver Mines Ltd v Cropper*[140] the Canadian Supreme Court allowed a director to pursue and profit from prospecting claims which he had first become aware of when they were offered to his company. After consideration, the board of directors had initially rejected them on the ground that the company did not have sufficient development resources. The defendant director, along with two other directors, then purchased them at the same price at which they had been offered to the company. The Supreme Court cited the rejection of an argument that had been put to Lord Greene MR in the Court of Appeal in *Regal (Hastings) Ltd v Gulliver* to the effect that where a *bona fide* decision had been taken by the board of directors not to make an investment, a director who put up his own money for that investment would still hold any profit on behalf of the company. Lord Greene MR stated that that was a proposition for which no particle of authority was cited and went beyond previous law on the duty of directors. The House of Lords had declined to take this further since Lord Russell felt that this hypothetical case bore little resemblance to the facts of *Regal* itself.[141]

A point made in the judgment of the Supreme Court was that when the geologist who initially approached the company with the claims approached the defendant he was not approaching him in his capacity as director, but by that time as an individual member of the public. The company then no longer retained any interest in the opportunity. Laskin J, in *Canadian Aero Service*, was of the view that that case was very different from *Peso* since, after the good faith rejection by the directors of *Peso* because of the company's strained finances, the company's interest in the mining claims ceased.[142] This, it is submitted, is against the spirit of the judgment in *Regal*, since as

---

138 See Lord Russell in *Regal (Hastings) Ltd v Gulliver* at 150, although not a corporate opportunity case.
139 (1978) 52 ALJR 399.
140 (1966) 58 DLR (2d) 1.
141 [1967] 2 AC 134n at 152.
142 (1974) 40 DLR (3d) 371 at 390.

was stated by Norris JA in a dissenting judgment in the Court of Appeal in *Peso*, there was no doubt that the defendant acquired the information in the course of the execution of his duties as a director and that the profit was acquired without the knowledge and assent of the shareholders.

DUTIES OF SKILL AND CARE

In contrast to the relatively high standards of conduct which a company is entitled to expect from a director with regard to circumstances from which he may profit, or where a conflict of interest and duty with the company may rise, the level of competence expected of a director for the purposes of the law of negligence is low. The law in this area is still suffering from the 19th century view of the director as an unqualified, non-professional person who was not expected to bring any particular skills to his office. An example of the approach of the courts at this time can be found in the judgment of Jessel MR in *Re Forest of Dean Coal Mining Co*, where he states that:

> 'one must be very careful in administering the law of joint stock companies not to press so hardly on honest directors as to make them liable for these constructive defaults, the only effect of which would be to deter all men of any property, and perhaps all men who have any character to lose, from becoming directors of companies at all.'[143]

As will be seen there is now increasing pressure on directors to raise their standards of conduct.

The starting point of any analysis of the duty of care imposed upon a director is usually the judgment of Romer J in *Re City Equitable Fire Insurance Co Ltd*.[144] Here the company had lost a large amount of money, due partly to the fraud of the chairman of the board. In the winding up, the liquidator brought this action against other directors, who although honest, had allowed the frauds to take place, he alleged through their negligence. In the event Romer J did find that two of the directors were guilty of negligence, but they were saved by a clause in the company's articles which exempted directors from liability for negligence except losses caused by the directors' own 'wilful neglect or default'. Parliament took swift action to make these clauses void in the Companies Act 1929. Although in certain respects outdated, the well-known three propositions which Romer J distils from the decided cases is still a useful starting point.

First he states that:

> 'a director need not exhibit in the performance of his duties a greater degree of skill than may reasonably be expected from a person of his knowledge and experience.'

In *Re Forest of Dean Coal Mining Co*, Jessel MR had stated that directors are bound to use fair and reasonable diligence in the management of their company's affairs, and to act honestly.[145] But this means that at common law a director is not expected to have any specialist knowledge or skill just because of the position which he is occupying, eg

---

143 (1878) 10 Ch D 450 at 451.
144 [1925] Ch 407.
145 *Ibid* at 452.

finance director or sales director. As Neville J stated in *Re Brazilian Rubber Plantations and Estates Ltd*:[146]

'A director's duty has been laid down as requiring him to act with such care as is reasonably to be expected from him, having regard to his knowledge and experience. He is, I think, not bound to bring any special qualifications to his office. He may undertake the management of a rubber company in complete ignorance of everything connected with rubber without incurring responsibility for the mistakes which may result from such ignorance; while if he is acquainted with the rubber business he must give the company the advantage of his knowledge when transacting the company's business ... He is clearly, I think, not responsible for damages occasioned by errors of judgment.'[147]

The point Neville J makes, concerning the higher expectation of a director who does have some specialist knowledge or skill to bring to the company, can, it seems, be used to reconcile the decision in *Dorchester Finance Co Ltd v Stebbing*[148] with the other authorities. Here Foster J held that, where two directors had signed blank cheques and shown disinterest in the company's affairs, which had allowed a third director to cause loss to the company by making illegal loans, all three were liable in negligence.

He accepted a concession by counsel for one of the defendants that he could take into account the fact that of the three directors, two were chartered accountants and the third had considerable accountancy experience, and stated that:

'For a chartered accountant and an experienced accountant to put forward the proposition that a non-executive director has no duties to perform I find quite alarming.'[149]

But Hoffmann J in *Norman v Theodore Goddard*[150] stated that this was an extreme case and not of itself strong evidence of a change of attitude by the courts.

There is evidence to suggest, however, more recently, that the standards to be expected of a director are changing and the catalyst for change is the wrongful trading provision. In *Re D'Jan of London Ltd*[151] a director and 99% shareholder had signed an insurance proposal submitted by the company to the insurer, which had been completed by another person, without reading it himself. In fact the proposal contained inaccurate information which allowed the insurer to repudiate liability. Hoffmann LJ (sitting as an additional judge of the Chancery Division) held that the duty of care a director owed a company was equivalent to that contained in s 214(4) of the Insolvency Act 1986. This means that a director against whom allegations of negligence are made can be judged by an objective standard, so that his actions should be judged against those which could be expected from a director having the general knowledge,

---

146 [1911] 1 Ch 425.
147 *Ibid* at 437.
148 [1989] BCLC 498.
149 *Ibid* at 505.
150 [1991] BCLC 1028.
151 [1994] 1 BCLC 561.

skill and experience that may reasonably be expected of a person carrying out the same functions as are carried out by that director.

In the words of Hoffmann J:

'In my view, the duty of care owed by a director at common law is accurately stated in s 214(4),'[152]

and in this case he was of the view that:

'[b]oth on the objective test and ... on the subjective test, I think that he did not show reasonable diligence when he signed the form. He was therefore in breach of his duty to the company.'[153]

The importance of this approach is that directors may be expected to display higher standards of competence even while the company is solvent.

Second, Romer J stated that:

'[a] director is not bound to give continuous attention to the affairs of his company. His duties are of an intermittent nature to be performed at periodical board meetings and at meetings of any committee of the board upon which he happens to be placed. He is not, however, bound to attend all such meetings, though he ought to attend whenever, in the circumstances, he is reasonably able to do so.'

This is a reflection of the *Marquis of Bute's Case*[154] where the Marquis became the president of the Cardiff Savings Bank when he was six months old on the death of his father. He attended only one board meeting in 38 years before the bank was wound up. It transpired that frauds had been committed against the bank by an officer but Stirling J held that the Marquis could be held liable in damages for failing to attend to the business of the company, stating:

'[n]eglect or omission to attend meetings is not, in my opinion, the same thing as neglect or omission of a duty which ought to be performed at those meetings.'[155]

This proposition is today likely to apply to non-executive directors. Executive directors are likely to have their attendance obligations specified in their contracts. Further, it would be unwise for any director to fail to have regard to the performance of the company, since if it continues to trade after a time when it is obvious that it cannot avoid going into insolvent liquidation, then the directors can be liable for wrongful trading.

Third, Romer J stated that:

'[i]n respect of all duties having regard to the exigencies of business and the articles of association, which may properly be left to some other official, a director is, in the absence of grounds for suspicion, justified in trusting that official to perform such duties honestly.'

---

152 *Ibid* at 563.

153 *Ibid*.

154 *Re Cardiff Savings Bank* [1892] 2 Ch 100.

155 *Ibid* at 109.

This principle is demonstrated in *Dovey v Corey*[156] where a director relied on the judgment and advice of the chairman and general manager of the company when he assented to the payment of dividends and to loans from the company's funds. He had no reason to doubt the balance sheets presented to board meetings nor did he have any reason to doubt the competence of the general manager. In fact the dividends were paid out of capital and the loans were made without proper security. It was held that this director was not negligent. Lord Halsbury LC thought that business life could not go on if people could not trust those who are put into a position of trust for the purpose of attending to details of management. This was repeated by Romer J in *City Equitable* and reiterated in *Norman v Theodore Goddard*[157] by Hoffmann J. Here Q, who was a chartered surveyor, was a director in a company whose shares were the principal asset of a trust of which the firm of Theodore Goddard were the trustees. The affairs of the trust were administered by a partner in the firm who specialised in trust and tax work. He advised Q, who had control over the company's cheque book, to pay substantial sums of the company's money to another offshore company for tax reasons. In the event this offshore company was controlled by the partner and it enabled him to steal nearly £400,000 of the original company's money. In these circumstances Hoffmann J held that Q was not liable in negligence since he had been entitled to rely on the partner for advice in relation to tax, and on the evidence nothing should have made him suspicious so that he could not act on the advice of the partner.

MISCELLANEOUS STATUTORY PROVISIONS

Misfeasance proceedings

While the company is solvent and not in danger of being wound up, a breach of duty by the directors can only be pursued by the company or exceptionally by a shareholder if that shareholder can bring a derivative action as an exception to the rule in *Foss v Harbottle*.[158] This will mean in practice that many breaches will not be pursued, since if the directors are a close-knit body of persons they will be reluctant to authorise proceedings to be brought by the company against themselves. Proceedings may be brought against directors, though, even where the company remains in good health, where there is a change of shareholders on a takeover and a new board is put in place. This is what occurred in *Regal (Hastings) Ltd v Gulliver*.[159]

Where a company goes into liquidation there is a much greater chance that the liquidator will pursue breaches of duty that have occurred in the past and the procedure by which this can be done is provided for in s 212 of the Insolvency Act 1986. Under this section if, in the course of the winding up of a company, it appears that a director has misapplied or retained, or become accountable for, any money or other property belonging to the company, or been guilty of any misfeasance or breach of any fiduciary

---

156 [1901] AC 477
157 [1991] BCLC 1028.
158 (1843) 2 Hare 461. See p 283.
159 [1967] 2 AC 134n.

or other duty in relation to the company, the court may on the application of an appropriate person, examine into the conduct of the director and compel him to repay, restore or account for the money or property with interest or to contribute such sum to the company's assets by way of compensation in respect of the misfeasance or breach of duty as the court thinks just. The persons who can apply to the court under this section are the official receiver, the liquidator or any creditor or contributory[160] (eg members of the company), although in the case of a contributory an application cannot be made without the leave of the court, but the power to make an application is exercisable notwithstanding that he will not benefit from any order that the court may make. The section can also be used against liquidators, administrators, receivers and promoters.

In *Bentinck v Fenn*[161] it was held that the section creates no duty or liabilities for directors and no new rights against them. The section only provides a means of obtaining a summary remedy against them for breaches of duty for which they would be liable at common law or in equity.

Relief from liability: the articles

It will be recalled that in *Re City Equitable Life Assurance Co*[162] the directors, despite being held to have been negligent, escaped liability as a result of a clause in the company's articles which exempted directors from most types of liability. The legislature responded in the Companies Act 1929 by making such clauses ineffective. The relevant provision in the Companies Act 1985 is s 310 which provides that:

'any provision whether contained in a company's articles or in any contract with the company or otherwise, for exempting any officer of the company ... from or indemnifying him against, any liability which by virtue of any rule of law would otherwise attach to him in respect of any negligence, default, breach of duty or breach of trust of which he may be guilty in relation to the company'

will be void. The section also applies to such clauses which purport to relieve auditors from similar liabilities. Thus it is not possible for a director to 'contract out' of potential liabilities arising out of his holding office with the company.

Section 310 does not prevent a company from purchasing and maintaining for officers and auditors an insurance policy against any such liability.[163] Further, a company may indemnify officers and auditors against the costs of defending any proceedings (whether civil or criminal) in which judgment is given in favour of the officer or auditor or where they are acquitted and for the costs of applications under s 727 where relief from liability is given by the court.[164]

---

160 See p 305 on which members are 'contributories'.

161 (1887) 12 App Cas 652.

162 [1925] Ch 407. See the Greene Committee Report (1928) Cmd 2657, paras 46–47.

163 Where any such insurance has been purchased or maintained in any financial year, that fact must be stated in the directors' report for that year: Companies Act 1985, Sch 7, para 5A.

164 See p 253.

The question arose in *Movitex Ltd v Bulfield*[165] as to whether clauses in a company's articles which alter the equitable self-dealing rule and allow a director to have an interest in a contract with the company were avoided by s 310, since they sought to avoid the normal consequences of a director entering into such a transaction, namely that it would become voidable at the instance of the company. Such a conclusion, of course, would have meant that several articles in Table A would be held to be void. Vinelott J resisted such a conclusion, reasoning that the rule against self-dealing imposes a disability on a director from entering into valid contracts with the company,[166] and that as a result if a director places himself in a position in which his duty to the company conflicts with his personal interest, the court will intervene to set aside the transaction without enquiring whether there was a breach of duty to the company. When the articles are formulated by the shareholders they can decide to modify or exclude this principle and so remove the director's disability but the articles would not be exempting a director from or from the consequences of a breach of duty.

Relief from liability

At the court's discretion, s 727 of the 1985 Act provides that in any proceedings where a director, officer or auditor is held liable for negligence, default, breach of duty or breach of trust the court may, if it appears to it that the person acted honestly and reasonably, relieve him, either wholly or partly, from liability on such terms as it thinks fit. Such officer or person can on his own motion apply to the court for relief from liability if he apprehends that any claim will or might be brought against him in respect of the above.

It was held in *Customs and Excise Commissioners v Hedon Alpha Ltd*[167] that the court's discretion under this section to grant relief from liability did not apply to the claims against a director by a third party. A person could only qualify for statutory relief in respect of claims brought against him by the company, the exception to this being prosecutions brought against directors for breaches of the provisions of the Companies Acts. Further, the claim has to be one brought against the director for his personal misconduct in relation to the performance of his duties as a director. As Griffiths LJ stated:

> 'Although the section is expressed in wide language it is in my view clearly intended to enable the court to give relief to a director who, although he has behaved reasonably and honestly has nevertheless failed in some way in the discharge of his obligations to his company or their shareholders or who has infringed one of the numerous provisions in the Companies Acts, that regulate the conduct of directors ... When banks lend money to private companies they usually require the directors to enter into personal guarantees of the loan. Unhappily the directors are not infrequently called upon to honour their guarantees. I know of no case in which it has been suggested that [s 727] would provide any defence to such a claim by the bank.'[168]

---

165 [1988] BCLC 104.
166 Citing Megarry V-C in *Tito v Waddell (No 2)* [1977] Ch 106 at 248–49.
167 [1981] QB 818.
168 *Ibid* at 827, 828.

In *Re Produce Marketing Consortium Ltd*[169] it was held that a director who is ordered to pay compensation under s 214 of the Insolvency Act 1986 for wrongful trading cannot claim relief under s 727.

DISQUALIFICATION ORDERS

In an attempt to prevent those who would abuse the registered company causing harm to investors or creditors, and to prevent those who have shown themselves incapable of managing a company properly from continuing to be involved in the running of a company, Parliament has given the courts considerable powers to make disqualification orders. There are currently over 1,200 people subject to disqualification orders. The Government-backed Insolvency Service is now pursuing more and more directors and this follows in the wake of the DTI taking measures to tighten up the procedures for seeking disqualification orders. The public attitude to corporate governance and mismanagement has changed in recent years and the law is evolving to take account of that change. The Company Directors Disqualification Act (CDDA) 1986 is a major example of that. As Henry LJ recently stated, after explaining that the ability to trade through a limited liability company is a privilege which brings the responsibility of accepting certain standards:

> 'The parliamentary intention to improve managerial safeguards and standards for the long term good of employees, creditors and investors is clear. Those who fail to reach those standards and whose failure contributes to others losing money will often both be plausible and capable of inspiring initial trust, often later regretted. Those attributes may make them attractive witnesses. But as s 6 [of the CDDA 1986] makes clear, the court's focus should be on their conduct, on the offence rather than the offender.'[170]

The orders which can be made under the CDDA 1986 are made against a certain named individual and will prevent that individual for a specified period and without the leave of the court from acting as a director, liquidator, administrator, receiver or manager of a company's property or in any other way from being concerned or from taking part, whether directly or indirectly, in the promotion, formation or management of a company. There are a number of grounds upon which a court can make a disqualification order and one ground under which the court must make such an order.

By s 2 the court may make a disqualification order where a person is convicted of an indictable offence (whether on indictment or summarily) in connection with the promotion, formation, management, liquidation or striking off of a company or with the receivership or management of a company's property. The relevant court for the purpose of this section is the court having the jurisdiction to wind the company up or the court by or before which the person is convicted, which includes a magistrates' court. The maximum period of disqualification is five years in the case of a magistrates' court and 15 years in every other case.

---

169 [1989] 1 WLR 745.
170 In *Re Grayan Services Ltd* [1995] 3 WLR 1 at 15.

By s 3 the court may make a disqualification order where it appears to it that a person has been persistently in default in complying with the provisions of the Companies Act in filing, delivering or sending any return, account or other document with the registrar. Conclusive proof of persistent default for the purposes of the section is provided by showing that in the five years ending with the date of the application to disqualify, the person has been convicted of an offence for failing to comply with the provisions of the Companies Act or had a default order made against him. The maximum period of disqualification under this section is five years.

A court may make a disqualification order of up to 15 years against a person if, in the course of a winding up, it appears that he has been guilty of fraudulent trading or other fraud in relation to the company or of any breach of his duty as officer, liquidator, receiver or manager.

Under s 6, by way of contrast to the other provisions mentioned above, the court must make a disqualification order against a person in any case where it is satisfied that he is or has been a director of a company which has at any time become insolvent (whether or not it was at a time when he was a director) and that his conduct as a director of that company (either taken alone or taken together with his conduct as a director of any other company or companies) makes him unfit to be concerned in the management of a company. The court may make a disqualification order under this section of between two and 15 years. Schedule 1 to the Act provides a number of matters which are to be taken into account for the purpose of determining whether a person is so unfit. In all cases they include any misfeasance or breach of any fiduciary or other duty by the director in relation to the company; a misapplication or retention by the director of any money or other property belonging to the company or any conduct by the director which gives rise to an application to account for such money or property; the extent of the director's responsibility for the company entering into any transaction at an undervalue which defrauds creditors; or the extent of the director's responsibility for the company failing to comply with such requirements as the keeping of accounts, the filing of annual accounts and the keeping of a register of charges.

In cases where the company has become insolvent, the court must take into account the extent of the director's responsibility for the causes of the company becoming insolvent; the extent of the director's responsibility for any failure by the company to supply any goods or services which have been paid for by the customer; and the extent of the director's responsibility for the company entering into any transaction at an undervalue or the giving of any preference which is liable to be set aside under ss 238–40 of the Insolvency Act 1986.

In *Re Lo-Line Ltd*[171] Sir Nicholas Browne-Wilkinson V–C gave guidance on the proper approach for a court in deciding whether someone is unfit to be a director under what is now s 6:

'The approach adopted in all the cases to which I have been referred is broadly the same. The primary purpose of the section is not to punish the individual but to protect

---

171 [1988] Ch 477.

the public against the future conduct of companies by persons whose past records as directors of insolvent companies have shown them to be a danger to creditors and others. Therefore, the power is not fundamentally penal. But if the power to disqualify is exercised, disqualification does involve a substantial interference with the freedom of the individual. It follows that the rights of the individual must be fully protected.'[172]

So, for example, in this case although a director is not entitled to have the case against him disclosed to the same extent as criminal charges, natural justice required the official receiver to give the director here prior notice of a fundamental shift in the case against him from one alleging commercial dishonesty to one alleging gross commercial misjudgment.

'Ordinary commercial misjudgment is in itself not sufficient to justify disqualification in the normal case, the conduct complained of must display a lack of commercial probity, although I have no doubt that in an extreme case of gross negligence or total incompetence disqualification could be appropriate.'[173]

Here the director was found to have behaved in a commercially culpable manner because he had traded through limited companies when he knew them to be insolvent and he had used unpaid Crown debts (ie unpaid PAYE, national insurance contributions and VAT) to finance such trading. But since the allegations of dishonesty had been dropped, this was not a case which called for a lengthy disqualification and he was disqualified for three years from being a director of a company subject to certain limited exceptions.

Subsequently it has been held that, as the failure to pay Crown debts is not of itself evidence that the director is unfit and not in itself worse than the failure to pay other debts, it will be necessary in each case to look more closely to see what the significance of the non-payment is. In *Re Sevenoaks Stationers (Retail) Ltd*,[174] C, who was a qualified chartered accountant, had been the director of a number of companies which had become insolvent owing approximately £60,000. Dillon LJ, after citing with approval the passage from *Re Lo-Line Ltd* quoted above, stated:

'This is not a case in which it was alleged that [C] had, in the colloquial phrase, 'ripped off' the public and pocketed the proceeds. On the contrary ... he had lost a lot of his own money. ... There was evidence that [C] had remortgaged his home to raise money to pay creditors of the companies, and he claimed to have lost from £200,000 to £250,000 of his own money.'[175]

However, in addition to failing to keep proper accounts, failing to send annual returns and causing the companies to continue trading while they were insolvent:

'[C] made a deliberate decision to pay only those creditors who pressed for payment. The obvious result was that the two companies traded, when in fact insolvent and known to be in difficulties, at the expense of those creditors who, like the Crown,

---

172 *Ibid* at 485.
173 *Ibid* at 486.
174 [1991] Ch 164.
175 *Ibid* at 179–80.

happened not to be pressing for payment. Such conduct on the part of a director can well, in my judgment, be relied on as a ground for saying that he is unfit to be concerned in the management of a company.'[176]

He was disqualified for five years.

Applications under s 6 are made by the Secretary of State or by the Official Receiver if the Secretary of State so directs in the case of a person who is or has been a director of a company which is being wound up by the court.

A person can also be disqualified for up to 15 years if he has an order made against him under s 213 (fraudulent trading) or s 214 (wrongful trading) of the Insolvency Act 1986.[177] The court can make such a disqualification order of its own motion regardless of whether any other person has made an application.

It is a criminal offence for any person to act in contravention of a disqualification order for which a term of imprisonment of up to two years can be imposed, if a conviction is obtained on indictment.[178] Further, a person who is involved in the management of a company at a time when he is subject to a disqualification order becomes jointly and severally liable with the company for the company's debts which are incurred at a time when that person was involved in the management of the company.[179] Such personal liability is also extended to a person who is involved in the management of a company who does not have a disqualification order made against him but who acts or is willing to act on the instructions of a person whom he knows is subject to such an order at that time.[180]

---

176 *Ibid* at 183.
177 Company Directors Disqualification Act 1986, s 13.
178 Company Directors Disqualification Act 1986, s 13.
179 Company Directors Disqualification Act 1986, s 15(1)(a) and (2).
180 Company Directors Disqualification Act 1986, s 15(1)(b).

CHAPTER ELEVEN

COMPANY CHARGES

INTRODUCTION

It has already been seen[1] that borrowing is an important means by which a company can finance its activities and that the overwhelming majority of companies have the power, express or implied, to borrow money.[2] If a company does not have such a power any borrowing is *ultra vires* and void although the transaction may be validated by s 35.[3] Any document by which a company creates or acknowledges a debt may be called a debenture although this term is rarely applied to short term debts.[4]

Whatever their precise form, loans (or loan capital as it is sometimes called) can be divided into two categories. First, sums owed by the company as a debt, such as a loan by an individual or institution, most probably the company's overdraft and second, marketable loans. Marketable loans are in essence potential debts which may be issued (sold) to investors. These loans will be issued on strict terms and conditions relating to the date when the interest (if any) is due, date of redemption and other rights attaching. A company could create one million pounds of marketable debt (be it called loan stock, bonds or something else) divided into £1 units[5] bearing interest at x% which it could sell as and when required and for whatever price it will fetch (there is no prohibition on issuing a loan at a discounted price unless it is convertible into shares) which debt is to be redeemed at face value at some future date.[6] If £1 of redeemable debt is sold at a discount, the owner at redemption, who receives the face value of the debt and not the issue price or the price he paid for it, will make a capital profit. Marketable loans are more relevant for larger companies whereas the overdraft is a fact of life for companies large and small.

A person lending money to a company has such rights as are given by the contract creating the loan. Typically, the contract will include provisions for repayment of the loan, the payment of interest (if any) and the ability (generally none) of the creditor to attend company meetings or otherwise influence company policy. A debentureholder should be sent a copy of the company's annual accounts and reports submitted to

---

1 See p 1.

2 *General Auction Estate & Monetary Co v Smith* [1891] 3 Ch 432.

3 See p 124 *et seq*.

4 Section 744 defines a debenture as including 'debenture stock, bonds and any other securities of the company whether constituting a charge on the assets of the company or not' although the term tends to be used in business circles only to secured loans.

5 Although loan stock need not be divided into units by reference to sterling.

6 But note that it is perfectly possible for a company, unlike other legal entities, to create a charge which is irredeemable, s 193.

members[7] and is entitled to ask for the company's accounts.[8] A debenture is transferable (unless the contract creating it prohibits transfer). A transfer may be by simple delivery from the current holder to the new holder (a bearer debenture) or by delivery and the completion of a transfer document.

It is not a legal requirement but a prudent lender may insist on having some claim upon the assets of the company if the loan is not repaid or if other terms of the contract are broken by the company, for example if interest on the loan is not paid, or to ensure re-payment of the principal if the company goes into insolvent liquidation. In the business world an unsecured loan is likely to be called an unsecured loan note rather than a debenture. Where the contract of loan, or a linked contract, provides that if the company fails to meet its obligations the lender can have recourse to the company's assets and can obtain the sums outstanding by selling the assets or receiving income generated by those assets, the lender has a direct security. The assets of the company covered by this security are said to be charged and the lender may be called a chargee; the person (the company) whose assets are secured can be called a surety or chargor. This chapter is concerned with company charges.

A company may have an express power to give security but any company with the power to borrow money has an implied power to give security for its repayment.[9] Any of the assets of a company, for example real property, machinery, goods in the course of production or book debts, can be charged to provide security for a loan but its uncalled capital can be used as security only if this is expressly authorised by the memorandum; express authorisation may be explicit or may be implied from its wording. After some initial judicial hesitation, reasonable readiness to find an implicit express power can be perceived. Thus, wherever a company has an express power to charge or receive money on loan against *any* security the courts have been willing to treat this as an express power to charge uncalled capital.[10] It is somewhat incongruous that a company can charge other future assets, for example future debts, without express authorisation but not uncalled capital, but that is the legal position.

In addition to (or instead of) a contract of direct security, a lender may have some claim upon a third party if the company does not meet its obligations under the contract of loan. Such a claim may be by way of indemnity or be a contract of guarantee. A guarantor may also charge his assets to the lender as security for meeting his obligations under the guarantee – this is a contract of collateral or indirect security. Thus, a company might charge its assets to secure its overdraft with its bank and a director of the company might guarantee that if the company failed to repay the debt he would do so and charge his property (perhaps the matrimonial home) as security should he be called upon to meet his guarantee.

---

7   Section 239.

8   Section 238.

9   *Re Patent File Co* (1870) LR 6 Ch App 83.

10   *Re Phoenix Bessemer Steel Co* (1875) 44 LJ Ch 683.

The contract for security

The contract for security must comply with the usual contractual rules if it is to be legally enforceable.[11] In practice most contracts to provide security are made by deed. The contract can only be enforced in accordance with its terms. Thus, the security (or charge) can only be enforced if the obligation it secures has not been met. It must be noted that an overdraft is generally repayable on demand so that a bank can recall an overdraft at any time and failure to repay will result in the obligation secured by the charge being broken which would allow the bank to enforce its security. Obviously if a loan is repaid or terminated by agreement in some other way the security contract, be it direct or collateral, also terminates and the security is discharged.[12]

Legal and equitable charges

Any charge created by a company over an asset may be a legal charge or an equitable charge. A legal charge will, potentially, bind any person who acquires a charged asset from the company even if that person knows nothing of the charge (but note the position is different where the charge is registrable; see further below). In contrast, an equitable charge does not bind a person who subsequently acquires an interest in the charged asset bona fide, for value and without notice of the existence of the charge. However, since most charges created by companies have to be registered in compliance with s 395, and registration gives constructive notice of the existence of the charge, a person acquiring an interest in a charged asset will generally have notice of its existence[13] and will be bound by it. Note that charges over some corporate assets may have to be registered in two registers. For example, a charge on land owned by a company must be registered in the company charges register and the appropriate district land registry (if the land is registered land) or the Land Charges Registry (if the land is unregistered). Registers of charged property are open to public inspection hence there can be no question of a person pretending he has an uncharged asset, when such is not the case, and leaving the lender with no excuse for not discovering a prior charge. Where a charge, legal or equitable, is required to be registered, and registration has not taken place, the contract for security is valid as between the person charging the asset and the chargee but any subsequent buyer or chargee of the asset is not bound by the prior charge even if that person has notice of its existence. Thus, for example, a person acquiring an interest in an asset subject to a registrable equitable charge which has not been registered takes free of that charge even if he knows of it. In addition, an unregistered charge does not bind the liquidator of a company[14] and the charge can be disregarded by an administrator of a company appointed under an administration order.

---

11 In addition to the usual rules for the formation of contracts there may be special requirements relating to the form of the contract. For example the Statute of Frauds 1677, s 4, requires a contract of guarantee to be in writing or evidenced in writing to be enforceable.

12 *Rourke v Robinson* [1911] 1 Ch 480.

13 See below for the special case of floating charges.

14 Section 395.

A legal charge will be created when the company transfers to the chargee a legal interest in the charged property. It is common to find a company creating a legal charge over its real property or choses in action, for example company shares. A legal charge of this type will generally be called a mortgage, the person mortgaging the property may be called the mortgagor and the chargee in such a case is a mortgagee. There is no precise definition of an equitable charge but in *Re Charge Card Services Ltd*[15] Millet J said that:

> '... the essence of an equitable charge is that, without any conveyance or assignment to the chargee, specific property of the chargor is expressly or constructively appropriated to or made answerable for the payment of a debt, and the chargee is given the right to resort to the property for the purpose of having it realised and applied in or towards payment of the debt.'

The status of the charged property

Does property which is subject to a charge remain the property of the surety even if his ability to deal with the property is restricted by the contract for security? If there are no competing claims upon the charged asset its status is of little importance. However, where a company seeks to create further charges upon an asset already charged, or a third party seeks to claim a corporate asset (perhaps to satisfy a judgment debt), or the company is in liquidation and the issue is whether a charged asset belongs to the company or the chargee, the status of a charged asset is critical.

The position is not entirely free from confusion. Where corporate real property is subject to a legal charge, ie the company's legal interest in an asset has been transferred to the chargee, the existence of any equitable right to regain the secured asset (the equity of redemption applicable to mortgaged real property) would seem to preserve the company's ownership of its asset[16] so that a claim upon the assets of the company could be made against the charged asset. Moreover, one form of equitable charge (the floating charge) clearly leaves the company free to deal with the charged asset. Consequently, assets subject to such a charge remain the property of the company, at least until crystallisation.[17] The rights of a holder of a floating charge are considered further below.

The rights of a debentureholder

The rights possessed by an unsecured debentureholder are those of an ordinary unsecured creditor. Thus, where the company defaults on its obligations the creditor can sue for the sums owing and levy execution against the company. In appropriate cases a creditor may be able to present a petition to wind up the company or seek an administration order.

---

15   [1987] Ch 150.

16   See *Cunliffe Engineering Ltd v English Industrial Estates Corp* (1994) BCC 972 for an acknowledgment of the company's rights in respect of real property.

17   For an explanation of floating charge and crystallisation, see below.

The rights possessed by a secured debentureholder (a chargee) are those of the unsecured debentureholder and such other rights as are provided in the contract for security and under the general law. Where the chargee is exercising his normal contractual rights the limitation period is six years. However, where the security contract is created by deed (as is usually the case) and the debt is created under and by virtue of the contract the limitation period is 12 years.[18]

The right to sell

Unless the contract for security so provides (which it generally does) a chargee has no right to sell the charged assets. However, where a charge is created by deed, s 101 of the Law of Property Act 1925 allows the chargee to sell the assets (unless the contract excludes this right) if certain conditions set out in s 103 have been complied with. Section 103 permits sale only if the surety has been given three months' notice to repay the amount of the loan and he has not complied, or two months interest is outstanding or some other term of the contract has been broken. These time limits may be shortened by the contract creating the security.

A chargee who does not have the power to sell the charged assets can apply to the court for an order to sell. Where the chargee exercises a right to sell he can take what he is owed from the sums realised and must account to the surety for the balance. A chargee can sell the secured assets whenever the power of sale becomes exercisable and need not wait for the market in that asset to pick up if it is then depressed. However, the chargee must exercise reasonable care in selling the asset and must take care to ensure the sale price is a fair reflection of its market value. If the chargee fails to exercise reasonable care in selling the property he is liable in damages to the chargor to the extent that he must pay the chargor the difference between the price actually obtained and the price he should have obtained had he exercised reasonable care.[19]

The right to take possession

A chargee who has a legal charge has an immediate right to possession of the asset charged which can be exercised at any time unless the contract provides otherwise. However, a chargee who takes possession incurs heavy obligations towards the surety and this procedure is little used. Instead a process developed whereby the chargee could appoint a third party, a receiver, who would take possession of the charged property having provided in the security contract that the receiver would be deemed to be the agent of the surety, thus ensuring the chargee incurred no liability to the company.

An equitable chargee has no right of immediate possession of the charged asset and can appoint a receiver only if the security contract so provides (most do so). If the equitable chargee has the contractual right to appoint a receiver he should ensure such a receiver is also deemed to be the agent of the surety to avoid liability for the acts of the receiver. A receiver appointed under a floating charge (or a composite fixed and

---

18 Limitation Act 1980, ss 5 and 8.

19 *Cuckmere Brick Co Ltd v Mutual Finance Ltd* [1971] Ch 949.

floating charge) over the whole (or substantially the whole) of the property of a company is called an administrative receiver.[20] Where the contract does not provide for an equitable chargee to appoint a receiver the court is empowered to do so on an application of the chargee. However, a court receiver is an agent of the court and will not be acting with the interests of the chargee at the front of his mind so that such a procedure is very much second best from the point of view of the chargee.

The right to receive income

Where the charged property is revenue-generating, for example, land which has been leased, the chargee may wish to collect the revenue and thereby satisfy his claims rather than sell the property. This might well be the case where the property was unsaleable. If the contract provides that the chargee or a receiver has the right to receive income generated by the property there is no difficulty in enforcing such a contractual right. However, even if the contract does not create such a right, s 101 of the Law of Property Act 1925 allows the appointment of a receiver of income if the charge was created by deed. Section 101 applies to both legal and equitable charges. This power can be exercised only if the conditions set out in s 103 of the Act which are mentioned above have been satisfied.

Subsequent chargeholders

A transferee of a secured debenture can enforce the rights outlined above but debentures (other than bearer debentures) are not negotiable instruments. Hence, a person who acquires a secured debenture is subject to any claim which the company had against a prior holder[21] unless the conditions of transfer exclude such a right. In practice, most debentures do allow a transferee to be paid the amount due on the debenture regardless of the company's claims on prior holders – indeed if such is not the case the debentures marketability is much reduced.

Transfers of debentures, other than convertible debentures, are generally exempt from stamp duty.[22]

CHARGES

As already indicated, a security interest in property may be legal or equitable. Corporate charges are subject to another classification, a charge may be fixed (legal or equitable) or floating (equitable only). The security known as a floating charge was developed in the mid-19th century (and introduced into Scotland by statute in this century) as a means by which a company could create a charge over a type of asset rather than a specified asset. For example, a manufacturing company may make thousands of objects in the course of a month or even a day, it is impossible to create a fixed charge over each and every object but it is possible to describe each object as

---

20   Insolvency Act 1986, s 29(2).

21   *Re Rhodesia Goldfields Ltd* [1910] 1 Ch 239.

22   Finance Act 1986, s 79.

forming part of a class of corporate asset. Thus, the merit of a floating charge is that it can attach to a nominated class rather than an individual asset within that class. Obvious classes are, all assets, machinery, goods in the course of production or book debts etc. Floating charges cannot be created by partnerships or individuals.[23]

A floating charge confers no ownership rights in respect of the charged class of assets upon the chargee. A floating charge would be valueless if the chargee could not convert it into a specific or fixed charge. This conversion, called crystallisation, has the effect of attaching the charge upon whatever assets form part of the charged class at that moment or are acquired thereafter. When crystallisation occurs the assets then within the specified class are deemed to be assigned to the chargee and they cease to form part of the assets of the company and become the property of the chargee.[24] Until the charge crystallises the company can deal with the charged asset in the ordinary course of business[25] – this could include replacing, selling or charging the asset – although this freedom is frequently restricted by the charge. A common restriction is a 'negative pledge clause' which is discussed below.

The line between fixed and floating charges is not always clear.

Distinguishing fixed and floating charges

A fixed charge, which can be legal or equitable, is a charge over a specific, identifiable asset of the company. Examples are mortgages of company land or a charge over an identifiable asset in the course of production, perhaps a ship. A fixed charge, generally prevents the company dealing with the charged asset without the consent of the chargeholder and is, thus, an inappropriate form of security for assets which are constantly changing. The distinction between fixed and floating charges raises a continuing uncertainty about the nature of floating charges. Should they be seen as a type of fixed charge with a licence granted to the company by the chargee to allow dealing with the charged asset or is a floating charge to be regarded as not creating a charge on any specific asset until crystallisation? The weight of authority supports the latter view.[26] The advantage to the company of allowing the company the freedom to deal with the asset is restricted if the charge is regarded as fixed but floating charges have drawbacks from the point of view of the chargee (see below). Recently, the courts have adopted a pragmatic approach to the effect of charges and are inclined to give effect to the wishes of the parties as manifested in the security contract unless the law provides otherwise.

An example of the pragmatic approach designed to give effect to the wishes of the

---

23   There is one minor exception.
24   For a recent example, see *Re ELS Ltd* [1994] 3 WLR 656.
25   *Wallace v Evershed* [1899] 1 Ch 891.
26   See *English and Scottish Mercantile Investment Co Ltd v Brunton* [1892] 2 QB 700; *Government Stock Investment Co v Manila Rly Co Ltd* [1897] AC 81 and *Re Yorkshire Woolcombers Association Ltd* [1903] 2 Ch 284, CA; approved on appeal by the House of Lords under the name *Illingworth v Houldsworth* [1904] AC 355.
27   [1994] 1 BCLC 485.

parties is *Re New Bullas Ltd*.[27] In this case the Court of Appeal accepted that it was possible to create a defeasible fixed charge – that is a fixed charge (which offers greater protection to the chargee), which on the happening of given events, ceased to exist. In this case the company had granted a fixed charge over its book debts which provided that when debts were paid the money was to be paid into a designated bank account, the operation of which could be dictated by the chargee. If the chargee failed to give instructions, the collected sums became subject to a floating charge. The chargee failed to give instructions and the court treated the book debts as subject to a fixed charge which ceased to exist in respect of collected debts on the happening of the 'event', ie the failure to give instructions as to what the company was to do with the money.[28]

There is no statutory definition of a floating charge and what the parties call the charge is not conclusive evidence of its status.[29] Judicial pronouncements have isolated certain factors which are likely to be present if a charge is to be classified as floating. These factors are[30] that the charge:

(a) is over a class of assets both present and future;

(b) which assets are in the ordinary course of business periodically changing;

(c) leaves the company free to use and deal with those assets in the ordinary course of business (this freedom need not be absolute).

A floating charge may extend over the whole corporate enterprise or it is quite common to encounter a company which has created a fixed charge over real property and a floating charge over the rest of the company's assets and undertaking. It is perfectly possible to create a floating charge over assets which do not yet exist or which have not yet been acquired by the company.

While it is tempting to see fixed charges as relating to permanent assets and floating charges as affixing to changing assets, cases, particularly since the important decision in *Siebe Gorman & Co Ltd v Barclays Bank Ltd*,[31] have stressed that the courts will not regard any single factor as crucial in seeking to classify a charge as fixed or floating. What seems to be of primary importance in determining the nature of the charge is whether the asset is identifiable at the time the charge is created and is not susceptible to disposal by the company free from the charge while the charge continues to exist.[32] On this basis, even present and future debts can be the subject of a fixed charge provided the debts are payable to the chargee or his nominee (which might include the

---

28 See also *Re Cimex Tissues* below for another situation in which the court preserved the freedom of the company to deal with its assets without treating the charge as floating.

29 See *Re New Bullas Ltd* [1994] 1 BCLC 485.

30 This 'definition' is derived from *Government Stock Investment Co v Manila Rly Co Ltd* [1897] AC 81 and *Re Yorkshire Woolcombers Association Ltd* [1903] 2 Ch 284, CA; approved on appeal by the House of Lords under the name *Illingworth v Houldsworth* [1904] AC 355.

31 [1979] 2 Lloyd's Rep 142, where the issue was whether the company had created a fixed charge over book debts.

32 This view is derived from *Siebe Gorman* itself and also *Re Permanent House (Holdings) Ltd* [1988] BCLC 563; *Re Portbase (Clothing) Ltd* [1993] BCLC 796; *Re Armagh Shoes Ltd* [1982] NI 59 and *Re GE Tunbridge Ltd* [1995] 1 BCLC 34.

company), that the company can not use any debts collected for its own general purposes and that the company must pay sums received into an account for the use of the chargee (even if the account is opened in the name of the company). It is not certain if some classes of asset are incapable of being the subject of a fixed charge although it seems inconsistent with the nature of a fixed charge to permit one to attach to materials consumed in the manufacturing processes of the company or the stock of a trading company.

In one case, *Re Cimex Tissues Ltd*,[33] a limited freedom to deal with assets without consulting the chargee, generally regarded as conclusive evidence that a charge is floating, did not preclude the creation of a fixed charge. Thus, a charge over plant and machinery which allowed the company to dispose of assets without the chargee's permission was held to be fixed – the machinery in practice rarely changed and some had been held for 30 years. Where the status of a charge is uncertain the fact that it would paralyse the business of the company if classified a fixed charge will tend to suggest that the parties intended it to be a floating charge.[34]

Crystallisation of floating charges

The essence of a floating charge is that it leaves the company free to deal with the charged asset in the ordinary course of business without consulting the chargeholder (although the security contract may restrict this freedom). Since a floating charge is over a class of assets, the chargee is uncertain as to the value of his security at any moment before the charge 'crystallises'. Crystallisation, when a floating charge becomes a fixed charge over the assets currently comprising the relevant class, occurs automatically on the happening of certain events, namely:

(a) if a receiver is appointed by the court or any chargee; or

(b) when winding up commences; or

(c) when the company ceases to carry on its business as a going concern.[35]

While the onset of receivership and winding up is a determinable fixed point it is more difficult to determine when a company has ceased to carry on business. In particular it is not clear whether the crystallisation of a floating charge automatically means that the company has ceased to operate thereby crystallising any other floating charges granted by the company. The English cases reject the view that crystallisation (other than by the appointment of a receiver which itself crystallises all floating charges) necessarily means the company has ceased to carry on business.[36] In the next paragraphs

---

33 [1995] 1 BCLC 409.

34 *Re GE Tunbridge Ltd*, above.

35 The first two grounds are well established, the third is more controversial but, it is submitted, is justified by the decisions in *William Gaskell Group Ltd v Highley* [1994] 1 BCLC 197 and *Bank of Credit and Commerce International SA v BRS Kumar Bros Ltd* [1994] 1 BCLC 211.

36 *Re Woodroffes (Musical Instruments) Ltd* [1986] Ch 366, this view has found support in Australia, see *National Australia Bank Ltd v Composite Buyers Ltd* (1991) 6 ACSR 94, but has been rejected in Canada where the crystallisation of a floating charge in itself has been held to crystallise any other floating charges.

crystallisation either by notice or automatically is discussed. It is surely possible for a chargee to include a provision in the security contract to the effect that the crystallisation of another floating charge either permits him to give notice of crystallisation of his charge or automatically crystallises his charge.

A charge also crystallises when the security contract provides that the chargee is entitled to give notice of crystallisation and such notice is given. Typically, the security contract will allow notice on the happening of certain specified events such as interest falling into arrears, the levying of execution on the assets of the company or the company being unable to pay its debts. In cases where the chargee seeks to crystallise the charge by notice, strict compliance with the security contract is necessary for crystallisation to occur.[37]

It is also generally accepted (although not yet entirely free from doubt) that a chargee can put a provision in the security contract providing for the charge to crystallise automatically on the happening of specified events (ie without notice being given). If this is so then a chargee can provide that a floating charge is to crystallise automatically if the company attempts to create a further charge over an asset to which his floating charge attaches or the assets of the company fall below a specified figure. The courts have indicated, *obiter*,[38] that if the security contract so provides a floating charge may crystallise on the happening of the specified event without any intervention by the chargee. Hoffman J in *Re Brightlife Ltd* and *Re Permanent House (Holdings) Ltd* said that he saw no reason why company law should intervene in the freedom of lender and borrower to put such terms in their contract as they saw fit. While this argument has much power there is a counter view. It can be argued that to allow a chargee to rely on his contractual rights is unfair to a third party (a second chargeholder) who has no means of knowing about the automatic crystallisation clause. It is true that a prudent third party would inquire of the company whether his charge would crystallise any prior floating charges but the company might provide an inaccurate answer. It is open to the Secretary of State to make regulations relating to such clauses, for example it could be required that such a provision is registered. What is certain, is that an automatic crystallisation clause, will be construed strictly against the party who seeks to rely on it.

On crystallisation the charge becomes fixed only from that moment and the charge is not retrospectively transformed into a fixed charge from its inception. This has important consequences on winding up. If there are two charges attaching to the same asset a floating charge being, until crystallisation, an equitable charge, is ranked in the order of priorities after a fixed legal charge over the same asset. The fixed charge has priority even if it was created after the floating charge and that charge had been

---

37 *Re Brightlife Ltd* [1987] Ch 200.

38 See *Re Woodroffes (Musical Instruments) Ltd* [1986] Ch 366; *Re Brightlife Ltd* [1987] Ch 200 and *Re Permanent House (Holdings) Ltd* [1988] BCLC 563. The validity of such clauses has been accepted in New Zealand, see *Re Manurewa Transport Ltd* [1971] NZLR 909 and Australia but rejected in Canada.

39 For another method by which floating charge-holders protect themselves see 'negative pledge' clauses, below.

registered. It is this problem which automatic crystallisation is designed to address.[39] The position of a floating chargee may have been further eroded by the decision in *Griffiths v Yorkshire Bank plc*[40] which seems to say that where there are two floating charges over the same asset, the second in time may acquire priority over the first (contrary to the usual rule for equitable charges) if it crystallises first. If this decision is correct, and it has been doubted, it will make automatic crystallisation clauses (and negative pledge clauses) of even greater importance to a floating chargee. The general position on priority as between two floating chargees is discussed below.

Drawbacks of floating charges

As indicated above, a floating chargee has no right to possession of the charged asset and may find that his claims upon the charged asset rank after a subsequent fixed chargee even if the fixed charge was created later than his charge: of course, the floating charge retains priority if the fixed charge was expressly stated in its security contract to rank behind the floating charge. Thus, if the asset is of insufficient value to satisfy both chargeholders in full, the floating chargeholder is paid only what remains after the fixed chargeholders claims have been satisfied in full. Registration of a floating charge does not protect the floating chargee even though it gives notice of the existence of the prior floating charge. After all what is a subsequent chargeholder entitled to conclude if he knows there is a floating charge over all or some of the assets of the company – only that the company is free to deal with those assets since this is a key feature of a floating charge. Thus, floating charges are subject to the drawback that they may be postponed to later charges. Floating chargeholders face other problems when the liquidator of an insolvent company is determining the order in which the creditors should be paid.[41] Let us consider some of these priority problems and possible solutions.

Priorities between chargees

Logically the argument which permits subsequent fixed charges to obtain priority over prior floating charges – freedom to deal with charged assets – also applies where the subsequent charge is itself floating. However, in *Re Benjamin Cope Ltd*[42] Sargant J held that a company's freedom to deal with charged assets did not extend to permitting a company to create a second floating charge over assets which ranked in priority or *pari passu* (equally) with the first charge even if the second charge purported to have such priority. Of course the first charge could specifically permit the creation of subsequent floating charges with priority which would allow the second charge to take priority over the first.

---

40   [1994] 1 WLR 1427.

41   However, it can be noted that whoever comes first among the creditors, unsecured creditors always come last although even these lowly creatures rank before share-holders who receive money on a winding up only after all creditors have been paid in full.

42   [1914] 1 Ch 800.

43   [1926] Ch 412.

This view was modified in *Re Automatic Bottlemakers Ltd*,[43] in which the Court of Appeal (which included Sargant J) held that a floating charge (even if over all the assets of a company) did not prevent the company creating a second floating charge with priority over the first in respect of *part* of the charged assets (perhaps book debts). This seems to apply even if the first charge did not specifically authorise the granting of a second charge with priority.[44] *Automatic Bottlemakers* would not give priority to a second floating charge where the assets subject to the second charge were largely the same as those subject to the first charge. Whether the second charge is over part of the assets or is essentially over the same assets as the first charge IS a question of fact.

Hence, a subsequent floating charge may, and a subsequent fixed charge will, generally, obtain priority over a floating charge. As the next paragraph shows, floating chargees have evolved a means by which they may be able to preserve their priority.

Negative pledge clauses

Since there is the risk of a later charge obtaining priority, prudent floating chargees commonly insert negative pledge clauses into the security contract.

A negative pledge clause is a clause specifically precluding the creation of a second charge with priority over the floating charge. Such a clause restricts the company's freedom to deal with the charged asset, but since the restriction does not prevent all dealings, but merely one, it is not thought to render the first clause fixed. However, the efficacy and status of the clause as between the company and the floating chargee does not necessarily mean it affects the rights of third parties. It can be argued that for the company to ignore such a clause and grant a further charge would be a case of equitable fraud and thus the second charge would be void and the floating charge is unaffected by it, however, the prevalent view is that the second charge is not void. The first charge will, thus, retain its priority only if the second chargeholder has notice both of the existence of the first charge (which is provided by registration) *and* of the restriction on the freedom of the company to further charge the relevant asset.

Registration does not provide, it seems, constructive notice, of a restriction since a restriction need not, at present, be registered (other than when the company charge requires registration in Scotland). Despite the frequency of negative pledge clauses, the cases support the view that even if a later chargee has actual knowledge of the existence of a prior floating charge (which he will have at least constructively through registration) this is neither notice of a restriction nor to require the potential chargeholder to make inquiries as to the nature and extent of the registered charge.[45]

Where, however, a potential chargeholder searches the Register of Charges, and thereby obtains actual knowledge of the existence of the charge he will also obtain actual knowledge of any restriction registered with the charge so that the restriction

---

44 For the situation where there is a specific prohibition on the granting of subsequent charges, fixed or floating, with priority, see below.

45 *English and Scottish Mercantile Investment Co Ltd v Brunton* [1892] 2 QB 700.

will be effective in retaining the priority of the floating charge over the subsequent charge.

Preferential debts

Debts which are classified as preferential must be paid out of the assets of a company in priority to the claims of a floating chargee[46] if the company goes into liquidation or a receiver is appointed (other than a receiver appointed in pursuance of an automatic crystallisation clause).[47] If a debentureholder takes possession of the charged assets rather than appointing a receiver the preferential debts do not take priority over the floating charge (Insolvency Act 1986, s 40). Assets subject to a fixed charge are not subject to the preference debts unless the fixed charge is on property to which a floating charge, which has priority over it, also attaches.[48] If the assets subject to a floating charge are insufficient to satisfy the preference debts any unsecured assets of the company must be used to satisfy these claims.

Preferential debts are defined in s 386 and Schedule 6 of the Insolvency Act. They are:

(a) Income tax and social security contributions collected from money paid during the 12 months prior to winding up (or receivership), ie PAYE and national insurance collected from employees but not yet handed over to the Revenue or the Department for Social Security;

(b) VAT, insurance premium tax, car tax, betting tax, lottery duty, excise duty on beer and air passenger duty collected within six months (12 months for car tax, betting tax and lottery duty) of winding up (or receivership) and not yet paid to Customs and Excise;

(c) A maximum of four months or £800 of unpaid salary (whichever is the greater);

(d) Certain coal and steel levies payable under EC law.

If there are insufficient funds available to pay all the preference debts they all rank equally and will be paid a percentage of the sums owing.

Assets of the company

On crystallisation, a floating charge becomes fixed and attaches to any assets of the company falling within the charged class. However, it is crucial to remember that assets within the charged class over which a third party has a better claim than the company are not subject to the charge.

Consequently, where a floating chargee has a charge over raw materials to be used by the company he may find that the supplier of the goods has retained title to them until he has been paid (a retention of title clause). Such a clause allows the supplier, if

---

46   Insolvency Act 1986, s 175.

47   *Griffiths v Yorkshire Bank plc* [1994] 1 WLR 1427.

48   *Re Portbase Clothing Ltd* [1993] Ch 388.

49   *Aluminium Industrie Vaasen BV v Romalpa Aluminium Ltd* [1978] 1 WLR 676.

unpaid, to remove the goods from the company's premises and out of the grasp of the chargee.[49] A retention of title clause will cease to exist if the goods to which it applies are used by the company so that those goods have ceased to exist as a separate entity, for example if wool is woven into carpets. If a supplier of goods has transferred title to goods to the company and the contract of supply then purports to allow the supplier to recover the goods for non-payment, the contract will be construed as creating a charge in favour of the supplier which will almost certainly be void for non-registration. Whether a supply contract has retained title or created a charge is a question of construction. An attempt to extend the use of retention of title clauses to cover all indebtedness of the company to a supplier, and not merely the price of goods supplied under a particular contract, or to extend the supplier's rights to the proceeds of resale of the goods will almost certainly lead to the contract being treated as having created a charge.

Similarly, goods are not company assets susceptible to the clutch of the chargee if they are already subject to a lien or a trust or have been leased or acquired on hire-purchase by the company. The position in respect of the enforcement of legal rights against a company, for example the levying of execution for unpaid bills or rent, is far from clear. However, it does seem certain that legal rights, for example a garnishee order, take priority over floating charges provided they are enforced before crystallisation.

However, a floating charge is not postponed to the holder of a *Mareva* injunction (an injunction restraining the removal of the assets from the jurisdiction of the UK courts).

AVOIDANCE OF CHARGES

As with any company contract a charge granted by a company may be attacked as *ultra vires* or its validity may be challenged on the basis that the person negotiating the charge lacked authority; the directors may incur liability for acting improperly in creating the charge. There are, in addition, special provisions relating to the validity of company charges. These sections are designed to 'prevent companies on their last legs from creating charges to secure past debts or for moneys which do not go to swell their assets and become available to creditors' and specifically to ensure that those closely connected with a company cannot protect themselves in the event of insolvency by granting charges to themselves or their associates. The principal provision is s 245 of the Insolvency Act but s 239 of the same Act may also affect the enforceability of a charge (the later section embraces a number of transactions and not merely charges).

Section 245

Section 245(1) invalidates a floating charge created within a defined period (the statutory period) prior to the commencement of winding up (or administration). The statutory period is currently 12 months or two years if the chargeholder is a connected person. A floating charge in favour of a non-connected person is not invalidated even if granted within 12 months if the company was able to pay its debts at the time the charge was granted and did not cease to be able to do so by virtue of the granting of the charge.[50] Solvency at the time of grant will not avail a connected person. Note that the validity of a charge granted within the statutory period arises only when liquidation (or administration) commences and that the section does not affect the validity of the underlying debt. Consequently, if a company grants a charge within the statutory period to secure a debt and then repays the debt before liquidation, thereby discharging the charge, the validity of the charge is irrelevant since it no longer exists.[51] However, a debt paid within six months of winding up may be challenged as being a preference contrary to s 239 on which see below.

The following are connected[52] for the purposes of s 245:

(a) a director or shadow director of the company; or

(b) an associate of a director or shadow director of the company; or

(c) an associate of the company.

An associate is defined in considerable detail in s 435. In outline, it includes a spouse and other close relatives of a director or shadow director, any business partners (and their spouses and close relatives) and companies over which the relevant person and his associates have control. A company is an associate of another company if they are both controlled by a relevant person (either alone or with associates) and a person is an associate of his employer or anyone whom he employs.

Section 245 does not invalidate the debt underlying the charge nor does it affect fixed charges (but see s 239, below). The section is construed objectively so that there is no need to prove impropriety to invalidate a charge or even, where the longer statutory period is in issue, to prove that a person knew he was a connected person.

Section 245(4)

A charge which appears to be invalidated by s 245 will remain valid to the extent of the total of 'the value of so much of the consideration for the creation of the charge as consists of money paid, or goods or services supplied, to the company at the same time as, or after the creation of the charge' (s 245(2)(a)) and 'the value of so much of that consideration as consists of the discharge or reduction at the same time as, or after, the creation of the charge, of any debt of the company' (s 245(2)(b)). This sub-section does not refer to funds or goods which have been provided to the company in consideration of a charge being granted in the future. The Court of Appeal (rejecting the view generally held) has ruled that money or goods supplied prior to the execution of the charge, however short the period before the charge is executed, cannot be taken into

---

50 Section 245(4).

51 *Mace Builders Ltd v Lunn* [1987] Ch 191.

52 Section 249. The critical date is when the charge was granted.

53 *Power v Sharp Investments Ltd* [1994] 1 BCLC 111.

account in determining the extent to which a charge is validated by this section even if the supply was in anticipation of the charge subsequently granted.[53]

The court will not permit s 245(4) to be used to turn an unsecured existing obligation into a new secured debt – some new and genuine benefit to the company must be provided by the chargee. Thus, in *Re Fairway Magazines Ltd*[54] a floating charge granted to X, a director of F Ltd, who had guaranteed the company's overdraft and who had agreed to lend money to the company in return for the charge, was invalid insofar as the money he lent the company was used to pay off the overdraft. Even though X's conduct had not been fraudulent or in any way dishonest the effect of this payment was merely to substitute a secured debt for an unsecured debt (a claim on the company if the guarantee was called in) and not to benefit the company. Banks, however, may be in the happy position of being able to manipulate s 245(4) to their own advantage. Where a company is overdrawn at its bank and grants a floating charge as security for that debt the existing overdraft pre-dates the charge and s 245(5) does not apply to it. However, money paid into the overdrawn bank account by a company pays off part of the overdraft and if the company is permitted to draw out an equal sum to that paid in, the drawing is to be regarded as new money paid to the company as consideration for the charge.[55]

Money may be regarded as paid to the company even if it is paid directly to a creditor of the company provided the payment was directed by the company and was for its benefit.[56]

Sections 238 and 239

These provisions are primarily of concern when discussing liquidation of companies and the following is a brief outline of their scope. Both sections allow a liquidator (or administrator if the company is in administration) to apply to the court to have certain transactions, which could include the granting of a charge, entered into by a company within the statutory period prior to the commencement of the winding up (or administration) set aside and the position of the company restored to what it would have been but for disputed transaction.

Section 238 permits the re-opening of transactions at an undervalue[57] unless the company entered into the transaction in good faith, for the purpose of carrying on its business and there were reasonable grounds to believe it would benefit the company.[58] In *Re MC Bacon Ltd*[59] Millett J refused to treat a charge granted to the company's bank

---

54 [1993] BCLC 643.

55 *Re Yeovil Glove Ltd* [1965] Ch 148. This decision was much criticised by the Cork Report into Insolvency, Cmnd 8558, but has remained unamended and still appears to be good law.

56 *Re Mathew Ellis Ltd* [1933] 1 Ch 458.

57 Defined in s 238(4) to include gifts and transactions where the consideration provided by the beneficiary is significantly below the value of the benefit conferred by the company.

58 Section 238(5).

59 [1990] BCLC 324.

to persuade it to allow the company to continue to operate its overdraft as a transaction at an undervalue; the company had not parted with anything of value – it had not diminished its assets but had merely appropriated them for the payment of a debt.

Section 239 applies to transactions which give a preference to a person, that is, doing something which has the effect of putting a person into a position which would, if the company went into insolvent liquidation, be better than if that thing had not been done (s 239(4)), for example granting a fixed charge over corporate assets to an unsecured creditor. Whether a transaction is at an undervalue or is a preference is determined objectively.

The statutory period for both sections is two years prior to the commencement of the winding up if the beneficiary is a connected person (defined as for s 245 but excluding employees). If the beneficiary is a non-connected person the statutory period is six months for s 239 and s 238 does not apply. Neither section operates if at the time of the disputed transaction the company could pay its debts and this position was not affected by the disputed transaction.

The intention to prefer

Section 239 only applies where the company which gave the preference was 'influenced in deciding to give it by a desire to create a preference in relation to the person whose position has been improved' (s 239(5)). There is a rebuttable presumption that such was the intention of the company if the person preferred was a connected person (other than an employee) but it must be proved by the applicant in all other cases.

There is scanty case law on this provision but it seems that a liquidator must establish that at the time the disputed charge was made the company desired the other party to the transaction to be treated more favourably than other creditors etc, ie it is a subjective test. This desire can be inferred from the surrounding circumstances and may be at variance with the expressed desires of those making the decision. Simply to grant a charge does not manifest a desire to prefer, it depends upon whether the decision was motivated by commercial considerations rather than a 'positive wish to improve the creditor's position'. It seems that a charge granted for commercial reasons and with the desire to prefer must be treated as falling within s 239.[60] In *Re MC Bacon Ltd*[61] the company, in granting a charge to secure its overdraft facility, had been motivated by the desire to fend off the bank which was pressing for repayment rather than by any desire to prefer and the charge was upheld.

REGISTRATION OF CHARGES

The position on registration is presently in a state of uncertainty in that the registration

---

60   *Re Fairway Magazines Ltd* [1993] BCLC 643. In this case the decision to grant a fixed charge was made for commercial reasons alone, namely the need to raise money quickly, and not by a desire to prefer X should insolvency ensue and was valid.

61   [1990] BCLC 324.

of company charges is currently subject to the 1985 Act but its provisions were to be replaced by a new system contained in the 1989 Act. However, no date for the substitution of the 1989 system has been set and it looks increasingly likely that these 1989 change will not be implemented but will be replaced by alternative amendments. Until some change is executed the 1985 Act prevails.

Prescribed details of most charges on the assets of a company must be delivered to the Registrar of Companies for entry into the charges register within 21 days of the charge's creation.[62] Failure so to do results in the security, but not the debt secured by the charge, being void against specified persons. Late delivery of the details may result in the charge being void against the liquidator if the company goes into insolvent liquidation within a specified time after the delivery of the details.[63] The register of charges is open to public inspection[64] but the possible 21 day gap between creation and registration means that a person searching the register may not receive accurate information on the state of a company's registrable charges.[65]

Registration of a charge gives constructive notice to the whole world of the existence of the charge but it does not provide notice of the terms of the registered charge. Hence, as we have seen, the registration of a negative pledge clause in a floating charge does not provide constructive notice of the clause (it does give actual notice to anyone who searches the register).[66]

What is registrable?

Section 396 provides a list of what is required to be registered. It includes:

(a) a charge to secure an issue of debentures;

(b) a charge on uncalled share capital;

(c) a charge which, if created by an individual, would require registration as a bill of sale;

(d) a charge on land (wherever situate);

(e) a charge on book debts;

(f) a floating charge; and

(g) a charge on certain assets such as goodwill or any intellectual property.

Note that liabilities created by a company such as hire-purchase transactions and conditional sale agreements which might well have an adverse affect on the company's

---

62 Section 398. This does not apply to a charge arising by operation of law.

63 Sections 399 and 400.

64 Section 401(3).

65 The register of charges which the company must keep, see s 407, should contain comprehensive details but non-registration in this register does not affect the validity of a charge.

66 It is arguable that the frequency of negative pledge clauses will lead to their registration giving constructive notice of their existence – some slight judicial support for this view may be discerned in *Ian Chisholm Textiles Ltd v Griffiths* (1994) BCC 96.

financial stability are not registrable and thus not capable of discovery by searching the register. The interpretation of s 395 is that any transaction for value which gives a third party the benefit of a corporate asset creates a charge however the transaction is phrased.[67] However, where the third party becomes entitled to an asset and not merely the benefit of it that is not a charge. Hence debt-factoring agreements are not charges nor are sale and leaseback agreements even, it seems, if the company has the right to regain the asset in the future.[68] Rights arising by operation of law are not registrable since they have not been created by the company.

Section 401 specifies the details of what should be registered. This includes:

(a) the date of creation;

(b) the sum secured;

(c) the names of the chargees; and

(d) short details of the property subject to the charge.

If the details submitted for registration are incomplete the Registrar will return the particulars for amendment but the obligation to register within 21 days of creation remains in force so that the lender will have to move swiftly to comply with the Act. If a company acquires property already subject to a charge s 400 requires the company to register the charge within 21 days of the acquisition of the charged property but failure to do so does not render the charge void.

Once a charge is registered the Registrar gives a certificate which is conclusive evidence that the registration requirements have been complied with even if this is not in fact the case.[69]

Rectification of the register

Section 404 permits rectification of the register of charges to supply an omission or correct a misstatement. An application for rectification must be made to the court and it is permitted only if the court is satisfied that the error sought to be corrected arose through inadvertence or other sufficient cause and will not prejudice the creditors or shareholders of the company.[70] Rectification may be allowed on terms.

Failure to register

---

67   *Gorringe v Irwell India Rubber Works* (1886) 34 Ch D 128.

68   *Welsh Development Agency v Export Finance Ltd* [1992] BCLC 148.

69   Section 401(2) and see *Re CL Nye Ltd* [1971] 1 Ch 442, charge overlooked and date amended then registered within 21 days of amended date – charge validly registered. The benefits of correction fluid are all-pervasive.

70   Rectification is also permitted where it is just and equitable.

71   Any costs are recoverable from the company, s 399(2).

72   Section 399(3).

It is the duty of the company to register a charge which it creates but a person interested in the charge may also seek to register the charge and would be wise to do so.[71] Failure to register renders the company and any officer in default liable to a fine.[72]

Section 395 provides that failure to register within the statutory period renders a charge void against the liquidator, an administrator and any other creditor of the company even if that person actually knew of the existence of the charge[73] and this applies even where the company being wound up is solvent. If a registrable charge is not registered the money secured by it is repayable immediately.[74]

Late registration

Where a charge has not been registered within 21 days of creation all is not lost for the lender. He can use s 404 and apply for late registration but must do so as soon as he discovers the omission to register. Late registration, when permitted, will normally be subject to the term that the charge now being registered cannot obtain priority over any charge created and registered between the time when the original charge should have been registered and its actual date of registration.[75]

Other than in exceptional circumstances, late registration is not permitted once a winding up order has been made. To allow late registration in such a case would give priority to the holders of the charge over the unsecured creditors whose rights might be said to vest on the commencement of winding up. In *Re Braemar Investments Ltd*[76] late registration was permitted, despite the imminence of winding up when it was clear that the failure to register was not attributable to the chargee but his solicitor and that the chargee had acted promptly on discovering the situation.

---

73 *Re Monolithic Building Co* [1915] 1 Ch 643.

74 Section 395(2).

75 But see *Re Fablehill Ltd* [1991] BCLC 830 where the subsequent charge in favour of the directors was not given priority over the original charge when, eventually, it was registered.

76 [1990] BCLC 556.

CHAPTER TWELVE

SHAREHOLDER REMEDIES

INTRODUCTION

If the registered company is to achieve its full potential as an effective vehicle for investment in business and industry, it is of considerable importance to ensure that there are appropriate mechanisms and procedures in place to enable an investor/shareholder who believes that his investment is being illegitimately jeopardised by the conduct of the persons running the company either to remove his investment altogether or to prevent the conduct and/or recover property which properly belongs to the company. The fact that the English registered company thrived for so long without any such effective shareholder remedy is not proof that none was necessary, but simply that the interests of the controllers of companies in the sense of both directors and majority shareholders were seen as a higher priority than the interests of smaller, passive investors.

Of course the problems are not so acute in relation to the public company where a disgruntled or disillusioned shareholder can easily dispose of his shares on the market, a fact which has undoubtedly contributed to the historic disinterest of the courts in developing any effective shareholder remedies at common law. In addition those running public companies which are listed on the Stock Exchange have to comply with the extra-legal requirements and controls contained in the 'Yellow Book'.

Majority shareholders in any company can, of course, remove the directors from the board by passing an ordinary resolution to that effect if they are unhappy about the way the company is being run.[1] So the real problems are faced by minority shareholders in private companies. These will be the main focus for consideration in this chapter but in principle the law is also applicable to shareholders in public companies.

THE COMMON LAW

The principle of majority rule

The starting point for any consideration of the position of minority shareholders is the rule in *Foss v Harbottle*.[2] This rule, which has two strands, precludes a shareholder from bringing an action to pursue wrongs which have been done to the company. First, the directors have been appointed to manage the company's affairs and they owe their duties to the company any misfeasance, appropriation of corporate property or breach of duty on their part is a wrong done to the company and, as a separate legal person,

---

1   Companies Act 1985, s 303.
2   (1843) 2 Hare 461.

the company is the proper plaintiff in any subsequent legal proceedings. Secondly, where there are irregularities in the way the company is run, and also in many cases where directors are in breach of their duties, the majority of shareholders in general meeting may by ordinary resolution ratify and adopt what has been done. In those circumstances the courts will not allow a minority shareholder to bring an action pursuing a matter which it is competent for the majority to approve on behalf of the company. A shareholder who buys shares in a company must accept that the majority will prevail.[3]

One of the clearest statements of the rule is in the judgment of Jenkins LJ in *Edwards v Halliwell*[4] where he states that:

> '[t]he rule in *Foss v Harbottle* ... comes to no more than this. First, the proper plaintiff in an action in respect of a wrong alleged to be done to a company or association of persons is *prima facie* the company or association of persons itself. Secondly, where the alleged wrong is a transaction which might be made binding on the company or association and on all its members by a simple majority of the members, no individual member of the company or association is in favour of what has been done, then *cadit quaestio*. No wrong had been done to the company or association and there is nothing in respect of which anyone can sue.'[5]

Another well-known examination of the rule is to be found in the Privy Council judgment of *Burland v Earle*[6] where Lord Davey states:

> 'It is an elementary principle of the law relating to joint stock companies that the Court will not interfere with the internal management of companies acting within their powers, and in fact has no jurisdiction to do so. Again, it is clear law that in order to redress a wrong done to the company or to recover moneys or damages alleged to be due to the company, the action should *prima facie* be brought by the company itself.'

Further on, Lord Davey turns again to the question of irregularities stating:

> '... no mere informality or irregularity which can be remedied by the majority will entitle the minority to sue, if the act when done regularly would be within the powers of the company and the intention of the majority of the shareholders is clear.'[7]

A clear example of this is the case of *MacDougall v Gardiner*.[8] Here a company's articles gave the chairman of the general meeting power to adjourn with the consent of the meeting. The articles also provided that a poll should be taken if one was demanded by five or more members. During a general meeting a member proposed the adjournment of the meeting. When this resolution was passed on a show of hands the chairman declared it to be carried. Five members then demanded that a poll be taken on the question of whether there should be an adjournment, but the chairman refused to hold

---

3   See also *Mozley v Alston* (1847) 1 Ph 790.
4   [1950] 2 All ER 1064.
5   *Ibid* at 1066; See also *Regal (Hastings) Ltd v Gulliver* [1967] 2 AC 134 at 150.
6   [1902] AC 83.
7   *Ibid* at 93.
8   (1875) 1 Ch D 13.

one and immediately left the room. The members then brought this action, asking for, *inter alia*, a declaration that the conduct of the chairman was illegal and improper. The action was dismissed, since Mellish LJ was of the opinion that this was a matter which the majority of the members of the company were entitled to put right by a resolution to that effect, and there was no point allowing the action to proceed if the end result would be that a meeting was called and ultimately the majority obtained its wishes.

A further point emphasised by Lord Davey in *Burland v Earle*[9] is that in principle it does not matter how the majority vote is obtained or how the majority is composed so that a shareholder is not debarred from voting or using his voting power to carry a resolution just because he has a particular interest in the subject-matter of the vote. This was seen in *North West Transportation Ltd v Beatty*[10] but also in the earlier case of *East Pant Du United Lead Mining Co Ltd v Merryweather*.[11] Here proceedings had been launched in the name of the company against a director who, it was alleged, had sold worthless mines to the company. The court adjourned the case so that a general meeting could be held and at the meeting a resolution was passed in favour of a stay of the action. The resolution was held to be validly passed even though it was passed as a result of the director using his votes as a shareholder.

Limits to the principle of majority rule

There have always been a number of cases where the courts have not applied the principle of majority rule so as to preclude a minority shareholder from obtaining relief. These are cases where either the rule has no application or the courts have developed an exception on the ground of fraud.

Cases where the rule has no application

The principle of majority rule can have no application where a bare majority of shareholders has no right to ratify and adopt a particular act for the company. So therefore the rule in *Foss v Harbottle* had no application where the company was proposing to do an *ultra vires* or illegal act since the shareholders could not, even by a unanimous vote, ratify an *ultra vires* or illegal act.[12] Even after the Companies Act 1989 introduced the new s 35 into the 1985 Act, *ultra vires* acts in the sense of being outside the company's contractual capacity can only be adopted by special resolution and *ultra vires* acts in the sense of unlawful returns of capital cannot be ratified at all. In these circumstances the shareholder has a right to bring a personal action since he has a right to have the company act in accordance with the terms of its constitution and within the law.[13] The right of a shareholder to bring an action restraining a proposed *ultra vires* transaction is expressly recognised in s 35(2) of the 1985 Act.

---

9   [1902] AC 83 at 94.

10   (1887) 12 App Cas 589.

11   (1846) 2 Hem & M 254.

12   *Simpson v Westminster Palace Hotel Co* (1860) 8 HL Cas 712.

13   *Parke v Daily News Ltd* [1962] Ch 927.

In *Smith v Croft (No 2)*[14] Knox J held that where the *ultra vires* or illegal act had been completed, then any loss accruing to the company was recoverable in an action brought by the company itself, so the shareholder would lose the right to bring an action and would have to pursue the matter, if allowed, in a derivative suit.[15]

Second, the principle of majority rule can have no application where what is done or proposed to be done can only be a special majority or special resolution. So, for example, a shareholder is entitled to have the articles altered only on the passing of a special resolution in accordance with s 9, and in *Edwards v Halliwell*[16] a member of a trade union was able to obtain a declaration that an alteration to the union contributions was invalid as it had not been made following a two-thirds majority vote as required by the union rules.

Third, and more wide-ranging, is the shareholder's right to enforce personal rights which accrue to him as a shareholder. In a sense the first two cases above are merely special features of this general right. An example of a shareholder enforcing his rights can be seen in *Wood v Odessa Waterworks Ltd*[17] where a shareholder enforced a right in the articles to be paid a dividend rather than being issued a debenture which was what the directors proposed. Again in *Oakbank Oil Ltd v Crum*[18] a shareholder enforced the calculation of a dividend which was provided for in the articles and in *Pender v Lushington*[19] the shareholder enforced a right to have his vote recorded at a general meeting.

In *Salmon v Quin & Axtens*[20] a shareholder in effect enforced his right to have the company act in accordance with the terms of the articles. A careful distinction has to be drawn between cases where a shareholder has the right to enforce the articles because they confer some personal right on him and cases where there is an infringement of the articles which amounts to no more than an internal irregularity which can be cured by an ordinary resolution. The action of the chairman of the general meeting in *MacDougall v Gardiner*, when he refused to hold a poll when requested to do so in the manner provided in the articles, was characterised by the court as an internal irregularity therefore the shareholder could not complain. It is difficult to accept a distinction between this case and, for instance, *Pender v Lushington* and *Salmon v Quin & Axtens*, but the article providing the procedure for demanding a poll did not confer a personal right on the individual shareholder since the demand for a poll could only be at the request of five or more shareholders. So it could be viewed as a procedure of the general meeting rather than an individual right.

---

14   [1988] Ch 114.
15   *Ibid* at 170F.
16   [1950] 2 All ER 1064.
17   (1889) 42 Ch D 636.
18   (1882) 8 App Cas 65.
19   (1877) 6 Ch D 70.
20   [1909] 1 Ch 311.

It was held in *Prudential Assurance Co Ltd v Newman Industries Ltd & Others (No 2)*[21] that a shareholder does not have a personal right to bring an action against persons who have caused harm to the company, alleging that their actions have caused him loss as a result of the diminution in the value of his shares. As was stated by the Court of Appeal:

'what [the shareholder] cannot do is to recover damages merely because the company in which he is interested has suffered damage. He cannot recover a sum equal to the diminution in the market value of the shares, or equal to the likely diminution in dividend, because such a 'loss' is merely a reflection of the loss suffered by the company. The shareholder does not suffer any personal loss. His only 'loss' is through the company, in the diminution in the value of the net assets of the company. ... The plaintiff's shares are merely a right of participation in the company on the terms of the articles of association. The shares themselves, his right of participation, are not directly affected by the wrongdoing. The plaintiff still holds all the shares as his own absolutely unencumbered property.'[22]

To hold that a shareholder could bring a personal claim for damage directly done to the company, would of course, totally circumvent the rule in *Foss v Harbottle*. But in *George Fischer (Great Britain) Ltd v Multi-Construction Ltd (Dexion Ltd a third party)*[23] the Court of Appeal seemed to allow just that. Here a holding company, F, operated through a number of wholly-owned subsidiaries. F entered into a contract with the defendant in which the defendant agreed to construct a warehouse and distribution centre for F. A sub-contractor, D, which was joined as a third party in these proceedings, installed defective machinery on the premises with the result that the subsidiary companies suffered extra operating costs of £262,000 and sales losses of £229,000. Since the subsidiaries were not parties to the contract between F and the defendant they could not bring an action in their own name. The Court of Appeal allowed F to bring an action against the defendant to recover the losses which it sustained indirectly as a result of the breach through the resulting diminution in the value of the shares in the subsidiaries. The court was able to distinguish *Prudential* by pointing to the fact that here the subsidiary companies had no right to bring an action so they were not the proper plaintiffs. F was suing not to pursue a wrong done to the subsidiaries but to recover a loss suffered as a result of the breach of contract and liability should be determined by the normal rules of remoteness of damage.

Cases which are an exception to the rule: the derivative action

In a number of cases where what has been alleged to have been done would, if proved, be a wrong done to the company and where a majority of the shareholders are apparently willing to ratify and adopt what has been done, the courts are still prepared to allow a minority shareholder to bring an action. These cases illustrate a genuine

---

21 [1982] Ch 204.

22 *Ibid* at 222; See also Harman J in *Re a Company (ex parte Holden)* [1991] BCLC 597.

23 [1995] 1 BCLC 260.

exception to the rule in *Foss v Harbottle* and are allowed in cases where what is alleged amounts to a 'fraud on the minority' by those in control.[24]

As Jenkins LJ said in *Edwards v Halliwell*:[25]

'It has been further pointed out that where what has been done amounts to what is generally called in these cases a fraud on the minority and the wrongdoers are themselves in control of the company, the rule is relaxed in favour of the aggrieved minority who are allowed to bring what is known as a minority shareholders' action on behalf of themselves and all others. The reason for this is that, if they were denied that right, their grievance could never reach the court because the wrongdoers themselves, being in control, would not allow the company to sue.'[26]

These actions are now known as derivative actions after their equivalent procedures in the USA.[27] This is because the right to bring the action derives from the company itself. It is in substance a form of representative action provided for by the Order 15, r 12 of the Rules of the Supreme Court where the minority shareholder is suing as a representative plaintiff for and on behalf of the company.

'Fraud on the minority'

Lord Davey in *Burland v Earle* described as a familiar example of the sort of fraud necessary in order to bring an action as an exception to the rule in *Foss v Harbottle* where:

'the majority are endeavouring directly or indirectly to appropriate to themselves money, property or advantages which belong to the company.'[28]

A clear and striking example of this occurred in *Cook v Deeks*,[29] where a shareholder was allowed to bring an action against directors who were in breach of their duties to the company by diverting to themselves a contractual opportunity which in equity belonged to the company. They were not allowed to use their majority voting power in general meeting to prevent an action being brought against them. Contrast this case with *Regal (Hastings) Ltd v Gulliver*.[30] There Lord Russell was of the opinion that the breach of duty by the directors could have been ratified by the shareholders in general meeting. Whether it was because of the difference in the type of breach of duty (eg an 'honest' breach where the directors were acting *bona fide* rather than *mala fide* as in *Cook v Deeks*) or whether it was because the directors in *Cook v Deeks* had diverted 'property' or advantages which belonged to the company whereas in *Regal* the directors made an incidental profit, was not made clear.

---

24 See generally the general principles stated by Peter Gibson LJ in *Barrett v Duckett* (1995) BCC 362 at 367.

25 [1950] 2 All ER 1064.

26 *Ibid* at 1067.

27 The term was first adopted in England in *Wallersteiner v Moir (No 2)* [1975] QB 373.

28 [1902] AC 83 at 93.

29 [1916] 1 AC 554.

30 [1967] 2 AC 134n at 150.

Another well-known example is *Menier v Hooper's Telegraph Works*[31] where H Co was the majority shareholder in E Co which was formed to lay a telegraph cable between Europe and South America, and there was an agreement which provided that H Co would make and lay submarine cables for E Co. The chairman of E Co appropriated to himself a concession belonging to the company and subsequently H Co did not support an action by E Co to recover the concession but instead and in agreement with the chairman, used its voting power in general meeting to pass a resolution to wind up E Co. This released itself from the obligation to supply cable to E Co and so it could supply another company.

The Court of Appeal allowed the action to proceed with James LJ stating that:

'[a]ssuming the case to be as alleged by the bill, then the majority have put something into their pockets at the expense of the minority. If so, it appears to me that the minority have a right to have their share of the benefits ascertained for them in the best way in which the court can do it.'[32]

In *Alexander v Automatic Telephone Co*[33] the scope of this exception was demonstrated to be wider than merely fraud *per se* but included cases where the directors acted in a belief that they were doing nothing wrong. Here all charges of fraud against the directors which were originally contained in the pleadings were dropped. The company had issued partly paid shares and the directors made calls on all the shares except those held by themselves and those held by persons whom they were associated with. In those circumstances Lindley LJ in the Court of Appeal looked for a beach of duty by the directors and found it by the directors obtaining money from the other shareholders and paying nothing themselves.

'The breach of duty to the company consists in depriving it of the use of the money which the directors ought to have paid up sooner than they did. I cannot regard the case as one of mere internal management which, according to *Foss v Harbottle* and numerous other cases, the Court leaves the shareholders to settle among themselves.'[34]

This case was followed by Templeman J in *Daniels v Daniels*[35] where he drew a distinction between cases where directors are in breach of their duties but do not themselves benefit from that breach, and cases where directors are in breach of their duties and even though no fraud is alleged or proven they do benefit. In the former case the rule in *Foss v Harbottle* would preclude any action by a minority shareholder against a director, whereas in the latter the court would not allow the rule to defeat a claim. The distinction can be illustrated by the facts of *Pavlides v Jensen*[36] and those of *Daniels v Daniels* itself. In *Pavlides* the directors, as a result of alleged gross negligence, sold a mine at an undervalue. They did not in any way benefit from the sale.

---

31   (1874) LR 9 Ch App 350.

32   *Ibid* at 353.

33   [1900] 2 Ch 56.

34   *Per* Lindley LJ at 69.

35   [1978] Ch 406.

36   [1956] Ch 565.

Danckwerts J held that this case could not fall within the exceptions to the rule in *Foss v Harbottle* and it was open to the majority of shareholders in general meeting to decide that no proceedings should be taken against the directors.

In *Daniels v Daniels* on the other hand, the two directors, who were also the majority shareholders, caused the company to sell land belonging to it at an undervalue to one of the directors who then resold the land making a substantial profit. Although there was no fraud alleged on the part of the directors, Templeman J, in refusing to strike out the claim, held that:

> '[i]f minority shareholders can sue if there is fraud, I see no reason why they cannot sue where the action of the majority and the directors, through without fraud, confers some benefit on those directors and majority shareholders themselves. It would seem to me quite monstrous – particularly as fraud is so hard to plead and difficult to prove – if the confines of the exception to *Foss v Harbottle* were drawn so narrowly that directors could make a profit out of their negligence. ... The principle which may be gleaned from [authority] is that a minority shareholder who has no other remedy may sue where directors use their powers, intentionally or unintentionally, fraudulently or negligently, in a manner which benefits themselves at the expense of the company.'[37]

Both Vinelott J in *Prudential Assurance Co Ltd v Newman Industries Ltd (No 2)*[38] and Megarry J in *Estmanco (Kilner House) Ltd v Greater London Council*[39] were prepared to embrace this more liberal view of the acts as conduct which could come within the fraud on the minority exception. Megarry J held that conduct by the sole shareholder with voting rights at general meetings could amount to fraud on the minority where it was using its voting power not to promote the best interests of the company but in order to bring advantage to itself and disadvantage to the minority. The disadvantage to the minority consisted in this case of a radical alteration of the basis on which the company was formed and on which shares had been issued to the non-voting minority members in order that the defendant council could implement its new policy objectives.

There has been a suggestion that there is a more general exception to *Foss v Harbottle* on the 'justice of the case'. This was limited even in the judgment of Wigram V-C in *Foss v Harbottle* itself and has been mentioned in a number of cases subsequently. But the Court of Appeal in *Prudential* were firmly against any such liberalisation of the rule commenting that it was 'not a practical test'.

Control

It is essential for a minority shareholder to be able to invoke the exception to the rule in *Foss v Harbottle* to show that the wrongdoers are in control. This element of control is part of the definition of fraud on the minority and is the reason why the company will not be allowed to bring an action to pursue the wrong done to it. There is some uncertainty as to the meaning of control for these purposes. There is no problem where

---

37 [1978] Ch 408 at 414.

38 [1981] Ch 257.

39 [1982] 1 WLR 2.

the wrongdoers have control of the general meeting by virtue of holding a majority of shares. The problem is that the larger the company becomes and the more dispersed the shareholding the more unlikely it will be that the wrongdoing directors will be able to control anything approaching a majority of votes in general meeting. Yet at a day-to-day level they will enjoy a *de facto* control, for instance being able to frame the circulars which are sent to shareholders before the general meetings inviting the return of proxy votes.[40]

At first instance in *Prudential Assurance Co Ltd v Newman Industries Ltd (No 2)*[41] it was argued by the plaintiff that an action could be brought to remedy a wrong done to the company under the fraud exception even where the defendant wrongdoers did not have voting control in general meeting. Vinelott J, after a lengthy examination of the authorities on the meaning of control, favoured the view that such an action would be brought where the persons against whom the action is sought to be brought are able 'by any means of manipulation of their position in the company' to ensure that the action is not brought by the company, and that the means of manipulation should not be too narrowly defined. He was of the view that there were a great many circumstances which would lead to a find of control for these purposes, for instance the court can look behind the register to find out who the beneficial owners of the shares are where the registered members are holding as nominees. Further there was no reason why:

'the court should not have regard to any other circumstances which show that the majority cannot be relied upon to determine in a disinterested way whether it is truly in the interests of the company that proceedings should be brought. For instance, some shareholders able to exercise decisive votes may have been offered an inducement to vote in favour of the wrongdoers. ... Moreover, today it would be uncommon for any large number of shareholders to attend and vote in person at a general meeting of a large public company, and directors alleged to be liable to the company might be able to determine the outcome of a resolution in general meeting in their own favour by the use of proxy votes. Similarly, most modern articles confide to the directors, the management of the business of the company (see, eg, article [70] of Table A) and it is possible that an article in these terms vests in the directors a discretion whether proceedings should be commenced by the company which cannot be overridden by resolution in general meeting.'[42]

In this last sentence Vinelott J is reflecting the change in company law and practice since the time of *Foss v Harbottle* where, in the judgment in that case, Wigram V-C stated that the general meeting itself had power to originate proceedings if the directors had not. So there was a logical justification at that time for seeing control purely in terms of votes exercised in general meeting.

Overall Vinelott J is expressing a more liberal view of control, which would allow actions to be brought even though it could not be shown that the wrongdoers

---

40 See p 101.
41 [1981] Ch 257.
42 *Ibid* at 324.

beneficially held a majority of the votes in general meeting. On appeal the Court of Appeal's decision, for reasons stated below, is only *obiter* on the question of control, and even then in answer to the question what is meant by control for these purposes it states only that it:

> 'embraces a broad spectrum extending from an overall absolute majority of votes at one end, to a majority of votes at the other end, made up of those likely to be cast by the delinquent himself plus those voting with him as a result of influence or apathy'[43]

without reaching a conclusion whether the latter is sufficient. But it is clear from the tenor of the judgment that the Court of Appeal was of the opinion that control should remain only defined in terms of a majority of votes at general meeting.

Procedural matters

The rule in *Foss v Harbottle* is a rule of procedure, not a rule of substance, which means that a court is not saying to a minority shareholder in any particular case that where an action is disallowed that there has been no wrong, but either that the shareholder is not the proper plaintiff to pursue the wrong and/or it is a wrong which the company in general meeting might choose not to pursue anyway. It is a rule which operates to preserve the rights of the majority.

The writ which the shareholder issues will name himself as plaintiff, and the wrongdoers and the company as defendants, even though the company will receive the benefit of any award. The shareholder cannot name the company as plaintiff because the wrongdoers can apply to the court to have the proceedings struck out as being improperly instituted.[44] The company is joined as a party so that it can be represented before the court and take the benefit of or be bound by any order which the court may make.[45]

In *Prudential Assurance Co Ltd v Newman Industries Ltd (No 2)*[46] it was alleged by the plaintiff shareholder that B and L, two of the directors of Newman, had conspired to cause loss to Newman by causing Newman to buy assets from another company, in which B and L had an interest, at an overvalue. This contract had not been properly disclosed and a misleading circular had been sent to shareholders which recommended a vote in favour of the agreement. A vote approving the agreement was required by Stock Exchange regulations. In these circumstances Vinelott J dismissed a summons issued by the defendants to determine as a preliminary issue whether the plaintiffs were entitled to bring an action as an exception to the rule in *Foss v Harbottle* and instead proceeded to hear the action in full (which lasted 72 days), in order to decide whether the plaintiff could bring the action, which he concluded in the affirmative.

---

43 [1982] Ch 204 at 219.

44 *Danish Mercantile Co Ltd v Beaumont* [1951] Ch 680.

45 *Prudential Assurance Co Ltd v Newman Industries Ltd (No 2)* [1982] Ch 204; *Atwool v Merryweather* (1867) LR 5 Eq 464n.

46 *Supra.*

He also held that damage had been sustained by the company and ordered an inquiry into quantum. The defendants appealed, but by the time of the appeal Newman itself had stated that it was prepared to adopt the benefit of any order made in its favour so that it became in essence a corporate action rather than a minority shareholders' action and therefore any discussion on the rule in *Foss v Harbottle* became *obiter*.

What is important in the Court of Appeal's judgment is the enthusiasm and support expressed for the rule. In criticising the handling of the case it was stated that:

> 'we have no doubt whatever that Vinelott J erred in dismissing the summons. ... He ought to have determined as a preliminary issue whether the plaintiffs were entitled to sue on behalf of Newman by bringing a derivative action. It cannot have been right to have subjected the company to a 30-day action (as it was then estimated to be) in order to enable him to decide whether the plaintiffs were entitled in law to subject the company to a 30-day action. Such an approach defeats the whole purpose of the rule in *Foss v Harbottle* and sanctions the very mischief that the rule is designed to prevent. By the time a derivative action is concluded, the rule in *Foss v Harbottle* can have little, if any, role to play. Either the wrong is proved, thereby establishing conclusively the rights of the company; or the wrong is not proved, so *cadit quaestio*.'[47]

The Court of Appeal therefore suggested that a plaintiff bringing a derivative action be required before proceeding with his action to establish a *prima facie* case:

(i)   that the company is entitled to the relief claimed; and

(ii) that the action falls within the proper boundaries of the exception to the rule in *Foss v Harbottle*

and in order to determine the latter point it may be right for the judge to grant a sufficient adjournment to enable a general meeting to be convened so that the judge can form a view in the light of the conduct of, and proceedings at, that meeting.

In *Smith v Croft (No 2)*[48] a further obstacle was placed in the path of a minority shareholder who sought to bring a derivative action. Knox J held that it would be appropriate at a preliminary meeting of the shareholders to take into account the views of a majority of the independent shareholders, ie, those shareholders not aligned with either the wrongdoing majority or the plaintiff, on the desirability of bringing a derivative action. If they were against such proceedings then the action could be struck out.

In *Wallersteiner v Moir (No 2)*[49] it was first recognised that a plaintiff who properly pursued a derivative action could be indemnified for his costs and expenses in bringing the action by the company. As Lord Denning MR explained:

> '[s]eeing that, if the action succeeds, the whole benefit will go to the company, it is only just that the minority shareholder should be indemnified against the costs he incurs on

---

47   *Ibid* at 221.

48   [1988] Ch 114.

49   [1975] QB 373.

its behalf. If the action succeeds, the wrongdoing director will be ordered to pay the costs: but if they are not recovered from him, they should be paid by the company. ... But what if the action fails? Assuming that the minority shareholder had reasonable grounds for bringing the action – that it was a reasonable and prudent course to take in the interests of the company – he shall not himself be liable to pay the costs of the other side, but the company itself should be liable, because he was acting for it and not for himself. In addition, he should himself be indemnified by the company in respect of his own costs even if the action fails.'[50]

To this, Buckley LJ added the following test:

'where a shareholder has in good faith and on reasonable grounds sued as plaintiff in a minority shareholder's action, the benefit of which, if successful, will accrue to the company and only indirectly to the plaintiff as a member of the company, and which it would have been reasonable for an independent board of directors to bring in the company's name, it would, I think, clearly be a proper exercise of judicial discretion to order the company to pay the plaintiff's costs.'[51]

The procedure to be followed in most cases would be that there is an application by summons prior to the action itself for a *Wallersteiner* order. In *Smith v Croft*[52] a master had granted an order but the company subsequently applied to the court to have it set aside. Walton J allowed the company's application and quashed the indemnity order on the grounds that the action had little chance of success. The plaintiff claimed that the directors had paid themselves excessive amounts of remuneration, but a report had been commissioned by the board from a reputable firm of accountants which investigated the company's affairs and gave the directors a 'clean bill of health'. Although the salaries were high, Walton J explained that:

'the company operated in the world of entertainment ... and the salaries which persons operating successfully in this world enjoy are so manifestly out of line with that which ordinary mortal, condemned to the mere pittance which falls to those who reach the top of their profession in almost any other field, that even fashionable silks feel a twinge of envy from time to time.'[53]

Given this evidence an independent director would not feel that proceedings by the company should be launched, especially since any action would result in the director working time being lost by attending court thus increasing the loss to the company. Walton J also took the point which Knox J was to take later in dismissing the action itself, that a majority of the independent minority did not approve of the proceedings.

The derivative action is not one which a shareholder can bring as of right. It is an equitable procedure allowed by the court so as to do justice. It will not therefore be allowed to be brought where the plaintiff does not come to the court with 'clean hands' and especially if he has participated in the wrong himself. In *Towers v African Tug*

---

50   *Ibid* at 391.
51   *Ibid* at 403.
52   [1986] 1 WLR 580.
53   *Ibid* at 592.
54   [1904] 1 Ch 558.

Co[54] the directors had paid illegal dividends out of capital. Subsequently, two shareholders commenced an action on behalf of themselves and all other shareholders of the company against the company and the directors, to compel the directors to repay to the company the amount of the illegal dividend. The Court of Appeal held that the plaintiffs were not entitled to bring the action since they had participated in the wrong by receiving and keeping the dividends.[55]

The court will not allow a derivative action to be brought if it is of the opinion that there is an alternative remedy available which is more appropriate in the circumstances. Therefore, for example, if other shareholders wished to have the company wound up it would be better to allow that to proceed and to have an independent liquidator to decide whether or not to use the company's available resources to pursue the alleged wrongdoers especially if there was evidence that the plaintiff who wished to bring a derivative action was doing so for personal reasons rather than *bona fide* for the benefit of the company.[56]

Where a company has gone into liquidation a shareholder is prevented from bringing a derivative action since it is then the responsibility of the liquidator to pursue wrongs done to the company.[57]

STATUTORY REMEDIES

Companies Act 1985, s 459

As long ago as 1945, in the Cohen Committee Report, it was proposed that there ought to be a statutory remedy for minority shareholders who were the victims of 'oppression' because of the way the company was being run.[58] This proposal resulted in s 210 of the Companies Act 1948. The remedy was known in the side-note to the section as the alternative remedy, and was supposed to provide an alternative to winding up the company under the 'just and equitable' ground. In fact the remedy proved to have considerable practical difficulties and inherent defects and only two cases appear to have been successfully brought under it. The problems associated with the section were examined by the Jenkins Committee which reported in 1962 and which recommended that the section should be amended, and in particular it should be made clear that it applied to cases where the affairs of the company were being conducted in a manner unfairly prejudicial to the interest of some part of the members.[59] These recommendations were finally enacted in s 75 of the Companies Act 1980 which is now, with some minor modifications, s 459 of the 1985 Act.

Subsection (1) reads as follows:

---

55   See also *Nurcombe v Nurcombe* [1985] 1 WLR 370.

56   *Barrett v Duckett* (1995) BCC 362.

57   *Fargro Ltd v Godfroy* [1986] 1 WLR 1134.

58   *Re H R Harmer Ltd* [1959] 1 WLR 62; *Scottish Co-operative Wholesale Society Ltd v Meyer* [1959] AC 324.

59   Cmnd 1749, para 212.

'(1) A member of a company may apply to the court by petition for an order under this Part on the ground that the company's affairs are being or have been conducted in a manner which is unfairly prejudicial to the interests of its members generally or of some part of its members (including at least himself) or that any actual or proposed act or omission of the company (including an act or omission on its behalf) is or would be so prejudicial.'

The meaning of unfair prejudice

Shortly after the enactment of s 459 the courts gave an indication that they would be using an objective test to determine whether conduct complained of was unfairly prejudicial or not. In *Re Bovey Hotel Ventures Ltd*,[60] which was cited by Nourse J in *Re R A Noble & Sons (Clothing) Ltd*,[61] Slade J held that:

'[t]he test of unfairness must, I think, be an objective, not a subjective, one. In other words it is not necessary for the petitioner to show that the persons who have had *de facto* control of the company have acted as they did in the conscious knowledge that this was unfair to the petitioner or that they were acting in bad faith; the test, I think, is whether a reasonable bystander observing the consequences of their conduct would regard it as having unfairly prejudiced the petitioner's interests.'[62]

It is clear that in contrast with the 'oppression' remedy under s 210, where a course of conduct was necessary, an isolated act or proposed act is sufficient for a successful petition under s 459.

The act or conduct complained of must not only be prejudicial but unfairly prejudicial.[63] So that, for example, if the petitioner is a shareholder in a small private company and is relying on the payment of dividends as a return on his investment, the non-payment of dividends in one year may well be prejudicial if the other shareholders are receiving a salary under contracts of employment with the company, but it might not be unfairly prejudicial if it is shown that the company badly needs to retain profit for re-investment in the company's business.

As regards examples of what acts or omissions might amount to unfairly prejudicial conduct, the swelling body of case law now provides a wealth of authority. However, it must be borne in mind that many of the reported cases have involved applications by the respondents to have the petition struck out as disclosing no cause of action, so the judge hearing the case was only deciding the question of whether the facts alleged in the petition, if all were true, were incapable of amounting to unfair prejudice. Only if the judge is satisfied that they could not amount to unfair prejudice does he exercise the power to strike out. Therefore a somewhat distorted picture may emerge since the judges are not saying that the facts as alleged do constitute unfair prejudice but merely that they could, and the hearing of the petition which follows determines that issue.

Slade J, in the case cited above, had stated:

---

60   1981, unreported.
61   [1983] BCLC 273.
62   *Ibid* at 290.
63   *Ibid* at 292.

'[w]ithout prejudice to the generality of the wording of the section, which may cover many other situations, a member of a company will be able to bring himself within the section if he can show that the value of his shareholding in the company has been seriously diminished or at least seriously jeopardised by reason of a course of conduct on the part of those persons who have had *de facto* control of the company, which has been unfair to the member concerned.'

This would allow a member to bring a petition under s 459 in those cases where the Court of Appeal in *Prudential* had precluded a plaintiff from bring an action at common law.

Where a company consistently pays low dividends to shareholders, and there is no explanation for this because the company does have distributable profits, then this may well be unfairly prejudicial conduct to a minority. In *Re Sam Weller Ltd*[64] the company had not increased its dividends for 37 years despite making large profits. The petitioners were substantial minority shareholders who complained that while they received low dividends on their shares their uncle, Sam Weller and his sons who ran the company, paid themselves salaries and increased the capital value of their shareholdings. In these circumstances Hoffmann J was of the opinion that the petition should not be struck not as disclosing no cause of action. This means that there may be good grounds for a s 459 petition even where the persons in control of the company have suffered the same prejudice (or even greater as a result of their holding a large proportion of the shares) as the complaining minority.

Mismanagement is a difficult issue for shareholder remedies because for amongst other reasons the courts generally do not wish to be drawn into deciding whether a particular commercial decision was proper or improper with the benefit of hindsight. In *Re Five Minute Car Wash Service Ltd*[65] the petitioner had alleged that mismanagement, inefficiency and carelessness on the part of a managing director could amount to 'oppression' under the old s 210. This was rejected by Buckley J who stated that even if all the matters alleged were true this could not amount to 'oppression'.

This question of whether mismanagement could amount to unfair prejudice has been raised a number of times under s 459 and has not been dismissed out of hand. As Warner J stated in *Re Elgindata*:[66]

'I do not doubt that in an appropriate case it is open to the court to find that serious mismanagement of a company's business constitutes conduct that is unfairly prejudicial to the interests of minority shareholders. But I share Peter Gibson J's view [expressed in *Re Sam Weller Ltd*] that the court will normally be very reluctant to accept that managerial decisions can amount to unfairly prejudicial conduct.'[67]

There appears to be two reasons for this view. First is the reluctance of the courts to become arbitrators in disputes between the petitioner and respondent over commercial

---

64   [1990] Ch 682.
65   [1966] 1 WLR 745.
66   [1991] BCLC 959.
67   *Ibid* at 993.

decisions referred to above. Second, a shareholder acquires shares in a company knowing that their value will depend in some measure on the competence of the management. Therefore the shareholder takes the risk that the management of the company may turn out to be poor and not be capable of maximising profit for the company by the use of its assets.

'Short of a breach by a director of his duty of skill and care ... there is *prima facie* no unfairness to a shareholder in the quality of the management turning out to be poor.'[68]

Warner J then proceeded to give an example of where mismanagement could give rise to a valid s 459 petition, namely:

'where the majority shareholders, for reasons of their own, persisted in retaining in charge of the management of the company's business a member of their family who was demonstrably incompetent.'[69]

The issue of mismanagement also arose in *Re Macro (Ipswich) Ltd*,[70] where after citing the views of Warner J, Arden J drew a distinction between questions of commercial judgment on the one hand and mismanagement of the company's property on the other. Here the company was a property company and the judge suggested that, in relation to questions of which type of property to invest in, mistakes by the directors would not amount to unfair prejudice. But here the alleged and proven mismanagement went beyond this. Those running the company's affairs had failed to supervise properly the company's property and as a result inspections of property had not taken place, money had been wasted on repairs, properties had not been let on protected shorthold tenancies, commissions had been taken from builders and 'key money' had been taken from tenants by those running the company or their own employees which had not been accounted for. There was also evidence that because the person who was in control of the company also controlled the property managers employed by the company, there was no realistic possibility of the appointment of alternative property managers even after these acts of mismanagement. In the circumstances Arden J was prepared to hold that there was unfair prejudice to the petitioners' interests.

The extent to which breaches of directors' duties can form the basis of a petition under s 459 has not been precisely determined. If breaches of duties are to become generally the subject of complaints under s 459 the rule in *Foss v Harbottle* becomes effectively sidestepped. Hoffmann LJ, who generally has given the section a broad application, stated in *Re Saul D Harrison & Sons plc*[71] that 'enabling the court in an appropriate case to outflank the rule in *Foss v Harbottle* was one of the purposes of the section'.[72] It must be remembered, though, that the petitioner must always show some

---

68   *Ibid* at 994.
69   *Ibid*.
70   [1994] 2 BCLC 354.
71   [1995] 1 BCLC 14.
72   *Ibid* at 18.

prejudice to at least his interests, or the interests of the members generally, or some part of the members, as a result of the breach of the director's duty. The larger the company, the more difficult it would seem to be able to do this. But in a smaller company many breaches of directors' duties will have a significant effect on the members' interests.

In *Re Saul D Harrison & Sons plc* Hoffmann LJ discussed the possibility of finding unfairly prejudicial conduct where the directors who, on being appointed under the articles, were entrusted with fiduciary powers which should be exercised for the benefit of the company, but who exercised them for some ulterior purpose and who therefore stepped outside the terms of the bargain made between the shareholders and the company. Not all conduct which was not in accordance with the articles would be unfairly prejudicial; trivial or technical infringements of the articles would not give rise to petitions under s 459. But in citing Lord Cooper's view of 'oppression' under the old s 210 expressed in *Elder v Elder and Waston*,[73] unfairly prejudicial conduct could exist where there was a:

> 'visible departure from the standards of fair dealing and a violation of the conditions of fair play on which every shareholder who entrusts his money to a company is entitled to rely.'

Where the directors use their powers to allot shares for ulterior, unlawful or improper purposes, or at a time when they know that the minority shareholder is not in a position to be able to take up a rights issue, this has been held to be unfairly prejudicial conduct.[74] Similarly, if the directors carry on in business in order to provide themselves with salaries after a time when no rational board could honestly have thought that carrying on was in the interests of the company.[75]

The issue of the payment of excessive salaries to the directors has been discussed in the cases on a number of occasions.[76] In *Re Cumana*[77] it was held that the payment of £356,000 to a person who was in control of the company was excessive and was therefore unfairly prejudicial to the other, minority shareholder. But it would seem in principle that the payments to directors would have to be excessive and unjustified and the value of the minority's shareholding would have to be affected.

If a shareholder brings a s 459 petition complaining about a wrong which is done both to himself and the company, can he claim an indemnity from the company for his costs which he may have received if he had brought a derivative action?

In *Re a Company (No 005136 of 1986)*[78] the company, which had an issued capital of 30 shares of £1 each, proposed to offer its members the right to subscribe for a total of 2,000 new shares, but they were to be allotted to existing members under criteria

---

73 1952 SC 49

74 [1985] BCLC 80.

75 *Re Saul D Harrison & Sons plc, supra.* But see the case cited above.

76 For example, *Re A Company, ex parte Burr* [1992] BCLC 724.

77 [1986] BCLC 430.

78 [1987] BCLC 82.

that would have produced an uneven distribution. The petitioner claimed that this would be a departure from the understanding on which the members came into the company and the company did not need the extra capital. The petitioner's allegation was, therefore, that the real motive was to alter the balance of voting power within the company. Since this was a misuse of the directors' powers and a breach of their duty to the company, the petitioner applied to the court for a *Wallersteiner* order, ie, that the petitioner should be indemnified in respect of all costs and expenses incurred by the petitioner in bringing the action to pursue the wrong done to the company.

Although Hoffmann J was 'provisionally inclined' to accept that a *Wallersteiner* order could be obtained by a shareholder who uses the procedure of a petition under s 459 rather than a derivative action by writ, here the complaint, whatever form it took, was not a derivative action.

The decision of the Privy Council in *Howard Smith Ltd v Ampol Petroleum Ltd*[79] is frequently cited to show that a shareholder has a personal right to bring an action where the breach of duty by a director is an improper allotment of shares.

> 'Although the alleged breach of fiduciary duty by the board is in theory a breach of its duty to the company, the wrong to the company is not the substance of the complaint ... the true basis of the action is an alleged infringement of the petitioner's individual rights as a shareholder. The allotment is alleged to be an improper and unlawful exercise of the powers granted to the board by the articles of association, which constitute a contract between the company and its members. These are fiduciary powers, not to be exercised for an improper purpose. ... An abuse of these powers is an infringement of a member's contractual rights under the articles.'[80]

So here both the company and the shareholder had the right to bring an action, but on the facts the shareholder was petitioning to defend his own interests and was not entitled to have the company indemnify him. But if there had been a misappropriation of the company's assets by the directors, it is possible that a minority shareholder could petition under s 459 and obtain an indemnity order.

In another *Re a Company*[81] case, Hoffmann J was unwilling to strike out a petition where some of the complaints were that a director had disposed of the company's assets without authority, where the ground on which the striking out was sought was that that was a matter which should be complained of separately in a derivative action. This would bring about an unnecessary duplication of proceedings.

This appears to be the correct approach, particularly since s 461(2)(c) specifically provides that the courts can authorise civil proceedings to be brought in the name of and on behalf of the company, so it must have been envisaged by the legislature that wrongs done to the company would be brought before the court under s 459.

A shareholder could also petition under s 459 where the directors have not given

---

79   [1974] AC 821.

80   [1987] BCLC 82 at 84.

81   [1986] BCLC 68.

full and impartial advice concerning the merits of two or more rival takeover bids for the company. The directors are not under a duty to advise shareholders to accept the highest offer but they must provide sufficient information and advice to enable shareholders to reach an informed decision about which was the better offer.[82]

Conduct of the petitioner

Where a petition is brought under s 459 the past conduct of the petitioner can be relevant to the success of the case or the order which the court is prepared to make. In *Re London School of Electronics Ltd*[83] the petitioner was a director and 25% shareholder in a company which was formed with the object of running a college which taught electronics courses. The other 75% of the shares were held by the respondent company of which A and G were the directors and major shareholders. The relationship between the petitioner and A and G broke down, and A and G sought to remove the petitioner from the board. A and G also diverted students registered with the company to the respondent company which ran its own college.

In these circumstances Nourse J held that the conduct of the respondent was unfairly prejudicial and was prepared to grant relief. There was no justification for the respondent transferring students to itself. This was despite the fact that, on the evidence, the petitioner himself had been difficult, unreliable and lazy in performing his teaching and other duties. He had also left the company's college and moved to another one, taking some of the company's students with him.

Nourse J held that there was no independent or overriding requirement that it should be just and equitable to grant relief under s 459 or that the petitioner should come to the court with 'clean hands'. But the conduct of the petitioner may be material in a number of ways. For instance, first the petitioner's conduct may render the conduct by the respondent, even if it is prejudicial, not unfair. For example, in *Re R A Noble & Sons (Clothing) Ltd*[84] a company had been formed by N and B to take over a business previously carried on by N. N and B each took 50% of the issued shares and whereas it was agreed that N should be responsible for carrying on the company's business, B was to provide money and to renovate the company's shop premises through another of his companies. Subsequently the relationship between N and B broke down and B caused a petition to be brought seeking relief under what is now s 459, or in the alternative an order to wind up of the company on the grounds that it was just and equitable to do so. The grounds on which B requested the relief were that he had not been informed of, or adequately consulted on, major transactions affecting the company and that N had improperly taken over control of the company excluding B from involvement in its affairs. Nourse J refused relief under s 459 since he held that although the matters complained of could amount to conduct which was unfair and prejudicial, having regard to the circumstances of this case, including a history of disinterest on the part of B, the conduct of N, whilst prejudicial to B, could not be said

---

82 *Re a Company* [1986] BCLC 382.

83 [1986] Ch 211.

84 [1983] BCLC 273.

to be 'unfair'. B had, therefore, partly brought the matter on himself. The judge was prepared, however, to order that the company be wound up.

Second, even if the respondent's conduct is both prejudicial and unfair, the petitioner's conduct may nevertheless affect the relief which the court thinks fit to grant. Since the court is given a discretion in what relief to grant, it might order that instead of the respondent buying the petitioner's shares as requested in the petition it would be more appropriate that the petitioner purchase the respondent's shares.

The member's interests

As originally drafted, the petitioner was required to show that the affairs of the company were conducted in a manner which was unfairly prejudicial to the '*interests of some part of the members (including at least himself)*'. On a literal construction this meant that conduct by those controlling the company which prejudiced all members could not be complained of in a s 459 petition. So, for instance, breaches of directors' statutory or common law duties which resulted in an indirect loss to members of the company as a result of the devaluation of their share values could be argued to be excluded altogether from the scope of the section.

This was seen as a major anomaly and so the section was amended by the Companies Act 1989 so that it now covers conduct in the affairs of the company which is unfairly prejudicial 'to the interests of its members generally or of some part of its members (including at least [the petitioner])'.

Under the old s 210 a rule known as the '*qua* member' requirement was developed. As explained by Buckley J in *Re Five Minute Car Wash Service Ltd*,[85] this was to the effect that:

> 'the matters complained of must affect the person or persons alleged to have been oppressed in his or their character as a member or members of the company. Harsh or unfair treatment of the petitioner in some other capacity, as, for instance, a director or a creditor of the company, or as a person doing business or having dealings with the company, or in relation to his personal affairs apart from the company, cannot entitle him to any relief ...'[86]

So, for example, in *Re Westbourne Galleries Ltd*,[87] a petition under s 210 was struck out where a director had been removed from office under what is now s 303 of the 1985 Act, since the removal and exclusion from management did not affect him as a member or '*qua* member'.

It has been held that in principle, a petitioner under s 459 must still show that the conduct has been unfairly prejudicial to his interests as a member and not in some other capacity, but important developments have been made in the definition of what those member's interests actually are. In *Re a Company*[88] Hoffmann J stated that the interests

---

85   [1966] 1 WLR 745.

86   *Ibid* at 751.

87   [1970] 1 WLR 1378.

88   [1986] BCLC 376.

of a member were not necessarily limited only to his strict legal rights under the constitution of the company. The court can construe interests more widely than rights and because s 459 referred to the word 'unfairly' and the court could therefore take into account the wider equitable considerations. Hoffmann J used the analogy of the courts' power to wind the company up on the grounds that it is 'just and equitable' to do so, and in particular the House of Lords' decision on this jurisdiction in *Ebrahami v Westbourne Galleries Ltd*.[89] In granting the order for winding up where the petitioner had been excluded from the management of the company Lord Wilberforce stated that:

> '... a limited company is more than a mere legal entity, with a personality in law of its own: ... there is room in company law for recognition of the fact that behind it, or amongst it, there are individuals, with rights, expectations and obligations *inter se* which are not necessarily submerged in the company structure.'[90]

So there is in reality (but not in law) a difference between the positions of the director of a large public company who happens to hold a small number of shares in the company, and the director of a small private company in which two or three members have invested their capital taking the issued shares between them on the understanding that each will be a director of the company, taking a part in its management.

In the former case the distinction between the director's interest as a managing director employed under a service contract and his interests as a member is easy to discern. But the same distinction in respect of a person holding a directorship in the latter case is less obvious. Therefore the removal of a director from the board and exclusion from management in the latter case can amount to unfair prejudice to that person's interests as a member since he may have had a legitimate expectation as part of his membership interests to remain a director of the company involved in its management. Hoffmann J, though, was prepared to limit the type of case which may give rise to these considerations in the same way that Lord Wilberforce wished to limit their scope in the context of 'just and equitable' winding up. Essentially this is where the company is what is known as a 'quasi-partnership', normally found in cases where there is:

> 'a personal relationship between shareholders involving mutual confidence, an agreement that some or all should participate in the management and restrictions on the transfer of shares which would prevent a member from realising his investment.'[91]

Absent these features whether the company is large or small, the member's rights under the articles of association and the Companies Acts can be treated as an exhaustive statement of his interests as a member.

So, for example, in *Re Blue Arrow plc*[92] where the petitioner, who had built up the business of the company, had been appointed under the articles as the 'president' of the

---

89   [1973] AC 360.

90   *Ibid* at 379.

91   [1986] BCLC 376 at 379.

92   [1987] BCLC 585; see also *Re Tottenham Hotspur plc* [1994] 1 BCLC 655.

company, it was not unfairly prejudicial to her interests as a member of the company for the articles to be altered allowing her to be removed by a majority vote of the board. The company had been introduced to the Unlisted Securities Market and Vinelott J held that the outside investors were entitled to assume that the whole of the constitution of the company was contained in the articles and the Companies Acts and there was no basis for finding that the petitioner had any legitimate expectation that the articles would not be altered allowing for a different method of terminating her presidency.

In *Re Posgate & Denby (Agencies) Ltd*[93] a non-voting shareholder petitioned to his interests as member for the directors to exercise their powers to sell the company's assets to themselves in a management buy-out. But the articles regarding conflicts of interest had been complied with, so had s 320 of the 1985 Act, and in those circumstances, although Hoffmann J was prepared to re-iterate that s 459 allows the court to take into account not just the members' rights under the company's constitution', but also could give 'full effect to the terms and understandings on which the members of the company became associated',[94] it could not rewrite them. Here there was no evidence that the petitioner was entitled to expect that the directors would not exercise their powers to sell the company's assets without first seeking the approval of the non-voting shareholders contrary to the terms of the articles vesting powers of management in the board.

Orders which the court can make

Where a petitioner successfully establishes that there has been unfairly prejudicial conduct, the court is given, by s 461(1), a wide discretion as to the order it can make in granting relief. It is not restricted to granting the relief requested by the petitioner. Section 461(2) then proceeds, without prejudice to the width of the court's discretion under s 461(1), to list some of the orders it may wish to make, that is to say it may:

(a) regulate the conduct of the company's affairs in the future;

(b) require the company to refrain from doing or continuing an act complained of by the petitioner or to do an act which the petitioner has complained it has omitted to do;

(c) authorise civil proceedings to be brought in the name and on behalf of the company by such persons as the court thinks fit;

(d) provide for the purchase of the shares of any members of the company by other members or by the company itself.

Sections 461(3) and (4) also envisage the court ordering in an appropriate case that the company should not make any alteration to the memorandum or articles without leave of the court or ordering that the company's memorandum or articles be altered. In the latter case the alteration then has the same effect as if it had been duly made by complying with the provisions of the Act.

---

93   [1987] BCLC 8.
94   *Ibid* at 14.

In an appropriate case, relief under s 459 can be sought against a person who is not a member of the company or against a person who was not involved in the conduct which is complained of in the petition.[95] So, for example, a third party to whom the company's property had been transferred at a gross undervalue could, in certain circumstances, be made a respondent and be made a party to an order compelling the respondents to buy out the petitioner's shares.

The courts can, on occasion, exercise their discretion in a flexible, creative way to solve in particular problems about which the petitioners have successfully complained. So, for instance, in *Re HR Harmer Ltd*,[96] a case brought under s 210, where it was established that the conduct of H had been 'oppressive' where he had transferred a business which he had founded and built up to a company, but continued to run it as if it were still his own in an autocratic way disregarding the wishes or interests of the other shareholders. Roxburgh J made an order that he should be made president for life with no duties, rights or powers and that he should not interfere in the affairs of the company otherwise than accordance with the valid decisions of the board. H was also given a contract of service to provide services to the company as a consultant.

This was an exceptional case. In the majority of cases the order which the court makes on a successful petition is that the petitioner's shares should be compulsorily acquired by the respondents. This achieves the result that the petitioner will be able to extract his investment from the company at the proper valuation and will not be 'locked in', and it will avoid the drastic and unnecessary alternative of winding the company up.

The important question then arises of how the valuation is to be carried out. There are three important decisions which the court might have to make. First, on what date should the shares be valued; second, should the valuation be done on a *pro rata* basis or should a discount be made for the fact that the petitioner's shares are a minority holding; and third, what is the effect, if any, of the presence in the articles of a method of valuation?

In *Re London School of Electronics*[97] Nourse J was of the opinion that if there was a general rule as to the date on which shares ordered to be purchased are valued, then it was the date of the order which was the most appropriate, since *prima facie* an interest in a going concern ought to be valued at the date on which it is ordered to be purchased. But he recognised that there was a general requirement that the valuation be fair on the facts of the particular case so that this general rule might effectively be reduced to no rule at all by the number of exceptions to it. In *Scottish Co-operative Wholesale Society Ltd v Meyer*[98] the shares were ordered to be purchased at the value which they would have had at the date of the petition if there had been no oppression. In *Re Cumana Ltd*[99] it

---

95   *Re Little Olympian Each-Ways Ltd* [1994] 2 BCLC 420.
96   [1959] 1 WLR 62.
97   [1986] Ch 211.
98   [1959] AC 324.
99   [1986] BCLC 430 at 436 *per* Lawton LJ.

was held that the choice of a date for valuation is a matter for the exercise of the trial judge's discretion. If there was evidence, for example, that the majority deliberately took steps to depreciate the value of shares in anticipation of a petition being presented, it would be permissible to value the shares at a date before such action was taken. In *Re OC (Transport) Services Ltd*[100] it was held that the valuation of the shares should be back-dated to the date when the unfair prejudice occurred, since the petitioner was entitled to a valuation before the diminution caused by the unfair prejudice otherwise the respondents would gain from their conduct.

In short, there is a range of dates on which the court can order the valuation to be done and it will choose one which appears to do justice in all the circumstances.

As regards the second point the court may have to give directions in the order as to whether the shareholder should receive a *pro rata* valuation for his shareholding or receive only a market valuation which takes into account the fact that he is holding a minority stake. The market value of a minority stake in a small private company will be below the *pro rata* value because of the absence of voting control, especially when the percentage does not confer enough votes even to prevent the passing of a special resolution.

In *Re Bird Precision Bellows Ltd*[101] at first instance Nourse J expressed some general considerations for valuing shares in a small private company for the purpose of s 459 relief which the Court of Appeal affirmed.[102] Where the successful petitioner was holding a minority shareholding in a quasi-partnership company and the conduct of the majority had been unfairly prejudicial to the interests of the minority or where there had been an agreement that the fair price should be determined by the court, without any admission by the majority as to the existence of any such unfairly prejudicial conduct, then the fair price should be determined on a *pro rata* basis. As Nourse J explained:

'I would expect that in a majority of cases where purchase orders are made under [s 459] in relation to quasi-partnerships the vendor is unwilling in the sense that the sale has been forced upon him. Usually he will be a minority shareholder whose interests have been unfairly prejudiced by the manner in which the affairs of the company have been conducted by the majority. On the assumption that the unfair prejudice has made it no longer tolerable for him to retain his interest in the company, a sale of his shares will invariably be his only practical way out short of a winding up ... In that kind of case it seems to me that it would not merely not be fair, but most unfair, that he should be bought out on the fictional basis applicable to a free election to sell his shares in accordance with the company's articles of association, or indeed on any other basis which involved a discounted price. In my judgment the correct course would be to fix the price *pro rata* according to the value of the shares as a whole and without any discount, as being the only fair method of compensating an unwilling vendor of the equivalent of a partnership share.'[103]

---

100 [1984] BCLC 80.

101 [1984] Ch 419.

102 [1986] Ch 658.

103 [1984] Ch 419 at 430.

But apart from this general rule there is no rule of universal application even in quasi-partnerships, since the circumstances might make it fairer to impose a market or discount basis where, for example, the conduct of the petitioner has not been above reproach and has brought exclusion from management upon himself. Where this nevertheless leads to a finding of unfairly prejudicial conduct by the majority the court could order a valuation as if there had been a free election to sell the shares because the petitioner has made a constructive election to sever his connection with the company.

It would also be inappropriate to apply a *pro rata* basis in a quasi-partnership where the petitioner purchased his shares from an existing shareholder as an investment rather than where he was one of the original shareholders. The price which he paid for the shares no doubt in this case would have reflected the fact that it was a minority holding and it would be fair to order that he should be bought out on the same basis. This was the order made in *Re Elgindata*.[104]

As regards the third issue there is a divergence of authority. Hoffmann J in *Re Abbey Leisure Ltd*[105] expressed the view that where the conduct complained of by the petitioner would be unfairly prejudicial only if accompanied by a refusal on the part of the respondents to buy his shares at a fair price and where the articles provide for a machinery as to valuation, that should be invoked even before the petition under s 459 is presented. The Court of Appeal in *Virdi v Abbey Leisure Ltd*,[106] overruling Hoffmann J at first instance, held that in certain circumstances it would not be unreasonable for the petitioner to ignore the provision in the articles, since the valuation under the articles may be made by an expert who is under no obligation to give reasons for the basis of his valuation, so it can later be challenged, and in that particular case there were claims against the company which required evaluation, and there was a real risk that if the claims were taken into account they would be inadequately appreciated. This approach was followed by Harman J in *Re a Company ex parte Holden*.[107]

Postscript

Although s 459 has spawned a considerable volume of litigation where petitioners have succeeded, and has undoubtedly improved the position of the minority shareholder, providing much needed relief in situations where the common law would be of no assistance, there is evidence of growing concern about the use of the section. This concern is expressed in the DTI consultative document *Company Law Review: The Law Applicable to Private Companies*,[108] where attention is drawn to the fact that proceedings under s 459 can be extremely lengthy and complex and can lead to evidence being presented of the entire history of the company and the conduct of the parties.

---

104 [1991] BCLC 959.

105 [1989] 5 BCC 183. See also his decisions in *Re a Company* [1987] BCLC 94 and *Re a Company ex parte Kremer* [1989] BCLC 365.

106 [1990] BCLC 342. But see *Re Castleburn Ltd* [1991] BCLC 89.

107 [1991] BCLC 597.

108 November 1994, URN 94/529.

109 [1994] 2 BCLC 354.

In *Re Macro (Ipswich) Ltd*[109] the judge was presented with evidence of events over 40 years of the company's history. She gave a warning that the parties in s 459 should not allow proceedings to become cumbersome. Reference is made in the consultative document to an unreported case, *Re Freudiana Music Company Ltd*,[110] which lasted 165 days, where the judge, Parker J stated that:

> '[t]he main reason for the length of the hearing was the sheer number of allegations made and issues raised on the pleadings ... the very width of the jurisdiction conferred by s 459 offers an opportunity to would-be petitioners and their advisers to mount a campaign on any number of different fronts, and to join battle on any number of different issues.'

Again Parker J had to examine virtually the whole of the history of the company. *Re Elgindata*[111] was another s 459 case in which the evidence put before the court was enormous and where the costs totalled £320,000 and the shares which were eventually ordered to be purchased by the respondents were valued at only £24,000.

In some cases petitioners can use the section itself as an instrument of oppression because of the costs of defending s 459 petitions, so that the threat of proceedings can be used as a bargaining tool by a minority shareholder.

Hoffman J in *Re a Company*[112] expressed his view, gained from experience in dealing with many s 459 petitions, that they resembled divorce petitions with each party blaming the other for the breakdown in the relationship and further:

> 'the prospect of a lengthy contested petition, sometimes brought by a legally-aided plaintiff, is a strong inducement to the respondents to pay the petitioner the price he asks for his shares. In [the present] case the respondents seem relatively well-off, but the companies against which such petitions are brought are often very modest and the burden of legal costs and expenditure of management time is crippling'[113]

It was for this reason that Hoffman J was of the opinion in *Re Abbey Leisure Ltd*[114] that if the articles provide a method for determining the fair value of a member's shares, a member who wishes to sell his shares after a breakdown in the relationship with other members should not be entitled to petition under s 459 if he has made no attempt to use the machinery provided by the articles.[115] Further, in the normal case of a breakdown of a quasi-partnership there should ordinarily be no 'legitimate expectation' that the member is entitled to have his shares valued by the court rather than by the company's auditors under the articles. So if the court is of the view that the petitioner is acting unreasonably in pursuing the petition under s 459, it may stay or strike out the

---

110 Unreported.
111 [1991] BCLC 959.
112 [1987] BCLC 94.
113 *Ibid.* See also n 105.
114 (1989) 5 BCC 183.
115 But this view was rejected by the Court of Appeal: see *Virdi v Abbey Leisure* [1990] BCLC 342.

petition as being an abuse of the process of the court.

Insolvency Act 1986, s 122(1)(g)

Long before the enactment of s 210 of the 1948 Act, a shareholder was able to exercise a statutory right as a 'contributory'[116] to petition the court for an order that the company be wound up on the ground that it was just and equitable to do so.[117] The provision which currently provides for this is s 122(1)(g) of the Insolvency Act 1986. There are a number of categories under which the courts will be inclined to hold that it is 'just and equitable' to wind up the company but by far the most important from the point of view of a minority shareholder's remedy is when there is a breakdown of the relationship between the members of a quasi-partnership.

From a procedural point of view, a member has to show that he has a 'tangible interest' in having the company wound up. If the member is holding partly-paid shares or the company is limited by guarantee, then the member will have an interest, since the winding up will prevent the director from causing the company to incur further debts so that they may increase the amount to which he is liable to contribute.[118] If he is holding only fully-paid shares, then his interest in winding up the company will have to be demonstrated by showing that there is a reasonable prospect that the company will have surplus funds to distribute amongst the members after the payment of its debts.[119]

Quasi-partnership

In *Ebrahimi v Westbourne Galleries Ltd*,[120] the leading case on 'just and equitable' winding up, E and N were partners in a business selling Persian carpets. A company was formed to take over the business and E and N became its first directors. They each took 500 shares and E purchased the shares with his own money. Soon afterwards N's son, G, was made a director and both N and E transferred 100 shares to him. The company prospered and all profits were paid out in the form of directors' remuneration. Subsequently the relationship between N and G on the one hand and E on the other broke down, and because N and G had a majority of votes in general meeting they passed a resolution removing E from the board of directors, a procedure which was provided for in the company's articles, but would have been available in any case because of the equivalent provision of what is now s 303 of the 1985 Act. This placed E in a disadvantageous position since he then lost the right to receive directors' remuneration and only retained the chance of obtaining dividends. Dividends had not previously been paid and, despite assurances by N that this practice would change, E

---

116 Insolvency Act 1986, s 79.

117 The 'just and equitable' provision first appeared in s 5 of the Joint Stock Companies Winding Up Act 1848.

118 *Re Chesterfield Catering Co Ltd* [1977] Ch 373.

119 *Re Rica Gold Washing Co* (1879) 11 ChD 36.

120 [1973] AC 360.

was at the mercy of N and G. He could not even dispose of his shares, under the articles, without the consent of N and G.

In these circumstances E presented a petition for relief under s 210 or an order that the company be wound up on the grounds that it was 'just and equitable' to do so. The first of these claims was dismissed at first instance by Plowman J[121] since E's complaint did not amount to a course of conduct which affected his interests as a member. Plowman J did order that the company should be wound up on 'just and equitable' grounds. This order was set aside by the Court of Appeal but restored by the House of Lords.

Lord Wilberforce, who delivered the leading speech, after an examination of the authorities, gave a cogent explanation of why it was appropriate to invoke the 'just and equitable' provision in these types of cases:

> 'The words [just and equitable] are a recognition of the fact that a limited company is more than a mere legal entity, with a personality in law of its own: that there is room in company law for recognition of the fact that behind it, or amongst it, there are individuals, with rights, expectations and obligations *inter se* which are not necessarily submerged in the company structure. ... [The provision] does, as equity always does, enable the court to subject the exercise of legal rights to equitable considerations: considerations, that is, of a personal character arising between one individual and another, which may make it unjust, or inequitable, to insist on legal rights, or to exercise them in a particular way.'[122]

In cases such as the present one where the company was formed on the basis of a personal relationship involving mutual confidence between the members and where the business had previously been run as a partnership it was possible to view the company as a 'quasi-partnership'. In a partnership, where a partner is expelled or excluded from management, even where under the partnership agreement there is a power of expulsion, the conclusion must be that that the partnership be dissolved. But the use of the language of partnership should not obscure the fact that the company was essentially a different legal form from the partnership. Therefore it was necessary to invoke the 'just and equitable' provision, where a petitioner could show that there was an underlying obligation on the part of the other members of the company to the effect that so long as the business continued he should be entitled to participate in the management of the business, and that if that basic obligation were broken the conclusion must be that the company should be wound up. This was despite the fact that the majority were doing nothing more than exercise their rights under the articles or under s 303. As Plowman J had stated:

> '... while no doubt the petitioner was lawfully removed, in the sense that he ceased in law to be a director, it does not follow that removing him the respondents did not do him a wrong.'[123]

---

121 [1970] 1 WLR. See p 298.
122 [1973] AC 360 at 379.
123 [1970] 1 WLR 1378 at 1389.

Lord Wilberforce was unwilling to define precisely the circumstances in which it would be appropriate to subject the company to these considerations, but just because the company is small is not enough. He then gave the usual criteria, which have been subsequently employed in the s 459 cases to establish a legitimate expectation to a right outside the constitution of the company.

Lord Cross pointed out that as this jurisdiction was 'equitable' a petitioner should come to the court with clean hands and therefore:

'if the breakdown in confidence between him and the other parties to the dispute appears to have been due to his misconduct he cannot insist on the company being wound up if they wish it to continue.'[124]

Therefore it is possible that a court will refuse a claim for 'just and equitable' winding up if the petitioner has acted in bad faith, but as the Privy Council explained in *Vujnovich v Vujnovich*:[125]

'it is quite clear that Lord Cross was considering the position in which the petitioner's misconduct (and thus the relative uncleanliness of his hands) was causative of the breakdown in confidence on which the petition was based.'[126]

Therefore past conduct by the petitioner which, although not particularly helpful, is not actually responsible for the breakdown in the relationship between the quasi-partners, will not prevent the petitioner proceeding with a claim for 'just and equitable' winding up.[127]

A different issue in relation to the conduct of the petitioner is raised if he pursues a claim for 'just and equitable' winding up in circumstances where he has an alternative remedy. Under s 125(2), if the court is of the opinion that the petitioner is entitled to relief either by winding up the company or by some other means, and that in the absence of any other remedy it would be just and equitable that the company should be wound up, it shall make a winding up order. But this does not apply if the court is also of the opinion both that some other remedy is available to the petitioner and that he is acting unreasonably in seeking to have the company wound up instead of pursuing that other remedy.

At first instance in *Re Abbey Leisure Ltd*[128] Hoffmann J had taken the view that the petitioner was acting unreasonably in refusing to accept an offer made by the respondents for his shares on a valuation to be made in accordance with the articles of association. The Court of Appeal reversed this decision[129] and allowed the petition to proceed, since it was likely in the circumstances that the petitioner should be awarded a

---

124 [1973] AC 360 at 387.

125 (1989) 5 BCC 740.

126 *Ibid* at 744.

127 See also *Re R A Noble & Sons (Clothing) Ltd* [1983] BCLC 273.

128 [1990] BCLC 342.

129 *Virdi v Abbey Leisure Ltd* [1990] BCLC 342.

value on the *pro rata* basis and he was not acting unreasonably in refusing to accept the risk that the valuation in accordance with the articles might produce a discount basis.

Loss of confidence in management

It was established very early on that even this drastic procedure of last resort could not be used by a shareholder where the directors had simply been guilty of misconduct, even if that misconduct would otherwise give rise to the possibility of an action being brought against them.[130] But in *Loch v John Blackwood*[131] the Privy Council was prepared to order that the company be wound up in circumstances where, despite the fact that the business had made considerable profits, the directors had not called general meetings of shareholders, no auditors were appointed, and accounts had not been produced and submitted. It was held that in applications under this section:

> 'there must be a justifiable lack of confidence in the conduct and management of the company's affairs. ... [T]he lack of confidence must spring not from dissatisfaction at being outvoted on the business affairs or on what is called the domestic policy of the company. On the other hand, wherever the lack of confidence is rested on a lack of probity in the conduct of the company's affairs, then the former is justified by the latter, and it is under the statute just and equitable that the company be wound up.'[132]

Loss of 'substratum'

If a company has a narrowly drawn objects clause in its memorandum, laying down quite specifically what business the company was formed to pursue, then if that particular object or business becomes impossible the court can wind up the company on the 'just and equitable' ground. The minority shareholders would have the right to say that they became members of the company on the understanding that the company would carry out a certain activity and it would not be fair to force shareholders to remain members of a company which then carries on a totally different activity. This is what happened in *Re German Date Coffee Co*[133] where a company was formed to acquire and exploit a particular patent. It subsequently transpired that the company could not acquire this patent and therefore the Court of Appeal was willing to order that the company be wound up. The shareholders had a right to say that they contributed their capital for a specific purpose, and that now being impossible they should be prevented from being able to withdraw their investment. But the success of an application under this heading will depend on the construction of the objects clause. Where a company is formed to carry on a type of business rather than for a specific purpose, then the probability will be that the company will still be able to carry on that

---

130 *Re Anglo-Greek Shipping Co Ltd* (1866) LR Eq 1.

131 [1924] AC 783.

132 *Ibid* at 788.

133 (1882) 20 Ch D 169.

134 *Re Kitson & Co Ltd* [1946] 1 All ER 435.

type of business, although not perhaps in precisely the way originally envisaged and therefore the substratum of the company has not failed.[134]

Deadlock

Where there is a complete deadlock in the running of the company's affairs and the company concerned is a 'quasi-partnership' then it is appropriate to make a 'just and equitable' winding up order, because if such a position were reached in the closely analogous situation of a partnership, the court would make an order for the dissolution of the partnership. In *Re Yenidje Tobacco Co Ltd*,[135] the relationship between the only two directors and shareholders who had equal voting rights in general meeting broke down to such an extent that they only communicated with each other through a third party. Astbury J made an order that the company should be wound up and in dismissing the appeal, Lord Cozens-Hardy MR expressly stated that he had treated the company as if it were a partnership.[136]

Companies Act 1985, Part XIV, ss 431–53

There is a remote possibility that shareholders could initiate an investigation by the Department of Trade and Industry into the company's affairs. These investigations are practically of much greater importance in larger, public companies where there is a clear public interest involved. As Lord Denning MR explained:

> 'It sometimes happens that public companies are conducted in a way which is beyond the control of the ordinary shareholders. The majority of the shares are in the hands of two or three individuals. These have control of the company's affairs. The other shareholders know little and are told little. They receive glossy annual reports. Most of them throw them in the wastepaper basket. There is an annual general meeting but few of the shareholders attend. The whole management and control is in the hands of the directors. They are a self-perpetuating oligarchy: and are virtually unaccountable. Seeing that the directors are the guardians of the company, the question is asked: *Quis custodiet ipsos custodes?* – who will guard the guards themselves? ... It is because companies are beyond the reach of ordinary individuals that this legislation has been passed so as to enable the Department of Trade to appoint inspectors to investigate the affairs of a company.'[137]

By s 431 the Secretary of State may appoint one or more competent inspectors to investigate the affairs of a company and to produce a report on them in such manner as he may direct. This appointment may be made on the application either of not less than 200 members of the company or members holding not less than one-tenth of the issued shares or, where the company does not have a share capital, on the application of not less than one-fifth of the persons on the company's register of members. An application for an appointment of inspectors by the Secretary of State can also be made

---

135 [1916] 2 Ch 426.
136 *Ibid* at 431.
137 *Norwest Holst Ltd v Secretary of State for Trade* [1978] 1 Ch 201 at 223.

by the company. The Secretary of State may, before appointing inspectors, require the applicants to give security of an amount not exceeding £5,000. He is given power to specify a higher sum but this would have to be by Order in a statutory instrument. The security is to go towards the payment of costs of the investigation. The application to the Secretary of State shall be supported by such evidence as he may require for the purpose of showing that there is a good reason for requiring the investigation. In the last five years, however, only one investigation seems to have been completed under this section.[138]

Investigations are not solely initiated by the shareholders or the company, however, so that by s 432(1) the Secretary of State shall appoint inspectors if the court orders that its affairs ought to be investigated. In addition, s 432(2) provides a number of other situations where the Secretary of State himself may make an appointment, namely, where there are circumstances suggesting: that the company's affairs are being or have been conducted fraudulently; or in a manner which is unfairly prejudicial to the interests of its members; or the persons who formed or who are managing the company have been guilty of fraud, misfeasance or other misconduct towards it or to its members; or the company's members have not been given all the information in respect of its affairs which they might reasonably expect.

Once appointed the inspectors can also investigate the affairs of the company's subsidiaries or holding company if they think that is necessary for the purposes of their investigation.[139]

The investigation by the inspectors is not a judicial or quasi-judicial inquiry. It is an administrative process in which the inspectors act inquisitorially.[140] No person submits or presents a case to the inspectors; they examine witnesses and collect evidence in private.[141] The rules of natural justice, which would mean that every party is entitled to hear the grounds on which the Secretary of State proposed to appoint inspectors and make submissions, do not apply. The Secretary of State's decision to appoint inspectors cannot be challenged if he has acted in good faith.[142]

The officers and agents (including the company's solicitors and bankers) of a company which is under investigation are under a duty to produce to the inspectors all documents of or relating to the company, and to attend before the inspectors when required to do so.[143] They are also under a general duty to give the inspectors all assistance in connection with the investigation which they are reasonably able to give.[144]

The inspectors have the power to require any officer or agent whom they consider

---

138 Companies in 1994–95, DTI, HMSO.
139 Companies Act 1985, s 433.
140 *Re Pergamon Press Ltd* [1971] Ch 388.
141 *Maxwell v Department of Trade and Industry* [1974] QB 523.
142 *Norwest Holst Ltd v Department of Trade* [1978] 1 Ch 201.
143 Companies Act 1985, s 434(1)(a) and (b).
144 Companies Act 1985, s 434(1)(c).

may be in possession of information which they believe to be relevant to the investigation to produce any relevant documents in his custody or power or to attend before them.[145] But the notice requiring documents must not be unreasonable or excessive in the circumstances. It should give the person who is required to produce the documents adequate time to do so and should not be too wide in the documents it requires. An inspector can administer an oath and examine any person under oath.[146]

Witnesses who appear before the inspectors have no privilege against self-incrimination even though the answers are, *prima facie*, admissible under s 434(5) in criminal proceedings.[147] The inspectors are concerned only whether the question is fair in the context of their enquiry to ask the question.

If a person refuses to comply with the requirements laid down in these provisions, or refuses to answer any question put to him by the inspectors, then the inspectors can certify this fact to the court and the court can then enquire into the case, hearing both the offender and any witnesses who may be produced for or against him. After this enquiry the court can punish the offender in the same way as if he had been guilty of contempt of court.[148]

Such a certificate was given in the case of the inquiry into the affairs of Pergamon Press Ltd, when the late Robert Maxwell and others refused to give answers to the inspector's questions unless they received assurances concerning the conduct of the enquiry and whether they would be allowed the opportunity to read the transcripts of the evidence given against them and to answer any allegations against them which may be made against them. The Court of Appeal held that they were not entitled to these assurances and remitted the case to the inspectors with the clear warning that if they persisted in the delays they would be treated in the same way as if they were in contempt of court. As an enquiry is ordered in the public interest, witnesses should not be discouraged from coming forward to give evidence. Since these proceedings are not judicial, but administrative, the witness only has qualified rather than absolute privilege. The inspectors should exercise their discretion to protect a witness as far as is possible so as to encourage him to be frank. But Lord Denning MR took it as axiomatic that the inspectors would not use the evidence of a witness so as to make it the basis of an adverse finding unless they gave the party affected sufficient information to enable him to answer it.[149]

When the inspectors have made their report to the Secretary of State, he may if he thinks fit forward a copy of it to the company's registered office and provide a copy on request to any member of the company; any person whose conduct is referred to in the report; the auditors or any other person whose financial interests appear to the Secretary of State to be affected by the matters dealt with in the report. He may also

---

145 Companies Act 1985, s 434(2).

146 Companies Act 1985, s 434(3).

147 *R v Seelig* [1992] 1 WLR 148.

148 Companies Act 1985, s 436.

149 *Re Pergamon Press Ltd* [1971] Ch 388.

150 Companies Act 1985, s 437.

151 *R v Secretary of State for Trade and Industry ex parte Lonrho plc* [1989] 1 WLR 525.

cause the report to be published.[150] The decision to publish and the timing of the publication are a matter of discretion for the Secretary of State.[151]

As regards the consequences of the investigation, it is quite possible that during the course of the investigation criminal offences may have come to light and these matters will be referred to the appropriate prosecuting authority. In addition the Secretary of State is given the following power under s 438:

> '[i]f from any report made or information obtained under this Part it appears to the Secretary of State that any civil proceedings ought in the public interest to be brought by any body corporate, he may himself bring such proceedings in the name and on behalf of the body corporate.'

The Secretary of State will indemnify the company in respect of the costs of such proceedings.[152] Further, the Secretary of State must also, in the first instance, bear the costs of the investigation. But by s 439 any person who is convicted of a criminal offence as a result of an investigation or who is ordered to pay the whole or any part of the costs of the proceedings brought under s 438 may in the same proceedings be ordered to pay the expenses of the investigation or any part of them.[153]

The Secretary of State is also given powers if it appears to him to be expedient in the public interest to petition to the court for an order that the company be wound up on the grounds that it is just and equitable to do so.[154]

Other powers given to the Secretary of State, although strictly outside the scope of shareholder remedies, are the powers to appoint inspectors to investigate and report on the membership of any company,[155] or to require that any person whom he has reasonable cause to believe to have obtained or to be able to obtain any information as to the present and past interests in the shares or debentures of the company, give such information to him for the purpose of determining the true persons who are or have been financially interested in the success or failure of the company or able to control or influence its policy.[156]

Separate from the powers to appoint investigators and again outside the ambit of shareholder remedies are the powers contained in ss 447-51 to require the production of company documents, which includes not only powers to require the company and its officers to produce, but also powers to obtain search warrants to enter any premises where there are reasonable grounds for believing that there are documents whose production has been required but have not been produced. Investigations under these powers are much more common than those under ss 431 and 432. In 1994-95 there were 308 enquiries commenced under this section.[157]

---

152 Companies Act 1985, s 438(2).

153 Companies Act 1985, s 439.

154 Companies Act 1986, s 124A.

155 Companies Act 1985, s 442.

156 Companies Act 1985, s 444.

157 Companies in 1994–95, DTI, HMSO.

CHAPTER THIRTEEN

WINDING UP

The law of insolvency and the relatively new concept of the administration order designed to nurture ailing companies back to health are largely outside the scope of this book. However, it is necessary to deal with some of the provisions and procedures which from the company law point of view bring the company's life to an end. The existence of a company is brought to an end by winding up and ultimately dissolution. The dissolution brings to an end the company's legal personality. The most likely reason for a company to be wound up is that it has become insolvent, unable to pay its debts. This is by no means the only reason though and a company can also be wound up when it is quite solvent. Despite this, and rather confusingly, the provisions relating to all types of winding up are contained in the Insolvency Act 1986, and subordinate legislation, such as the Insolvency Rules 1986.[1] References to sections in this chapter will be to the Insolvency Act 1986 unless otherwise indicated.

THE TYPES OF WINDING UP

There are two basic types of winding up: compulsory winding up and voluntary winding up.

Compulsory winding up

This type of liquidation is ordered by the court. Section 122(1) provides a number of circumstances or grounds on which a company may be wound up by the court, the main ones being:

(a) the company has by special resolution resolved that the company be wound up by the court;

(b) the company is unable to pay its debts;

(c) the court is of the opinion that it is just and equitable that the company should be wound up.[2]

An application for a winding up order is by petition and can be made by the company or the directors or by any creditors, contributories (ie members or certain former members)[3] or even by the clerk of a magistrates' court (to enforce fines which have been imposed on but not paid by the company).[4]

By s 123 a company is deemed to be unable to pay its debts if a creditor of the company who is owed more than £750 serves on the company at its registered office a

---

1   SI 1986/1925.

2   See p 305.

3   *Ibid.*

4   Insolvency Act 1986, s 124.

written demand in the prescribed form requiring the company to pay the sum due and the company has not paid it for three weeks, or an execution or other process issued on judgment in favour of a creditor is returned unsatisfied.

The court is given a wide discretion by s 125 on the hearing of a winding up petition but if it makes the order then a liquidator has to be appointed. In fact, by s 135 the court is given powers to appoint a provisional liquidator at any time after the presentation of the petition. Once a winding up order is made, the official receiver becomes the liquidator and remains in office unless or until another person is appointed.[5] By s 136(4) and (5) the official receiver is given a number of powers and duties to perform regardless of whether he is retained as a company's liquidator or not, for example, summoning meetings of the company's creditors and contributories.

The functions of the liquidator of a company which is being wound up by the court are stated by s 143 to be:

'to secure that the assets of the company are got in, realised and distributed to the company's creditors and, if there is a surplus, to the persons entitled to it.'

To ensure that this is possible on the making of the winding up order the powers of management which were enjoyed by the company's directors pass to the liquidator who then has complete control over the company and can, for example, initiate proceedings on its behalf to recover assets belonging to the company.

A liquidator is not a trustee of the company's assets for individual creditors and contributories,[6] but he does owe fiduciary duties to the company and therefore must act in good faith and not make secret profits.[7] He is acting as an agent of the company, therefore if in exercising his functions he properly makes a contract on behalf of the company, he is not personally liable if there is a breach of that contract.[8] He can be held liable in misfeasance proceedings under s 212, if he has improperly retained property or had improperly or unnecessarily paid out the company's money, and these proceedings can be instituted by any creditor or contributory. The basic position, function and role of the liquidator are the same whether the winding up is compulsory or voluntary.

Voluntary winding up

The company can resolve by special resolution that the company be wound up or, more quickly, by extraordinary resolution that it cannot by reason of its liabilities continue its business and that it is advisable to wind up.[9]

By ss 86 and 87 a voluntary winding up is deemed to commence at the time of the passing of the resolution to wind up and the company shall from that date cease to

---

5   Insolvency Act 1986, s 136(2).

6   *Knowles v Scott* [1891] 1 Ch 717.

7   *Silkstone and Haigh Moore Coal Co v Edey* [1900] 1 Ch 167.

8   *Re Anglo-Moravian Hungarian Junction Rly Co ex p Watkin* (1875) 1 Ch D 130.

9   Insolvency Act 1986, s 84.

carry on its business, except so far as may be required for its beneficial winding up. A petition can be presented after the commencement of a voluntary winding up for a compulsory winding up order and if one is made then the date of commencement of compulsory winding up is 'back-dated' to the date of voluntary winding up. This may have significant consequences because by s 127 any disposition of the company's property made after the commencement of the winding up is void (unless the court orders otherwise).[10]

There are two different types of voluntary winding up. A members' winding up is a voluntary winding up where a directors' statutory declaration of solvency has been made and a creditors' winding up is one where such a declaration has not been made.

Members' voluntary winding up

The statutory declaration of solvency essential to this form of winding up is made by the directors (or in the case of a company having more than two directors, a majority of them), at a meeting to the effect that they have made a full enquiry into the company's affairs and that they have formed the opinion that the company will be able to pay its debts in full, together with interest, within such period, not exceeding 12 months from the commencement of the winding up, as may be specified in the declaration.[11] To be effective the declaration must be made within five weeks immediately before the passing of the resolution to wind up and it includes as recent a statement of the company's assets and liabilities as practicable.[12] This declaration must then be delivered to the registrar within 15 days after the passing of the resolution to wind up.[13]

Unlike certain statements directors are required to make where a company's capital is affected,[14] there is no direct involvement of the company's auditors, but a director who makes a declaration without having reasonable grounds for the opinion that the company will be able to pay its debts is liable to imprisonment or a fine or both. Further, if the company is wound up within five weeks after the making of the declaration and its debts are not paid in full then there is a presumption that the director did not have reasonable grounds for his opinion.[15]

By s 91 the company in general meeting in a members' winding up appoints one or more liquidators. This is the advantage of the directors being able to make the statutory declaration of solvency, since if they control the general meeting they will be able to appoint a liquidator who they believe will be less inquisitive as regards their own conduct than one appointed by the creditors. This is a reason why directors would not wish a petition to be presented under s 122(1)(a) after the passing of a special

---

10 See *Re Gray's Inn Construction Co Ltd* [1980] 1 WLR 711 for guidance on when the court will exercise its discretion under s 127.

11 Insolvency Act 1986, s 89.

12 Insolvency Act 1986, s 89(2).

13 Insolvency Act 1986, s 89(3).

14 For example, Companies Act 1985, s 156.

15 Insolvency Act 1986, s 89(4).

resolution to wind up the company. But there are provisions for converting a members' into a creditors' winding up if the liquidator is of the opinion that the company will be unable to pay its debts within the period stated in the statutory declaration.[16]

The liquidator must call a general meeting of the company as soon as the company's affairs are fully wound up.[17] At this meeting the liquidator must lay before it an account of the winding up, showing how it has been conducted and how the company's property has been disposed of and he must explain the account to the meeting.

Creditors' voluntary winding up

In this type of liquidation the company must cause a meeting of its creditors to be summoned for a day not later than the 14th day after the day on which the meeting is to be held at which the resolution for voluntary winding up is proposed.[18] Further, it must cause notices of the creditors' meeting to be sent to the company's creditors not less than seven days before the meeting is to be held and to advertise the meeting in the Gazette and two newspapers. By s 100 the creditors can nominate a person to be the liquidator of the company. If they do so, then he becomes the liquidator; if they do not then the company can nominate someone.

The creditors of the company can also appoint a 'liquidation committee' consisting of not more than five persons, whereupon the company can appoint up to another five persons to the committee.[19] This committee can then liaise with the liquidator without the need for the liquidator to convene full creditors' and members' meetings. The liquidator is under an obligation to report to the committee all such matters as appear to him to be, or as they have indicated to him as being, of concern to them with respect to the winding up.[20]

The liquidator is under a similar obligation in a creditors' winding up as he is under a members' winding up in respect of calling a general meeting of the company when the company's affairs are fully wound up,[21] except that he must also call a meeting of the creditors for the same purpose of laying the account before it.

DISSOLUTION

Where a company is wound up voluntarily and the liquidator has sent his final account and return to the registrar who registers them, the company is deemed to be dissolved after the expiry of three months from the date of registration.[22] This period can be

---

16 Insolvency Act 1986, s 95.
17 Insolvency Act 1986, s 94.
18 Insolvency Act 1986, s 98.
19 Insolvency Act 1986, s 101.
20 Insolvency Rules 1986, r 4 155.
21 Insolvency Act 1986, s 106.
22 Insolvency Act 1986, s 201(1) and (2).

extended on application by the liquidator or any other person who appears to the court to be interested.[23]

Where the winding up is by the court the liquidator must, when the winding up is for practical purposes complete and the liquidator is not the official receiver, call a final general meeting of the company's creditors which receives the report of the winding up and determines whether to release the liquidator.[24] After this meeting has been held, the liquidator must give notice to the court and the registrar stating whether the creditors gave him the release or not and he must also send copies of the report to the registrar and the official receiver. The liquidator then vacates office as soon as he has given notice to the court and the registrar and the company is dissolved after the expiry of three months.[25] This is subject to a possible application by the official receiver or any other interested person to the Secretary of State who can defer the dissolution of the company if he thinks fit.[26]

Where the official receiver is the liquidator of the company in a winding up by the court, there is no final meeting of creditors but the official receiver gives notice to every creditor of the company of his intention to give notice to the Secretary of State and to the registrar and to state that the winding up is for practical purposes complete and thereupon he obtains his release.[27] The registrar then registers the notice given by the official receiver and the company is dissolved after the expiry of three months.[28] Again there is power vested in the Secretary of State to defer dissolution on the application of the official receiver or any interested party.[29]

STRIKING OFF DEFUNCT COMPANIES

Section 652 of the Companies Act 1985 gives the registrar the power to strike defunct companies from the register of companies. By s 652(1) if he has reasonable cause to believe that a company is not carrying on a business he can set in motion a procedure which will ultimately lead to the company being struck off. But where a company is struck off the liability of every director or member of the company continues as if the company had not been dissolved.[30]

---

23 Insolvency Act 1986, s 201(3).

24 Insolvency Act 1986, s 146(1).

25 Insolvency Act 1986, s 172(8) and s 205(2).

26 Insolvency Act 1986, s 205(3).

27 Insolvency Act 1986, s 174(3).

28 Insolvency Act 1986, s 205(2).

29 Insolvency Act 1986, s 205(3).

30 Companies Act 1985, s 652(6).

CHAPTER FOURTEEN

THE INFLUENCE OF EUROPE

The Treaty of Rome (as amended by the Treaty of European Union), in the Preamble and Articles 2 and 3, sets out the objectives and the activities necessary to achieve those objectives of the European Community which include ensuring the economic and social progress of Member States by common action to eliminate the barriers which divide Europe, the promotion of a harmonious and balanced development of economic activities, establishing a common market and the approximation of the laws of the Member States to the extent required for the functioning of the common market.

'HARMONISATION'

The most important action taken by the Council of Ministers and the Commission in relation to company law has been to issue a number of directives which have sought to 'harmonise' the laws in a number of fields in Member States. It has been seen as vital to ensure that each Member State's laws provide similar protection to investors and persons dealing with companies otherwise, amongst other reasons, it is feared that with the freedom of movement and the right of establishment which the Treaty provides companies would tend to be incorporated only in Member States with lax protection for outsiders against companies or with pro-management laws operating to the detriment of investors. Also, perhaps more importantly, it is believed that 'harmonised' laws relating to companies will make cross-border ventures simpler and co-operation will be undertaken more easily, as will cross-border mergers.

There have been 13 directives in company law proposed so far but not all have been adopted. Those which are still to be adopted are the fifth, ninth, tenth and thirteenth. In addition there are a number of directives on company law – related matters which affect the regulation of capital markets and insider dealing. The authority to issue these directives in company law areas has usually been stated to be Article 54(3)(g) which provides that the Council and the Commission should carry out the duties devolving upon them in creating and safeguarding freedom of establishment 'by co-ordinating to the necessary extent the safeguards which, for the protection of the interests of members and others are required by Member States of companies or firms [as defined by Article 58] with a view to making such safeguards *equivalent* throughout the Community'.

Some directives rely on Article 100, which provides that the Council can issue directives for the approximation of such laws of Member States as directly affect the establishment or functioning of the common market or Article 100a, whereby the Council can adopt measures for the approximation of laws in Member States which have as their object the establishing and functioning of the internal market. Finally, the Council could rely on Article 235, which provides that if in the course of the operation of the common market action should prove necessary to achieve one of the objectives of the Community and the Treaty has not provided the necessary powers, then the Council shall take the appropriate measures.

There is some significance to which Article is being relied upon, since action under Articles 54 and 100a can be taken by the Council with approval of a qualified majority,[1] whereas action under articles 100 and 235 can only be taken where there is unanimous approval in Council.

Whatever is the basis for issuing the directives, Article 189 states that:

'[a] directive shall be binding, as to the result to be achieved, upon each Member State
... but shall leave to the national authorities the choice of form and methods.'

So once adopted, the Member State has to set about amending its own law so as to enact the substance of the directive. The harmonisation process is not aimed at producing identical sets of company laws throughout the Member States but simply laws which are equivalent in each jurisdiction.

The directive itself will contain a time limit by which each Member State has to have brought its laws into conformity with it. If a Member State fails to meet this obligation then the Commission may bring infringement proceedings against it, under Article 169, before the Court of Justice. Further, the amended version of Article 171 provides that the Court of Justice may impose a lump sum or penalty payment on the Member State.[2]

In addition it has been held that after the time limit for implementation has passed, an individual can rely on directives as against Members States and national authorities in national courts even though the terms of the directive are in conflict with national law.[3] But it has to be shown that the terms of the directive sought to be invoked are clear and unconditional. A number of cases brought before the Court of Justice have involved company law directives most notably *Marleasing SA v La Commercial Internacional de Alimentation SA*.[4] Here the Court of Justice held in line with its previous decisions that a national court had to interpret its national law by reference to the wording and purpose of the First Directive. The particular Member State concerned had not implemented the directive at the relevant time but it was held that the courts in that State could not use a ground for nullity which was not one of those contained in Article 11 of the First Directive to strike a company off the register. So, despite the restriction on individuals enforcing the terms of a directive directly against another individual (the so-called horizontal direct effect) the individual may be able to achieve broadly the same end by obtaining a judgment from the European Court on how national courts can decide a particular case, the circumstances of which are covered by a directive.

---

1   In accordance with the procedure under Article 189b.

2   See *Francovich v Italian State* [1991] ECR I 5357.

3   *Van Duyn v Home Office* [1974] ECR 1337; *Marshall v Southampton and South West Hampshire Area Health Authority* [1993] 4 All ER 586.

4   [1990] 1 ECR 4135; and see *Karellas v Greek Minister of Industry* (1993) BCC 677; *Von Colson and Kamann v Land Nordrhein-Westfalen* [1984] ECR 1891.

The methods used by the UK Parliament to implement directives are either by means of primary legislation or by the use of subordinate legislation, statutory instruments, under s 2(2) of the European Communities Act 1972. This latter provision enables an Order in Council or regulations to be made by the Crown or by a Minister for the purpose of implementing any Community obligation of the UK, but by Schedule 2 this provision is subject to a number of limitations, for example, the power cannot be used to impose or increase tax or to create any new serious criminal offence.[5] Further the Order in Council or regulations have to be laid before and approved by each House of Parliament.[6] Hitherto this power has not been used to implement a directive if it were necessary to repeal and replace a large number of existing statutory provisions. This was generally done by primary legislation. However, it seems that increasing use is being made to introduce large scale amendments.[7]

Where a directive has been implemented the courts will look at the text of the directive to ensure that the UK complies with its obligations. In *Litster v Forth Dry Dock & Engineering Ltd*,[8] a case concerning the implementation of an employment protection directive, Lord Oliver stated at 559:

'[t]he approach to the construction of primary and subordinate legislation enacted to give effect to the UK's obligations under the EEC Treaty have been the subject matter of recent authority in this House (see *Pickstone v Freemans plc* [1989] AC 66) and is not in doubt. If the legislation can reasonably be construed so as to conform with those obligations – obligations which are to be ascertained not only from the wording of the relevant directive but from the interpretation placed upon it by the European Court of Justice at Luxembourg – such a purposive construction will be applied even though, perhaps, it may involve some departure from the strict and literal application of the words which the legislature has elected to use.'[9]

And further on:

'*Pickstone v Freemans plc* has established that greater flexibility available to the court in applying a purposive construction to legislation designed to give effect to the UK's Treaty obligations to the Community enables the court, where necessary, to supply by implication words appropriate to comply with those obligations.'[10]

This is in contrast to *Phonogram Ltd v Lane*,[11] the first case to construe s 9(2) of the European Communities Act 1972 implementing the First Directive provisions in relation to pre-incorporation contracts, where Lord Denning refused to look at the text of the Directive to help construe the section.[12] The Directive was drafted at a time

---

5   European Communities Act 1972, Sch 2, para 1(1)(a) and (d).

6   *Ibid*, para 2.

7   See, for example,

8   [1990] 1 AC 546; See also Lord Bridge in *Factortame Ltd v Secretary of State for Transport* [1990] 2 AC 85; [1991] 1 AC 603.

9   *Ibid* at 559.

10 *Ibid* at 577.

11 [1982] QB 938.

12 The 'high-water mark' of this approach is seen in *Duke v GEC Reliance* [1988] AC 618; and *Webb v EMO* [1993] 1 WLR 49.

before English was an official language. But in a another case concerning the provisions implementing the First Directive, *International Sales Agencies Ltd v Marcus*,[13] Lawson J was prepared to look at the English version of the text as an aid to interpreting s 9(1) of the 1972 Act.

OTHER COMMUNITY ACTION

Two other European initiatives are of some importance for company lawyers. First, the European Economic Interest Grouping (EEIG) and second, the European Company statute or the *Societas Europaea* (SE).

The EEIG is a new form of business association and is an example of European action in the company law field by way of regulation rather than by directive, the difference being that, by Article 189, a regulation is binding in its entirety and directly applicable in all Member States.

The EEIG Regulation, in contrast to the company law directives, is stated to be made under Article 235 of the Treaty. *Prima facie* as a result of the direct effect of a regulation no further action is needed by the Member State to enact the substance of the regulation. But in the case of the EEIG Regulation which was adopted in 1985 considerable supplementation was required by the Member States on issues such as taxation and registration, and for example Articles 35 and 36 of the Regulation leave the issue of insolvency and cessation of payments to national law. In Great Britain the Secretary of State brought in the European Economic Interest Grouping Regulations[14] to supplement the Regulation which came into force on 1st July 1989.

These regulations *inter alia* make provision for the registration of an EEIG in Great Britain since the members can choose which Member State the EEIG will be registered in.[15] By Article 4 of the Regulation the only members of an EEIG can be companies or firms formed and having their central administration within the Community or natural persons who carry on industrial, commercial, craft or agricultural activity or who provide professional services within the Community. An EEIG must have at least two members who have their central administration or who carry on business in different Member States.

By Article 3 the purpose of the EEIG is:

'to facilitate or develop the economic activities of its members and to improve or increase the results of those activities; its purpose is not to make profits. Its activity shall be related to the economic activities of its members and must not be more than ancillary to those activities.'

This means that it is envisaged that the EEIG will be used for such purposes as research and development or joint activities designed to further the members' own businesses such as joint tendering for contracts with the overall aim to foster cross-frontier co-

---

13 [1982] 3 All ER 551. See p 128.

14 SI 1988 No 1359.

15 *Ibid*, Part III.

operation. The EEIG cannot have any power of management or supervision over its members or their business activities nor can it employ more than 500[16] people.

It is prevented from holding shares in any of the member companies. So from all of the above there is no possibility of using the EEIG form as a means to create a European parent or holding company. Its role is to remain ancillary to the members' businesses.

By Article 1(2) an EEIG has the capacity to make contracts or accomplish other legal acts and to sue and be sued, in its own name. Whether or not the EEIG has a separate legal personality is a matter for Member States but in Great Britain an EEIG is a body corporate by regulation 3 of the 1989 Regulations. The EEIG does not, though, have limited liability so the members remain jointly and severally liable for any debts which might be incurred in the course of its activities.[17] A creditor has first to request payment from the EEIG itself and if payment is not forthcoming within an appropriate period then take steps against the members.

An EEIG is formed by a contract which is then filed at the registry in the Member State where the EEIG is to be registered. So far it appears that there has not been a great deal of use of the EEIG in Great Britain but over 200 have been formed throughout the EC.

Apart from the EEIG there has been for a long time a much more ambitious proposal for a supranational corporate form. This company would be incorporated under a European Company Statute which would exist independently from national laws. If achieved this would overcome many of the problems of attempting piecemeal harmonisation of national laws by directives. A proposal for a European company was made as early as 1959[18] and following this the Commission by 1967 had a draft statute prepared for it by a committee of national experts. This resulted in the first official draft proposal being published in 1970. This, together with a revised draft in 1975, was a proposal for a complete and independent body of law which would form and regulate the European company and there would be no reference to any national law. However, agreement could not be reached between the Member States so it was abandoned.

Spurred on by the move towards the completion of the internal market in 1992, the Commission revived its proposal for the European Company in a Commission Memorandum issued in July 1988. After consultation a new proposal was produced with the latest text being issued in February 1992. Amongst other advantages, the availability of a pan-European company would, it is thought, assist cross-frontier mergers and avoid a number of tax and double taxation problems.

Under the present version of the proposal the European Company Statute is far less ambitious. It would have no central registration. Registration would be in individual

---

16 Article 3(2).

17 Article 24.

18 In the inaugural address by Professor Dieter Sanders at the University of Rotterdam.

Member States[19] and this must be where the company has its central administration.[20] It must be a public company limited by shares with a minimum capital of at least ECU 100,000. Many of the former draft provisions have been dropped from the current proposal for the ECS which will leave the national laws of Member States to control and regulate the Company where there are gaps, for instance in respect of capital, shares, debentures, accounts and groups of companies. Such a proposal is far removed from the original conception of an ECS.

The present proposal would be introduced by way of a regulation under Article 100a of the Treaty and a supplementary directive under Article 54(3)(g) providing for mandatory employee participation. Not surprisingly, given its opposition to the Fifth Directive on employee participation generally in public companies, the UK Government is opposed to the implementation of the ECS on these bases which it regards as inappropriate. Measures under both Article 100a and 54 can be adopted by qualified majority voting.

---

19   Article 8.
20   Known as the 'real seat' rule.

INDEX

S